P9-CRF-796

# American Government

This book brings the study of American politics and government alive by presenting American politics as a dramatic narrative of conflict and change. It adopts an American political development approach to show how the past, present, and visions of the future interact to shape governing institutions and political forces. There is a strong emphasis on the role of ideas. Two key political development principles – path dependency and critical choice – are central to explaining how and why the past affects the present and future. Each chapter begins with an opening vignette that epitomizes the key themes of the chapter.

The book's developmental approach does not diminish the attention it gives to current matters, but it does provide a richer context for the appreciation and understanding of the whole gamut of attitudes, behaviors, organizational activities, and institutional relationships that comprise American political and governmental life.

Marc Landy is Professor of Political Science at Boston College and the winner of the 2009 Boston College Phi Beta Kappa Teaching Award, Phi Beta Kappa Omicron of Massachusetts. He graduated with a B.A., magna cum laude, from Oberlin College and has a Ph.D. in Government from Harvard. He teaches courses on American political development, the American presidency, and American federalism, and he is the former chair of the Political Science Department at Boston College. He also serves as Faculty Chair of the Boston College Irish Institute, coordinating the academic component of its executive programs on various topics in American government, most of which are sponsored by the U.S. State Department. He and Sidney M. Milkis coauthored *Presidential Greatness* (2000). He is also coauthor of *The Environmental Protection Agency from Nixon to Clinton: Asking the Wrong Questions* (1994) and the editor of *Creating Competitive Markets: The Politics of Regulatory Reform* (2007) and *Seeking the Center: Politics and Policymaking at the New Century* (2001).

Sidney M. Milkis is the White Burkett Miller Professor in the Department of Politics and a GAGE Faculty Associate at the Miller Center of Public Affairs at the University of Virginia. His books include *The President and the Parties: The Transformation of the American Party System since the New Deal* (1993); *The Politics of Regulatory Change* (with Richard Harris, 1996); *Political Parties and Constitutional Government: Remaking American Democracy* (1999); *Presidential Greatness* (with Marc Landy, 2000); *The American Presidency: Origins and Development, 1776–2011, 6th edition* (with Michael Nelson, 2011); and, most recently, *Theodore Roosevelt, the Progressive Party, and the Transformation of American Democracy* (2009). He is the coeditor, with Jerome Mileur, of three volumes on twentieth-century political reform: *Progressivism and the New Democracy* (1999), *The New Deal and the Triumph of Liberalism* (2002), and *The Great Society and the High Tide of Liberalism* (2005). His articles have been published in *Perspectives on Politics, Political Science Quarterly, The Journal of Policy History, Studies in American Political Development*, and numerous edited volumes.

**Figure 0.1.** "The Great Bartholdi Statue, Liberty Enlightening the World." Lithograph, 1885, by Currier & Ives. Image No. 0011724.

*Source*: The Granger Collection, NYC – All rights reserved.

# American Government

*Enduring Principles, Critical Choices*

Third Edition

**Marc Landy**
*Boston College*

**Sidney M. Milkis**
*University of Virginia*

CAMBRIDGE
UNIVERSITY PRESS

# CAMBRIDGE
## UNIVERSITY PRESS

32 Avenue of the Americas, New York, NY 10013-2473, USA

Cambridge University Press is part of the University of Cambridge.

It furthers the University's mission by disseminating knowledge in the pursuit of education, learning, and research at the highest international levels of excellence.

www.cambridge.org
Information on this title: www.cambridge.org/9781107650022

© Marc Landy and Sidney M. Milkis, 2004, 2008, 2014

This publication is in copyright. Subject to statutory exception and to the provisions of relevant collective licensing agreements, no reproduction of any part may take place without the written permission of Cambridge University Press.

First published 2004
Second edition 2008
Third edition 2014

Printed in the United States of America

*A catalog record for this publication is available from the British Library.*

*Library of Congress Cataloging in Publication data*
Landy, Marc Karnis.
American government: enduring principles, critical choices / Marc Landy, Boston College, Sidney M. Milkis, University of Virginia. – Third edition.
    pages   cm
Includes bibliographical references and index.
ISBN 978-1-107-65002-2 (pbk.)
1. United States – Politics and government.   I. Milkis, Sidney M.   II. Title.
JK276.L36   2014
320.973–dc23        2014002455

ISBN 978-1-107-65002-2 Paperback

Cambridge University Press has no responsibility for the persistence or accuracy of URLs for external or third-party Internet Web sites referred to in this publication and does not guarantee that any content on such Web sites is, or will remain, accurate or appropriate.

# Contents

# PART IV   Political Forces

# Preface

To understand contemporary American politics and government, students need to understand how political ideas, institutions, and forces have developed over time. In Chapter 1 we invoke that unsung political scientist, William Faulkner, who said, "the past is not dead, it is not even past." Because the past shapes one's ideas and sentiments, it is among the most important causes of how things happen in the present. This text uses the past to explain the present. In political science, this approach has come to be called American Political Development (APD). Delving into the past reveals what key political and governmental principles endure over time and what critical changes have occurred (hence the subtitle of this new edition). It was difficult to part with the previous subtitle, "Balancing Liberty and Democracy." The tensions involved in maintaining that balance remain a critical theme of the book, but the new subtitle more accurately expresses its essential message and purpose.

This new edition represents a total reworking of the text. It is much more concise. Authors love their words, and in the previous edition we loved them too much. The text was too long and discursive. This edition is roughly one-third shorter. It is also much more focused analytically. It more systematically ties the past to the present. Each chapter now begins with a contemporary portrait of the particular aspect of politics or government that is the subject of that chapter. This portrait grounds the students in the most important facts and analytic principles regarding the chapter subject. Taken together, these portraits comprise a brief guide to current politics and governments.

The next section of each chapter, entitled "Political Development," delves into the past to render the contemporary portrait more comprehensible and meaningful. For example, we do not simply discuss public opinion in terms of the current, and therefore transitory, state of opinion on various issues of the day. We examine how the very idea of public opinion came into being in reaction to the Federalist efforts to limit political participation and how this concept was understood and used by Lincoln and subsequently transformed by the Progressives. Thus, students do not merely learn about current public opinions, which may well have shifted by the time they read this book; they also learn about the efforts to restrict and expand the role of public opinion that have affected the political institutions and dynamics with which they live. Likewise, the discussion of the media's role in politics is informed by an understanding of how that role has evolved, beginning with the creation of a party press in the 1790s. The discussion also includes Theodore Roosevelt's use of the newly created mass-circulation national newspapers to popularize his messages to Congress, Franklin Roosevelt's mastery of radio in his fireside chats, and John F. Kennedy's ingenious use of television to expand the audience for his news conferences – to appeal over the heads of journalists and speak directly to the tuned-in public.

This edition also adds a comparative dimension. It points out similarities and differences between American political ideas, institutions, and practices and those of other developed countries. Such comparisons should help students think about which aspects of American political life are shared widely among prosperous nations and which are truly exceptional.

The text contains no separate chapters about civil rights, civil liberties, or public policy, because these subjects are so integral to American politics that we use them as key threads to be woven into the fabric of the entire book. On the other hand, we devote an entire chapter to political economy (Chapter 6). We believe that such a chapter is necessary because so much of the substance of political discussion, partisan conflict, and policy making is about economics. As the name implies, this chapter highlights the political forces that have shaped the institutional and legal framework in which economic activity takes place. Throughout the book, students are made aware that what they are learning in their history courses complements their political science understanding, and vice versa. Chapter 6 shows them how the study of economics and that of political science inform one another as well.

This book grows out of a friendship that developed from a deep intellectual affinity. We met in 1984 when we were put on the same panel at the American Political Science Association meeting. We found that we were both preoccupied by the New Deal. Sid was trying to understand how it gave rise to the modern administrative state. Marc was trying to figure out how Franklin Roosevelt both embraced the labor movement and staved off the transformation of the Democratic Party into a British-style Labor party. Soon after, Sid came to Brandeis University, where Marc had become a Fellow of the Gordon Public Policy Center. We had adjoining offices at the center and were able to continue our conversations over lunch and coffee and at the center's seminars. We discovered that our common interests were not limited to Franklin Roosevelt and the New Deal; we had both come to believe that the study of political science had been severed from its historical roots, and that our job was to graft the study of contemporary politics back on to those roots. Both of us were already doing this in our American politics teaching, with very good results. We saw that students developed a much keener and firmer grasp of current matters when they became aware of the intellectual and institutional connections that the contemporary issues and events had with the past. Sid applied this approach to his book

*The President and Parties* and to the textbook he coauthored with Michael Nelson, *The American Presidency: Origins and Development.* Marc applied the approach to essays about the labor movement's impact on the development of American politics. Together we drew on the American political development framework in our investigations for our book *Presidential Greatness* and our chapter, "The Presidency in the Eye of the Storm," in Michael Nelson's edited volume, *The Presidency and the Political System.* In the meantime, our devotion to connecting past and present came to appear less eccentric; many other scholars also began to find greater meaning and interest in bringing history to bear on the study of American politics. APD has now established itself as one of the most active and intellectually vibrant movements within political science. We are delighted to be part of this fruitful and stimulating scholarly effort and hope that this book can convey its insights to a new generation of beginning students.

# Acknowledgments

We thank Ed Parsons who helped us develop a strategy for the thoroughgoing revision of the previous edition that this new edition represents. Lew Bateman, the editor of this edition, has been immensely helpful in seeing this project through. The three anonymous readers of a draft of this edition provided very useful suggestions and criticisms. Likewise the careful reading of the draft by Dennis Hale and Gregory Burnep of Boston College and Stephen Thomas of Ohio Dominican led to very important corrections and improvements. We are deeply grateful to Rachel Pagano of Boston College for her indispensable help in finding and choosing the illustrations and for her other editorial help as well.

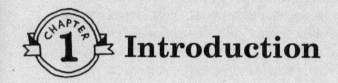

# Introduction

## CHAPTER OVERVIEW

This chapter focuses on:

☆ Fundamental concepts of politics and of American government.
☆ Why this book approaches the study of American politics and government from the perspective of APD.
☆ Why the American political system is biased in favor of the status quo.
☆ How critical choices operate to overcome the bias in favor of the status quo and lead to transformative change.
☆ What American government looks like today.
☆ How American government differs from the governments of other modern prosperous countries.

## "I HAVE A DREAM"

On August 28, 1963, 250,000 people marched on Washington to protest discrimination against African Americans and to celebrate the rise of the civil rights movement. Race relations in the South were dominated by so-called Jim Crow laws, enacted at the end of the nineteenth century, which imposed racial segregation in all aspects of life. In *Brown v. Board of Education of Topeka* (1954), the Supreme Court declared the "separate but equal" doctrine in education policy unconstitutional. Nonetheless, many Southern schools remained segregated. Not since the turbulent Reconstruction Era that followed the Civil War had the South been so alienated from the rest of the country.

When, starting in the mid-1950s, civil rights demonstrations broke out throughout the South to protest this racial caste system, local police brutally repressed efforts to break down what the distinguished African-American sociologist W. E. B. Du Bois had called the "color line." When African-American students tried to enter Little Rock High School in September if 1957, a crowd of white parents cursed and threatened them as the governor of Arkansas, Orval Faubus, blocked the door. The civil rights movement gained great momentum in 1960 when black and white students joined together to sit in at lunch counters throughout the South demanding to be served. The wave of protests continued in 1961 as Northern blacks and whites took bus trips to the South and refused to segregate themselves when they reached Southern bus terminal waiting rooms and restaurants. A particularly ugly confrontation took place in Birmingham, Alabama in September of that year, where one of the civil rights movement's most important leaders, Martin Luther King, Jr., was jailed. President John F. Kennedy had been reluctant to take on civil rights, arguing that it was up to local officials to enforce the law. After Birmingham, however, Kennedy gave his support to a comprehensive civil rights bill making racial discrimination in hotels, restaurants, and other public accommodations illegal and giving the attorney general the power to bring suits on behalf of individuals to speed up lagging school desegregation. The measure also authorized agencies of the federal government to withhold federal funds from racially discriminatory state programs.

To heighten awareness of their cause and to press for passage of Kennedy's bill, civil rights leaders organized the largest single protest demonstration in American history. King's speech at the Lincoln Memorial was its climax. Late in the afternoon, the summer heat still sweltering, King appeared at the microphone. The crowd, restlessly awaiting King's appearance, broke into thunderous applause and chanted his name. King began by praising Lincoln's Emancipation Proclamation as "a great beacon of hope to millions of Negro slaves who had been seared in the flames of withering injustice." But, he continued,

[O]ne hundred years later, we must face the tragic fact that the Negro is still not free. One hundred years later, the Negro is still sadly crippled by the manacles of segregation and the chains of discrimination. One hundred years later, the Negro lives on a lonely island of poverty in the midst of a vast ocean of material prosperity. One hundred years later, the Negro is still languishing in the corners of American society and finds himself an exile in his own land. So we have come here today to dramatize an appalling condition.

This litany of oppression might have elicited anger; indeed, some of King's followers had been growing impatient with his peaceful resistance to Jim Crow and its brutish defenders. But King, an ordained minister, spoke the words of justice, not revenge: "Let us not seek to satisfy our thirst for freedom by drinking from the cup of bitterness and hatred." A reverend might have been expected to invoke the warnings of the biblical prophets in calling America to account; instead King appealed to America's charter of freedom. He called on Americans to practice the political and social ideals of the Declaration of Independence:

When the architects of our republic wrote the magnificent words of the Constitution and the Declaration of Independence, they were signing a promissory note to which every American

**Figure 1.1.** The Unfinished Work of Martin Luther King: Cartoon by Dave Granlund, 2011 Political Cartoons. Com #88037.

was to fall heir. This note was a promise that all men would be guaranteed the unalienable rights of life, liberty, and the pursuit of happiness.

King lamented that America had not lived up to those famous words. Even after the Brown case had interpreted the Constitution so as to fulfill the promise of the Declaration of Independence, segregationists prevailed. The promissory note had come back marked "insufficient funds."

Still, he counseled continued faith in the promise of American life. African Americans should "refuse to believe that the bank of justice is bankrupt." At the same time, King warned, their faith in American justice could not last much longer; the time had come "to make real the promises of Democracy." "Now is the time to rise from the dark and desolate valley of segregation to the sunlight path of racial justice." His indictment went beyond the South. "We can never be satisfied as long as a Negro in Mississippi cannot vote and a Negro in New York believes he has nothing to vote for." The crowd shouted and clapped in cadence with him. Inspired by this surge of feeling, King abandoned his prepared text; but even as he spoke "from his heart," in words that would make this address memorable, King's sermon had a familiar ring, drawing again on the Declaration of Independence:

I say to you today, my friends, that in spite of the difficulties and frustrations of the moment, I still have a dream. It is a dream deeply rooted in the American dream. I have a dream that one day this nation will rise up and live out the true meaning of its creed: "We hold this truth to be self-evident, that all men are created equal." When we let freedom ring, when we let it ring from every village and every hamlet, from every state and every city, we will be able to speed up that day when all of God's children, black men and white men, Jews and gentiles, Protestants and Catholics, will be able to join hands and sing in the words of the old Negro spiritual, "Free at last! Free at last! Thank God almighty, we are free at last!

## THE AMERICAN POLITY: A DEMOCRATIC REPUBLIC

The entire political story of civil rights, of which this speech is such an epochal part, takes place within the frame established by one overarching institution, a polity, the United States. It was the law of the United States that had the ultimate authority to decide the outcome of the civil rights struggle. It was the legislature of the United States that deliberated about and formulated the law. The citizenry of the United States chose the members of that legislature. The United States is a *polity* because it successfully claims the political allegiance of its members. Those members may feel a deeper tie to their church or to some other institution to which they belong, but it is the constitution and the laws of the United States that they are compelled to obey. The governing institutions of the United States provide them with their political rights and responsibilities. Once in the history of the United States its claim to being a polity was challenged. Southern states seceded and, temporarily, formed a new polity, the Confederate States of America. It took a brutal war, the Civil War, to defeat secession and restore the United States' status as a single polity.

The United States is unusual in that it went through a formal process of constitution writing to become a polity. Many other polities such as Britain, France, China, or Japan did not begin on any specific date, nor did they go through a process of discussion and debate to become a polity. If this were a text on comparative politics, it would be necessary to delve deeply into how those other polities came into being, but this book focuses exclusively on the formation of the American polity. Chapter 2 describes the ideas and beliefs that formed the background to the actual formation of the United States. Chapter 3 focuses specifically on the writing and ratification of that polity's founding document, the U.S. Constitution. Chapter 4 identifies key moments of constitutional crisis when there were major reconsiderations of the American polity's constitutional underpinning.

To claim that speech and choice are building blocks of a polity, that polity must allow persons to speak freely, to have a say in how the laws are made and to feel secure that those laws will be obeyed. A polity characterized by free speech, rule of law, and collective decision making is called a *republic*. The American Republic, and all modern ones, operate on the basis of representation. The citizenry plays a minor role, if any, in governing. For the most part its role is restricted to electing representatives who do the actual work of governing.

Because the representatives are popularly elected, the United States is a representative, democratic republic.

## FUNDAMENTAL DEMOCRATIC REPUBLICAN CONCEPTS: SPEECH, LEADERSHIP, AND INSTITUTIONS

King's speech is a fine place to begin this text because it shows that politics is not just about power, greed, and ambition, but also about the noblest sentiments of the human spirit. It also vividly illustrates what American politics and government are made of, their fundamental concepts. It was a speech, and in a free society, most of political life is lived through speech. The various forms of speech that politics employs – argument, explanation, exhortation, and discussion – are what gives a free society its distinctive character. Just as clay is the medium of sculpture, words are the medium of republican and democratic politics. The brilliance of King's speech stems from his ability to artfully make use of what that medium has to offer: metaphor, adjective, symbol, and analogy. Hundreds of thousands of people listened to the speech. It was a *public event*. Unlike many other activities – friendship, sex, reading or listening to an MP3 player – politics typically takes place in public. Not everyone is capable of commanding the attention of a crowd the way Martin Luther King, Jr. did. Those who can command such public attention we call leaders. Followers have a big political role to play as well, but the United States is a very big place, and ordinary people have only a very limited capacity to influence political life and make their voices heard. Therefore, they are very dependent on leaders to represent, inspire, and command them. King was not a professional politician. No matter. The key tasks of *political leadership* are frequently performed by those who do not even think of themselves as politicians and who do not hold political office.

King's speech took place in a very particular context and was intended to achieve very particular goals. King's goal was to pass civil rights legislation. The very need to push hard for that goal implies that there is opposition to it. Other people, and their leaders, have other, often conflicting goals. Speech and leadership give politics some of the qualities of theater – vivid language, evocative acting. But, as the word "goal" suggests, politics also resembles sports. Competition can be fierce. Foul play occurs and gets penalized if the perpetrators get caught. There are winners and losers. Thus conflict and competition are also central to politics.

Politics also resembles sports in that it is highly organized. The rules are carefully laid out. Different teams develop a collective identity and persist over time. The term used for the organizations that endure, command loyalty, and develop their own collective identities is *institution*. Martin Luther King, Jr. was not simply speaking to a crowd of individuals on that warm August day; he was speaking to people with strong institutional affiliations – union members, church congregants, lodge brothers, and sorority sisters. And he was appealing to leaders of two powerful political institutions – the Democratic and Republican parties – to press for action by one of the three central national governing institutions, the U.S. Congress. King himself was not only the leader of a movement; he was also the head of an important religious institution, the Ebenezer Baptist Church. Chapter 3 introduces an additional fundamental republican democratic concept: deliberation.

## AMERICAN POLITICAL DEVELOPMENT

Martin Luther King, Jr. gave a speech in the present in an effort to influence the future, and yet so much of that speech focuses on the past. It refers back to leaders, documents, and songs from long ago – Lincoln, the Declaration of Independence, the framers of the Constitution, a spiritual sung by slaves. This was no accident. King knew that the best way to impress all the audiences for his speech – the crowd on the Mall, the Congressmen whose votes he was trying to garner, the next day's newspaper readers, the next generation of children reading history textbooks – was to link his thoughts and aspirations to great leaders, ideas, and cultural symbols from the past.

As the great American writer William Faulkner observed, "the past is not dead, it is not even past." It shapes our ideas and sentiments endowing the present with meaning. Stories from the past pervade our imaginations. They provide vivid examples of what to do and what not to do. They help define our sense of who we are, whom we love, and whom we hate. They supply our minds with a cast of heroes to emulate. Faced with a tough decision, a president or even an ordinary person might not only consider the present facts but also look for moral and intellectual guidance by asking, "What would Lincoln have done? What would Martin Luther King have done?"

The pull of the past is demonstrated by the frequency with which historical analogies find their way into political debate. People often make use of such analogies to reason through a problem and to defend their position. Those who favored Obama's stimulus package chose a favorable historical case to compare it to – President Franklin D. Roosevelt's New Deal. Those who opposed the War in Iraq often likened it to an unsuccessful prior war – Viet Nam. Those who favored it claimed that a failure to attack Iraq would do to the Middle East what the appeasement of Hitler at Munich did to Europe. The manner in which the past influences our thoughts, feelings, and imagination this text calls *political memory*. Martin Luther King, Jr. crafted his words to create the strongest possible connection between his ideas and sentiments and those that serve as the wellsprings of American political memory.

Modern political science strives to incorporate this recognition of just how critical an understanding of the past is to the understanding of the present. In the words of leading political scientists Stephen Skowronek and Karen Orren, "because a polity in all its different parts is constructed historically, over time, the nature and prospects of any single part will be best understood within the long course of political formation." They term this approach to studying politics *political development.* This text takes a political development approach. It shows how the political building blocks discussed in the previous section – speech, leadership, conflict, and institutions – have operated over time to shape current American politics and government.

As critical as political memory is to understanding present politics, the APD approach also demonstrates two other crucial avenues by which the past affects the present – *path dependency* and *critical choices.*

## Path Dependency

Like individuals, political institutions are also heavily influenced by the past. Once a particular way of doing things has been set in motion, considerable inertia develops that encourages the continuation of that course. Political scientists call this phenomenon *path dependency.* A striking everyday example of path dependency is typewriting. When inventor C. L. Sholes built the first commercial typewriter prototype in 1868, the keys were arranged alphabetically in two rows. But the metal arms attached to the keys would jam if two letters near each other were typed in succession. So, Sholes rearranged the keys to make sure that the most common letter pairs such as "TH" were not too near each other. The new keyboard arrangement was nicknamed QWERTY after the six letters that form the upper left-hand row of the keyboard. QWERTY's original rationale has disappeared because keyboards now send their messages electronically. Many typing students find it very hard to master. Despite its shortcomings, QWERTY remains the universal typing keyboard arrangement simply because it is already so widely used and so many people have already taken pains to master it. Future typists might benefit from a change, but they do not buy keyboards; current typists do. Many political institutions and practices are just like QWERTY. Although their original purposes no longer exist, people are used to them, and the costs of starting afresh are just too high.

There are countless examples of path dependence in American politics. Perhaps the single most important example is the way in which the United States is carved up into individual states. State boundary lines exist for all sorts of peculiar historical reasons. On the East Coast, they represent, for the most part, the grants given by Britain to specific individuals and groups to establish colonies. On the Pacific Coast and in the Southwest, they represent the boundaries of colonies obtained from Spain. In the Great Plains, they often represent little more than the preference of surveyors for drawing squares and rectangles. One can imagine many good reasons for adjusting state boundaries to accommodate practical realities. Why should Kansas City be split between Kansas and Missouri? The suburbs of northern New Jersey and southwestern Connecticut are dominated culturally and to a large measure economically by New York City and yet they remain part of other states. There have been very few changes in state boundaries over the entire course of American history.

This bias in favor of the status quo is not simply because people are creatures of habit, though indeed they are. It is also because, as a rule, those who benefit from an existing policy will fight harder to keep the policy in place than those who might benefit from a change will fight to alter it. Beneficiaries of existing policies know what they have and what they stand to lose if policies change. Potential beneficiaries can only estimate the benefits a policy change might bring them. Therefore, politically speaking, fear of loss is a more powerful motivator than hope of gain.

## Critical Choices

By showing how the odds favor the status quo, the developmental approach encourages a greater appreciation of what it takes to beat the odds. As passage of the 1964 Civil Rights Act and the 1965 Voting Rights Act so forcefully demonstrates, the powerful inertial biases of American politics are sometimes overcome. A key theme of this book is how and why Americans have made *critical choices* that shifted America's political path. How and why did the antipathy to political parties yield to the establishment of a two-party political system? How and why did a strictly limited federal government mushroom into an elaborate administrative state? How and why were voting rights for African Americans and women finally granted after having been denied for so long? Those critical choices that reshaped the constitutional underpinnings of the American polity the text refers to as *conservative revolutions* (see Chapter 4). Calling them conservative revolutions is a reminder that such is the power of path dependency that even when critical change does occur, it is strongly shaped by past events.

In sum, this text bases its discussion of American politics on several key building blocks: the influence of *political speech*, the role of political leaders, the dynamics of *political competition*, and the functioning of political institutions. To fully explain how those building blocks operate, it examines them *developmentally*. The essential elements of the development approach are: political memory, path dependency, and critical choices.

## THE PLAN OF THIS BOOK

This book is divided into four parts. The first, "Formative Experiences," contains Chapters 2, 3, and 4, which focus respectively on political culture, constitutional design, and critical episodes in American political development. Chapter 2 examines the formation and meaning of the core political beliefs that Americans profess. It shows how those beliefs coalesce to form what Tocqueville called "habits of the heart," an enduring political culture shaping the political opinions and actions of Americans. Chapter 3 looks at the Constitution: the political debate its creation provoked, the conflicts between rights and democracy that it settled, and those that it left unsettled. It explains why it is so important that the American government was erected on the basis of an original and carefully designed blueprint and how that conscious plan both reflects American political culture and has helped shape it. Chapter 4 focuses on the major points of transition that have occurred since the constitutional founding.

Part II, "Pivotal Relationships," looks at how the federal government engages with the states and with the economy. The Constitution does not establish fixed boundaries between national and state governmental power, nor does it clearly define the limits of government regulation of private property. The disputes provoked by these uncertain boundaries have proven to be among the most hotly contested controversies in all of American political life and have given it much of its distinctive style and substance. As we shall see, those who fight for greater national power as well as those who resist in the name of either states rights or property rights all invoke the principles of rights and democracy to support their side.

The four chapters that form Part III, "Governing Institutions," each examine one of the three branches of national government – the Congress, the presidency, and the federal judiciary – enumerated in the Constitution, as well as the bureaucracy, which developed, in large measure, outside of formal constitutional arrangements. These chapters describe how those institutions operate now and how they have changed over time. The great debates over the structure and purposes of these institutions demonstrate how political arguments and political decisions shape and alter the "nuts and bolts" of government.

Part IV, "Political Forces," focuses on the most important political phenomena that exist outside of the formal governing structures and how they shape political debate and governmental decision making. These include political parties, social movements, interest groups, and the media. All of these political actors have been discussed extensively earlier in the book but always in supporting roles. It would be impossible to have a full-fledged discussion of any of the topics in Parts I through III without paying due attention to their mighty influence. Here they gain center stage. The spotlight is on their development and dynamics and how they have embodied and exemplified key questions of liberty and democracy.

Each chapter begins within an overview of its key themes. A vignette follows that embodies one or more of those themes. Then it presents a contemporary portrait of how the chapter's subject actually functions today. After, the chapter traces the political development of that subject to demonstrate the debt that current reality owes to persistent paths and critical choices forged over time. It provides a concluding statement. It ends with a summary of the most important points the chapter has made.

## AMERICAN POLITICS AND GOVERNMENT: POLICIES AND PROGRAMS

There is no better guide to what Americans want and expect from government than the Constitution's Preamble:

We the People of the United States, in Order to form a more perfect Union, establish Justice, insure domestic Tranquility, provide for the common defense, promote the general Welfare, and secure the Blessings of Liberty to ourselves and our Posterity, do ordain and establish this Constitution for the United States of America.

The following is a brief introductory sketch of the programs and policies that have been put in place to implement these high-minded but vague objectives, as well as some of the most serious current controversies surrounding them. The sketch highlights the distinctiveness of American government and politics by pointing out some of the most important differences in governmental aims and approaches that distinguish the United States from the other prosperous democratic republics – including France, Great Britain, Germany, and Japan – with whom it is most often compared.

### "Form a More Perfect Union"

At present, the United States is the only major nation that refers to itself as a "union." Someday the European Union may become a nation, but it is not one now. The United States was founded as a union of states and, to this day, the individual states have many of the powers that in other countries belong exclusively to the central government. They levy taxes, educate college students, build and maintain roads, and have their own law codes. Most crimes are tried in state criminal courts. Most lawsuits are brought in state civil courts. Those states with capital punishment laws exercise a legal power to kill. States perform a multitude of important regulatory functions. They regulate insurance companies, hospitals, and real estate transactions. All states issue drivers licenses. States also require licenses to engage in a wide variety of professions and businesses. In North Carolina, for example, one must obtain a license in order to engage in any one of more than 150 occupations including school teachings, practicing law, parachute rigging, embalming, and acting as an agent for a professional athlete.

Each state has its own constitution, which differ greatly from one another. For example, unlike the federal government and forty-nine other states, Nebraska's legislature is not bicameral. It consists solely of one legislative chamber. The Louisiana legal code is derived from France's Code Napoleon, not from British Common Law that serves as the basis for the law codes of all the other states. The complex relationship between the states and the national government is called Federalism (see Chapter 5). The United States is not the only federal nation. Germany, India, and Canada are among the other nations that grant significant powers to their states or provinces.

The original reason for seeking to establish *a more perfect union* was the weakness of the central government formed by the Articles of Confederation (see Chapter 2). The current national government is at least as strong as those of other nations. It commands the largest and strongest military and spends the most money on defense of any country in the world. Some of its activities – such as running the military, diplomatic corps, post office, and national parks, forests, and public lands and providing old age pensions – it does entirely on its own. But many others – providing health care and income subsidies to the poor, training workers, regulating air and water pollution, aiding the handicapped and establishing student achievement standards – it does in partnership with state and local governments. Sometimes it funds these policy partnerships through what are called federal grants in aid (see Chapter 5). Sometimes it simply requires the states and localities to do them with their own money through what are called mandates (see Chapter 5).

There is no clear-cut distinction between which powers belong to the states and which to the federal government. This blurriness gives a distinctive cast to American political debate. Here, political conflict occurs not only over *what* government should do, but *who* should do it. For example, the arguments over abortion, gay marriage, and gun control include both the question of what should be done about them and also whether the states or the federal government should control the matter. Before the passage of the No Child Left Behind law (NCLB) in 2002, the federal government had restricted its intervention in K–12 education to enforcing school desegregation and providing various forms of aid to poor school districts. NCLB made it a condition of federal aid that every state establish student achievement standards and test students to ensure that they were meeting those standards. Many parents, teachers, and concerned citizens consider NCLB to be an unwarranted intrusion of the federal government into a matter that ought to remain the exclusive province of the states and localities.

Perfecting the Union pertains not only to harmonizing national and state governments but also to determining which persons can legitimately claim to be a part of it. Other nations traditionally defined their citizenry on the basis of blood. A Frenchman was a Frenchman because he is descended from Frenchmen.

**Figure 1.2.** Uncle Sam Welcomes America's Future: An 1880 American cartoon by Joseph Keppler in favor of unrestricted immigration.

*Source*: The Granger Collection, NYC – All rights reserved.

The United States, being a nation formed by immigrants, did not adopt that approach. Citizenship has been open both to those born here and those who take an oath of allegiance to the United States. Becoming an American means committing one's self to the set of principles that define the *American creed* as that creed is expressed in the Declaration of Independence, the Preamble to the Constitution, and the Bill of Rights.

## Controversy: Open versus Restricted Immigration

Not everyone has the opportunity to become a U.S. citizen. Current law restricts the number of aliens who can establish residency in the United States and thus become eligible for citizenship. To escape poverty and political oppression, millions of foreigners, most of them from Mexico, the Caribbean, and Central America, enter the country illegally. As of 2011 the Department of Homeland Security estimated that there were 11.5 million illegal aliens in the United States. The attitude of American citizens toward them is ambivalent. They perform work that American citizens are unwilling to perform – slaughtering cows and hogs, harvesting crops, and maintaining lawns. But they also put a great strain on schools, housing, police, hospitals, and welfare systems.

THE PROPOSED EMIGRANT DUMPING SITE.

STATUE OF LIBERTY—"Mr. Windom, if you are going to make this island a garbage heap, I am going back to France."

**Figure 1.3.** The Proposed Immigrant Dumping Site: An 1890 anti-immigration cartoon by F. Victor Gillam.

*Source*: The Granger Collection, NYC – All rights reserved.

The arguments in favor of exerting tighter control of illegal immigration and loosening such control are based on different conceptions of how best to perfect the Union. Neither denies that the essence of American citizenship is a commitment to the American creed. But restrictionists insist that the Union can only continue to flourish if the rate of immigration does not exceed the capacity of government and society to successfully absorb and assimilate the newcomers. Anti-restrictions maintain that any serious attempt to keep people out violates the deepest principles of liberty and equality underlying the Union and thus renders the Union all the more imperfect.

## "Ensure Domestic Tranquility"

Unlike other countries, the United States has no national police force. The ordinary tasks of "insuring domestic tranquility" such as preventing and solving crimes, regulating traffic, and controlling crowds are performed by state and local police. States also have their own codes of criminal law covering most ordinary crimes such as burglary, arson, rape, murder, and assault and their own courts for enforcing those codes. In 1878, Congress passed the *Posse Comitatus Act*, which is still in effect. *Posse Comitatus* means "power of the county." It forbids the military from conducting domestic law enforcement except for constitutionally explicit or congressionally mandated exceptions. The Insurrection Act of 1807 clarifies the authority of the federal government to use the military to suppress domestic insurrections, as Lincoln did in the South's secession in the Civil War. In the 1950s and 1960s federal troops were used to overcome the refusal of southern governors to integrate schools as required by decisions of the Supreme Court, and were sent in to control some of the riots that have broken out in the African-American neighborhoods of major American cities.

The federal government does perform certain specific law enforcement functions that are beyond the capacity of state and local police. The Federal Bureau of Investigation (FBI) was formed to cope with crimes that crossed state lines such as kidnapping, and subsequently expanded the scope of its activities to include the prosecution of organized crime. The Secret Service guards the safety of the president, the vice president, their families, presidential candidates, and visiting world leaders. It also protects the money supply by prosecuting counterfeiting of U.S. currency and bonds. The Coast Guard was granted an exception by Congress to enable it to fight drug trafficking. But the targeted nature of these assignments attest to how powerful the resistance of Americans is to allowing the federal government to perform ordinary police functions.

Since 9/11, efforts to prevent terror attacks has served to greatly increase federal law enforcement responsibilities. This expansion is signified by the creation of the Department of Homeland Security (DHS), the first new cabinet-level department since the Department of Veterans Affairs was established in 1989. Both the Secret Service and the Coast Guard have been transferred to DHS. It also houses the newly created Transportation Security Administration created to protect the nation's airports, railroads, and other transportation networks; the Customs Service; Immigration Service; and various other bureaus and parts of other agencies concerned with domestic preparedness. Although not part of DHS, the FBI has greatly expanded its anti-terror efforts.

## Controversy: "Insure Domestic Tranquility" versus Civil Liberties

The most serious current controversy about ensuring domestic tranquility concerns the clash between protecting citizens against terror attack and protecting the full range of individual rights the Constitution guarantees. Normally a search warrant is required in order for law enforcement to place a tap on a telephone or otherwise listen in on what would otherwise be private communication. In order to obtain information about terror attack planning President George W. Bush ordered the National Security Agency (NSA) to monitor international telephone calls and international e-mail of persons suspected of terrorist ties without first obtaining a search warrant. When news of this practice was leaked to the *New York Times,* many critics claimed that it was a violation of one's right to communicate in private. The administration stressed that the NSA did not eavesdrop on the actual phone conversations or read e-mails but rather searched for patterns of phone numbers and e-mails addresses to see who was talking to whom. This did not reassure critics who viewed the compiling of any data about interpersonal telecommunications as a violation of civil liberties. Despite the great outrage expressed, Congress confirmed the president's authority to order these forms of surveillance when it amended the Foreign Intelligence Surveillance Act in 2008.

## "Provide for the Common Defense"

The goal of "providing for the common defense" is obvious. Americans want to be safe from foreign threat. But what does "defense" mean? As any football fan knows, offense and defense are inseparable. The other team cannot score if your team has the ball. The same is true for war. The national defense does not consist only of fending off enemy attack. In many cases the best defense consists of keeping one's enemies on the defensive by strengthening one's own offensive capabilities. The U.S. military is trained and equipped to attack others as well as defend against attack.

Modern war is horrifically destructive. It is a last resort for protecting national security. Therefore a critical aspect of providing for the common defense involves diminishing the likelihood of war through the conduct of diplomacy. Diplomatic time and effort is devoted to building alliances with other friendly nations and trying to find common ground even with potential enemies via negotiation. The military aspect of providing for the common defense is primarily the responsibility of the Department of Defense and the armed services that it supervises. The diplomatic aspect is primarily the province of the Department of State. These duties are so vital to the safety of the nation that the secretaries of defense and state, along with the secretary of the treasury, are, after the president, the most powerful and prestigious positions in the executive branch.

Until the Cold War ended in the early 1990s, the United States was one of two world superpowers and was engaged in a costly and dangerous rivalry with the other superpower, the Soviet Union. With the collapse of the Soviet Union, the United States has become the world's sole superpower. Its military strength dwarfs that of any other nation. It spends more on defense than the rest of the world combined, almost ten times more than the second-biggest military spender, China.

Because it has such a voracious appetite for supplies and technology, it has spawned huge industries devoted to producing weapons, transport, communications systems, and other high-tech equipment for it. In order to maintain its technological edge over other nations, the military invests heavily in scientific and engineering research, much of which is done by universities who, in turn, have become heavily dependent upon the funds they receive from the defense department to conduct such studies. Indeed, the United States spends more on defense research and development than any other nation spends for all its military needs. President Dwight David Eisenhower coined the term "military industrial complex" to refer to this complex network of government, industry, and higher education.

Its size and strength enables the United States to operate on a global basis. No other nation has the wherewithal to do so. Even at the height of the Iraq War, when 160,000 soldiers were fighting in that country and another 12,000 were fighting in Afghanistan, the United States maintained what are called combatant commands prepared to wage war almost anywhere in the world. These include: European Command, Pacific Command, and Southern Command, among others. Each command has a well-staffed headquarters and large numbers of troops, with others available to be mobilized in time of war.

## Controversy: Superpower or Super Bully?

The most serious controversy involving the common defense stems from the United States' superpower status and global reach. Does this overwhelming power really make the country safer or does such strength serve as an almost irresistible temptation to throw its weight around? In recent decades the United States has been engaged militarily in places such as Kosovo, Somalia, and Libya where the relationship between the fighting they were engaged in and U.S. national security was tenuous at best.

The war on terror launched by the Bush Administration committed the United States to long, costly, and bloody wars in Iraq and Afghanistan. Nations whom the United States considers allies either opposed these efforts or made only very small troop commitments. Some argue that the United States should not be so willing to act on its own. It should work more closely with its allies because that is the best way to maintain peace and ensure that the burden of fighting is more equally shared should war become unavoidable. Others contend that those allies have become so used to having the United States fight their battles for them that they are no longer willing or able to bear their fair share of the load and that, therefore, the United States has no choice but to take on the primary responsibility of protecting its national security, and theirs.

## "Promote the General Welfare"

The United States took a very different approach to providing for the general welfare than did the nations of Western Europe. It defined "welfare" to mean restricting the intrusion of government rather than providing help to people. This effort to reign in government power is called *limited government*. It assumes that unless the constitution specifically grants government the right to engage in a specific activity, the government is not permitted to do so. Limiting government to only those constitutionally specified activities is called *enumerated powers*. Article One of the Constitution restricts the legislative power of government to only those specific powers enumerated in Article Section 8 (see Appendix). Throughout most of its history the national government did not provide student loans, unemployment benefits, aid to the disabled, old-age pensions, medical care for the poor, or any of the other social service programs it now offers.

In the twentieth century American government has greatly expanded its powers beyond those enumerated in the Constitution. As a result, differences between American welfare policy and those of Western Europe have diminished considerably. The major remaining differences relate not to the total amount of welfare aid provided– the United States is now in line with most advanced countries in total welfare funds expended – but rather how and for what purposes welfare aid is provided. The United States is much less likely to provide help to everyone and much more inclined to *target* specific categories of recipients – the elderly, disabled, children, and unwed mothers. Whereas many rich countries will provide income to any poor person, in the United States a guaranteed income is only accorded to those over sixty-five and welfare payments only go to poor single-parent families, and for a maximum of only five years. In many European countries, college tuition is free or very low. The U.S. national government does not attempt to control college tuition but subsidizes low-income college students and provides low-interest loans to middle class ones. Nor does the United States provide free universal day care and preschool as so many of its counterparts do. Rather, it funds preschool programs for the poor.

Rather than make direct payments for many welfare purposes, the United States prefers to make use of the Federal Tax Code for philanthropic purposes. Gifts to charity are tax deductible. A very sizeable part of funds spent on medical care, scholarship aid, mental health services, and many other welfare programs comes from charitable donations. Low-income working people receive tax credits to offset their income tax obligations. If those credits exceed the taxes owed, they keep the difference.

The federal government also provides for the general welfare by regulating the behavior of the private sector. Federal agencies such as the Environmental Protection Agency (EPA), the Food and Drug Administration, the Occupational Safety and Health Administration (OSHA), the Civil Rights Division of the Justice Department, and the Consumer Product Safety Commission have been established to enforce a variety of regulatory laws passed by Congress. The missions of these various regulatory bodies include, among others: enforcing laws to limit the air, water, and other forms of pollution emitted by factories, power plants and automobiles; guaranteeing the safety of food, drugs, toys, and workplaces; and combating race, gender, and other forms of discrimination.

The federal government also intensively regulates various aspects of the economy. It does this in two different ways. It oversees the behavior of specific sectors such as banking and stock and bond trading to try to make sure that the firms engaged in those activities provide accurate information to customers and do not engage in excessively risky activities. It also regulates the overall functioning of the economy by controlling the money supply and setting the interest rates the government charges for the sale of government bonds.

Other rich nations engage in these same regulatory activities. But they also take aggressive actions to control labor markets and the conditions of employment. They intervene to set wages for the employees of certain industries; establish a mandatory number of vacation days and restrict the ability of employers to fire workers. The United States restricts itself to establishing a minimum wage that, in practice, only affects the lowest paid workers. Otherwise companies are free to pay what they wish, hire and fire whom they want, and set whatever vacation policies they desire as long as they do not discriminate among workers on the basis of race, religion, national origin, gender, or age.

## Controversy: Welfare versus Self-Reliance

What government provides for individuals and businesses they need not provide for themselves. Ever since the creation of old-age pensions in the 1930s, every major proposal for greater government welfare aid has aroused opposition on the grounds that it diminishes the self-reliance and sense of personal responsibility of those receiving the aid. This criticism is at the heart of the most recent major controversy about federal subsidy – the bailouts of certain banks, investment houses, insurance firms, and automobile companies that took place during the financial collapse and economic recession of late 2008 and early 2009. Opponents argued that by bailing out those who made excessively risky loans, insurance contracts, and investments the government was signaling that it would do so again in the future, thus relieving the perpetrators of these risky practices of the need to act more prudently and responsibly. Likewise, the bail-out of Chrysler and General Motors signaled that if a company employed a large enough number of workers, dealers, and suppliers, the government will not let it fail even if it is has failed the market test of supply and demand. Supporters of the bailouts do not deny that bailouts give the wrong message to firms; rather, they argue that if major banks, insurance companies, and investment houses failed, the stock and bond markets would tumble, credit would disappear, and a wave of home foreclosures would occur. Furthermore, the auto industry is so central to the economy that the failure of the first and third-largest auto companies would set off a similar wave of unemployment. So, even if bailouts risk encouraging irresponsibility, they were necessary and in this instance the lesser of two evils.

## "Secure the Blessings of Liberty"

The American Constitution is made up of seven separate articles and twenty-seven different amendments. But when Americans are asked what is in the Constitution they rarely mention either the Articles or the last seventeen Amendments. For the average American the Constitution *is* the Bill of Rights – the rights to free speech, religion, gun ownership, property, and other liberties granted to persons and the states in the first ten Amendments. Americans have always prided themselves on being a liberty-loving people and they still do. A great theme of American political development is that of the expansion of rights to include full civil and political rights to African Americans and women. Although the Constitution contains no right to old-age pensions, social security has become such an accepted part of American life that it has more or less risen to the status of a right. In recent years, laws have been passed to greatly increase the rights enjoyed by the physically and mentally disabled. The Supreme Court has also declared that the Constitution ensures that every American enjoys a right to privacy.

## Controversy: A Right to Health Care?

In our discussions of immigration and electronic surveillance we have already commented on the problems that arise when rights clash. Another great source of controversy arises from efforts to further expand rights. The current con-troversy over health care reveals differences of opinion about how much of it

Americans should have by right. Currently, most Americans have health insurance. It is either a benefit they receive from their employer, tax free, or something they purchase for themselves. But many employers do not provide health insurance. Therefore, many Americans are uninsured either because they cannot afford to buy it or they are young and healthy enough that they would rather go without it.

Even if one agrees that health care is a right of all Americans, what does that right actually entitle one to? Breakthroughs in modern medicine have greatly expanded the possible meanings of healthcare. Laser surgery enables tennis players with knee problems to be back on the court in a few weeks. Viagra extends the active sex life of men into their old age. Fertility treatment enables women to get pregnant later in life. Botox eliminates wrinkles. Does everyone have a right to all these forms of health care? Some argue that the right to health care is limited to "no frills" items such as checkups and catastrophic illness or trauma. Others argue that virtually any form of physical or mental correction or enhancement should be available to all Americans regardless of income, especially because the government provides much of the funding that goes into the discovery and development of the chemicals and techniques that makes such enhancements possible.

## "Establish Justice"

We save "establish justice" for last because for two of the three dominant schools of contemporary American political thinking it is very closely tied to goals we have already discussed. *Libertarians* would argue that establishing justice means the same thing as securing the blessings of liberty. They would consider justice to mean what the Declaration of Independence posits as the right to "pursue happiness." Justice is not something that government grants; rather, it is the opportunity to make the best of things on one's own, free of government interference. *Liberals* would link the establishment of justice to providing for the general welfare. They consider that a society is just only if it assists those who have not had a fair chance to pursue happiness because they are poor, female, or members of racial, religious, or ethnic minorities. They demand that government do more than refrain from interfering in the race of life. They want it to act affirmatively to ensure that all handicaps have been removed so that the race is run fairly. Only *conservatives* view the establishment of justice as a distinct aim of politics. Conservatives are often lumped together with Libertarians because they, too, oppose government policies aimed at redistributing wealth and subsidizing the poor. Both fear that such policies undermine self-reliance and personal responsibility. But unlike Libertarians, conservatives seek to use government to establish justice by upholding moral virtue and combating moral decay.

## Controversy: Permit, Subsidize, or Ban Abortion

These differing views of justice crystallize in the debate over abortion. Libertarians support unfettered access to abortion, believing that women should have the freedom to control what is done to their bodies. They oppose the attempts by conservatives to moralize the issue. Most liberals also oppose restrictions on abortion, but as a matter of justice they also insist that the government subsidize abortions for those too poor to afford them. Many conservatives consider abortion to be immoral and therefore they want government to ban it or at least establish restrictive conditions to control it, including requiring pregnant minors to discuss the matter with their parents and the prospective father.

## THE INSTITUTIONS OF GOVERNMENT

After setting out the aims of American government in the Preamble, the Constitution proceeds to establish specific institutions designed to carry out those aims. The Constitution creates three branches of government: the executive, headed by the president (see Chapter 8), the legislative, comprised of two separate branches of Congress – the House of Representatives and the Senate (see Chapter 7) – and the judicial, comprised of a system of federal courts presided over by the Supreme Court (see Chapter 9).

Each of these branches has its own duties, and this allocation of responsibilities is known as *the separation of powers*. Each branch is also granted specific means for intruding into the workings of the others. This system of intrusions is referred to as *checks and balances*. Thus, the president has the power to veto bills passed by Congress. The House of Representatives can *impeach* the president, and the Senate may then vote to remove him from office. The Senate must confirm certain presidential appointments, most especially appointments to the federal courts and the president's cabinet. Although the Constitution does not explicitly provide for it, the Supreme Court has acquired the power to declare acts of Congress and actions of the president unconstitutional.

The following is a brief sketch of each of the three branches of the federal government. The sketches display both continuity and change. They depict critical ways in which the three branches adhere to the constitutional blueprint. They also describe departures from that blueprint and raise the question of whether or not those departures violate the spirit of checks and balances.

### Congress

Article One grants *Congress* the exclusive power to legislate. All the laws of the United States must pass both houses of Congress – the *House of Representatives* and the *Senate*. If the president vetoes a bill approved by Congress, both houses must reapprove the measure by a two-thirds vote for it to become law. All bills having to do with raising revenue must first pass the House of Representatives before being eligible for consideration by the Senate. The Senate reviews all cabinet, court, and diplomatic appointments made by the president and must consent to them.

Congresspersons also engage in many activities not discussed in the Constitution. They provide diverse services to their constituents including help with immigration problems and difficulties in obtaining veterans, social security, and other forms of benefits that constituents believe they qualify for. Congress also engages in extensive oversight of executive agencies. It holds hearings and calls executive officials to testify and defend their actions. Although the Constitution does not specifically grant such powers to Congress they may well be defended as constituting important checks on the executive, preventing it from dealing arbitrarily or unfairly with citizens or evading the letter or spirit of laws passed by Congress. Congress's capacity to adequately check executive excess is more fully discussed in Chapter 7.

## The President

Congress legislates, but it no longer serves as the only, or even perhaps the most important, initiator of legislative proposals. The role of chief legislator has passed to the *president*. He often sets the legislative agenda and uses his enormous political influence to press for passage of legislation he favors and fight against legislation he opposes.

This shift in the nature of legislative leadership is but one aspect of a broad increase in the expansion of the president's political importance. The president commands the bulk of the attention that the media pays to national political affairs. His speeches are televised. His travels and activities are reported on in minute detail. Presidential elections are by far the most important and celebrated of all national political events. The Constitution makes the president commander in chief of the armed forces, but in addition to acquiring the power of legislator in chief he has now also become political celebrity in chief. Only the most popular entertainers and athletes can claim a similar level of fame.

Celebrity poses both opportunities and problems for the president. It enables him to command public attention more or less at will, and to communicate more successfully with the citizenry than anyone else. But it also greatly increases the public's expectations of what he can accomplish. If the economy declines, the public is ready to blame him even though he may not necessarily be in a position to do anything about it. The impact of this expansion of the president's role on the system of checks and balances will be discussed more fully in Chapter 8.

## The Supreme Court

Article Three of the Constitution creates a federal court system, culminating in a *Supreme Court*, which is responsible for "all cases arising under the Constitution." The federal courts do indeed hear and decide cases involving disputes between states, that take place at sea, and a host of other questions that are clearly beyond the capacity of any state court to deal with. But the Supreme Court in particular has also taken on two enormous responsibilities that the Constitution does not specifically give it. It decides whether acts of Congress and the president are constitutional or not. During the Bush Administration the Court overruled actions of both the president and Congress regarding the War on Terror.

The Supreme Court has also taken on the power to declare the existence of rights not enumerated in the Bill of Rights. For example, in declaring unconstitutional a Connecticut law that made it a crime to sell or use contraception because the law violated the right to privacy, it admitted that the Constitution mentions no such right. Rather, it argued, the spirit of a right to privacy pervades the document as a whole. Defenders of these rulings view them as critical both to checking congressional and presidential excess and protecting the people's liberties. Critics charge that these decisions undermine the Constitution by allowing the Court to usurp legislative and executive authority as well as short circuit the constitutional amendment process by rewriting the Constitution itself. This controversy over the Court's role in the checks and balances system will be taken up more fully in Chapter 9.

## A REQUEST

As the reader now proceeds to the fuller account of American government and politics that this chapter has introduced, we urge that in addition to trying to understand how politics works, the reader also try to appreciate politics. Because no person is an island, politics is inescapable. We must live with the collective decisions made in our midst whether we choose to participate in them or not: inescapable, yes; tedious, no. Politics combines the suspense of sports with the colorful array of characters found in great literature. Savor its richness, dramatic intensity, and capacity to surprise.

## CHAPTER SUMMARY

☆ Key building blocks of American politics include: the influence of political speech, role of political leaders, dynamics of political competition, and functioning of political institutions.

☆ The American polity is best understood to be a democratic republic.

☆ The United States is a federal union in which both the states and national government exercise considerable powers.

☆ The American Constitution prescribes limited government based on enumerated powers and seeks to create a system of checks and balances between the different branches of government.

☆ American political development is an approach to the study of politics and government that proceeds historically in order to illuminate how the past affects the present and future.

☆ The past strongly influences the present because of how political institutions work and how individuals think about politics and government. Three key aspects of political development are: political memory, path dependency, and critical choices.

☆ Path dependency means that once a way of doing things has been set in motion a considerable inertia develops that encourages the continuation of that course.

☆ Americans have made critical choices that shifted America's political path.

☆ The battle over immigration is not one between right and wrong but between different conceptions of rights – the right to enter a free society versus the right of those already there to protect their quality of life by defining the terms and conditions of entry.

☆ Unlike most other countries, the United States has no national police force. The ordinary tasks of "insuring domestic tranquility" such as preventing and solving crimes, regulating traffic, and controlling crowds are performed by state and local police.

☆ With the collapse of the Soviet Union, the United States has become the world's sole superpower. Its military strength dwarfs that of any other nation.

☆ Historically, the United States took a very different approach to providing for the general welfare than did other advanced republican democracies, but those differences have diminished considerably in recent decades.

✮   A great theme of American political development is that of the expansion of rights to include full civil and political rights to African Americans and women. In recent years laws have been passed to greatly increase the rights enjoyed by the physically and mentally disabled.

✮   A key difference between Libertarians, liberals, and conservatives regards their views of justice.

## MAJOR CONCEPTS

| | |
|---|---|
| American Creed | Checks and Balances |
| Congress | Conservative |
| Critical Choices | Form a More Perfect Union |
| House of Representatives | Institution |
| Insure Domestic Tranquility | Liberal |
| Libertarian | Path Dependency |
| Political Competition | Political Development |
| Political Leadership | Political Memory |
| Political Speech | Polity |
| Posse Comitatus Act | President |
| Promote the General Welfare | Provide for the Common Defense |
| Public Event | Representation |
| Republic | Secure the Blessings of Liberty |
| Senate | Separation of Powers |
| Supreme Court | |

## SUGGESTED READINGS

Bryce, James. *The American Commonwealth*. Indianapolis, IN: Liberty Fund, 1996.
Chesterton, G. K. *What I Saw in America*. New York: Dodd Mead, 1923.
Croly, Herbert. *Progressive Democracy*. New York: Transaction, 1998.

Crenson, Matthew A., and Benjamin Ginsberg. *Downsizing Democracy: How America Sidelined Its Citizens and Privatized Its Public*. Baltimore: Johns Hopkins University Press, 2002.

Du Bois, W. E. B. *The Souls of Black Folk*. New York: Penguin, 1996.

Hamilton, Alexander, James Madison, and John Jay. *The Federalist Papers*, ed. Charles Kesler. New York: Mentor Books, 1999.

Hartz, Louis. *The Liberal Tradition in America*, 2d ed. New York: Harvest Books, 1991.

Heclo, Hugh. *On Thinking Institutionally*. Boulder CO: Paradigm Publishers 2008.

Landy, Marc, and Martin Levin, eds. *The New Politics of Public Policy*. Baltimore: Johns Hopkins University Press, 1995.

Lowi, Theodore. *The End of Liberalism*, 2d ed. New York: W. W. Norton, 1979.

McWilliams, Wilson Carey. *The Idea of Fraternity in America*. Berkeley: University of California Press, 1973.

Morone, James. *Democratic Wish: Democratic Participation and the Limits of American Government*, rev. ed. New Haven, CT: Yale University Press, 1998.

Orren, Karen, and Stephen Skowronek. *The Search for American Political Development*. New York: Cambridge University Press, 2004.

Pierson, Paul. *Politics in Time: History, Institutions, and Social Analysis*. Princeton, NJ: Princeton University Press, 2004.

Putnam, Robert. *Bowling Alone: The Collapse and Revival of American Community*. New York: Simon & Schuster, 2000.

Schuck, Peter H., and James Q. Wilson. *Understanding America: The Anatomy of an Exceptional Nation*. Washington, DC: Brookings Institution Press, 2006.

Smith, Rogers M. *Civic Ideals: Conflicting Visions of Citizenship in the United States*. New Haven, CT: Yale University Press, 1999.

Storing, Herbert, ed. *The Complete Anti-Federalist*. Chicago: University of Chicago Press, 1981.

Tocqueville, Alexis de. *Democracy in America*, ed. Harvey Mansfield and Delba Winthrop. Chicago: University of Chicago Press, 2000.

# Formative Experiences

# Political Inheritance and Political Culture

## CHAPTER OVERVIEW

This chapter focuses on:

★ The central components of American political culture and the key points of comparison with the political cultures of other advanced democratic republics.

★ The origins of American political culture.

★ The Declaration of Independence as the seminal statement of the American creed.

★ The key factors that shifted American opinion to be in favor of creating a strong national government.

The Declaration of Independence does not say "all *Americans* are created equal." It extends the promise of equality and the inalienable rights attached to it to all men, meaning all people. In a series of speeches in the days and weeks following September 11, 2001, President George W. Bush argued that the terrorist attacks on the World Trade Center and Pentagon were not merely acts of senseless destruction but direct challenges to the universal principles of human freedom that the Declaration defined.

Three days after the attack, speaking at a prayer service at the National Cathedral, the president explained that the War on Terror was about nothing less than the future of human freedom and that defending freedom was America's oldest responsibility and greatest tradition: "In every generation, the world has produced enemies of human freedom. They have attacked America, because we are freedom's home and defender. And the commitment of our fathers is now the calling of our time."

The following week, addressing a joint session of Congress, he explained why America in particular had been the target of the attacks: "Why do they hate us? They hate us for what we see here in this chamber – a democratically elected government. Their leaders are self-appointed. They hate our freedoms – our freedom of religion, our freedom of speech, our freedom to vote and assemble and disagree with each other."

He told the members of Congress that the War on Terror was not merely to protect American lives and property but to defend the universal principles at the heart of the American creed: "Freedom and fear are at war.... The advance of human freedom now depends on us."

In early November, President Bush addressed the United Nations to impress on the peoples of the world that America's fight was their fight as well because the natural rights at stake belonged to everyone:

[T]he dreams of mankind are defined by liberty, the natural right to create and build and worship and live in dignity.... These aspirations are lifting up the peoples of Europe, Asia, Africa and the Americas, and they can lift up all of the Islamic world. We stand for the permanent hopes of humanity, and those hopes will not be denied.

In his January 2002 State of the Union address, he spoke of how America was once again being called on to play a "unique role in human events," a role first recognized by John Winthrop when he announced that the New World was "a city upon a hill," a beacon of freedom beamed at a world threatened by despotism.

There are many different approaches that Bush could have chosen for explaining to the American people what the problem was and how the government would respond. His decision to so strongly emphasize issues of human freedom and natural rights provides an important clue to just how deeply embedded such ideas are in what this chapter calls American political culture. *Political culture* refers to the core beliefs in a society, what the French author Alexis de Tocqueville referred to as "the habits of the heart." These central beliefs forge a people – "We the People," as the preamble to the Constitution reads – from a large and diverse society. Chapter 1 discussed the concept of path dependence. This chapter describes how the core beliefs and "habits of the heart" that have persisted throughout the course of American political development were forged. It examines the three most important sources of American political culture: *Calvinist Protestantism*, *Classic Liberalism*, and *slavery*. It shows how the single-most-important statement of the American creed, the Declaration of Independence, reflects these three sources and how the Declaration itself helped shape American political culture. Finally, it looks at the factors that steered American thinking away from the radically democratic course the ex-colonies embarked on immediately after Independence and toward the sort of balanced constitution that was more in line with Classic Liberalism.

## AMERICAN POLITICAL CULTURE: A CONTEMPORARY PORTRAIT

American political culture is in most respects similar to its sister rich, democratic nations in Europe. Like them, Americans believe in a political system that is free, democratic, and respectful of minority rights. These political cultures believe that people should be tolerant of religious, ethnic, and cultural diversity and individuals should be judged on their merits, not on what family they come from or ethnic group they belong to. They also share a strong skepticism about the national government and other large institutions, especially corporations. However, there are critical cultural, economic, and political matters about which American opinion departs from its closest relatives. These departures combine to form a political culture that is highly distinctive and helps account for critical political and policy differences between the United States and other mature democracies.

Americans are far more patriotic than citizens of those mature European democracies. They are more likely to display pride in their country and say that they would prefer to live in America than elsewhere. They believe that the fundamental principles and attributes of American society are sound even though they are highly critical of specific governmental institutions, especially Congress and the bureaucracy. Americans are proud of their particular ethnic, religious, and racial identities. And yet, political scientist Jack Citrin cites a 1994 public opinion survey in which 96 percent of the respondents identified themselves as "just Americans." Some live abroad for periods of time, but the number of those who resettle permanently in other countries is remarkably low.

Americans are also more optimistic about their futures than Europeans. The Harris poll asked whether one expected one's own life to get better over the next five years. Sixty-five percent of Americans said "yes." Only 44 percent of Europeans agreed. This optimism is also reflected in the greater willingness of Americans to bring children into the world. The U.S. birth rate is higher than the birth rates in Europe, Canada, or Japan.

Americans differ from their sister democratic republics in their understanding of the proper relationship between the individual and the government. Only 20 percent of Americans think the government should provide individuals with a guaranteed income as compared to 60 percent of Britons and 56 percent of Germans. Like their European counterparts, Americans value equality. But they are far more likely to define equality in terms of equal opportunity than equal result. Most Europeans claim that government should reduce the gap between the rich and the poor. Most Americans disagree. They are less likely to see income inequality as unfair because they are more likely to interpret such inequality as resulting from differences in talent, ambition, and effort. They are more likely than Europeans to see poverty as resulting from laziness and passivity than from bad luck. Although they profess an appreciation for diversity they oppose the use of racial, gender, or ethnic quotas as a means for achieving it. Individual merit is the only acceptable grounds for attaining professional and economic success. Freedom for the individual is considered a superior objective to social equality. Even those racial minorities – African Americans and Hispanics – that have experienced significant economic discrimination are more likely than Europeans to believe that they can and will better themselves economically and individuals are responsible for their own destiny.

Americans are far more religious than Europeans. The World Value Study asked people around the world how important religion was in their life; 47.4 percent of Americans said it was very important. By contrast, only 21 percent of Britons said it was very important. Americans were twice as likely as Britons to say they were active members of a church or religious organization and nine times more likely to say so than Frenchmen.

Americans are also far more likely to profess the moral values that religion inspires. In the United States, it is less common for a man and a woman to live together as a couple without being married. Prostitution is illegal in forty-nine states. Many towns and counties ban the sale of alcohol. The differences in moral attitudes between Europe and the United States were evident in the public reaction to President Clinton's sexual encounters with a young woman who was serving as his intern. In the United States there was shock and outrage. The case figured significantly in the bill of impeachment brought against him by the House of Representatives. The same news was greeted in Europe with a combination of unconcern and amusement at the Americans' lack of sophistication. By European standards, Americans appear "puritanical."

Thus, although their levels of education and wealth are roughly equal to those of Europeans countries, Americans are not nearly as "modern" in their beliefs. If by modern one means irreligion, a nonjudgmental attitude toward sexual conduct, and a desire for the government to provide for one's needs. The more traditional religious and moral principles that Americans adhere to are usually associated with premodern social arrangements based on family ties and social caste. One might therefore expect Americans to have stronger ties to family and place and expect that their lot in life will be no better than that of their parents. Yet Americans are the most staunchly individualistic and have the strongest commitments to free and open economic competition and social mobility of any rich nation. The answer to how such varied and even contradictory attitudes have come to coexist lies in the origins and early development of American political culture.

## POLITICAL CULTURE AND AMERICAN POLITICAL DEVELOPMENT

### The British Inheritance – Puritans, Liberals, and Slaves

Colonial America was settled primarily by emigrants from the lands that then composed Britain: England, Scotland, Ireland, and Wales. The colonists referred to Britain as the "mother country," and it is therefore not surprising that their views about fundamental political questions were shaped by such a strong maternal bond. The charters issued by the king that formed the basis of their existence as colonies guaranteed them "the rights of Englishman." The Seal of Massachusetts showed an "English American" holding a copy of the Magna Carta and a sword. The Magna Carta, issued in 1215, enumerated the fundamental rights and privileges of the English people. Two powerful sets of beliefs and ideas that originated in Britain, Puritanism and Classic Liberalism, exerted critical influence on the formation of American political culture. *Puritanism* was the religion of those who first settled New England beginning in the early 1600s. Classic Liberalism exerted its importance over the ensuing decades as more and more Britons emigrated to both Massachusetts and the other twelve colonies established by the king, stretching from New Hampshire in the north to Georgia in the south.

### Puritans

Puritan religious understanding was grounded in the thought of the great theologian John Calvin (1509–1564), who was born a Frenchman but lived most of his life in Geneva, Switzerland. Calvinism's defining principle was that because humankind was so deeply sinful, individuals could not, on their own, redeem themselves in the eyes of God and bring about their own salvation; salvation was something that only God could bestow. One of Calvin's greatest criticisms of the Roman Catholic Church was its acceptance of the idea that through confession, penance, and good works a person could be saved and expect to go to heaven. One might imagine that a rejection of good works would cause Calvinists to become selfish and self-indulgent, but the Puritans' interpretation of the impossibility of saving themselves led in just the opposite direction. They determined to create a covenant with God in which they would pledge to act as righteously as possible and to be single-minded in their devotion to him.

A covenant is not a contract. It puts God under no obligation. The totality of the Puritan commitment came with no strings attached. Individuals did not enter the covenant; it was entered into by the entire congregation; hence, the origin of the term "congregationalist." The congregation was identical with the community. Therefore, each community member had to accept responsibility for the behavior of every other member. And, because any one member could destroy the covenant, it implied that each member was as important as everyone else. The idea of the covenant therefore established a political community in which every person had equal value and the good of the whole took precedence over that of any one individual.

America appealed to the Puritans precisely because it was a new land that had not been corrupted by the decadent and heretical forms of Christianity that dominated the Old World. In a speech entitled "A Model of Christian Charity," John Winthrop, the first governor of Massachusetts, gave voice to the Puritan mission, suggesting that England would soon take heed of what they were accomplishing in the New World: "For we must consider that we shall be as a city upon a hill, the eyes of all people are upon us." Thus, the mission of the Puritan was twofold. To establish a religious community pleasing in the eyes of God and provide the mother country with a shining example of how she could mend her ways. The Puritans thus bequeathed to later Americans both a strong commitment to democratic solidarity but also a deep sense of America as an exemplary nation with a mission to encourage others to adopt its freedom-loving ways.

The Puritans did not dominate American religion. But the critical principles of a covenential relationship with God and a duty to serve as an example of egalitarian democratic virtue had a great impact across the colonies. The impulse to encourage community spirit, denigrate materialism, and serve as a beacon to the godless became a critical element of American political culture, one that was bolstered by the overall strength of church life. Because the American colonies were a haven for religious dissenters, no one church dominated life in the colonies.

The *Continental Congress* did not attempt to establish a single official American church. Most states did initially establish a single church, but even by the time of the adoption of the Constitution many had emulated the national government in separating church from state. Religious freedom strengthened religious influence on American society. It cultivated the belief that churches did not threaten individual liberty, as was the case in feudal Europe, but protected it. This relationship gave the clergy significant influence over rights-conscious Americans. Shorn of state sponsorship, churches became strong, independent institutions that contributed significantly to the emergence of a distinctive American culture. The Anglican Church in America, painfully weaned from government support, became the Episcopal Church. After the Revolution, Roman Catholics previously under the administration of the vicar apostolic of England came under the authority of Father John Carroll of Baltimore, named the first American Roman

Catholic bishop in 1789. Lutherans, Presbyterians, Quakers, Jews, Baptists – and a few decades later Methodists – thrived along with the Congregationalists.

The strength of American religious institutions and attachments tempered the individualism fostered by the second strand of British influence, Classic Liberalism, with Christian principles of fellowship and charity. Tocqueville observed, "While the law allows the American people to do everything, there are things which religion prevents them from imagining and forbids them to dare."

## Classic Liberalism

Classic Liberalism was originally developed by the great seventeenth-century and early eighteenth-century British political philosophers Thomas Hobbes, John Locke, and David Hume and the great French political philosopher Baron de Montesquieu. Its fundamental principles are *natural rights* and government as a *social contract*. It asserts that people lived completely freely, on their own, until they chose to make a contract with one another to form a government. They made the contract because on their own they could not protect their natural rights to live free of oppression and violent death and enjoy their property. Those entering the contract promised to give up their freedom to do exactly as they wished, in return for the promise that government would protect their natural rights. If the government failed to secure their rights, they were free to dissolve the contract and return to their prior natural state of complete freedom.

The term "Classic Liberalism" should not be confused with Liberalism as the term is currently used. Liberalism in its modern guise connotes a belief in using the national government to achieve benevolent purposes. It is directly at odds with Classic Liberalism's stress on limited government. *Modern Liberalism* has far more in common with *Progressivism*, a political viewpoint we will discuss in Chapter 4. The shift from the older to the newer meaning of liberalism came about because Franklin Delano Roosevelt deemed it more politically prudent to shed the "Progressive" label and call his defense of an activist, ambitious national government "liberalism."

Classic Liberalism's rights-based approach was a sharp departure from earlier political philosophical traditions. Like the Puritans, those traditions had stressed the duties and obligations owed to the political community and/or to the Church rather than the rights of individuals. Traditionally, people conceived of themselves as members of a greater whole – a clan, a tribe, a city – not as solitary persons. Hobbes and Locke influenced the American Founders to believe that everyone is born endowed with a right to live as one pleases, and therefore the community may not trample on those rights unless the individual does harm to others. This view of government as a contract between free individuals was in stark contrast to the Puritan concept of covenant. The purpose of the covenant was to commit to collective obligations. The purpose of the social contract was to protect individual rights. American political culture absorbed both of these contradictory points of view, and the tensions between them continue to animate American political life.

Classic Liberals recognized the difficulties of maintaining and perpetuating a political order dedicated to individual freedom. Their knowledge of history informed them that the right to life and liberty was constantly being trampled as a result of the lust of kings and nobles for power and glory and the competing claims of different religions to provide the sole path to salvation. To counter these threats it was necessary to encourage people to find satisfaction in pursuits that did not so readily stimulate them to oppress and kill one another. Therefore, Classic Liberals encouraged people to enjoy their private lives; to seek comfort and happiness from their work and their recreation and satisfy their competitive instincts by vying with one another in the marketplace rather than on the battlefield. They believed that the pursuit of wealth, comfort, and security would prove less threatening to liberty than the pursuit of glory or salvation.

Previously, the world of business had been looked down on. Soldiers and churchmen were seen as far nobler than those engaged in "mere" trade. The Classic Liberals sought to elevate the prestige of business in order to encourage ambitious and energetic men to enter this "safe" profession rather than expend their energies and talents on warmongering and theological disputation. Furthermore, to succeed in business they would need to develop talents and habits far more conducive to political peace and stability than those associated with soldiering and religious disagreements. The traits of frugality, prudence, patience, and temperance necessary for commercial success were also more conducive to preserving a decent political order than the swagger and recklessness of the soldier or intolerant single-mindedness of the religious zealot. Imagination, inventiveness and ambition were also highly prized as long as they were channeled in a practical, marketable direction, toward increasing human well being and comfort.

The Classic Liberals sought to organize governmental affairs to protect liberty. Montesquieu in particular stressed the importance of a separation of powers among the executive legislative and judiciary. But he also believed that the peaceful and liberty-loving habits created through a devotion to commerce were a necessary complement to political protections if natural rights were to be preserved. A liberal republic would need to be a commercial republic.

Because Americans were highly literate, Classic Liberal ideas spread rapidly and widely during the eighteenth century. Newspapers flourished in all the cities and towns of any size. Large cities established publishing houses of their own. Even if they did not read the actual writings of Hobbes, Locke, Hume, and Montesquieu, the settlers were exposed to classical liberal ideas in a welter of books and articles written by disciples of these philosophers. These popularizations were devoted to making the key principles of classical liberalism accessible and attractive to the ordinary reader. Classic Liberal ideas were especially appealing to British Americans because, unlike the people they left behind, a large percentage of the males among them owned some property and participated in town governments, criminal and civil juries, and colonial assemblies.

Despite the deep differences in outlook between Puritans and Classic Liberalism, they also shared important similarities that allowed them to coexist and influence one another. Unlike supporters of feudalism or hereditary monarchy, they both believed that government was only legitimate if it was based on the willingness of the individual to be governed. Membership in the Puritan community was voluntary; you could leave it, or you could be expelled from it. In that sense it was not completely different from the liberal idea of a government formed by individuals who have agreed to join on certain rational terms.

## Slavery

Virginia was the first of the English colonies, founded in 1607. Unlike Massachusetts, it was founded by seekers of gold and silver, not religious perfection. No sooner had it been settled than it began to deprive men and women of the fruits of their labor. Slavery was introduced in Virginia in 1620 by a Dutch ship that landed twenty Africans on the banks of the James River. Over time, it spread to all the British colonies in North America. Virginia's leaders, including such great figures as George Washington, Thomas Jefferson, and James Madison, professed to believe in the key principles of Classic Liberalism, but they also owned slaves. At the time of the outbreak of the American Revolution in 1776 slavery was legal in all thirteen former colonies and there were more than half a million slaves in what was to become the United States. American political culture acquired a contradictory quality that it has never entirely shed. An exemplary democratic politics deeply imbued with community responsibility, endowed by the Puritans, and a profound commitment to individual rights, endowed by Classic Liberalism, came to coexist with toleration for the most thoroughgoing dehumanizing oppression and victimization of a large minority of the population.

## COLONIAL AMERICA: GROWTH OF A DISTINCTIVE POLITICAL CULTURE

The American colonies had already been in existence for more than a century prior to American independence. Because Britain did not pay much attention to their internal affairs, they had acquired extensive experience in governing themselves. Many of the most important practices and principles at the heart of American government and politics were already functioning during this long prerevolutionary period. Especially in Puritan New England, the individual towns were run democratically. Colonies had their own elected legislatures, independent judiciaries, and practiced trial by jury. Thus, colonists developed the habit of running their own affairs, arriving at collective judgements based on mutual deliberation. The great observer of American democracy, Alexis de Tocqueville, was especially impressed with trial by jury. He recognized that the need to deliberate about guilt and innocence in criminal cases and relative fault and obligation in civil ones was the best possible learning experience for citizens. He called juries "the schoolrooms of democracy."

During the 1760s and 1770s, the British attempted to tighten their control of the colonies. Among other actions, Britain restricted the functioning of colonial legislatures and limited trial by jury. Thus, the Declaration of Independence talks not only of "injuries" that the British king has done to the Americans, but of "usurpations" of rights and privileges that the colonists had previously enjoyed:

He has obstructed the Administration of Justice, by refusing his assent to Laws for establishing Judiciary Powers.

He has made Judges dependent on his Will alone, for the Tenure of their Offices, and the Amount and Payment of their Salaries.

He has dissolved Representative Houses repeatedly, for opposing with manly Firmness his Invasions on the Rights of the People.... [He has assented to legislation] ... depriving us, in many Cases, of the Benefits of Trial by Jury."

Threatening to take away political authority and liberty that the colonists previously enjoyed served only to strengthen the colonists' commitments to them. As a result, a profound commitment to trial by jury and an independent judiciary and legislature became even more deeply embedded in American political culture.

## AMERICA'S CREED: THE DECLARATION OF INDEPENDENCE

The cause of revolution was given a powerful push in January 1776 by the publication of an enormously influential and widely read political pamphlet called *Common Sense*. It was written by Thomas Paine, a newly arrived English immigrant. *Common Sense* aroused strong sentiment not only against King George, but also against the idea of monarchy itself. It proclaimed that the time had come for Americans to grow up. It attacked the Crown and vilified monarchy, calling King George a "Royal Brute," "the hardened sullen tempered Pharaoh of England."

Paine called for a democratic representative government with power concentrated in a large national popular assembly. Elections would be frequent, terms short, and rotation in office required. Paine opposed the creation of any independent executive power. The Congress should choose the president from its own members, Paine recommended; moreover, a new president from a different state should be selected every year. Everything possible should be done to preserve the new government's democratic character and suppress all monarchic tendencies. As the size of America grew, so should its assembly, assuring a strong relationship between the people and their representatives.

Urging Americans to declare their independence, Paine appealed to their exemplary urges, insisting that their cause "was in great measure the cause of mankind.... We have it in our power to begin the world all over again.... The birth-day of a new world is at hand, and a race of men perhaps as numerous as all of Europe contains, are to receive their portion of freedom from the event of a few months."

Paine shared the Puritan ambition to transform the world, but not to achieve Puritan ends. He was a Classic Liberal. He viewed *natural rights*, not community as sacred. He believed that the founding of America signaled humanity's emancipation from the limits of nature and the duties of community. In America, individuals served their fellow citizens by pursuing gain and increasing the general prosperity. Paine's view of natural rights implied a sharp distinction between government and society and an unyielding defense of limited government: "Society is produced by our wants, and government by our wickedness; the former promotes our happiness positively by uniting our affections, the latter negatively by restraining our vices.... Society in every state is a blessing ... but government even in its best state is but a necessary evil." *Common Sense* not only conveyed a revolutionary message, it also featured a new style of writing aimed at a wider reading public. It was written in simple and direct language shorn of the flowery trappings characteristic of late eighteenth-century political writing. It succeeded spectacularly in its objective: about 150,000 copies were sold in the critical period between January and July 1776. The population of the colonies at that time was roughly 2.5 million. One of every seventeen people bought the pamphlet. To achieve a similar proportion of buyers, a pamphlet today would have to sell more than 15 million copies.

Opinions similar to Paine's had been expressed at the Second Continental Congress, which first met in Philadelphia in May 1775 in response to a call from Massachusetts (only Georgia failed to send representatives). The Congress passed a declaration of grievances that amounted to a complete condemnation of Britain's actions since 1763. The delegates also endorsed Massachusetts's proposal that the American people take up arms to defend their rights against

Britain's violation of them. Paine's great contribution was to argue the case for independence in a form that reached beyond political leaders to reach the ordinary person.

## THE GREAT DECLARATION

When the members of the Second Continental Congress met in Philadelphia in May 1776, they recognized the powerful appeal of Paine's words. Many, in fact, sent copies to their home constituencies. The tone of the debate in the national legislature and country changed dramatically as Paine's call to arms took effect. On June 7, 1776, Richard Henry Lee introduced a resolution in favor of independence from Britain.

The Continental Congress did not want to take such a dramatic step until it had achieved a strong consensus, and some colonies, most notably Maryland and Pennsylvania, were still reluctant to break all ties with the mother country. In the meantime it appointed a committee to prepare a declaration of independence. That committee had five members: Thomas Jefferson of Virginia, John Adams of Massachusetts, Benjamin Franklin of Pennsylvania, Roger Sherman of Connecticut, and Robert R. Livingston of New York. The committee asked Jefferson, the most gifted writer of the group, to prepare a draft. By the beginning of July a consensus was reached, and the independence resolution was approved on July 2, 1776.

The enduring political cultural significance of the *Declaration of Independence* is attested to by the choice of July 4, the date it was issued, rather than July 2, as the nation's official birthday. The principles justifying the revolution were exalted above the revolutionary act itself. The Declaration of Independence did include a lengthy indictment of the "injuries and usurpations" of George III. But the condemnation of the British king's actions was preceded by a statement of general principles justifying the right of any people to revolt against tyranny and form a government based on the consent of the people.

## THE LIBERAL ORIGINS OF THE DECLARATION

The Declaration established Jefferson as an icon of American democracy, but its ideas did not originate with Jefferson. Like Paine, Jefferson derived his ideas from Classic Liberal principles. The Declaration's rationale for breaking with Britain restated Locke's argument that individuals had natural rights that all legitimate governments were obligated to protect. In Jefferson's epochal words: "We hold these truths to be self evident, that all men are created equal, that they are endowed by their creator with certain inalienable rights, that among

TEARING DOWN STATUE OF GEORGE III.

**Figure 2.1.** Down with Monarchy: Wood engraving of the destruction of the statue of George III after the reading of the Declaration of Independence. Credit: The Granger Collection, NYC – All rights reserved.

these are Life, Liberty and the Pursuit of Happiness." Locke had argued that a government was only legitimate if it better protected the individual's rights than did the "state of nature," which "however free, is full of fears and continual dangers." Therefore, in Jefferson's view, Britain's role as the "mother country" gave it no special claim on the loyalties of Americans if it failed to secure their natural rights. Jefferson placed the blame for the colonies' departure squarely on Britain: "Whenever any Form of Government becomes destructive of these ends, it is the Right of the People to alter or to abolish it, and to institute new Government." Jefferson's contribution was to state compellingly ideas and beliefs that had already worked their way into American political culture.

He dignified what Paine had aroused. As Jefferson wrote many years later, the essential thing was "to place before mankind the common sense of the subject, in terms so plain and firm as to command their assent.... Neither aiming at originality of principles or sentiments, nor yet copied from any particular and previous writing, it was intended to be an expression of the American mind." He elevated commonly accepted truths into a constitutional document. The Declaration creates the foundation on which the constitutional edifice was built. As Lincoln argued more than half a century later, the Constitution is only fully intelligible if one recognizes that it presupposes the "self evident" truths the Declaration proclaims. The depths to which its key sentences have penetrated American political culture justify referring to the Declaration as the statement of the American creed. No other country has a set of key principles and statements to which its citizens adhere to the same degree that Americans adhere to the principles of "life, liberty and the pursuit of happiness." Unlike most other nations, Americans are not bound together by ties of blood, religion, and ethnicity. Thus, it is their mutual adherence to this creed that provides the very definition of what it means to be an American.

All the members of the Continental Congress signed the Declaration, even though it officially required only the signature of the Congress's president, John Hancock. Hancock's signature was the largest to appear at the end of the Declaration – to save King George III the trouble, he noted cheekily, of putting on his reading glasses. The other members of Congress, embracing their president's rebellious spirit, added their names. After all, the Declaration was no mere official document, but "an avowal of revolution." In making their signatures part of such a dangerous state paper, the members of the Continental Congress took a solemn oath as citizens of a new government. They gave the first official display of the American political community. As the last sentence of the document read, "For the support of this declaration, with a firm reliance on the protection of divine providence, we mutually pledge to each other our lives, our fortunes, and our sacred honor."

The gravity of this pledge was demonstrated by the manner in which the Declaration was publicized. It was read before groups of people in public ceremonies. The mobilization of British soldiers on American soil for the purpose of suppressing the incipient rebellion added solemnity to these occasions. With this menace in mind, Congress directed that the Declaration should be proclaimed not only in all the colonies but also by the head of the army.

On July 9, General George Washington ordered officers of the Continental Army brigades stationed in New York City to obtain copies of the Declaration from the Adjutant General's Office. Then, with the British soldiers "constantly in view, upon and at Staten-Island," as one participant recalled, the brigades were "formed in hollow squares on their respective parades," where they heard the Declaration read.

## THE DECLARATION AND SLAVERY

Jefferson was painfully aware of the contradiction involved in a slave owner such as himself declaring that all men were created equal and that they had an inalienable right to liberty. He knew that slavery was wrong. He hoped that it would die out over time. But he believed that it had become too important to the livelihood of white Southerners to be abolished. Many Southerners shared his view that slavery was a necessary evil. Jefferson did attempt to abolish the slave trade in his original draft. In a long paragraph, which John Adams admiringly called "the vehement philippic against Negro slavery," Jefferson charged King George III with waging "cruel war against human nature itself, violating its most sacred rights of life and liberty in the persons of distant people who never offended him, captivating and carrying them into slavery in another hemisphere, or to incur miserable death in their transportation thither." Congress eliminated all discussion of the slave trade in the final draft, acquiescing to South Carolina and Georgia, who sought to perpetuate the slave trade, and many in the North, who profited from the transportation of slaves.

Jefferson accused the British of compounding their crime of introducing slavery into the colonies by sowing seeds of rebellion among slaves. His uncharacteristically venomous prose was aimed at the "Christian king of Great Britain," who, through his subordinates in America, "was now exciting these very people to rise in arms among us, and to purchase that liberty of which he deprived them, by murdering the people upon whom he also obtruded them; thus paying off former crimes committed against the liberties of one people, with crimes which he urges them to commit against the lives of another." These are the most hollow words to be found in the Declaration. Everyone knew that the colonists themselves were responsible for the evils of slavery and therefore had to bear the responsibility for the violence and death that would occur when slaves sought their freedom. The fact that Jefferson felt compelled to deflect the blame for it from the colonists to the King reflects just how badly tarnished its claims to liberty and equality were tarnished by the perpetuation of this oppressive institution.

The Declaration did not condemn slavery, but neither did it endorse it. It states that all men not all white men are endowed with inalienable rights to life liberty and the pursuit of happiness (in the language of the eighteenth century, "men" was a collective noun that included women as well, thus including them among those endowed with inalienable rights). This unconditional declaration of human rights would indeed become an important weapon against slavery. In the first decades after the Declaration, one northern state after another abolished slavery, and the new northern states admitted all had antislavery provisions in their state constitutions. Appropriately, New York's act to emancipate slaves was gradually approved on July 4, 1799, and New Jersey's on the same day five years later. The southern states resisted emancipation Even gradual abolition would have violated the "property rights" of thousands of influential men, including Jefferson, and left the South with the unwanted task of devising a new labor system. Moreover, the South was afraid that a large population of free blacks would exact retribution, perhaps violently. Jefferson would write in 1820:

I can say with conscious truth that there is not a man on earth who would sacrifice more than I would to relieve us from this heavy reproach in a practical way.... But as it is, we have the wolf by the ears, and we can neither hold him, nor safely let him go. Justice is in one scale, and self-preservation on the other.

Jefferson's fears were tragically realized by the violent slave uprising led by Nat Turner, which was originally planned to begin on July 4, 1831. The revolt actually began on August 22, when a band of eight slaves led by Turner killed five members of the Travis family in Southampton, Virginia. During the next three days, the ranks of the rebels swelled to between sixty and seventy, and they killed an additional fifty-eight whites in Jerusalem, Virginia. Militias caught most of the rebels within a few days, and Turner was captured on October 31. He was executed on November 11, 1831.

Still, the Declaration ensured that opponents (see Chapter 12), not defenders of slavery, would be able to claim the moral high ground. John C. Calhoun of South Carolina, one of slavery's most effective champions, admitted as much in the late 1840s. He lamented that the Declaration had "spread far and wide, and fixed itself deeply in the public mind." The Declaration became a revered document, not just because its message was "popular," as Calhoun thought, but also because it articulated and affirmed the American creed. Frederick Douglass, a former slave who had escaped bondage to become an eloquent defender of emancipation, made clear to America in his famous July 4, 1852, oration that the United States could not enslave African Americans and still be true to its deepest beliefs:

What to the American slave, is your 4th of July? I answer; a day that reveals to him, more than all the other days in the year, the gross injustice and cruelty to which he is the constant victim. To him your celebration is a sham; your boasted liberty an unholy license; your national greatness, swelling vanity; your sounds of rejoicing are empty and heartless; your denunciations of tyrants, brass fronted impudence; your sermons and thanksgivings, with your religious parade, and solemnity, are, to him, mere bombast, fraud, deception, impiety, and hypocrisy – a thin veil to cover up crimes which would disgrace a nation of savages.

Like Abraham Lincoln and Martin Luther King, Douglass made clear that slavery robbed the Revolution of its true meaning. The fight for independence was not about separating from Great Britain alone; it was a critical step in fulfilling a special mission – a duty, as Winthrop had preached – that inspired political life in the United States. Some Americans might resist such an argument; but they could not ignore it.

## THE DECLARATION AND THE RIGHTS OF WOMEN

The Declaration and the Revolution also led many people in the United States to challenge the subjugation of women. For example, it became somewhat easier for women to obtain divorces in the aftermath of the struggle for independence. During the colonial period, divorces were rare, but easier for men to obtain than for women. The difference did not vanish after the Revolution, but it did diminish. Before independence, no Massachusetts woman was known to have obtained a divorce on the grounds of adultery; thereafter, wives were more likely to sue errant husbands successfully.

As with racial inequality, changes in sexual relations were limited. When Abigail Adams urged her revolutionary husband John and his fellow rebels to "remember the ladies," or the women would "foment a revolution of their own," he did not take his wife's plea seriously. Politics, he insisted, was "not the Province of the ladies." In truth, Abigail Adams was not advocating political rights; she was advocating fairer treatment for women in the household. "Do not put such unlimited power into the hands of husbands," she wrote. "Remember all men would be tyrants if they could."

Although the Revolution did not directly alter the political status of women, it did create important new educational opportunity for them. The New Englander Judith Sargent Murray urged the cultivation of women's minds to encourage self-respect and "excellency in our sex." Her fellow reformer, Benjamin Rush, gave political expression to this view: only educated and independent-minded women, Rush argued, could raise the informed and self-reliant citizens that a republican government demanded.

This emphasis on "republican motherhood" and its potential to bestow dignity on the democratic individual had a dramatic influence on female literacy. Between 1780 and 1830, the number of colleges and secondary schools, including those for women, rose dramatically. Women's schools and colleges offered a solid academic curriculum. By 1850, there were as many literate women as men. Nonetheless, American women remained excluded from participation in political life. Most Americans considered the female's rightful place to be in the home. But like opponents of slavery, advocates of women's rights found the Declaration a powerful text to enlist on behalf of their cause.

The organizers of the first convention for women's rights, in 1848 at Seneca Falls, New York, were veterans of the antislavery movement. In preparing the convention's statement of principles and demands, Elizabeth Cady Stanton invoked the Declaration. "We hold these truths to be self-evident," the proclamation declared, "that all men and women are created equal." The Seneca Falls proclamation went on to submit "facts" to a "candid world" to prove "the history of mankind is a history of repeated injuries and usurpations on the part of man toward woman, having in direct object the establishment of an absolute tyranny over her."

**Figure 2.2.** Left Behind: 1869 Satire on Women's Rights by Currier & Ives. Credit: The Granger Collection, NYC – All rights reserved.

Even some of the convention's leaders, such as Lucretia Mott, felt that the right to vote was too advanced for the times and would lead to ridicule of the nascent women's movement. But, Frederick Douglass, one of thirty men brave enough to attend the Seneca Falls gathering, argued convincingly that political equality was essential if women were to enjoy true freedom. The convention adopted the suffrage resolution by a small majority. The Seneca Falls Statement of Principles, as Stanton observed, "would serve three generations of women" in their fight for natural rights promised by the Declaration

The Declaration did not specify the institutional forms that would best protect the rights it proclaimed. The ensuing debate about how the ex-colonies should govern themselves revealed the ongoing tensions between the democratic and liberal strands of American political culture. The leaders of the Revolution disagreed about whether a government based on consent of the people had to operate by means of their consent, that is, by democratic institutions. John Locke had argued that the people could consent to place the hands of government in a monarchy (rule of one), aristocracy (rule of few), or democracy (rule of the many). He believed that a mixed government – one in which powers were shared among different institutions representing different interests – best protected individual liberty. John Adams encouraged the national and state governments to adapt the British system of separated powers. Perhaps the united colonies should not have a king, but they needed a strong executive who would share power with separate legislative and judicial institutions. "Without three orders and an effectual balance between them," he wrote in 1786, America "must be destined to frequent unavoidable revolutions."

Thomas Paine disagreed. He prescribed a complete departure from the British system, with its clashes among the king, House of Lords, and House of Commons. America should be governed by a popular assembly and organized to express the sentiments of the people. Here he was building on the long experience with self-government that many of the former colonists had enjoyed.

## THE ARTICLES OF CONFEDERATION

During its first years, the new Union took a democratic direction. In the wake of the Declaration, and its charges against King George III, most of the states wrote constitutions that sought to ensure that executive power would not threaten popular liberty. In some states, the executive office, an outpost of royal administration during the colonial period, was eliminated entirely. Where an executive was provided for, governors were often given little power. They tended to be limited to one-year terms and some were not eligible for reelection. They had no authority to convene or dissolve the legislature; nor could they exercise a veto over laws passed by the assemblies. They were not allowed to appoint state officials or manage executive branch activities.

The states vested vast authority in popular assemblies. In the spirit of Paine, the great Boston patriot Samuel Adams declared, "[E]very legislature of every colony ought to be the sovereign and uncontrollable Power within its own limits of territory." To ensure that legislatures were truly popular, state constitutions put them on a very short leash. They called for annual elections and required candidates to live in the districts they represented. Many states went so far as to assert the right of voters to instruct the men in office how to vote on specific issues and elect judges. No state granted universal manhood suffrage, but most substantially reduced the size of the property requirements for voting that had previously been in place.

As John Adams warned, the decisive rejection of the British system of mixed government enabled legislatures to act irresponsibly. Most telling was the inability of many state legislatures to pay their debts and provide for a stable currency. But in the wake of independence, there was little support for anti-majoritarian institutional checks and balances. The revolutionary struggle, aroused by pamphlets such as *Common Sense*, made political leaders more conscious of the power of the people. Political leaders competed with each other in demonstrating their sympathy for the people – and in so doing, greatly expanded their public audience.

The emergence of democratic sentiments actually preceded the Revolution. In 1766, for example, the Massachusetts House of Representatives erected a public gallery for the witnessing of its debates – "a momentous step," according to the historian Gordon Wood, "in the democratization of the American mind." The Pennsylvania Assembly followed reluctantly in 1770, and eventually other legislatures followed suit, usually provoked by revolutionary leaders, who were anxious to build popular opposition to Great Britain. Although attention to public opinion began prior to the Revolution, the fight for independence intensified the celebration of "the People." Consequently, the line between "gentlemen" and the rest of the society, never as clear in the colonies as it was in the mother country and Europe, was radically blurred by the Revolution and its aftermath.

Allegiance to states and localities, not the Union, dominated the first efforts to form a national government in the United States. In fact, the Declaration of Independence referred explicitly not to the United States but to these "free and independent states." It envisioned not one large republic, which revolutionary leaders feared would render popular rule impractical, but a loose federation of thirteen. The first national government after the Revolution, formed after the Articles of Confederation ratified in 1781, embodied this desire to retain the full independence of the states.

The Articles provided for a national legislature modeled on the Continental Congress. It remained the creature of the state legislatures, which chose its members, had the power to remove them at any time, and paid their salaries and expenses. It had the authority to declare war, conduct diplomacy, coin money, regulate Indian affairs, appoint military officers, and requisition men from the states. But it had little power to fulfill these responsibilities. It could neither levy taxes nor regulate trade. The states retained the power of the purse, as well as the ultimate authority to make and administer laws.

The national government had no distinct executive branch. The president was a figurehead, a delegate chosen to preside over congressional sessions. Executive power, such as it was, rested with congressional committees, constantly changing in their membership. With no means for carrying out policies of finance, war, and foreign policy, the national government's power was extremely limited.

The lack of centralized authority stemmed from the democratizing influence of the Revolution. Just as the state constitutions were written to keep representatives closely tied to popular opinion, the Articles of Confederation took pains to broaden citizen involvement in national affairs. It provided that members of Congress be annually elected and forbidden to serve in the national legislature more than three years in any six-year span.

## THE DIFFICULTIES OF DECENTRALIZED GOVERNMENT

The democratic trend of state and national governance in this period came under increased criticism due to the various governmental failings that increasingly came to threaten the viability of the Union. The Continental Congress had also relied on the states, but its dependence occurred during wartime, which made the states relatively willing to provide men and money for the common defense. But such a loose alliance of states proved far less practical during peacetime. From 1781 to 1786, for example, Congress requested $15 million from the states to carry out its foreign and domestic responsibilities but received only $2.5 million.

The absence of national power also weakened national security. No sooner had the 1783 treaty ending the Revolutionary War been signed than British ministers, seeking to exploit the new weak alliance of colonies, surreptitiously instructed the Canadian colony to maintain its forts and trading posts, so they could serve as bases for raids and espionage against the United States. Many frontier settlements suffered terrible losses from Indian attack. Trouble also developed in the Southwest, where the Spanish closed the Mississippi River to American navigation in 1784. The Confederation's weak response prompted set-tlers along the western frontier to consider seceding from the Union and joining Spain's empire.

Chaos ensued from the Confederation's inability to control commerce among the states and with foreign nations, aggravating the economic hardship that the war had wreaked. The states imposed competitive duties and tariffs on goods coming from other states and fought with each other over foreign trade. These squabbles enabled Britain to engage in a policy of divide and conquer. British merchants got around the regulations of states that sought to restrict their goods by bringing their products in through states that did not. Britain expanded exports to America while holding imports to a minimum. The Confederation lacked the authority to retaliate.

Economic depression and the unfavorable balance of trade led to increased pressure on states to make life easier for debtors, especially for small farm-ers who were well represented in the democratic state legislatures. Farmers demanded that more paper money be printed to expand the money supply, mak-ing it cheaper for them to repay their debts. More than half the states yielded to this pressure between 1785 and 1786. Rhode Island printed so much money that creditors fled the state to avoid being paid in worthless currency. Although this case was extreme, many states experienced the ironic spectacle of debtors hunting down creditors, who hid for fear of being paid!

State legislatures that maintained a sound currency fared no better. Massachusetts's decision to maintain a tight money supply led to an armed rebellion. In the summer of 1786, mobs in its western communities tried to halt farm foreclosures by taking up arms and forcibly closing the debtor courts. The rebellion's leader was Daniel Shays, a war hero who had fought at Bunker Hill. The Massachusetts governor appealed to Congress, but the national gov-ernment had no legal authority to put down rebellions in the states. When the state government finally mobilized its own troops, with funds raised by frightened private merchants, and sent them to squash the uprising, the rebels attacked the Springfield arsenal. Shays was defeated and fled to Vermont, but the Massachusetts legislature did respond to the rebels' plight by providing some debt relief.

Shays's Rebellion greatly strengthened the hand of leaders, such as George Washington, Alexander Hamilton, and James Madison, who believed stronger national government was needed to solve the international and domestic troubles experienced under the Articles of Confederation. Still, there were many Americans, including such prominent patriots as Patrick Henry, John Hancock, and Samuel Adams, who resisted efforts to convene a constitutional convention for the purpose of tightening "the buckle of the continent." Indeed, to do so might jeopardize the democratic spirit aroused by revolution and agitated by economic crisis.

Jefferson, as a champion of American democracy, considered active engagement in politics critical to the protection of rights. From Paris where he was serving as ambassador, he wrote Madison urging him not to overreact to the Massachusetts uprising. Democracy has "its evils," he acknowledged, and the acts of Shays's band were "absolutely unjustifiable." But such popular rebellions, although "evil," were "productive of the good." They prevented "the degeneracy of government" and nourished "a general attention to the public affairs.... I hold it that a little rebellion now and then is a good thing, and as necessary in the political world as storms in the physical."

Washington and Madison disagreed with Jefferson. "What, gracious God, is man! that there should be such inconsistency and perfidiousness in his conduct," the usually stoic Washington declared after hearing of the Massachusetts riots. "We are fast verging to anarchy and confusion." Still, the supportive response of the Massachusetts legislature to the rebellion showed that Jefferson's sentiments were not merely the musings of a patriot abroad. After all, Shays's rebels were not radicals, calling for a redistribution of property, they were former soldiers and respected citizens trying to protect their property.

The disagreement between Jefferson and Washington about Shays's Rebellion highlights the uneasy relationship between the religiously based democratic egalitarian strand of American political culture and the Classic Liberal strand. It challenges the notion that equality and rights, both celebrated in the Declaration, were truly compatible. During the process of creating and ratifying the Constitution that followed this dispute, the American people displayed a remarkable ability to rise to that challenge.

The decision of all the states, except Rhode Island, to send representatives to a convention in Philadelphia in the summer of 1787 to redress the weaknesses of the Articles of Confederation was motivated both by the sense of crisis engendered by Shays's Rebellion and the fiscal difficulties of the states, and also by critical instances of intellectual and political leadership that pushed political opinion in a nationalizing and centralizing direction. The debate about whether and how to reform American government was greatly influenced by John Adams's three-volume work *A Defense of the Constitutions of Government of the United States*. Adams's decision to write it was provoked by Shays's Rebellion: "The commotion in New England alarmed me so much that I have thrown together some hasty speculations upon the government." He proposed strengthening the national government by establishing a two-chamber legislature – one popularly elected, the other based more on aristocratic principles – and a strong, impartial executive who could veto acts of the legislature. The whole system was to be overseen by an independent judiciary. Such a constitution would moderate the sort of raw and disruptive conflict between rich and poor that the Massachusetts uprising portended.

Noah Webster was particularly effective in making the connection between a growing sense of nationalism and the imperative of strengthening the central government. Webster would become famous later for his American dictionary; but during the 1780s, his *Spelling Book* made him a household name. The *Spelling Book* emphasized American, as distinct from British, language. Its preface urged Americans to appreciate and further develop their own literature. Webster's *Reader*, published soon thereafter, included selections from the speeches of revolutionary leaders whom Webster praised as orators the equal of Demosthenes and Cicero. Both of Webster's books sold several million copies and remained bestsellers through the nineteenth century.

Webster considered a strong sense of nationality vital to the preservation of the Union. Americanism was not just a matter of political principles and governing institutions. A true spirit of nationality could develop only from distinctiveness in the daily life of the people. It was intimately associated with everyday matters of dress, speech, manners, and education. Cultural independence was the "mortar for the stones of union.... An American ought not to ask what is the custom of London and Paris, but what is proper for us in our circumstances and what is becoming our dignity."

In an influential 1785 tract, Webster joined his appeal to America's sense of national identity to a defense of stronger union. The Articles of Confederation was too "feeble to discharge its debts" and was, therefore, unworthy of a rising nation. It encouraged Americans to think small, clinging to "provincial views and attachments" that arrested the country's development. Some form of allegiance to states and localities was necessary. Provincial liberties were an important part of Americans' sense of themselves as citizens. But the country would only reach its fulfillment if people in the various states recognized and embraced their shared sense of mission: "The citizens of this new world should enquire not what will aggrandize this town or this state, but what will augment the power, secure the tranquility, multiply the subjects, and advance the opulence, the dignity, and the virtues of the United States." Only in this way would American individualism transcend narrow, destructive selfishness.

## THE ORDINANCE OF 1787

Webster's celebrity indicates that the people's sense of national identity grew during the 1780s, preparing the country to accept a stronger national government. The Northwest Ordinance of 1787, based on an initial draft written by Thomas Jefferson, reveals this impulse toward a stronger national constitution. This legislation established rules for the Northwest Territory, which included the present-day states of Ohio, Indiana, Illinois, Michigan, and Wisconsin. These states were carved from territory that once belonged to the original colonies, who ceded them to the national government. The western lands, which just a few years before had encouraged conflicts among the states, became a force for unity once they were given to the national government. In keeping with Jefferson's belief that slavery was an evil that could not be abolished where it already existed but ought not to be allowed to spread, the Ordinance banned slavery in the Northwest Territory. Thus, westward expansion was able to proceed in conformity with the inalienable rights proclaimed in the Declaration of Independence.

Popular attachment to a strong national government was immeasurably strengthened by the adoption of that cause by America's first great heroes, Benjamin Franklin and George Washington. Benjamin Franklin was the first great spokesman for American national unity. As early as 1754, in response to the growing threat to the colonies posed by France, Franklin proposed a plan to place the colonies under a colony-wide government headed by a president general appointed by the king, and a grand council to be composed of representatives of the individual colonies. The plan was approved at a meeting of delegates from the colonies that took place in Albany, New York, but it was then met with overwhelming opposition from both the colonial assemblies and the British government. The individual colonies were not yet ready to give up any substantial part of their autonomy to a central body. The British opposed uniting the colonies into a central government that would be far more capable of resisting British authority than were thirteen separate and warring colonial governments. Franklin's commitment to unity is brilliantly depicted in a cartoon he printed in his newspaper, the *Pennsylvania Gazette*. Entitled "Join or Die," it shows a snake that is cut up into eight separate parts, each representing a separate colony, except for the five New England colonies, which are fused into a single segment, and Georgia and Delaware, which are omitted.

Franklin advocated on behalf of the colonies during two prolonged stints in London serving as an agent of the Pennsylvania colonial assembly. He helped draft the Declaration of Independence and, as the U.S. representative to France was instrumental in bringing France into the Revolutionary War on the American side. However, Franklin's greatest fame and popularity came not from his political endeavors but from his remarkable accomplishments in private life. He was a successful businessman, author, philanthropist, scientist, and inventor. His life embodied the virtues and possibilities that Classic Liberalism celebrated and promoted. He was a self-made man, the son of a printer. Everything he accomplished he attributed to his hard work, persistence, and willingness to take risks. He moved from Boston to Philadelphia because he believed that the latter city was more likely to give an ambitious nobody a chance to succeed. In the words of the Declaration, he would be freer to pursue happiness there. In a very short period of time, despite being a newcomer without connections, he became one of the city's most influential personages. He was fascinated with science, but as a conscientious liberal he was not content with acquiring scientific knowledge for its own sake, but sought to apply that knowledge to improving the comfort and safety of humankind. Among his many inventions were: the lightning rod, Franklin stove, and bifocal eyeglasses. He was perhaps most celebrated as the author and publisher of the widely popular *Poor Richard's Almanack*. The almanac was a yearly publication that contained weather forecasts, astrological information, poems, and stories, but it was most famous for Poor Richards sayings, many of which, such as "A penny saved is a penny earned," "Early to bed and early to rise, makes a man healthy wealthy and wise," "God helps them that help themselves," and "Haste makes waste," are quoted in ordinary speech to this day. Consider also "If you would persuade, you must appeal to interest rather than intellect," and "Plough deep while sluggards sleep." Taken as a whole, the sayings are a compendium of the virtues that comprise the Classic Liberal commercial republic – patience, self-reliance, self-interest, hard work, and frugality. Franklin the writer as well as Franklin the man was the embodiment of those virtues.

George Washington was the greatest of all early American heroes both for what he was and for what he was not. His extraordinary leadership talents kept the revolutionary army together despite the immense suffering and numerous defeats it endured, and eventually enabled it to emerge victorious. He was a person of immense dignity with the ability to inspire awe and respect from all who came in contact with him. But he was a new kind of military hero, one who did not seek to remain in power once the war was over. At the height of his influence, after the successful conclusion of the Revolution, he voluntarily returned to private life. His retirement from power had a profound effect everywhere in the Western world. The greatest English military heroes such as Cromwell, William of Orange, and Marlborough had sought political rewards commensurate with their political achievements. In contrast, Washington was sincere in his desire for all the soldiers "to return to our Private Stations in the bosom of the free, peaceful and happy country." Thus, he practiced the Classic Liberal commandments he preached. Even the greatest leader should not cling to power for its own sake. Once he had done what was necessary to ensure the liberty and security of his countryman, he should return to the comforts and pleasures of private life.

When these two heroes agreed to attend the Constitutional Convention in Philadelphia, they bestowed those proceedings with invaluable legitimacy. Washington, in fact, agreed to serve as the president of the convention, to preside over what was sure to be a contentious debate over the country's future. His unifying presence in Philadelphia did not discourage that debate, but it surely gave it more prestige and enhanced the prospect that the final document would receive a fair hearing from the American people. The cause of creating a more perfect Union was immeasurably strengthened by the personal commitments that America's two greatest heroes made to achieving it.

## CONCLUSION

Chapter 3 examines the Constitutional Convention and the Constitution it produced. Considering that it was meant to serve as the blueprint for a government, that document is remarkably brief. But its few pages outline a set of governing principles and institutions that are remarkably diverse and seemingly incompatible. It provides for both a central government and a union of states; a government of strict limits and immense powers; democratic accountability and antidemocratic insularity; and guarantees of liberty and protections for slavery. Its complexities and tension reflect the complexities and tensions that characterize the political culture in which it was produced.

As this chapter shows, popular democracy and a religiously based idealism were present in America from the beginning of European settlement. America was not just a place to escape to, but a place to build a "City on a Hill," which the people back home could look up to and seek to emulate. And, the city would be governed by those who lived in it, its cit(y)zens. But self-government for some did not preclude involuntary servitude for others. From its inception, America had to cope with the anomalous combination of egalitarian aspirations and dreadful oppression. Nor did a strong sense of mutual obligation and community spirit preclude an equally strong commitment to the rights of individuals, including a right to property and the flowering of a spirit of enterprise and self-reliance. To this day, Americans struggle with the warring tensions between civic commitments and selfish concerns, belief in equality and toleration of persisting inequalities that were present from the beginning. American political culture remains bedeviled by the ambivalent forces that set it on its path.

## CHAPTER SUMMARY

☆ Americans are more patriotic, optimistic, individualistic, religious, moralistic, and committed to a competitive free-enterprise economy than other advanced democratic republics. They are also more tolerant of income inequality and less supportive of using government to provide a guaranteed income to individuals.

☆ The path of American political culture was formed by three often conflicting influences : Puritanism, Classic Liberalism, and slavery.

☆ The Puritans stamped American political culture with a strong strain of commitment to democracy, equality, community solidarity, and serving as an example for other nations to follow.

☆ Classic Liberalism, developed by political philosophers in the seventeenth and eighteenth centuries, stamped American political culture with a commitment to natural rights, freedom of the individual, separation of powers, and limited government.

☆ The term "Classic Liberalism" should not be confused with Liberalism as the term is currently used. Liberalism in its modern guise connotes a belief in using the national government to achieve benevolent purposes. It is directly at odds with Classic Liberalism's stress on limited government.

☆ The establishment of slavery created a profound contradiction in American political culture. Christian and Classic Liberal principles warred with an acceptance of the most thoroughgoing dehumanizing oppression and victimization of a large minority of the population.

☆ The Declaration of Independence is the seminal statement of the American creed. It creates the theoretical foundation upon which the constitutional edifice is built. No other country has a set of key principles and statements to which its citizens adhere to the same degree that Americans adhere to the principles of "life, liberty and the pursuit of happiness."

☆ As embodied in the Articles of Confederation, allegiance to states and localities, not the Union, dominated the first efforts to form a national government in the United States.

☆ Among the critical shortcomings of the national government under the Article of Confederation were its inabilities to: collect adequate revenue; protect Western settlers; maintain free and open interstate and international commerce; stabilize the currency; and suppress Shays's Rebellion.

☆ The cause of creating a more perfect Union was immeasurably strengthened by the personal commitments that two of America's greatest heroes, Benjamin Franklin and George Washington, made to achieving it.

## MAJOR CONCEPTS

| | |
|---|---|
| Calvinist Protestantism | Classic Liberalism |
| Congregationalist | Continental Congress |
| Declaration of Independence | Modern Liberalism |
| Natural Rights | Northwest Ordinance of 1787 |

## SUGGESTED READINGS

Almond, Gabriel, and Sidney Verba. *Civic Culture: Political Attitudes and Democracy in Five Nations*. Princeton, NJ: Princeton University Press, 1963.

Du Bois, W. E. B. *The Souls of Black Folk*. New York: Penguin, 1996.

Franklin, Benjamin. *The Autobiography of Benjamin Franklin and Other Writings*, ed. Ormond Seavey. New York: Oxford University Press, 1998.

Hartz, Louis. *The Liberal Tradition in America*, 2d ed. New York: Harvest Books, 1991.

Howe, Daniel Walker. *The Political Culture of American Whigs*. Chicago: University of Chicago Press, 1984.

Kloppenberg, James. *The Virtues of Liberalism*. Cambridge, MA: Harvard University Press, 2000.

Maier, Pauline. *American Scripture: How America Declared Its Independence from Britain*. New York: Random House, 2002.

McWilliams, Wilson Carey. *The Idea of Fraternity in America*. Berkeley: University of California Press, 1973.

Meyers, Marvin. *The Jacksonian Persuasion*, rev. ed. Stanford, CA: Stanford University Press, 1990.

Miller, Perry. *The New England Mind: The Seventeenth Century*. Cambridge, MA: Belknap Press, 1983.

Morone, James. *Hellfire Nation: The Politics of Sin in American History*. New Haven, CT: Yale University Press, 2003.

Paine, Thomas. *Common Sense*. New York: Penguin, 1976.

Schuck, Peter H., and Wilson, James Q., *Understanding America: The Anatomy of an Exceptional Nation*. New York: Public Affairs, 2008.

Smith, Roger M. *Civic Ideals: Conflicting Visions of Citizenship in the United States*. New Haven, CT: Yale University Press, 1999.

Tocqueville, Alexis de. *Democracy in America*, eds. Harvey Mansfield and Delba Winthrop. Chicago: University of Chicago Press, 2000.

Wood, Gordon. "The Democratization of Mind in America." In *The Moral Foundations of the American Republic*, 2d ed., ed. Robert H. Horowitz. Charlottesville: University Press of Virginia, 1979.

Wood, Gordon. *The Creation of the American Republic, 1776–1787*. Chapel Hill: University of North Carolina Press, 1998.

# CHAPTER 3
## Contesting the Constitution

## CHAPTER OVERVIEW

This chapter focuses on:

☆ The design of the constitutional path the country still follows.
☆ The contending visions of what that path should be.
☆ A contemporary portrait of the U.S. governing framework.
☆ The role of leadership in the design and ratification of the Constitution.
☆ The compromises that enabled the Convention delegates to agree to adopt the Constitution.
☆ The "new science of politics" that the Constitution embodies.

Benjamin Franklin remarked at the 1787 Constitutional Convention that the president's chair depicted a "rising sun and not a setting sun," indicating his high hopes for the fledgling U.S. government:

While the last members were signing [the Constitution] Doctor Franklin, looking towards the President's Chair, at the back of which a rising sun happened to be painted, observed to a few members near him, that painters had found it difficult to distinguish in their art a rising sun from a setting sun. "I have ... often and often in the course of the session, and the vicissitudes of my hopes and fears as to its issue, looked at that [sun] behind the president without being able to tell whether it was rising or setting: But now at length I have the happiness to know it is a rising sun and not a setting sun.

Benjamin Franklin spoke these famous words at the Constitutional Convention while the delegates who labored during the summer of 1787 to draft the Constitution were coming forward to sign their names to the document. Franklin's remarks expressed the grave doubts that even the most optimistic Founders felt about whether the people would approve the new Constitution.

Even if they did, would the result, as the preamble promised, form a more perfect Union? Franklin himself confessed that "there are several parts of this constitution which I do not at present approve." It was, after all, the product of many compromises, made necessary by the diverse interests represented at the convention. Moreover, the Constitution – embodying an attempt to serve the competing traditions of liberalism and democracy – represented a novel experiment in self-rule, one that was bound to be controversial.

As the oldest man at the convention, Franklin was aware of just how daunting a task it was to launch not only a new government but also a new way of governing. The Framers of the Constitution had invented the large-scale federal democratic republic. Before the establishment of the United States, the ideas of democracy and republicanism had been applied only to small places, such as ancient Athens and the small American states under the Articles of Confederation. Large places were governed by kings or queens. Franklin trembled at the possibility that this effort to tie size to liberty might well fail.

In spite of his doubts, Franklin saw the sun rising over America because he believed that the Constitution gave institutional form to the values that aroused the Revolution and pushed the country toward the creation of a national community. Today, more than 200 years later, Americans have reason to share Franklin's sense of accomplishment and possibility. Despite dim and dark moments, the sun has never set on the American experiment in large-scale constitutional democracy.

The essential governing structure and key governing principles established at that convention remain in place to this day. Chapter 4 will examine the critical challenges and reconsiderations of the Constitution that have taken place at key moments in American political development, but none of those great constitutional moments pushed the United States off the central path that the Constitution paved. Indeed, the most important of those moments, the Civil War and its aftermath, is best understood as a fulfillment of the promise made in the Declaration of Independence that all men are created equal. As Lincoln understood, the Declaration and Constitution are inextricably bound together. Even those sections of the Constitution most at variance with the spirit of the Declaration, those that condoned slavery, never sought to justify it.

This chapter focuses on the designing of the constitutional path the country still follows. It describes the process of invention that took place at the Constitutional Convention held in Philadelphia in the summer of 1787. There was no precedent in all of history for the endeavor the Framers had embarked on. Therefore, they had to carefully consider a wide variety of alternative institutional forms and principles. That consideration, reflected both in the debates at the Constitutional Convention and subsequent debates over ratification, was the fullest and freshest exploration of how best to organize a free government that has ever taken place.

The last chapter concluded with a discussion of the debate that arose during the 1780s between those who believed that liberty was best preserved by an active and competent citizenry and those who believed that protecting liberty required limiting political participation in order to prevent mob rule. This quarrel was at the heart of the conflict between those who framed and championed the Constitution, who came to be called *Federalists*, and those who opposed it, the *Anti-Federalists*. But it was a lovers' quarrel. The two sides shared so much in common, most especially a deep and abiding love of country and freedom and pride in having thrown off the yoke of British rule. Both adhered to the basic tenets of Classic Liberalism: natural rights, the social contract, and limited government (see Chapter 1). Like a lover's quarrel, the fierceness of their disputes stemmed from the passionate attachments binding them together. The Anti-Federalists believed that Classic Liberal principles could best be protected by relying on a vigilant and active citizenry, not by the limitations on popular rule proposed by the Federalists.

Like most quarrels, neither side came away entirely satisfied with the outcome. On the whole, the Constitution was a victory for the Federalists. Its central premise, the creation of a strong national government, ensured that America would be a large republic that emphasized natural rights and placed obstacles in the path of majority rule. Key aspects of the Constitution – most notably the Senate and Supreme Court – were adopted despite telling criticisms about how antidemocratic they were. But the Constitution did not close the door on democracy. It gave the greatest degree of responsibility for funding the government to the most democratic element of the government, the House of Representatives. The Federalist effort to centralize power in the hands of the national government was tempered by the *Bill of Rights,* which, as first enacted, was viewed not as a list of individual entitlements but instead as a constraint on the power of the national government – as a bulwark of local self-rule. In particular, the Tenth Amendment's guarantee that "the powers not delegated to the United States by the Constitution, nor prohibited by it to the States, are reserved to the States respectively, or to the people" offered powerful protection against the destruction of the existing forms of local and state politics that the Anti-Federalists cherished.

## THE CONSTITUTION OF THE UNITED STATES: CONTEMPORARY PORTRAIT

What we take most for granted about the Constitution is actually its most remarkable quality: its unbroken span of existence for a period of more than 200 years. As it did in 1788, the American government still consists of a bicameral legislature, an independent judiciary, an independently elected executive, and a division of governing authority between the federal government and the states. As later chapters will discuss in detail, every one of these elements and the relationships among them has gone through considerable change over time. But this does not undermine the extraordinary stability that the constitutional has endured for more than two centuries. The Constitution was never intended to provide a detailed enumeration of how politics and government ought to act or how they do act. Rather, the Constitution provides a broad framework for political and governmental action and establishes a set of fundamental principles to guide that action.

No other nation has displayed anywhere near this high level of constitutional stability and continuity. In 1787, France was still a monarchy. Since 1789 it has had five different constitutions. In 1787 Britain was a monarchy with actual governing authority distributed among the monarch, the Lords, and the Commons. Now the monarch's tasks are almost entirely ceremonial and the Lords have been stripped of virtually all their governing authority. Germany and Japan have constitutions that date back a mere half-century.

Although the 1787 format remains in place, the current Constitution does differ from the original in a few profound ways. Most important of all, the Thirteenth Amendment, ratified in 1865, freed the slaves (the full Constitution appears as Appendix Two). The Fifteenth Amendment, ratified in 1870, guarantees the right to vote to all citizens regardless of race or color. The Nineteenth Amendment, ratified in 1920, extends full voting rights to women. The Fourteenth Amendment forbids the states from depriving their citizens of rights that the federal constitution guarantees. It states, in part: "No State shall make or enforce any law which shall abridge the privileges or immunities of citizens of the United States; nor shall any State deprive any person of life, liberty, or property, without *due process* of law; nor deny to any person within its jurisdiction the *equal protection of the laws*." Prior to its ratification, the Bill of Rights only applied to the actions of the federal government, not the states. Even after the Fourteenth Amendment's adoption, many states placed great obstacles in the path of its full implementation. But eventually states did come to accept the principle it embodied, that they were fully subject to all the requirements contained in the Bill of Rights.

Originally, the Constitution required that senators be elected by individual state legislatures. The Seventeenth Amendment, ratified, in 1913, required that senators be elected by the citizens of their respective states. The original Constitution established that the president be chosen by electors, comprising the *Electoral College*, rather than by a nationwide popular vote. Each state was granted a number of electors equal to their number of congressional districts plus two additional electors for their two senators. The states were free to choose those electors any way they wished. To win, a candidate had to obtain an electoral-vote majority, otherwise the choice went to the House of Representatives, who chose among the top five finishers (House members do not vote as individuals;

rather, each state delegation votes separately and each state is granted one vote). The Electoral College remains in place, but the Twelfth Amendment changed the process by which electors vote. The original constitution called for each elector to vote for two different candidates, one of whom must not be from the elector's home state. The Twelfth Amendment requires electors to cast only one vote for president and a second vote for vice president and, in the absence of an electoral majority, the House of Representatives chooses among the top three finishers. The Twenty-Second Amendment limits the president to two terms in office.

Taken as a whole, these changes redefine American government and politics in ways that expand both its Classic Liberal and democratic aspects. As a result of empowering ex-slaves and women and insisting on the popular election of senators, the overall political system has become far more democratic. It includes virtually the whole adult citizenry. By requiring states to incorporate the Bill of Rights, it seeks to ensure that the Classic Liberal principle of natural rights be universally enforced. By establishing separate and single ballots for president and vice president, it improves the odds that a single candidate will gain a majority of electoral votes and therefore the presidential choice will be made by the voters and not by the House of Representatives. By limiting the president to two terms, it diminishes the risk of a president becoming a despot.

As the judiciary chapter (Chapter 9) will demonstrate, Americans love to argue about the meaning of their rights. The extent and nature of the rights contained in the Bill of Rights is at the heart of public debate about and judicial consideration of issues as diverse as gay marriage, gun control, treatment of terror suspects, and the extent of the government's right to interfere with the rights of property owners. Given how much debate takes place about the meaning of the Constitution, it is especially remarkable to note how little of that debate revolves around the governing structure as outlined in the Articles of the Constitution as opposed to the proliferation of argumentation that surrounds the Bill of Rights. Indeed, the only serious constitutionally based argument regarding the structure of national governing institutions occurred in the wake of the 2000 presidential election when prominent politicians and opinion makers, including Hillary Clinton, urged that Article Two be amended to abolish the Electoral College and have the president be chosen by national popular vote. These calls did not result in any widespread movement to amend the Constitution. However, Democratic legislators in many states are supporting an effort to change state law to achieve the goal of national popular election in the absence of constitutional change. Nine states have passed a law that commits that state's electoral votes to the presidential candidate who wins the national popular vote regardless of how the popular vote in the state was cast. Thus, in a state whose voters chose, say, the Democratic candidate, the state's votes would be cast for the Republican candidate if the Republican had won the national popular vote. The law only goes into effect when enough states have enacted identical legislation to create

**Figure 3.1.** "A Defense of the Union and the Constitution." This 1861 lithograph by P. S. Duval and Son shows a certificate given to Union Army volunteers serving to subdue the rebellion of 1861. Reproduction Number:LC-DIG-pga-03676 (digital file from original print) LC-USZ62–64426 (b&w film copy neg.)

the 270 electoral-vote majority necessary to elect a president. The nine states that have passed the law account for more than a quarter of the electoral vote total. The same bill has been introduced in all the other state legislatures. If the 270 majority is reached, the issue of whether a state's right to choose electors includes the right to bind those electors based on results in other states is a matter that will undoubtedly be settled in court.

## "A New Science of Politics"

The contest over the Constitution was waged not only indoors, in the Philadelphia convention and state ratifying conventions, but "out of doors" as well, through the media. The New York ratification contest led to the most famous Federalist defense of the Constitution. The eighty-five separate essays that compose *The Federalist Papers* were written by John Jay, James Madison, and Alexander Hamilton using the pseudonym Publius (a Roman statesman who championed the cause of the people).

Publius acknowledged that a full-fledged defense of the constitution demanded nothing less than "a new science of politics." In *Federalist* No. 10 (see Appendix 3), Madison laid out the principle that most clearly separated not only the Federalists from the Anti-Federalists but the new political science from the old. He refuted the Anti-Federalist belief, shared by all previous republican thinkers, that a good republic was a small republic. He argued that a large republic was better suited for maintaining liberty because it discouraged the creation of a single majority faction capable of dominating the minority and depriving it of its rights. Madison understood faction to be "a number of citizens, whether amounting to a minority or majority of the whole, who are united by some common impulse of passion, or of interest, adverse to the rights of other citizens, or to the permanent and aggregate interests of the community." As we pointed out in Chapter 2, Madison's concerns about unreliable majorities were not merely theoretical; they were based on the terrible clashes between creditors and debtors that arose in the 1780s, culminating in Shays's Rebellion.

Madison, like all previous great republican thinkers, feared *tyranny of the majority*. But Madison parted company with them by denying that the problem of majority tyranny could best be solved by abolishing faction. Madison's analogy was that liberty bears the same relationship to faction that air does to fire. It is possible to snuff out a fire by depriving it of air, but then the people cannot breathe, either. Likewise, faction can be destroyed, but only at the price of snuffing out liberty for everyone.

According to Madison, previous thinkers had failed to appreciate that a large republic deals with faction better than a small one does. The larger the republic is, the more separate factions it will contain. As factions multiply, they become less able to coalesce into a stable and coherent majority capable of tyrannizing others. Size and diversity, traditionally the enemy of republics, turn out to be its dearest friends.

The sheer arithmetic of large republics dictated that the actual work of government will be carried out not by the people themselves but by their representatives. In Federalist No. 10, Madison argued that representation is what enables popular government both to remain popular and avoid the otherwise inescapable difficulties posed by popular rule. Caught up, as they inevitably are, in the task of earning a living and tending to their families, subject to prejudice and passion, ordinary people are simply not capable of assuming the burdens of governance. Even if they were all geniuses, their vast numbers and the sheer size of the districts they lived in means they could not all gather in one place and deliberate for days on end. Therefore, the best they can do is make reasonably good choices about who should govern for them and whether the record of those who govern is worthy of their continuing support.

Properly structured, the process of electing representatives enables ordinary people to hold their government accountable but does not place unreasonable burdens on them. Here again, size comes to the rescue. Bigger electoral districts are better than small ones because they contain a larger number of individuals fit to assume the mantle of leadership. They provide voters with a richer array of talent from which to choose. The keys to the new science of politics are therefore size and representation.

But what was to prevent the representatives themselves from forming a faction that would tyrannize the populace? To answer this puzzle he built on John Adams's idea of *checks and balances*. Although each branch would enjoy distinctive powers, none would enjoy a monopoly of power. Each branch – the president, Congress, and the judiciary – would be granted some power to meddle in the affairs of the others, ensuring that government power remained dispersed. Madison stated this view in a famous passage from the *Federalist Paper* No. 51 (see Appendix 4):

[T]he great security against a gradual concentration of the several powers in the same department consists in giving to those who administer each department the necessary constitutional means and personal motives to resist encroachments of the others.... Ambition must be made to counteract ambition. The interest of the man must be connected with the constitutional rights of the place.... If men were angels, no government would be necessary. If angels were to govern men, neither external nor internal controls on government would be necessary. In framing a government which is to be administered by men over men, the great difficulty lies in this: you must first enable the government to control the governed; and in the next place oblige it to control itself.

## The Anti-Federalists' Defense of the Small Republic

The Anti-Federalists were led by some of the greatest heroes of the Revolution, including Samuel Adams and Patrick Henry, who warned that the Constitution would destroy the "Spirit of '76" and drain the country of the popular enthusiasm for politics that the fight for independence had inspired. The Anti-Federalists opposed the large republic. Small size was necessary for democracy, they believed, because all self-government relies on friendship and trust among the citizens. Like the Federalists, they also feared tyranny of the majority, but they sought to avoid it by nurturing ties of mutual affection and common interest among the community, not by multiplying faction. To trust and empathize with another person, one has to know that person's character. Such knowledge is possible only in small places. As anyone who lives in a small town knows, not everyone has to be on a first-name basis with everybody else. But there can be no real strangers. By consulting a friend, or the friend of a friend, one can obtain a rich assessment of the character of a person that one does not know personally. This knowledge does not imply that everyone likes and trusts one another. Even in the smallest of towns, one is likely to make enemies. But because there is so much knowledge of one another, one knows whom to trust and whom not to trust. Although grudges and feuds are bound to develop, their importance in the overall scheme of things is likely to be small compared to the sense of mutual responsibility, affection, and solidarity that small places instill.

In a large place, people remain anonymous and are therefore incapable of disciplining one another. Small places are nosy and gossipy. This lack of privacy can be aggravating, but because people are so knowledgeable about each other, they can anticipate political problems before those problems mushroom into open conflict. The Anti-Federalists counted on the capacity of citizens in small republics to exercise mutual vigilance to nip the formation of oppressive faction in the bud.

*Small republics* are also better at political education. Schools made citizens literate, but a complete democratic education required active participation in the affairs of state. The Anti-Federalists considered *citizenship* to be like a muscle: it could only become strong through exercise. Only by partaking in the myriad tasks of local governance could people learn the hard lessons of citizenship: how to speak in public; listen carefully to others; and know when to hold fast to principle and when to compromise. Because Anti-Federalists counted on the people themselves to preserve and protect the republic, they were much more concerned than the Federalists were about the character and outlook of citizens. Left to themselves, the American people would retreat to private concerns, especially because the proposed Constitution would spawn a large, diverse society more concerned with trade and pleasure seeking than civic virtue. Corrupt and decadent people would be incapable of being good citizens. Therefore, the Anti-Federalists believed that a constitution should sanction vice and promote virtue. Because religion is such a powerful source of good conduct and also a potential source of terrible factional discord, the Anti-Federalists believed that government had to both support and regulate it. Some Anti-Federalists favored the establishment of an official church and punishment of religious dissent. They believed that successful democracy required the limitation of some forms of personal liberty, and they were prepared to pay that price.

## The Constitutional Convention: Leadership and Deliberation

Nearly 200 years later, the historian Catherine Drinker Bowen used the term "miracle" to describe the success of the Constitutional Convention in producing a single constitutional blueprint. But the miraculous events in Philadelphia were distinctively practical, the result of political debate, compromise, and decision. The convention succeeded because most of the delegates displayed a great talent for deliberation, and a few showed a great talent for leadership. Studying the Philadelphia convention allows students to see the workings of these two key political principles – leadership and deliberation – that are so central to the success of a large, complex republic.

*Deliberation* is the art of reasoning together. Political deliberation is the application of this art to public decision making. It is not enough to have good talks; political deliberation is successful only when an assembly comes to a decision about whatever public issue is at stake.

Political deliberation involves a complex set of skills and attitudes. The key attitude is open-mindedness. Whatever one's preconceived ideas, one must be open to changing one's mind. This may not happen often. But if one remains close-minded, the other debaters will see that efforts at persuasion are hopeless and they, too, will be tempted to close their minds. The deliberation will turn into irreconcilable conflict. If the constitutional deliberation had degenerated into a stalemate, it would have been a contest with no winners. Those delegates who sensed they were losing the debate would have diverted their energies either to sabotaging the convention or convincing the voters in the several states not to ratify the document that was produced. Because delegates allowed themselves to be influenced by other delegates, creative solutions were found to problems that at first seemed intractable. Today's government was born out of the painstaking and imaginative political deliberation engaged in by the men who wrote the Constitution and worked for its ratification.

To encourage deliberation, the convention delegates took the drastic step of adopting a secrecy rule: nothing spoken within Philadelphia's convention hall was "to be printed, or otherwise published or communicated without leave." The Convention took place without visitors, journalists, or even public discussions by the delegates in earshot of nonparticipants. Citizens who suspected that the Convention would strengthen the central government beyond what a democracy could tolerate complained that such a "Dark Enclave," as Patrick Henry put it, could only be the work of conspirators.

Even Thomas Jefferson, in Paris at the time, who thought the Convention "an assembly of demigods," complained of the "abominable ... precedent ... of tying up the tongues" of the delegates. His criticism expressed the principle that democracy is strengthened by, as Woodrow Wilson would later put it, "open covenants, openly arrived at." Public deliberations, these men believed, allow citizens to judge representatives and the arguments brought to bear in support of their positions. Moreover, public debates educate and improve public judgment.

Still, the convention delegates adopted the secrecy rule easily and never wavered from their decision to hold meetings behind closed doors. Reflecting on that hot summer in Philadelphia many years later, Madison insisted that "no Constitution would ever have been adopted by the convention if the debates had been public." The secrecy rule encouraged the delegates to take controversial positions, discuss them freely, change their minds, and work out compromises without fear of challenging received wisdoms, such as the sovereignty of the states, and without temptation to play to any gallery save that of posterity.

The enduring union that the Constitution achieved required more than the luxury of secret deliberations; it also required leadership. Madison, Washington, and Franklin provided that crucial leadership. Each had his own gifts and style, but collectively they gave the convention a sense of direction. Like most serious deliberations, the Constitutional Convention risked having to consider too many options in too little time. Madison, Washington, and Franklin controlled the agenda to ensure that the initial choices that were made would shape and guide later choices. They provoked the other delegates when the deliberation became listless, and they calmed their colleagues when it became overheated. They took initiative when others were timid and suggested compromise when others were intransigent.

George Washington made his greatest leadership contribution simply by showing up. As we noted in Chapter 2, he was the most famous and celebrated man in America. He had led the Continental Army to victory, and in the wake of that victory, he refused to help disgruntled army veterans overthrow the feckless national government and make him king. Having seen Washington's commitment to republican rule, no citizen could believe that he would use the Convention for selfish political purposes. At no other time in American history has one person towered over all others in terms of public affection and respect. The public was keenly aware that he was putting his great reputation at risk by agreeing to participate in this uncertain venture. Thus, his very presence at the convention greatly increased its prestige and legitimacy. It was a foregone conclusion that Washington would chair the Convention. As the presiding officer, he was called not chairman but president.

## Agenda Setting, Conflict, and Compromise

The delegates were slow to arrive in Philadelphia. Eleven days elapsed between the scheduled start of the convention on May 14, 1787, and its actual opening on May 25, when enough delegates had finally arrived to produce the minimum number of seven states required for official business to begin. Because Madison insisted, the Virginia delegation, including Washington, arrived on time. Madison had more than punctuality on his mind. He used the spare eleven days to work with the Virginia delegation to gain its united support for his plan. The session opened with Virginia's plan as the only one on the table and a Virginia delegate as the presiding officer. Under these favorable circumstances, the *Virginia Plan* became the framework for the Convention's subsequent discussions. The final document retained the most essential features of Madison's plan: three separate branches of government; federalism; and a bicameral legislature.

If all the delegates had arrived on time, there would have been no fully formed proposal to claim first place on the agenda. The delegates may well have chosen to begin with a broad discussion of the state of the country and wrangled about how best to revise the Articles. Such a meandering discussion might have produced only minimal changes, especially because the mandate given by Congress to the Convention was to revise the Articles not to write a new document Instead, the Virginia Plan, which clearly and self-confidently challenged Congress's instructions, put the delegates on the spot. They would immediately have to decide whether to abide by their instructions from Congress or write a new and powerful constitution. Because the choice was posed so starkly and the Virginia Plan was so comprehensive and compelling, the convention made its most decisive choice first, to face the full challenge of constituting a national government.

The heart of the Virginia Plan was contained in a resolution that Edmund Randolph, delegate from Virginia, proposed on May 30 "that a national government ought to be established consisting of a supreme legislature, judiciary, and executive." The words "national" and "supreme" left no doubt about the proposal's sweep. The national government would rule over the states and the national legislature would have enormous power, including the power to tax. Had the delegates been able to avoid such a stark choice so early in the Convention, a majority might have chosen to do so. But faced with an either-or decision, they chose to accept Randolph's challenge, and his resolution passed easily. For the next several weeks, the deliberations of the convention focused on the Virginia Plan. Although many of its specific elements were changed or rejected, there was no retreat from the principles encapsulated in Randolph's May 30 resolution. The fork in the road heading toward a new constitutional order had been taken.

On June 15, the opponents of the Virginia Plan finally introduced the *New Jersey Plan.* It was framed as a series of amendments to the Articles of Confederation and called for a revision, not a transformation, of the existing government. It left intact the one state-one vote legislature and made no broad claim about national supremacy. Had this scheme served as the initial basis of discussion, the convention's product might have been far less revolutionary. It is a testament to the political skill of the Virginians – Washington and Madison in particular – that the New Jersey Plan now seemed, by comparison to their plan, excessively tame, even though it did include proposals to give Congress power to tax and regulate commerce, establish a supreme court, and create an executive authorized to compel states to obey federal law.

## Compromise

In addition to the deep divide between delegates who favored a strong central government and those who opposed it, two other profound political divisions existed among the delegates. Those from the small states feared that if government was nationalized and consolidated, the views and interests of the large states – Massachusetts, Pennsylvania, and Virginia, in particular – would prevail. Slaveholders feared that the new nation's nonslaveholding states would try to persuade Congress to inhibit slavery.

Even if delegates from small states and slave states agreed in principle that the United States was a full-fledged union, not merely a compact of states, they recognized that reserving strong powers for the individual states was still the best way to protect their specific interests. They were not persuaded by the argument that the states would be adequately protected because the new national government was to be one of strictly enumerated powers. In principle, the idea of strict enumeration ensured that all matters not delegated to the national government would be reserved to the states, but the small-state delegates realized that such delegations of authority would never be entirely clear-cut. The national government would always be tempted to interpret its power in the most expansive manner possible. Indeed, nationalists could draw on general language, such as the final clause of Article I, Section 8, which authorized Congress "to make all Laws which shall be necessary and proper for carrying into Execution the foregoing Powers," to consolidate their influence. The Virginia Plan did not provide for any direct representation by the states in the national government, as the U.S. Senate now provides. Instead, it called for a Congress consisting of two houses; that is, a bicameral legislature. Members of the first branch would be chosen by popular election. Members of the second branch would be chosen by the members of the lower chamber from lists of nominees provided by state legislatures.

The most dramatic moment of the entire proceedings occurred on July 16, 1787, when a majority of the state delegations were persuaded to support the compromise over representation in the bicameral legislature, a plan based on Benjamin Franklin's motion. Franklin's plea for "the assistance of Heaven" had helped restore a deliberative atmosphere in which the delegates could consider the most difficult issue confronting them.

*The Great Compromise* provided for two houses. The lower house, called the House of Representatives, would provide representation proportional to each state's population. In order to provide some tilt in importance to this lower house, it was stipulated that all bills relating to the raising of revenue would have to originate there. The upper house was called the Senate, and its members would be chosen by the states. Each state, regardless of its size, would be entitled to two senators. As a result of this compromise, the bicameral legislature came to embody the two opposing views of what role states should have in the new constitutional order. In the Senate, the states would continue to be represented as distinct and equal political societies, whereas in the House they would be reduced to nothing more than the sum of their allotted representatives. As we discussed earlier, a similar compromise was adopted when the delegates created a two-stage process for presidential elections. The first stage was governed by the principle of population. States were assigned a number of presidential electors based on the number of representatives they had in Congress, plus their two senators. If one candidate received a majority of electoral votes, that candidate became president. But if no one received a majority, only the top-five vote getters survived to enter the second stage, in which each state had an equal voice regardless of its size.

The other major compromise, involving the toleration and protection of slavery, marked a major exception to the lovers' quarrel among liberals typical of the constitutional debates. How could such otherwise ethically progressive and sophisticated people abet this evil? The question is all the more perplexing because so many of them, including some slave owners, recognized the evil of slavery. They acquiesced because they feared that to oppose slavery would foment a greater evil, the dissolution of the Union. Slavery's advocates, a majority in all the slave states, had made it clear that they would oppose the Constitution if they perceived that it would threaten either the present or the future of slavery. Therefore, even those delegates most opposed to slavery were obliged to consider what life would be like if that threat were carried out. Their willingness to compromise with slavery came from their considered conclusion that to do so was the lesser of two evils.

Their willingness to *compromise over slavery* was partly rooted in their feelings of loss at being politically separated from so many of their revolutionary allies, especially the great Virginians – Washington, Jefferson, and Madison. But more important was their recognition that the Union had almost no chance of survival if the southern states left. Already the young fragile nation faced a hostile power, Britain, on its northern border. West of the Mississippi lay the French and Spanish empires. If the South seceded, the Union would be reduced to little more than a strip of coastline that extended southward only as far as Pennsylvania (Delaware would remain a slave state until the ratification of the Thirteenth Amendment in 1865). And it would share a long southern border with what would then be a hostile country. To make matters worse, the easiest route west went through the South. The North was hemmed in by the Appalachian Mountains and powerful, hostile Indian nations. The most active western settlement was occurring in the slave-owning territories of Tennessee and Kentucky. In the near future, the South was likely to become larger and more powerful than the North. Therefore, the northern delegates recognized that they had no practical choice but to appease the South on the issue that it regarded as most important, namely, slavery.

The Constitution contains three clauses protecting slavery. The first dealt with how slaves were to be counted for purposes of apportioning congressional districts. The white population of the Southern states was insufficient to maintain voting parity with the North in the House of Representatives. Therefore, in order not to be outvoted by the North, the southern states required that slaves be counted in the census, on which the apportionment of seats in the House would be based. Ironically, this demand forced them to admit that slaves were indeed human beings, but they were prepared to live with this awkwardness for the sake of protecting their political strength. The opponents of slavery were unwilling to count slaves on an equal basis with non-slaves, but they compromised by allowing each slave to be counted as three-fifths of a person for the purposes of congressional apportionment.

The second proslavery clause guaranteed the continuation of the importation of slaves for a period of twenty years. To ensure that this protection would not be abridged, this clause was declared non-amendable. This provision was politically the most complex because it did not have the unified support of all slaveholders. States such as Virginia that already had more slaves than were needed to run their plantations would have been happy to ban the importation of slaves as a way to increase the value of their slave property. But states such as South Carolina and Georgia that needed more slaves for their plantations had strong interests in continuing the international slave trade in order to keep the price of slaves down. In the end, the greater intensity of feeling on the issue among the deep southerners enabled them to prevail.

The third provision, and the one that was to cause the most enduring controversy, was the fugitive slave provision. This provision required all states, including those that prohibited slavery, to return escaping slaves to their owners. The fugitive slave provision in the Constitution states, "No person held to service or labor in one state, under the laws thereof, escaping into another, shall, in consequence of any law or regulation therein, be discharged for such service or labor, but shall be delivered up on claim of the party, to whom such service or labor may be due." The original proposal from the South Carolina delegation required "slaves and servants to be delivered up like criminals." The final version makes no reference either to slaves or criminals, only to persons "held to service or labor." Another version required that fugitive persons be delivered up to the person "justly claiming" their labor. The final version makes no reference to the justice of the claim. Instead of "justly claiming," it substitutes "to whom such service or labor may be due" and therefore ignores the issue of whether that claim is just. And the Convention's committee on style changed the definition of a fugitive from one "legally held to service or labor" to a person held "to service or labor in one state, under the laws thereof." This wording thereby removed any direct constitutional endorsement of the legality of the practice of slavery. If indeed a promise to return fugitive slaves was a necessity, it is difficult to imagine how such an endorsement could have been worded to offer less support for slavery in principle.

The fugitive slave provision of the Constitution represents the fine line the Framers walked between codifying slavery and denying its moral legitimacy. As dreadful as these concessions and compromises with slavery were, they could have been worse. Although allowing the continuation of slavery and even abetting it by promising to help catch fugitive slaves, the Constitution ostentatiously refrains from providing slavery with a moral stamp of approval. The term "slavery" is never even mentioned in the document. The embarrassed delegates resorted to euphemisms such as "persons held to service," a tacit acknowledgment of their feelings of shame in acquiescing to it.

One cannot entirely exonerate the antislavery delegates, because it is impossible to say for sure that their willingness to go along with these three provisions was indeed the absolute minimum degree of cooperation required to placate the proslavery delegates. After all, quitting the Union would have exacted a high price from the South, as well; the South, too, had an incentive to compromise to keep the Union intact. But if one accepts the premise that abiding with slavery was necessary to preserve the Union, then the northerners may be given credit for not making a far worse deal, one that indicated positive approval for slavery and provided it with moral legitimacy.

Obviously, scrupulous attention to the wording of proslavery provisions provided no solace for those doomed to remain in chains. But the Constitution's wording, which deprived the defenders of slavery of any additional moral ground to stand on, provided later opponents of slavery with a crucial moral advantage. If the document had directly endorsed slavery, Abraham Lincoln would not have been able, decades later, to claim that the cause of the Union, a cause rooted in the Constitution, required that slavery be curtailed. The convention's insistence on treating slavery as a necessary evil, rather than a positive good, enabled Lincoln to argue that the Framers intended to confine slavery in the expectation that it would ultimately die. This expectation, Lincoln insisted, demonstrated their belief that "a house divided against itself could not stand," and it justified Lincoln's position that a defense of the Constitution required that slavery was wrong and must ultimately be abolished.

## A Strong Executive

For the most part, the completed Constitution was based on the initial Virginia Plan as modified by the defenders of the states and slavery, but there was one critical deviation from Madison's initial blueprint. Neither Madison nor his Anti-Federalist critics envisaged the establishment of a strong executive branch of government as came to be provided for in Article II of the Constitution. The establishment of a strong executive owes its existence to the deliberative activity of the convention itself. In the end, the delegates agreed to create something that almost none of them would have been willing to accept beforehand. It was only as a result of continual debate over executive power that they came to accept this radical and uncomfortable idea.

The Virginia Plan was quite vague about the executive. It allowed for either an individual or a committee. Whatever it was, it would be elected by the legislature. This decision to keep it captive of the legislature reflected Madison's deep fear of despotism. Independence had come in a war against a king. Madison, like most of the other delegates, even those who favored a strong national government, feared creating another king. In fact, before the Constitution was written, the conventional wisdom held that strong executive power and democracy did not mix. Initially, Madison preferred to rely on the Senate to perform those tasks normally assigned to an executive. A few delegates, most notably Alexander Hamilton, Gouverneur Morris, and James Wilson, favored a strong and independent executive. But early on, they were a distinct minority.

Opposition to a strong executive melted slowly. As the overall shape and format of the national government became clearer, the majority of the delegates began to recognize that such a bold effort needed a single identifiable person in charge as well as the means to make that person accountable and responsible. Thus, the delegates agreed to a single person rather than a committee because no one would be able to figure out whom to hold responsible if several different people participated in an executive decision. Allowing the executive to run for reelection gained favor because it provided a means for holding an incumbent accountable. The hardest problem the executive posed involved the method of election. Allowing the legislature to choose the president would violate the principle of checks and balances between the branches, rendering the president subservient to Congress. Direct election by the people would allow a demagogue to win – a popular but unscrupulous leader who would make false promises and exploit prejudices to gain power. Moreover, delegates from smaller states feared that the larger states would dominate such a process. The Electoral College, as described earlier in the chapter, allowed for an indirect election and protection of the smaller states.

Although these various elements of the executive were considered during the course of the entire convention, they were assembled into a single package only at the last minute by a committee appointed to propose final solutions for the important matters that the Convention deliberations had left unresolved. When the overall proposal was presented to the delegates, they approved it overwhelmingly. In the course of a few months, most of them had traveled an enormous political distance, from opposing any independent executive to endorsing one that had a single person in control, was elected independently of the legislature, and was eligible for reelection. On no other question was the cumulative impact of all that deliberating so great.

## The Constitutional Frame

The Constitution established a set of governing institutions and pattern of relationships between those institutions that gave practical form to the Federalists' "new science of politics." The creation of a two-house Congress embodied both the principles of popular representation and of checks and balances. The *House of Representatives* was intended to be the more popular of the two houses. Its members would be kept relatively close to the people because they would have to run for election frequently, every two years, most likely from districts that were relatively small. (The Constitution does not mention district elections for the House, and they were not mandated by law until 1842).

By contrast, the *Senate* would be comprised of two members from each state who would be elected for six-year terms. Once the delegates reached the Great Compromise – signaling their intention to define a middle ground between the impotence of confederation and the danger of excessive centralization – most also agreed that they wanted a Senate that might perform the role of an "upper house." The Senate would not simply uphold states' rights but would also check the excesses of the more popular House. Six-year terms would insulate senators somewhat from the ebb and flow of popular passions. The system of staggered elections, by which only one-third of the Senate could change in any given election, would further enhance the ability of its members "to refine and enlarge the public views." Those senators from the bigger states would be especially free from popular pressure. The large size of their constituencies meant that they would represent a diverse set of interests and would not slavishly serve any one narrow point of view.

Because they enjoyed freedom from constituency pressure and their house was of manageable size, senators would be able to consider public questions in a "cool and deliberate" fashion. They could be calm and reasonable in ways that members of the House could not, providing them, in Madison's view, with a special responsibility:

Stimulated by some irregular passion, or some illicit advantage, or misled by the artful mis-representations of interested men, [the people] may call for measures which they themselves may afterwards be the most ready to lament and condemn.... [At such times, they need] the interference of some temperate and respectable body of citizens ... to check ... the blow mediated by the people against themselves, until reason, justice, and truth can regain their authority over the public mind.

For a bill to become a law it had to be passed by both houses. Likewise, a presidential veto could only be overcome by a two-thirds vote of both houses. Thus, each house of Congress would exert an independent check on the other as well as on the actions of the other branches.

To further enable "ambition to check ambition," the Constitution also established an independent executive and judiciary. When they created these independent branches of government, the Founders gave each branch sufficient power – and involvement in each other's affairs – so that each branch's own ambitions would act to stalemate the ambitions of the others. Congress checks the other two branches through its role in judicial and executive appointments and power of impeachment. The Senate has final approval over the president's choices for judges, members of the *Supreme Court*, and members of the cabinet. If no presidential candidate garners a majority of the Electoral College, the House of Representatives elects the president. The House determines whether a judge, an executive official, or the president should be subject to an impeachment trial. If the House impeaches, then the Senate decides whether to remove the impeached person from office. Any treaty negotiated by the president with a foreign power must be ratified by a two-thirds vote of the Senate.

The president's greatest power over Congress resides in the ability to *veto* legislation. This power is far from absolute, however, because Congress can override that veto by a two-thirds vote of each house. The president also appoints the members of the Supreme Court and other federal courts and members of the cabinet, all subject to Senate approval. The importance of the president in making the complex system of representation work further reveals the Founders' objective of moderating democracy. The Founders' intention was that the presidency was to be a great national office that would draw strong leaders – those who would not be content merely to respond to public opinion but would seek to leave an enduring record of achievement.

The Constitution was not explicit in providing checks for the judiciary over the other two branches. Indeed, as we describe in Chapter 9, the issue of whether the Supreme Court had the power to declare acts of Congress unconstitutional remained hotly contested even after the Constitution was adopted. In *Federalist* No. 78, however, Alexander Hamilton argued that the court did have such power and that its ability to declare laws unconstitutional was a crucial aspect of the checks and balances system. Because even a presidential veto could be overridden by Congress, the court needed this authority in order to prevent congressional despotism. Hamilton recognized that granting such great power to judges appointed for life was highly undemocratic. But he argued that because the judiciary was inherently the weakest branch of government, it was not in a position to abuse that power. Hamilton further argued that judges alone had the knowledge and institutional means to uphold the law. Only they were fully competent to interpret the Constitution, and their lack of executive authority meant that they would not do so in a dictatorial fashion.

In addition to the checks and balances among the institutions of the federal government, the Constitution provided the overarching check of states' rights. The system of *federalism* made for a "compound republic," Madison observed, in which "the power surrendered by the people is first divided between two distinct governments, and then the apportion allotted to each subdivided among separate and distinct departments." The system of federalism thus ensured "a double security" in protecting "the rights of the people."

Madison, and most Federalists, generally understood that the powers of the national government were limited to those specifically enumerated in the Constitution. The states retained sole power over all legitimate governmental activities that the Constitution did not grant to the national government. Although the exact extent of that grant was ambiguous, it was understood to be limited to those matters that spilled over state boundaries, most prominently interstate and foreign commerce and national defense. All the rest – the routine but critical matters that affected the daily lives of people, such as education, policing, and road maintenance – were left to the states. The Constitution also granted the states a good measure of influence within the national government itself. The president was to be elected by the Electoral College, whose members were chosen by the states and whose votes were cast on a state-by-state basis. The Senate gave equal representation to each state, and in the original Constitution, the senators were actually chosen by the individual state legislatures.

Finally, Article V of the Constitution gave the states an important role in the amendment process. Constitutional amendments, which required approval by two-thirds of both the House and Senate, also had to be ratified by three-fourths of the states. The Constitution also provided an alternative amendment method by which two-thirds of the states may call for a constitutional convention that would have the authority to propose amendments.

## Ratification

In order for the draft Constitution to go into effect, to be *ratified*, it had to be adopted by nine states. The outcome of the state-by-state voting was by no means certain. All the states had prominent Anti-Federalists.

As the Anti-Federalist Patrick Henry forcefully argued at the Virginia ratifying convention, the opponents of the Constitution rejected the wording "We,
the People" in favor of "We, the States." They recognized that the Constitutional
Convention had gone against the instructions issued by the Continental Congress
and the very first words of the preamble had revolutionary consequences. Their
preference was to marginally strengthen the national government without a
major alteration of the Articles of Confederation.

Despite their preference for direct citizen involvement, the Anti-Federalists
did recognize the need for political representation. Even state capitals were
too far away to enable most citizens to participate in state government. But
their innate distrust of representation led them to take a very different view of
national government than did the Federalists. The Anti-Federalists' goal was
to minimize the separation, both physical and psychological, between representative and constituent. Therefore, representative districts should be as small
as possible, enabling the representative to stay in touch with each constituent.
Elections should be held yearly, giving constituents frequent opportunity to oust
an incumbent who did not adequately reflect their concerns. No matter that the
result would be a House of Representatives so large as to be unwieldy and whose
members would serve such brief terms that they would not have a chance to
become knowledgeable and competent. The loss of effectiveness and deliberative capacity, argued the Anti-Federalists, were small prices to pay to preserve
democratic accountability.

The Anti-Federalists loathed the Senate. They recognized that its small size
and infrequent election would encourage a strong sense of collegiality among
its members. This was not the type of classroom or kind of mutual instruction
they favored. Anti-Federalists took the word "represent" literally. The task of
the representative was to *re-present* the views of constituents to the representative body. The Anti-Federalists envisaged representatives returning home frequently to districts small enough to enable them to instruct constituents about
the events taking place at the national capital and receive instruction about how
best to represent their constituents.

The Anti-Federalists similarly feared and loathed the proposed presidency.
Having severed from a king, why now voluntarily succumb to a monarch? They
opposed not only a commander in chief, but also the very idea of a standing
army available for such a commander to lead. They admitted that the Union
might face military danger, but they much preferred placing responsibility for
defense in citizen militias, mobilized by the states, whose sole purpose was
to respond to a military emergency. When the emergency passed, the militias
would disband, and the country would not then have to worry about how to
cope with the threat inevitably posed to its freedom by a standing army led by
a powerful commander.

Ironically, Anti-Federalists attacked the Constitution both for protecting and inadequately securing slavery. Southern Anti-Federalists such as Patrick Henry also warned that a strong centralized government made possible the abolition of slavery, which would cripple the South's economy. Conversely, the Massachusetts Anti-Federalist, Consider Ames, who had participated in Shays's Rebellion, indicted the new Constitution for sanctioning and protecting an institution that denigrated the core principle of the Declaration. Massachusetts had outlawed slavery by judicial decree just a few years earlier. Ames feared that the Constitutions necessary and proper clause could be interpreted so as to undermine the antislavery efforts of individual states.

The debates that preceded the ratification votes were long and heated. What ultimately enabled the Federalists to triumph was the same advantage they possessed in the Philadelphia convention: they had a specific, comprehensive, and detailed plan for governing the nation, and their opponents had none. Therefore, the Anti-Federalists were continually on the defensive, criticizing this or that feature of the Constitution but offering no broad alternative for how the new nation would sustain itself into the future.

The Federalists were politically astute enough not to trumpet the radical innovations that the document contained but rather to emphasize its fundamental compatibility with the ideas and principles that Anti-Federalists held dear. This shrewd combination of arguments is shown to best advantage in *The Federalist Papers*, written, as we have noted, for the express purpose of gaining support for the Constitution in the politically volatile state of New York. Each paper concentrated on either a particular reason for seeking change in the status quo, a particular advantage offered by the new Constitution, or a refutation of some criticism about the Constitution levied by the Anti-Federalists.

Taken as a whole, *The Federalist Papers* provided a systematic and comprehensive case for the necessity of revamping the Articles and adopting a strong central government. They also persuasively argued that the new government would preserve the most essential features and virtues of the existing system, most important, the power and influence of the states. Then, as now, a political campaign is usually won by whoever can most successfully appeal to the undecideds. The Federalists won because they could convince citizens in the middle that their plan was both radical enough to solve the problems posed by the weakness of government under the Articles of Confederation and conservative enough to protect the sovereignty of the states.

## A Bill of Rights

The Federalists found it wise to make an additional concession during the ratification debates. They pledged that if the Constitution were adopted, they would support the addition of a bill of rights, in the form of a series of constitutional amendments. Many state constitutions already contained bills of rights. In some cases, these rights were listed in the preamble of the state constitution, as if to show that the details of institutional design that followed should be viewed as the specific devices by which the goals set out in the bill of rights were to be achieved.

The leading architects of the federal Constitution, including Madison and Hamilton, had opposed including a bill of rights. They claimed to oppose it because such a list was unnecessary for a government whose authority was expressly limited to its enumerated powers. But this argument cannot be taken at face value because in various parts of the Constitution this principle of relying on enumeration is violated and specific protections against government excess are provided. The deeper reason the Federalists opposed a bill of rights may have been that the government they were trying to put in place would not be strong enough and that its enemies would make use of a bill of rights to weaken it still further.

Supporters of a bill of rights saw it as an essential means for explaining to citizens what the purposes of the new government were and how the public should judge it. This explanation was especially important to wavering Anti-Federalists who acknowledged the need for a stronger union but found the proposed Constitution devoid of any clear statement about how it was to serve the greater goal of protecting liberty. They feared that later generations would not fully realize that behind the Constitution lay the Declaration of Independence. In their minds at least, the Constitution was worthless if its various institutional contrivances were not explicitly dedicated to "unalienable rights." Therefore, they insisted that the Constitution be amended to enumerate the most essential components of those rights to ensure that future generations would be fully informed about what it was that their government had been established to protect.

The enduring importance and success of the Bill of Rights, its special place in the hearts of Americans, proved that its supporters were right. It is fitting that the lovers' quarrel among Americans over adoption of the Constitution should have led in the end to such a critical improvement in the nature of their relationship.

## CONCLUSION: THE ENDURING CONTEST

The Bill of Rights is one demonstration of the critical role played by the Anti-Federalists as well as the Federalists in founding the new government. The quarrels between these rivals were mostly resolved in favor of the Federalists. Not only did they succeed in convincing the convention to do more than amend the Articles of Confederation, but they also prevailed over the Anti-Federalists on two of the most contentious issues – the extended republic and the establishment of a direct connection between citizens and federal government. But the Anti-Federalists' enduring contribution both to the creation of the Constitution and subsequent development of American politics and government should not be underestimated. Even at the Convention itself, where their ranks were thin, delegates with Anti-Federalist sympathies succeeded in forcing the Federalists to provide a much more powerful role for the states than delegates such as Madison or Washington were initially inclined to accept.

The inclusion of a Senate elected by and with equal representation of the states was a compromise forced on Federalists. Likewise, giving the states such a prominent role in the amendment process and providing for the election of the president by an electoral college organized on a state-by-state basis were also grudging concessions made to win over the support of wavering delegates with Anti-Federalist sympathies. These specific provisions add up to the creation of a new form of federalism that represented one of the Constitution's most imaginative and daring innovations.

In order to win passage of the Constitution in several undecided states, the Federalists made an additional public concession to the Anti-Federalists. They promised to cooperate in establishing a bill of rights in the form of a set of amendments to the Constitution and to do so as quickly as possible. Americans have come to view the Bill of Rights as an integral and cherished part of the Constitution, and they have the Anti-Federalists to thank for it.

Although the more extreme Federalists, such as Hamilton, had hoped to use the Constitution to enshrine the dominance of centralized national authority, they did not succeed. The Constitution itself left the relationship between central and local politics in a purposefully ambiguous tension. Sadly, this ambiguity would eventually result in civil war. But it also provided the opportunity for democratic politics to survive and thrive within a constitutional context. As the American republic developed in the nineteenth century, the national government remained small and relatively insignificant, whereas state and local politics flourished. State constitutions were rewritten to permit and encourage democratic participation to an extent that would have warmed the hearts of Anti-Federalists (see Chapter 5). Democratic impulses gained a far greater grip on the national imagination than the Federalists expected or hoped. The key success in the framing of the Constitution was not to settle the lover's quarrel between a liberalism grounded in localism and civic vigilance and one grounded in representation and institutional checks and balances, but rather to create a strong and resilient framework within which these two indispensable point of view could continue to fruitfully collide and coexist.

## CHAPTER SUMMARY

✫ The Constitution provides a broad framework for political and governmental action and establishes a set of fundamental principles to guide that action.

✫ Taken as a whole, the critical choices that have been made to change the Constitution serve to redefine American government and politics in ways that expand both its Classic Liberal and democratic aspects.

✫ The principles and sentiments that the Federalists and Anti-Federalists shared were more important than those that divided them.

✫ The deepest division between Federalists and Anti-Federalists occurred with regard to the relative merits of the large and small republic.

✫ Madison, Washington, and Franklin each provided leadership that was critical to the success of the Convention.

✫ The Virginia Plan became the framework for the convention's subsequent discussions. The most significant departure from it was the creation of a strong, independent executive.

✫ Adoption of the Constitution by the Convention delegates hinged on two compromises. The first established a bicameral legislature with the upper house, the Senate, chosen by the states. The second inserted three separate clauses protecting slavery.

✫ Two critical guiding principles of the Constitution are checks and balances and federalism.

✫ The success of the Constitutional Convention was due to the political capacities of the delegates – their capacity to deliberate, compromise, and understand how specific decisions about the design of the government would affect the ability of that government to endure.

✫ What ultimately enabled the Federalists to win the battle over ratification was the same advantage they possessed in the Philadelphia Convention: they had a specific, comprehensive, and detailed plan for governing the nation, and their opponents had none.

## MAJOR CONCEPTS

| | |
|---|---|
| Anti-Federalists | Bicameralism |
| Bill of Rights | Checks and Balances |
| Constitutionalists | Due Process of Law |
| Enumerated Powers | Equal Protection of the Law |
| Federalism | Federalists |
| Natural Rights | New Jersey Plan |
| Ratification | Separation of Powers |
| Slavery | Virginia Plan |

## SUGGESTED READINGS

Bailyn, Bernard. *The Ideological Origins of the American Revolution.* Cambridge, MA: Harvard University Press, 1992.

Bowen, Catherine Drinker. *Miracle at Philadelphia: The Story of the Constitutional Convention, May to September, 1787.* New York: Book of the Month Club, 1966.

Chernow, Ron. *Alexander Hamilton.* New York: Penguin Books, 2004.

Fallon, Richard. *The Dynamic Constitution: An Introduction to American Constitutional Law.* New York: Cambridge University Press, 2004.

Farrand, Max, ed. *The Records of the Federal Convention of 1787,* 4 vols. New Haven, CT: Yale University Press, 1966.

Hamilton, Alexander, James Madison, and John Jay. *The Federalist Papers,* ed. Charles Kesler. New York: Mentor Books, 1999.

Jensen, Merrill. *The Articles of Confederation.* Madison: University of Wisconsin Press, 1963.

McDonald, Forrest. *The Formation of the American Republic.* New York: Penguin, 1967.

Rakove, Jack. *Original Meanings: Politics and Ideas in the Making of the Constitution.* New York: Knopf, 1997.

Rossitor, Clinton. *1787: Grand Convention.* New York: Macmillan, 1966.

Siemers, David. *The Anti-Federalists: Men of Great Faith and Forbearance.* Lanham, MD: Rowman and Littlefield, 2003.

Storing, Herbert, ed. *The Complete Anti-Federalist,* 7 vols. Chicago: University of Chicago Press, 1981.

Storing, Herbert, *What the Anti-Federalists Were For.* Chicago: University of Chicago Press, 1981.

Wood, Gordon. *The Americanization of Benjamin Franklin.* New York: Penguin Books, 2004.

Wood, Gordon. *The Creation of the American Republic.* New York: W. W. Norton, 1982.

# 4 Political Development

This chapter focuses on:

★ The greatest contests of opinion that have taken place in the course of American political development and the critical choices they produced. It calls such episodes "conservative revolutions," and shows why this term is appropriate and how it helps one to understand each episode and the overall course of American political development.

★ The path that American political development has taken since the most recent conservative revolution, the New Deal of the 1930s.

In January of 1830, the United States Senate began debate on a motion by Senator Samuel Foote of Connecticut calling for a temporary halt to federal government sales of lands in the West. What followed was no mere debate about the wisdom of such a step but a great debate about the nature and meaning of the Constitution. Senator Robert Hayne of South Carolina rose in opposition to Foote's motion. But rather than confining himself to the lands question, he launched a tirade against national government oppression of the states:

I am opposed, therefore, in any shape, to all unnecessary extension of the powers or the influence of the legislature or executive of the union of the states; and, most of all, I am opposed to those partial distributions of favors whether by *legislation* or *appropriation*, which has a direct and powerful tendency to spread corruption through the land – to create an abject spirit of dependence – to sow the seeds of dissolution – to produce jealousy among the different portions of the union, and, finally, to sap the very foundations of the government itself.

Hayne had a lot more than land sales on his mind in issuing this diatribe. Congress had recently passed a tariff law that was highly detrimental to the South Carolina economy. A *tariff* is a tax imposed on a good that is imported from abroad. Because it raised tariffs on manufactured goods, thus aiding northern manufacturers, it invited South Carolina's European trading partners to retaliate by raising tariffs on the state's agricultural exports. Southerners in general and South Carolinians in particular feared that this act of regional discrimination was only the beginning of northern aggression against the South. They feared that eventually northerners would attempt to use the power of Congress to limit or even abolish slavery. Hayne used the occasion of the land sale moratorium, bitterly opposed by westerners, to forge an alliance with the West in opposition to all unwanted federal intrusion.

Senator Daniel Webster of Massachusetts responded to Hayne that the Union was no mere alliance of convenience but something to be cherished and revered:

I know that there are some persons in the part of the country from which the honorable member comes, who habitually speak of the union in terms of indifference, or even of disparagement. The hon. member himself is not, I trust, and can never be, one of these. They significantly declare, that it is time to calculate the value of the union, and their aim seems to be to enumerate and to magnify all the evils real and imaginary, which the government under the union produces. The tendency of all these ideas and sentiments is obviously to bring the union into discussion, as a mere question of present and temporary expediency – nothing more than a mere matter of profit and loss. The union to be preserved while it suits local and temporary purposes to preserve it; and to be sundered whenever it shall be found to thwart such purposes. Union, of itself, is considered by the disciples of this school as hardly a good. It is only regarded as a possible means of good; or, on the other hand as a possible means of evil. They cherish no deep and fixed regard for it, flowing from a thorough conviction of its absolute and vital necessity to our welfare.

Hayne retorted that Webster misunderstood the intentions of Constitution's framers:

The object of the framers of the constitution, as disclosed in that address, was not the *i*, but "the consolidation of the Union." It was not to draw power from the states, in order to transfer it to a great national government, but, in the language of the constitution itself, "to form a more perfect Union"; – and by what means? By "establishing justice, promoting domestic tranquility, end securing the blessings of liberty to ourselves and our posterity." But, according, to the gentleman's reading, the object of the constitution was, to *consolidate the government,* and the means would seem to be, the promotion of injustice, causing domestic *discord,* and depriving the states and the people "of the blessings of liberty" forever.

Webster replied that it was Hayne, not he, who misunderstood the Framers. "I deem far otherwise of the union of the states, and so did the framers of the constitution themselves. What they said I believe ... that the union of the states is essential to the prosperity and safety of the states.... I would strengthen the ties that hold us together."

Hayne supported his view of the Constitution by describing it as a compact between the states and that it was up to each state to decide whether or not a particular national government action violated the compact. In that case the state had every right to refuse to obey:

The constitution of the United States was formed by the sanction of the states, given by each in its sovereign capacity. It adds to the stability and dignity, as well as to the authority, of the constitution, that it rests upon this legitimate and solid foundation. The states, then, being the parties to the constitutional compact, and in their sovereign capacity, it follows of necessity that there can be no tribunal above their authority to decide. In the last resort, whether the compact made by them be violated and consequently that, as the parties to it, they must themselves decide, in the last resort, such questions as may be of sufficient magnitude to require their interposition.

Webster pointed to the chaos that would result from Hayne's view that a state could refuse to abide by a federal government mandate:

Four-and- twenty interpreters of constitutional law, each with a power to decide for itself, and none with authority to bind anybody else, and this constitutional law the only bond of their union! What is such a state of things but a mere connection during pleasure, or, to use the phraseology of the times, *during feeling*? And that feeling, too, not the feeling of the people, who established the Constitution, but the feeling of the State governments.

He also derided the constitutional theory on which such an absurd result rested.

This absurdity ... arises from a misconception as to the origin of this government and its true character. It is, Sir, the people's Constitution, the people's government, made for the people, made by the people, and answerable to the people. The people of the United States have declared that this Constitution shall be the supreme law. We must either admit the proposition, or dispute their authority. The States are, unquestionably, sovereign, so far as their sovereignty is not affected by this supreme law. But the State legislatures, as political bodies, however sovereign, are yet not sovereign over the people. So far as the people have given power to the general government, so far the grant is unquestionably good, and the government holds of the people, and not of the State governments. We are all agents of the same supreme power, the people. The general government and the State governments derive their authority from the same source. Neither can, in relation to the other, be called primary, though one is definite and restricted, and the other general and residuary. The national government possesses those powers which it can be shown the people have conferred on it, and no more. All the rest belongs to the State governments, or to the people themselves. So far as the people have restrained State sovereignty, by the expression of their will, in the Constitution of the United States, so far, it must be admitted, State sovereignty is effectually controlled.

He ended his defense of the Union with a paean of praise to its many blessings:

Every year of its duration has teemed with fresh proofs of its utility and its blessings; and although our territory has stretched out wider and wider, and our population spread farther and farther, they have not outrun its protection or its benefits. It has been to us all a copious fountain of national, social, and personal happiness.... "Liberty and Union, now and for ever, one and inseparable!"

This debate between two powerful and prestigious senators epitomizes the great contests of opinion that have periodically threatened to either unravel the Union itself or undermine its capacity to function. These contests have also been about very particular policy questions – tariffs, the extension of slavery to western territories, old age pensions. But, as Webster and Hayne both demonstrated, those specific policy differences have been linked to the deepest questions about the nature and meaning of the Constitution.

This chapter focuses on the great contests of opinion and the critical choices stemming from them that have periodically surfaced in the course of American political development. It reinforces the arguments made in Chapter 3 that the Constitutional order has remained fundamentally unchanged. It combines this claim of stability with the equally valid claim that the American political system has undergone several critical reconsiderations and transformations. It attempts to reconcile these claims about continuity and change through its depiction of each of these critical episodes of reconsideration and transformation as a *conservative revolution*. Each was revolutionary in that it resulted in some major shift in the understanding of individual rights, the meaning of democracy and equality, and of the role of government. It was conservative in its fidelity to fundamental constitutional norms and principles.

The first section of this chapter connects Chapter 3's study of the Constitution with the critical political episodes that form the core of this chapter. The subsequent sections focus on those episodes that are central to the development of the American nation: Thomas Jefferson's *Revolution of 1800*, Andrew Jackson's *mass democracy*, the *American Civil War*, and *the New Deal*. Finally, the chapter explores political developments since the New Deal.

## AMERICAN POLITICAL DEVELOPMENT: CRUCIAL EPISODES

### The First Conservative Revolution: Jefferson's Democratization of the Constitution

No sooner had the Constitution been ratified than Americans began to fight over its meaning. This contest led to the emergence of two fiercely divided parties, the Federalist and Republican parties, which became engaged in a heated contest of principle. The Federalists, led by Alexander Hamilton, and the Republicans, led by Thomas Jefferson, both spoke the language of rights and accepted the "self-evident" truth that government existed to protect property and free enterprise. But the two parties disagreed fundamentally about the relationship between liberty and democracy and whether rights were best protected by limiting or encouraging active citizen participation. Federalists believed that republican government rested in the deliberations of political representatives held at a considerable distance from popular opinion. Republicans championed the view, as Jefferson put it, that political authority "could be trusted nowhere but with the people in mass."

Constitutional struggle broke out during George Washington's first term, thwarting his desire to place the presidency and the Constitution above partisan conflict. Washington's two most brilliant cabinet ministers – Alexander Hamilton, secretary of the treasury, and Thomas Jefferson, secretary of state – differed over Hamilton's program to strengthen government's finances. At the request of the first Congress, Hamilton issued a series of reports between 1790 and 1791 that called on the legislature to fund the national debt, assume the war debts of the states, encourage manufacturing through the creation of a system of tariffs, and create a national bank. Jefferson opposed the national bank because he feared it would establish an unhealthy concentration of power in the national government, creating a dangerous tie between the capital and the country's wealthiest citizens, and because it was unconstitutional. Jefferson believed that democracy required a predominant agricultural sector, comprising small landholders of roughly equal wealth. Hamilton's commercial republic, Jefferson claimed, would breed inequality and moral decay, thus destroying the moral foundation of a free society.

Hamilton and his allies, identifying themselves as the respectable defenders of constitutional order, called themselves Federalists. Washington refused to adopt the label but tilted toward Hamilton. The Jeffersonians rejected the name Anti-Federalist and instead called themselves Republicans, sentinels of liberty standing against the Federalist threat. Republicans did not want to destroy the Constitution but did want to restore its balance between rights and popular rule, liberalism and democracy. They opposed the expansion of national government authority because Congress would be forced to delegate more responsibility to the executive branch. The Republicans believed that such an "administrative republic" would make the more decentralized and popular institutions – Congress and the states – subordinate to the executive, would frustrate popular sovereignty, and would push the United States toward a British-style monarchy.

The first conservative revolution took place between 1800 and 1808, during Thomas Jefferson's two terms as president. It promoted democracy by endorsing and nurturing those political institutions and constitutional principles that Jefferson and his followers considered to be most democratic in character, such as free speech, legislative supremacy, and a powerful defense of states' rights. And, it was inextricably connected to two new forms of political communication and conflict: a popular press and political parties.

The Republican attack on the Washington administration was not confined to the councils of government; it was also communicated directly to the public through newspapers. In early 1791, Hamilton helped start the *United States*

*Gazette*. Jefferson and James Madison aided in the establishment of a competing Republican newspaper, the *National Gazette*, which appeared in October 1791. As the political struggle between the Republicans and Federalists intensified, the number of newspapers expanded dramatically, from fewer than 100 in 1790 to more than 230 in 1800. By 1810, Americans were buying 22 million copies of 376 newspapers annually, the largest newspaper circulation in the world.

Madison's essays in the *National Gazette*, published in 1791 and 1792, demonstrated his opposition to the Federalists' concentration of executive power. Previously, Madison's fears of majority tyranny led him to support the Constitution's institutional arrangements for dividing and filtering the voice of the people. But now he sought to arouse a "common sentiment" against the consolidation of government power. Formerly a defender of nationalism, Madison became a champion of the states as agents for mobilizing public opinion against excessive consolidation. By working with Jefferson to organize the Republican Party, Madison championed the political centralization that building a national political party entailed as the best way to defend state and local interests against governmental centralization.

Previously, Madison had opposed Jefferson's notion that the "Constitution belongs to the living." He had warned against frequent public appeals about constitutional issues, fearing that popular contests over them would "carry an implication of some defect in the government" and thus "deprive the [Constitution] of that veneration which time bestows on everything." Continual constitutional discord would prevent the Constitution from establishing itself as the American political religion. But Madison came to believe that the Federalists had undermined the Constitution's system of checks and balances and had created a struggle between the many and the few. Now it was necessary to provoke just the sort of popular constitutional debate he had previously opposed.

The terms of this debate were illustrated by the different ways in which Republicans and Federalists chose to celebrate the Fourth of July, which became a national holiday during the 1780s. The Federalists emphasized nationalism and made few, if any, references to the Declaration of Independence, whose anti-British character embarrassed the Federalists, who now sought economic and political reconciliation with the mother country. Also, the claim that all men were created equal seemed too democratic. Federalists preferred to celebrate the Constitution – whose more perfect Union was dedicated to moderating America's democratic impulses – rather than praise Jefferson's handiwork.

Republicans, by contrast, celebrated the Declaration as a "deathless instrument," written by "the immortal Jefferson." They eagerly invoked its indictments of the British monarchy and recalled America's great debt to its sister republic, France. Above all, they stressed the Declaration's opening paragraphs – proclaiming that all men were created equal with unalienable rights – which they celebrated as America's creed. The essence of that creed, one Republican newspaper claimed, was not to be celebrated merely "as affecting the separation of one country from the jurisdiction of another; but as being the result of rational discussion and definition of the rights of man, and the ends of civil government."

The Republican triumph over the Federalists in the 1800 election strengthened the democratic character of the Constitution. This shift toward democratic principles did not dismantle republican government, but it did put an end to Federalist efforts to restrain popular opinion and secure ordered liberty through the creation of an administrative establishment in the nation's capital. Jefferson was the first president to invoke the authority of the "will of the majority." He denied that the president, not to mention the judiciary, could claim authority that did not rest ultimately with "the people in mass."

"Absolute acquiescence in the decisions of the majority," Jefferson declared in his first inaugural address, "is the vital principle of republics, from which there is no appeal but force, the vital principle and immediate parent of despotism." Representatives' views, even those of presidents, should not be privileged over ordinary Americans, for when the voices of democratic citizens were added together they represented the ultimate sovereign. These combined voices represented *public* opinion – a concept that would soon come to dominate American political culture.

The *Revolution of 1800* was dedicated to strengthening the decentralist and democratic institutions of the Constitution – the states and the House of Representatives. The Republicans sought to limit the scope of central government authority so that it rarely touched people's lives. They cut taxes and spending. Jefferson pardoned everyone (mostly Republican newspaper editors) convicted under the recently expired Sedition Act.

But the Revolution of 1800 was a decidedly conservative one. Republican faith in democracy was not absolute. Office was sought as a matter of honor, on the basis of accomplishments and service to one's country, not through active campaigning. Full citizenship rights, including the vote, were limited to men with property. Property qualifications were relatively modest – about two in three white males could vote in America compared to one in four in England – but most Republicans considered property to be an important barometer of independence and responsibility. Except for changing how the Electoral College voted for president, the Republicans presided over no formal constitutional changes. Despite their criticisms of the undemocratic nature of the judiciary they left it intact. Likewise, they did not fully dismantle the Federalists' economic program. The National Bank remained until 1811, when its charter expired. In 1816, after the War of 1812 with Britain made clear the need for some sort of currency control, the Republicans chartered a second bank.

Jeffersonians did not advocate a permanent mass party system. The Republican Party was a temporary expedient for defeating the Federalists

**Figure 4.1.** The Heartland: U.S. postage stamp printed in 1904 in memory of the 1803 Louisiana Purchase. Credit: The Granger Collection, NYC – All rights reserved.

and restoring balance to the constitutional order. Having accomplished those tasks, it could safely wither away, restoring the nonpartisan character of the Constitution. Jefferson's first inaugural address made overtures to Federalists, promising constitutional continuity and political moderation: "Every difference of opinion is not a difference of principle.... We have all called by different names brethren of the same principle. We are all republicans – we are all federalists."

Jefferson's purchase of Louisiana, a territory encompassing not only New Orleans but most of what now constitutes the Great Plains and Northwest, doubled the country's size, adding some 830,000 square miles. The Constitution made no provision for acquiring foreign territory and incorporating it into the Union. But constitutional niceties were overlooked so that this vast territory could be added to "make room for the generations of farmers yet unborn," strengthening the rural and therefore democratic character of the republic. Jefferson reconciled this effort to preserve the agrarian character of the country with his fear that America could thus become an empire on the order of France or Great Britain by declaring that this vast addition of empty space would enable America to become an *Empire of Liberty*. The terrible consolidation of power that had resulted from the formation of the European empires would be avoided because the new territory would quickly be divided into self-governing units set on a path toward statehood. In that manner, the United

States would remain decentralized with political primacy remaining in the states and localities.

## The Second Conservative Revolution: Mass Democracy

Like the Jeffersonians, Jackson and his political allies sought to strengthen the democratic tradition that the Constitution had sought to tame. But the Jacksonians' political philosophy encouraged a much bolder assault on the principles and institutions of republican government that were dedicated to harnessing majority rule than the Jeffersonians had undertaken. By the 1830s, the word "democracy" had largely supplanted "republicanism" as a description of American government. Indeed, the Jacksonians changed their party's name from Republican to Democrat. This change followed from the Jacksonian celebration of majority rule. The constitutional battles between Republicans and Federalists obscured their agreement about the need to moderate democracy through institutional checks and balances. The Jacksonians sought to reverse this equation and make the Constitution and its institutional arrangements servants of public opinion. Democracy did not displace liberalism in the Age of Jackson. Rather, Jacksonians sought to capture liberalism for the people. Thereafter, demands for rights would have to come to terms with a highly mobilized, competitive, and locally oriented democracy.

Andrew Jackson embodied this version of democracy. He was the first "outsider" president. His predecessors were highly educated and had undergone extensive apprenticeships in national politics and diplomacy. A self-made man, Jackson had little formal education, only brief experience in Congress, and no experience in the executive branch. In his first inaugural address, he stated the matter forthrightly: "The majority is to govern."

The most powerful expression of Jacksons' egalitarian instinct was his decision to *veto the rechartering of the Second Bank of the United States.* He believed that destroying the bank did not threaten a free economy but instead honored it. He hoped to unleash the commercial spirit of the people from the shackles of government-created monopolies such as the bank, which favored idle speculators over the productive members of society: farmers, laborers, and mechanics. The clarion call of Jacksonian democracy, "equal rights to all and special privileges to none," promised political and economic independence to the producing "bone and sinew of the country." Jackson coupled his attack on economic centralization with an attack on governmental consolidation. He vetoed federally funded road projects. He cut the federal budget, creating a revenue surplus. He used the surplus to pay off the national debt and returned what was left over to the states.

Jackson's championing of the will of the people greatly increased the pressure to open up the political process. By the late 1820s, most states had eliminated property qualifications for office holding and had expanded suffrage to include all adult white males. *Voter turnout* soared. In 1824, only 27 percent of the eligible voters bothered to go to the polls. By 1828, when Jackson was elected, turnout doubled to 56 percent. In 1840, 78 percent of eligible voters cast ballots, a remarkable rate of participation that did not decline until the end of the nineteenth century.

The *party system* arose as a means to both stimulate and discipline this extraordinary burst of democratic vitality. The Jefferson-led Republicans had viewed their party as a temporary expedient for defeating the Federalists' program of "consolidation." Their successors, the Jackson-led Democrats, defended not just parties but a *party system* as a critical extra constitutional device to make democracy work (see Chapter 11). Parties were the only means for cultivating strong attachments between the people and fundamental law. "Political parties are the schools of political science," a Jacksonian newspaper editorialized, "and no principal can be safely incorporated into the fabric of national law until it has been digested, limited, and defined by the earnest discussions of two parties.... [Parties] diffuse knowledge, cultivate the popular mind, and as they tend to give the people larger liberties, prepare them for enjoyment."

The Democratic party itself embodied these decentralizing principles. During the Jeffersonian era, national politics centered on the congressional caucus, which had the power to nominate candidates for president and vice president. As we discuss in Chapter 8, the Democrats replaced "King Caucus" with national nominating conventions dominated by state party conventions whose delegates sprang directly from the rank and file.

To extend this grassroots politics into government, the Jacksonians were committed to rotation in government office, using the president's appointment and removal power to give jobs to partisan loyalists. New York Senator William Marcy, a militant Jacksonian, described the credo of the new patronage system: "To the victors belong the spoils of the enemy." By the end of the nineteenth century, reformers would attack the *spoils system* as a corrupting influence on government. But *patronage politics* was conceived originally to extend the people's control over the executive branch. As Jackson put it in his first annual message to Congress, "The duties of all public officers are, or at least admit of being made, so plain and simple that men of intelligence may readily qualify themselves for their performance."

Patronage did not always serve democratic principles well. The lust for government jobs could exalt party organization as an end in itself – to the detriment of firm attachments to principles and programs. Nonetheless, the mechanism of periodic replacement of a substantial part of the government established the material basis for a mass party that mobilized large turnouts in presidential elections and thus counteracted "general indifference" to political life, which Tocqueville identified as the greatest threat to liberty in the United States. Prior to the 1830s, the spoils of office usually referred to the benefits that legislators bestowed on their constituents. Following the rise of the Democratic Party, spoils came to refer to the perquisites that party leaders lavished on campaign workers.

Decentralist, patronage-based democracy became so dominant that the *Whigs*, the opposition party formed against Jackson's bank veto, also committed themselves to it. They, too, claimed descent from Jefferson and praised his celebration of the dignity of the democratic individual. To avoid appearing elitist, Whig leaders such as Henry Clay of Kentucky and Daniel Webster of Massachusetts sought to convey the impression that they were less well educated and privileged than they actually were.

The Whigs set the precedent for how an opposition ought to behave in a party system. They did maintain and express important political differences from the Democrats. They believed in a much stronger federal government than did the Jacksonians. They supported a federally controlled national banking system and federal funding of roads, canals, and other forms of internal improvements. They also sought to strengthen Congress and keep a stronger check on the executive. But in the midst of these differences, they did not challenge the core Jacksonian commitment to local self-government. Nor did they question the legitimacy of the other party, tacitly admitting that both they and the Democrats were loyal supporters of the Constitution.

## The Third Conservative Revolution: The Contest over Slavery and the Triumph of the Union

Neither Whigs nor Democrats sought to engage Americans in a contest of opinion over slavery. Both were national parties, and their leaders feared that such a sectional struggle would fracture the Union. But the party system could not long suppress such a profound moral issue. Fittingly, the movement against slavery grew out of the churches. Evangelical Christianity, today considered a conservative force, was then a powerful reform agent. Animated by the religious revival efforts of the 1830s, called the Second Great Awakening, religious groups organized Sunday schools, spread the Gospel, opposed drinking, worked for peace, and fought slavery.

Abolitionists (see Chapter 12) sought to extend their influence through religious societies. There were 47 abolitionist societies in 1833, and more than 1,000 by 1837. Antislavery preachers moved from town to town, organizing new chapters and enlisting reform-minded church members, especially women, in petition drives to place antislavery motions before Congress. Although abolitionists operated outside regular political channels, they benefited from the spread of mass democracy. Appealing to a public already accustomed to following national political debates, the abolitionists flooded the country with newspapers, pamphlets, tracts, and pictures calculated to arouse African Americans, free and slave, and northern public opinion against forced servitude.

The Jacksonian Democrats sought to repress abolitionism. In his 1835 annual message to Congress, President Jackson, whose hero, Jefferson, had fought against censorship, called for a national law barring "incendiary" materials from the mails. When Congress did not pass the law, Jackson imposed it administratively, ordering postmasters to remove antislavery material from the mails. Jackson's action drew little opposition from the political establishment. Even in the North, most Democratic and Whig newspaper editors viewed abolitionism as a threat to peace and union. But Jacksonian democracy had unleashed popular forces beyond its leaders' control. Hundreds of petitions with tens of thousands of signatures poured into Congress, pressing for the abolition of slavery in the nation's capital and asking that neither Florida nor Texas be added to the Union as slave states.

In a last, desperate attempt to stifle debate, House leaders proposed a "gag rule" that prohibited the House from discussing or even mentioning the anti-slavery petitions. The gag rule passed in 1835 with Jackson's strong support, and was tightened in 1840 during the term of his successor, Martin Van Buren. This affront to democracy was turned to the advantage of the antislavery forces by Jackson's old political rival, John Quincy Adams, who had been elected to the House in 1834. Adams adroitly exploited reverence for the Declaration of Independence and popular rule to defeat the gag rule. In January 1842, Adams presented an antislavery petition from a town in his district and ordered the House clerk to read the Declaration of Independence – reminding the House that popular rule rested on unalienable rights that slavery defiled. Adams exploited the gag rule controversy to remind white people that the basic right of free speech was also under attack. Thus, he was able to enlist support from Americans who, regardless of their views on slavery, believed that the House should remain a free and open arena for democratic debate. The House repealed the gag rule in 1844.

A national debate over slavery exploded with the enactment of the *Kansas-Nebraska Act of 1854*. Sponsored by Senator Stephen Douglas and supported by President Franklin Pierce, the act repealed the Missouri Compromise that had adopted a specific line of longitude above which all territories that had been part of the Louisiana Purchase would be admitted as free states, and allowed the Kansas and Nebraska territories to adopt slavery if they chose to do so. This new formula permitting territories to decide for or against slavery by popular vote was called *popular sovereignty*. The bill represented the corruption of Jacksonian democracy by slavery and the spoils system. It passed Congress because of Pierce's heavy-handed use of patronage and was justified as a logical extension of the Democrats' commitment to local self-government.

In his debates with the Republican candidate, Abraham Lincoln, during the 1858 Illinois senatorial election, Steven Douglas justified northern Democratic defense of popular sovereignty on the grounds that government in the United States was "formed on the principle of diversity in the local institutions and laws, and not on that of uniformity.... Each locality having different interests, a different climate, and different surroundings, required different local laws, local policy and local institutions, adapted to the wants of the locality."

The new Republican Party, which had replaced the Whigs in the wake of the Kansas-Nebraska controversy, believed that Douglas's position defiled the Declaration of Independence. Lincoln mocked the idea that "if one man would enslave another, no third man should object" and that it was the height of hypocrisy to call that "popular sovereignty." He granted that the national government had no right to interfere with slavery where it was already established because that ignoble institution was protected by the Constitution. But the Constitution extended no such protection to the territories. Therefore slavery could constitutionally be banned from the territories and the moral foundation of the Constitution, the Declaration of Independence, could be preserved:

Drawing on a verse from the Bible's Book of Proverbs – "A word fitly spoken is like apples of gold in pictures of silver" – Lincoln praised the Declaration's principle of "liberty to all" as the essence of American political life. "This principle was "the word *fitly spoken* which has proven an *apple of gold* to us. The *Union*, and the *Constitution*, are the *picture* of silver, subsequently framed around it. The picture was made, not to *conceal*, or *destroy* the apple; but to *adorn* and *preserve* it. The *picture* was made for the apple – *not* the apple for the picture."

Before Lincoln, Thomas Jefferson and Daniel Webster had invoked the Declaration as the nation's creed and shown the link between its moral principles and the institutional arrangements of the Constitution. But Republicans were less willing to compromise this relationship than Jefferson or the Whigs had been. As historian Daniel Walker Howe has observed, Lincoln reinterpreted Jefferson to make "the proposition that all men are created equal ... a positive goal of political action, not simply a pre-political [or natural] state that government should preserve by inaction." The Declaration, Lincoln maintained, "did not mean to assert the obvious untruth, that all were actually enjoying that equality, nor yet, that they were about to confer it immediately upon them. They meant simply to declare the right, so that enforcement of it might follow as fast as circumstances should permit."

Douglas insisted that the "signers of the Declaration had made no reference to the Negro whatever, when they declared all men to be created equal," instead reserving such equality for whites. Lincoln retorted that denying African Americans a share in the Declaration threatened to transform slavery from a necessary evil into a positive good, a moral right, and thus risked "a gradual and steady debauching of public opinion." In the United States, where popular sovereignty was everything, the consequences of such a change in the public mind would be devastating. Douglas's impropriety was compounded in 1857 by the Dred Scott decision (see Chapter 9).

In part, the debate between Lincoln and Douglas involved a struggle for the soul of Jacksonian democracy. Douglas supported the worst side of Jacksonianism, the commitment to white supremacy; Lincoln championed the best side, commitment to the rights of the common American. Like his hero Jefferson, Lincoln sought to engage the American people in another profound constitutional reconsideration, revolutionary in the magnitude of its constitutional change but conservative in its rededication to unalienable rights and its preservation of the Union.

## Rhetorical Leadership

The importance that Lincoln placed on informing and rousing public opinion led him to focus on rhetoric. Lincoln was perhaps the greatest political orator in American history; much of his leadership ability derived from his ability to use language to justify and ennoble his political actions. His speeches endowed the Union with a religious aura, incorporating the principles of the Declaration into America's political and constitutional practices.

Lincoln used his 1863 *Gettysburg Address* to define the war's aim not as a quest for military glory but as a defense of America's constitutional heritage, a devotion that required the country to adopt a steady, measured course toward a new founding. Its opening lines, "Four score and seven years ago our forefathers brought forth on this continent a new nation, conceived in Liberty, and dedicated to the proposition that all men are created equal," established the Declaration, not the Constitution, as the nation's founding document. In 65 of the 272 carefully chosen words, he expressed the larger purpose of the sacrifices made on the hallowed Gettysburg battlefield:

From these honored dead we take increased devotion to that cause for which they gave the last full measure of devotion – that we here highly resolve that these dead shall not have died in vain – that this nation, under God, shall have a new birth of freedom – and that government of the people, by the people, for the people, shall not perish from the earth.

As political theorist Wilson Carey McWilliams has pointed out, Gettysburg established a storyline for the development of the nation. Americans were not "born free"; rather, their rights depended on an honored past and a collective will to fight for those rights. The American story that Lincoln told at Gettysburg thus honored not only the Founders and those soldiers who died there but also the dignity of democratic individuals willing to acknowledge their debts to the people they had wronged, the enslaved Americans who had been denied "the fruits of their own labor." The Gettysburg Address, recited in public schools and etched in stone at the Lincoln memorial became what legal scholar George P. Fletcher calls the "secular prayer" of post–Civil War America, giving new prominence to the Declaration's self-evident truths as the foundation of a new constitutional order.

The Thirteenth Amendment abolishing slavery transformed America's scripture, the Declaration of Independence, into a formal constitutional obligation. That obligation was further extended by the Fourteenth Amendment, ratified in 1868, which granted all Americans the "privileges or immunities of citizens of the United States," "due process," and "equal protection of the laws." The Fifteenth Amendment, added in 1870, proclaimed that the "right of citizens of the United States to vote shall not be abridged by the United States or any State on account of race, color, or previous condition of servitude." The three Civil War amendments changed the course of constitutional development and expanded government's obligation to protect the rights of the common citizen. As Lincoln told a special session of Congress in July 1861, the amendments aimed "to lift artificial weights from all shoulders – to clear the paths of laudable pursuit of all – to afford all an unfettered start, and a fair chance, in the race of life."

Lincoln's last great utterance, his *Second Inaugural*, was aimed at educating his fellow Unionists about how they should act once victory was achieved. They, as well as their Confederate enemies, were Christians, and even in their moment of triumph they must behave like Christians. To prepare themselves to display the proper humility and generosity of soul, they must first own up to their own complicity in the evils wrought. Then they would be in a position to accept their religious obligation to forgive those whom they have vanquished, and to bend all their efforts toward healing the wounds the terrible war had inflicted on the body politic:

Both read the same Bible and pray to the same God, and each invokes His aid against the other.... Woe unto the world because of offenses; for it must needs be that offenses come, but woe to that man by whom the offense cometh.... If we shall suppose that American slavery is one of those offenses which, in the providence of God, must needs come, but which, having continued through His appointed time, He now wills to remove, and that He gives to both North and South this terrible war as the woe due to those by whom the offense came.... With malice toward none, with charity for all, with firmness in the right as God gives us to see the right, let us strive on to finish the work we are in, to bind up the nation's wounds.

Lincoln neither expected nor intended that emancipation would secure the rights of black Americans quickly. As the language of the Second Inaugural suggests, He planned to carry out his conservative revolution gently, preferring to address the prejudices of Americans with persuasion rather than force. But

A DEFERRED ENGAGEMENT.

COLUMBIA—*" As I cannot take both the partners you are urging upon me, I must put off the match until I can investigate their respective claims a little further."*

**Figure 4.2.** "A Deferred Engagement" Columbia, the symbolic personification of the United States, awaits the victor in the contested 1876 election between Rutherford B. Hayes and James Tilden. Hayes was eventually awarded the twenty contested electoral votes and the U.S. presidency. Credit: The Granger Collection, NYC – All rights reserved.

his assassination and his bigoted successor, Andrew Johnson, severely limited Lincoln's constitutional refounding. The presidential election of 1876 effectively ended Reconstruction, the attempt of the national government to restructure government in the former confederate states and protect the rights of the former slaves. The Democrat, Samuel Tilden, won the popular vote, but if the Republican, Rutherford B. Hayes, carried the electoral vote of four disputed states – South Carolina, Louisiana, Florida, and Oregon – he would win the election. Unlike the 2000 election, which was decided by the Supreme Court, the 1876 election was resolved by an electoral commission consisting of eight Republicans and seven

Democrats. The commission awarded the election to Hayes on a straight party vote. To make this controversial decision acceptable to the Democrats, Hayes agreed to remove military troops from the South. This agreement enabled white majorities in southern states to enact *Jim Crow laws*, a system of forced segregation that prevented enforcement of the Fourteenth and Fifteenth Amendments and denied African Americans a full share of American citizenship for nearly a century. Thus, a debased form of Jacksonian local self-determination returned to American politics.

## Prelude to the Fourth Conservative Revolution: The Promise and Disappointments of Progressive Democracy

We call this section on the Progressive Era a prelude because the Progressive Era did not constitute a full-fledged conservative revolution on the order of those we have already examined. But it did generate political ideas and precedents that have remained critically influential ever since. It began the process of national government expansion that proved to be the most crucial political development of the twentieth century. The Progressive Era had no official beginning or end, but its influence began to be felt in the 1890s. It lost direct political influence when Warren Harding, a conservative Republican, was elected president in 1920, but its ideas remained influential throughout the 1920s. *Progressivism* formed a crucial part of the fourth conservative revolution, the New Deal, which began in 1933.

## The Birth of Progressivism

The reform assault on the post–Civil War, decentralized republic was motivated by indignation against economic injustice. The U.S. population doubled between 1870 and 1900. Urbanization and immigration increased at rapid rates and were accompanied by a shift from local, small-scale manufacturing and commerce to large-scale factory production and mammoth national corporations. Technological breakthroughs and frenzied searches for new markets and sources of capital caused unprecedented economic growth. From 1863 to 1899, manufacturing production rose by more than 700 percent. But this dynamic growth also generated profound economic and social problems that challenged the capacity of the decentralized republic to respond.

As we discuss in Chapter 6, by the turn of the century, economic power had become highly concentrated, threatening the security of employees, suppliers, and customers. Many Americans believed that great business interests had captured and corrupted government. Those people who fought to reform the economy and government became known as *Progressives*. No event so aroused their ardor as the nationwide celebration, in 1909, of the 100th anniversary of Lincoln's birth. A Progressive magazine editorial rejoiced:

Coming as it did in the flood tide of the most dangerous and determined reaction from fundamental democratic ideals and principles that have marked our history, it has given a new inspiration and hope to thousands who were all but despairing of the success of popular rule in the presence of the aggressive, determined and powerful march of feudalism and privileged wealth, operating through political bosses and money controlled machines, and the pliant tools of predatory wealth in state, press, school and church.

Yet this celebration of Lincoln went hand in hand with an attack on the decentralized republic that he had supported. Forgetting that Lincoln and the Republicans had defended localized parties as critical agents of "government of the people, by the people, for the people," Progressives scorned party leaders as servants of special interests and usurpers of the Constitution. They championed the creation of direct mass democracy, of "government at first hand: government of the People, directly by the People." Among the tools they sought to introduce to undermine parties were the direct primary and the allocation of government jobs on the basis of objective examinations rather than patronage.

In their attack on intermediary organizations such as political parties and interest groups, Progressives supported women's suffrage; the *direct primary*, in which voters, not party leaders, would choose candidates; and direct election of senators. They also championed methods of "pure" democracy, such as the *initiative*, by which a bill could be forced to the attention of legislatures by popular petition, and the *referendum*, which allowed the electorate to overrule decisions of state legislatures (see Figure 4.3). Especially controversial was the idea of subjecting constitutional questions to direct popular control, including referenda on laws that state courts had declared unconstitutional. *Direct democracy* became the centerpiece of the insurgent Progressive party campaign of 1912, which pledged a "covenant with the people," making the people "masters of their constitution."

Progressives blamed the celebration of property rights for the perversions of the industrial age. Consequently, they stressed collective responsibilities and duties rather than rights. Despite their reverence for Lincoln, they did not emulate his devotion to the Declaration of Independence. Instead, they invoked the preamble of the Constitution to assert their purpose of making "We the People" effective in strengthening the national government's authority to regulate the society and economy.

Like previous champions of democracy, the Progressive reformers' idealism owed much to religion. They saw the Progressive party and other reform associations as political expressions of the movement to promote Christian social action. The Progressives' celebration of national democracy dovetailed with

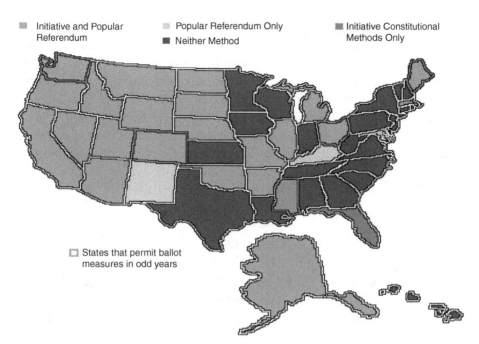

**Figure 4.3.** Referendum/Initiative Map.

*Source: The Book of the States, 2000–2001* (Lexington, KY: The Council of State Governments, 2000), 233.

the social gospelers religious devotion, which downplayed, if it did not scorn, particular theological doctrines and denominations. "We have been a wasteful nation," argued Walter Rauschenbusch, the esteemed social gospeler, in a speech praising the Progressive party. "We have wasted our soil, our water, our forests, our childhood, our motherhood, but no waste has been so great as our waste of religious enthusiasm by denominational strife. The heed of social service is seen in the fact that as the social spirit rises the sectarian spirit declines." The social gospelers thereby invested religious fervor in Progressivism's crusade for political reform.

Whereas Jeffersonian democracy and the principles set forth in the Declaration of Independence dominated the nineteenth century, a popular, idealistic version of Hamiltonianism, dedicated to realizing the nationalist potential of the Constitution, came to prevail in the beginning of the twentieth century. In the words of the first Progressive president, Theodore Roosevelt (TR), "I have never hesitated to criticize Jefferson; he was infinitely below Hamilton; I think the worship of Jefferson a discredit to my country." Yet TR was no blind disciple of Hamilton. Unlike Hamilton, who supported an energetic executive in order to curb popular influence, TR viewed the president as the visionary champion of social and economic reform. In the words of TR's confidant reformer Herbert Croly, the aim of progressive nationalism was "to give democratic meaning and purpose to the Hamiltonian tradition and method."

TR lost the 1912 election because the incumbent Republican president, William Howard Taft, refused to bow out in his favor. Because Taft and TR split the Republican vote, the election was won by the Democrat, Woodrow Wilson. In the campaign, Wilson championed a form of Progressivism, which he labeled *The New Freedom,* that was less trusting of centralized authority than TR's version, *The New Nationalism.* Nonetheless, once elected, Wilson supported national economic control initiatives, such as the creation of a federal trade commission with broad responsibilities for overseeing business practices, much like the one TR had proposed. Wilson also supported creation of the Federal Reserve System to administer the national banking and currency system (see Chapter 6).

## ADMINISTRATIVE MANAGEMENT

The policy changes wrought by TR and Wilson greatly enhanced the power and reach of the central government and led to the creation of a much larger bureaucracy in order to carry out central government dictates. This expansion of national public administration revealed a contradiction between the Progressives' celebration of direct democracy and their desire to cope with economic problems and inequalities by means of a more powerful and independent bureaucracy. In fact, Progressive reforms made government services less connected to elected officials and more tied to administrative agencies and bureaucracies, over which the voter at the polls had little control. Progressive reformers tended to believe that the most popular branches of government – state and national legislatures – were also the least capable and most corrupt. They were convinced that such exacting new tasks as setting railroad shipping rates and establishing standards for drug purity were too demanding for untrained legislators, who often sat only a few months at a time and who lacked policy expertise. The most extreme version of this resort to expertise was the city manager form of government, which supplanted elected mayors with appointed administrators. This movement mirrored reforms that efficiency expert Frederick W. Taylor was advancing for private industry – systematic and "scientific" forms of management from the head office to the shop floor. To bring such reform to government, Taylor urged the president to put an efficiency expert in the cabinet.

Progressives never carried the idea of nonpolitical service to the same lengths that other modern democracies did; for example, civil service reform was far more extensive in France and Great Britain. But by the end of TR's two terms in office, the merit system had begun to supplant the spoils system; Wilson, especially in his second term, built on TR's commitment to professional administration. Presidential leadership, previously dependent on patronage-seeking state and local party machines, now required careful attention to administrative management, sometimes to foster economy and efficiency and sometimes to bolster the power of the increasingly active federal government.

Despite Progressivism's championing of mass democracy, its mix of attack on political organizations and commitment to administrative management conspired to make American politics and government seem more removed from the everyday lives of citizens. Civil service reform, more stringent voter registration requirements, and the decline in monetary and social rewards for political activity significantly reduced the individual's incentive to participate in campaigns and elections. Thus, Progressive democracy actually decreased voter turnout, which was lower in 1920 and 1924 than at any time since the emergence of mass democracy in the 1830s. "Early in the 19th century, soaring turnout among white men reinforced the impression of The People governing," Robert Wiebe has observed. "Early in the 20th, falling turnouts reinforced the impression of people being governed."

## PROGRESSIVE DEMOCRACY AND LIBERALISM

The Progressive faith in majoritarian democracy dealt severe blows to the liberal principle of equal rights. TR and Taft tolerated racial segregation in the South because they acknowledged its political popularity. Woodrow Wilson, a native Virginian elected to the White House in large part because of white southern support, allowed his administration to actively promote it. He permitted a number of federal departments to segregate their employees in Washington and demote or fire their black federal workers in the South.

Progressive indifference to individual rights was not limited to southern issues. Immigration restrictions and racial segregation were often supported by "reformers," who viewed the growing diversity of America as a threat to national unity. By 1920, to disenfranchise immigrants, nine northern states passed literacy tests for voting and eleven states repealed older laws permitting aliens to cast ballots once they pledged to become citizens. The United States and Japan reached a so-called gentlemen's agreement in 1907 that excluded Japanese immigrants. In 1920, Congress passed the most restrictive immigration bill in the nation's history. Nativist sentiment – which scorned beer drinking as a vice of German, Irish, and Italian immigrants – led to the 1919 ratification of the Eighteenth Amendment to the Constitution, which prohibited the manufacture, sale, and transportation of intoxicating liquors. As the political scientist James Morone has written, "Prohibiting liquor looked like one more progressive social amelioration, blending easily into the movement's disdain for inferior people and corrupt politics."

## PROGRESSIVE DEMOCRACY AND WAR

The repressive tendencies of Progressive democracy were revealed dramatically during World War I. President Wilson's war aim was to make the "World Safe for Democracy." To convey the message to the American people, Wilson formed the Committee on Public Information (CPI), which enlisted 75,000 speakers to "persuade" the public that the war was a crusade for freedom and democracy against the Germans, a barbarian people bent on world domination. Most Americans supported the war. But a significant minority opposed it, including German and Irish Americans, whose ethnicity caused them to doubt the cause of the Allied powers, and Progressive reformers such as the prominent social worker Jane Addams, who thought American democracy would be corrupted by the necessities and cruelties of total war. The CPI and a number of self-styled "patriotic groups" sought to discourage, and sometimes repress, this dissent. People who refused to buy war bonds were often exposed to public ridicule and even assaulted. People with German names, scorned as hyphenate Americans, were prosecuted indiscriminately. Some school boards outlawed the teaching of the German language.

Wilson's Progressive democracy did not deter this oppression. Indeed, his view that the war was a moral crusade – to "make the world safe for democracy" – inspired intolerance. Wilson signed the Espionage Act of 1917, which imposed fines of up to $10,000 and jail sentences ranging to twenty years on persons convicted of aiding the enemy or obstructing military recruitment. He banned seemingly treasonable or seditious material from the mails. In May 1918, he signed the Sedition Act, which made it a crime to "utter, print, write, or publish any disloyal, profane, scurrilous, or abusive language" about the government, the Constitution, or the uniform of the Army and Navy, or "say anything" to discourage war bond purchases. Socialist leader Eugene V. Debs was sentenced to ten years in prison for making an antiwar speech.

## THE FOURTH CONSERVATIVE REVOLUTION: THE NEW DEAL AND THE TRIUMPH OF LIBERALISM

The *Great Depression* that began in 1929 was the worst economic cataclysm in American history. Out of its ruins rose the *New Deal*, the defining political episode of the twentieth century. The New Deal built on the two pillars of Progressive democracy: mass politics and national administration, but it added a critical dimension, a new understanding of rights. It marked a critical departure in governing principles, political alignments, institutional arrangements, and public policy. Franklin Delano Roosevelt (FDR) gave legitimacy to Progressive ideas by imbedding them in the language of constitutionalism and interpreting them as a fulfillment rather than a subversion of natural rights. The task of statesmanship, FDR insisted, was to redefine the rights of the Declaration in terms of a "changing and growing social order."

## NEW DEAL LIBERALISM

FDR was the first president to call himself a "liberal," adding the word to the common political vocabulary. In doing so, he reworked – or, as his political enemies claimed, "perverted" Classic Liberalism. To FDR, the Great Depression made it painfully obvious that it was necessary to rewrite the social contract to take account of a national economy remade by industrial capitalism and economic concentration. This new contract would establish a stronger national state to countervail concentrated economic power. As FDR put it, "The day of enlightened administration has come." The traditional emphasis on self-reliance should give way to an acceptance of the need for government to guarantee individuals protection from the uncertainties of the market. A fourth "self evident truth," security, was added to the litany of "Life, Liberty and the Pursuit of Happiness."

When FDR took the oath of office on March 4, 1933, about a fourth of the workforce, 13 million workers, were unemployed. In thirty-two states all banks were closed; in sixteen more, banking operations were severely curtailed. That morning, the New York Stock Exchange closed its doors. But the New Dealers looked beyond the immediate crisis. They sought to accomplish not only economic recovery but also enduring political and economic reform. Unlike the Progressives, they recognized that American politics could not be remade unless political and economic transformation was interwoven with traditional constitutional principles, especially the guarantee of rights.

The new understanding of the Declaration and Constitution was the principal message of FDR's reelection bid in 1936, and his success was the decisive triumph that established the Democrats as the majority party in American politics for a generation.

Lincoln, as this chapter has pointed out, defended the Declaration as America's founding document, claiming that the centrality of the rights it proclaimed justified a "new birth of freedom." The 1860 Republican platform championed the Declaration of Independence as America's founding document. The 1936 Democratic platform, drafted by FDR, was written as a pastiche of the Declaration, and thus emphasized the need for a fundamental reconsideration of rights. "We hold this truth to be self-evident," it said, "that government in a modern civilization has certain inescapable obligations to its citizens." Among these new responsibilities was "to erect a structure of economic security for its people, making sure that this benefit shall keep step with the ever increasing capacity of America to provide a high standard of living for all its citizens."

**Figure 4.4.** Names and numbers: a 1935 cartoon insinuating that Social Security and other New Deal Programs had reduced American citizens to mere numbers. Credit: The Granger Collection, NYC – All rights reserved.

The 1936 election validated FDR's redefinition of the social contract. He won every state but Maine and Vermont. The 1936 Republican platform declared that "America is in peril," and dedicated the party to "the preservation of ... political liberty," which "for the first time" was "threatened by government itself." But FDR successfully defended the New Deal in terms of enhancing liberty. Harking back to the American Revolution, FDR defined his opponents as "economic royalists" who

have conceded that political freedom was the business of government, but they have maintained that economic slavery was nobody's business. They granted that the Government could protect the citizen in his own right to vote, but they denied that government could do anything to protect the citizen in his right to work and his right to live.... If the average citizen is guaranteed equal opportunity in the polling place, he must have equal opportunity in the marketplace.

## ENLIGHTENED ADMINISTRATION AND PROGRAMMATIC RIGHTS

The New Deal, building on what the Progressives had begun, was the first conservative revolution to emphasize national administrative power. Its predecessors had not challenged Classic Liberalism's commitment to private property rights, limited government, and administrative decentralization. Even the Civil War, the most serious constitutional crisis of American history, did not lead to a departure from this consensus. As we explain in Chapter 8, FDR managed to push through Congress political reforms that led to the creation of the White House office, the hub of the executive office of the president. The reconstituted executive office deprived party leaders of the very tasks that gave them status and influence: linking the president to interest groups, staffing the executive branch, developing policy, providing campaign support, and linking the White House to public opinion. Moreover, New Deal political reforms were directed not just at creating presidential government but also at embedding progressive programs – which were considered tantamount to rights – in a bureaucratic structure that would insulate reform and reformers from party politics, conservative presidents, and even, to a point, public opinion.

The most important of these new *programmatic rights* was *Social Security*. The 1935 Social Security Act provided old age insurance, unemployment insurance, and Aid to Families with Dependent Children (AFDC), popularly known as welfare. Unlike old age insurance, unemployment compensation and AFDC were jointly administered by the national and state governments. Social Security was carefully nurtured by FDR to appear as a right, the cornerstone of the economic constitutional order. He insisted that it be financed by a payroll tax rather than by general revenues: "We put those payroll contributions there so to give the contributors a legal, moral right, and political right to collect their pensions. With those taxes in there, no damn politician can scrap my social security program."

And none did. By the 1950s, Social Security was the "third rail" of American politics, bringing political death to those who challenged it. By European standards, the Social Security program was quite limited. It did not include any support for healthcare, and its levels of welfare spending were low. It left considerable discretion and funding responsibility to the states, which dealt out social justice unevenly. Nevertheless, the program marked a watershed in the national government's assumption of the responsibility to protect individuals from the uncertainties of the market. Its programs, especially old age pensions, grew over the years, so that Social Security became the largest of all federal programs.

The *National Labor Relations Act of 1935* established another economic right, that of unions to bargain collectively. The act created a National Labor Relations

Board (NLRB) to ensure fair collective-bargaining elections, a move that transformed American society and economy (see Chapter 6). When the New Deal began, few factory workers belonged to labor unions, which left them vulnerable to workplace abuses and business-cycle uncertainties. By the late 1930s, industrial unionism was firmly in place.

In his 1944 State of the Union message, FDR called for a new bill of rights that provided adequate food, clothing, recreation, employment, housing, and education to all, "regardless of station, race, or creed," and which provided protection from the economic fears of old age, sickness, and accident. These new rights did not officially become part of the Constitution, but they formed the foundation of a new public philosophy that redefined the role of the national government. The previous understanding of rights – which was dedicated to limiting government – gradually gave way to a more expansive understanding that presupposed the creation of a large and powerful executive establishment.

To ensure that these newly established rights would survive his leadership, FDR sought to protect the many appointees he had brought to Washington to staff the newly created welfare and regulatory state from being fired by his successors. Through executive orders and legislation, FDR extended so called *merit protection* to 95 percent of federal service employees by 1941. Since Jefferson, federal appointments had been used to nourish parties; the New Deal, FDR's civil service reforms, deprived parties of that opportunity. Federal bureaucrats would now be controlled by the rules governing the programs they administered, not by party leaders. This change did much to enshrine an administrative state dedicated to perpetuating the programmatic rights the New Deal had established.

## Civil Rights

In the midst of the New Deal's expansion of rights, the right to racial equality proclaimed in both the Thirteenth and Fifteenth Amendments continued to languish. As late as 1938, the Federal Housing Administration Act had required the home mortgages that it insured to have racially restrictive covenants. But, as the threat of world war worsened, the Roosevelt administration took actions that served as critical precedents for the later triumph of civil rights. In 1940, the Roosevelt administration established the Fair Employment Practices Commission (FEPC), which was charged with eliminating discrimination in the employment of workers in the defense industry or government because of "race, color, creed, or national origin." As the wartime internment of Japanese Americans and continued racial segregation of the armed forces showed, the government was still in support of many racist policies. Nor was the FEPC an adequate response to racial discrimination. Nevertheless, it was the first federal government effort since Reconstruction that was specifically aimed at alleviating racial discrimination.

These administrative efforts were joined to judicial politics. At FDR's behest, his attorney general, Frank Murphy, set up the Civil Liberties Section of the Justice Department in 1939. Later called the Civil Rights Section, this office played a critical part in bringing and successfully adjudicating Supreme Court cases that challenged white supremacy in the South. The most important case, *Smith v. Allwright*, decided in 1944, declared the white primary, a critical foundation of Jim Crow electoral practices, unconstitutional. FDR's successor, Harry Truman, went further. His 1948 executive order demanded that "there shall be equality of treatment and opportunity in the Armed Services without regard to race, color, or national origin."

## Liberal Internationalism

Progressives championed internationalism that would make the world safe for democracy; New Deal rhetoric stressed international rights. As FDR put it in his famous 1941 Four Freedoms speech, the traditional liberal freedoms of speech and religion were to be supplemented by two new freedoms. "Freedom from want" was a commitment to "economic understandings which will secure to every nation a healthy peace time life for its inhabitants." "Freedom from fear" was dedicated to "a world-wide reduction of armaments to such a point and such a fashion that no nation will be in a position to commit an act of physical aggression against any neighbor."

In his draft of the 1941 Atlantic Charter, FDR committed the Allies to "respect the right of all peoples to choose the form of government under which they will live" and "to see sovereign rights and self-government restored to those who have been forcibly deprived of them." Believing that rejection of imperialism was crucial to defeating the Axis powers, FDR persuaded a nervous Winston Churchill to endorse the charter even though the language might be, and eventually was, used against the British Empire.

Of course, FDR's idealism frequently gave way to practical considerations. In his negotiations with Stalin toward the end of the war, FDR failed to prevent Soviet dominion over Eastern Europe. Likewise, the internment of Japanese Americans in concentration camps revealed all too clearly that New Deal rights did not provide ironclad protection for minorities against xenophobic hysteria. Still, liberal internationalism proved more resilient than did the Progressive ambition to make the world safe for democracy. World War I stifled Progressive domestic reform and fueled nativist attitudes. World War II strengthened the sense of entitlement, thereby justifying New Deal reforms, and advanced an inclusive popular nationalism and readiness to use the federal government to secure prosperity and meet important domestic and international needs. As Lincoln showed, words are more important than battles. After the war, the rights rhetoric that FDR pioneered was used effectively against imperialist and discriminatory impulses.

Just as New Deal liberalism made the national government an enduring presence in domestic affairs, FDR's liberal internationalism made it difficult for America to retreat from the world stage. Indeed, domestic and international commitments merged to enhance the influence of modern liberalism on American life. For example, in 1944, Congress enacted the GI Bill of Rights that entitled war veterans to home loans, business loans, unemployment compensation, and subsidies for education and training. This legislation did not provide the broad security and employment programs that FDR championed in his 1944 second bill of rights speech, but it did greatly expand the economic and educational benefits available to a very large and significant portion of the population, returning veterans and their families.

## Beyond the New Deal

The governing system and rights commitments established by the New Deal remain in place. The most significant effort to go beyond the New Deal occurred in the 1960s during the presidency of Lyndon Baines Johnson (1963–1968). Although it did not constitute a full-fledged conservative revolution it did have important consequence regarding the expansion of the administrative state and Americans' understanding of their rights.

In the signature speech of his presidency, a May 1964 commencement address at the University of Michigan, Lyndon Baines Johnson (LBJ) pointed to the New Deal's promise to end poverty and racial justice as "just the beginning." Challenging the students and parents to embrace more ambitious goals for America, LBJ described his vision of "a *Great Society* ... where the city of man serves not only the needs of the body and the demands of commerce but the desire for beauty and the hunger for community."

The eminent Progressive philosopher, John Dewey, had prophesied that Progressive reforms would reach fulfillment in a "Great Community" that would "order the relations and enrich the experience of local associations." Reformers in the 1960s hoped that the *Great Society* would produce the same thing. Their ambitions were fueled by the success of the Civil Rights Movement. This movement called not merely for a fulfillment of rights promised African Americans but also for direct action to overcome the bureaucratic inertia of the New Deal state. Its success "demonstrated not only the power and possibility of organized protest, but the unsuspected fragility of resistance to liberating changes," claimed Richard Goodwin, who drafted LBJ's University of Michigan speech.

Indeed, the Civil Rights Movement was a model for the social movements that grew out of the 1960s, including organized opposition to the Vietnam War, feminism, consumerism, and environmentalism. In the early days of the Great Society, LBJ and influential aides such as Goodwin supported these movements (except for the antiwar protests), viewing their clarion call for participatory democracy as paving the way for a new generation of reform.

The Great Society's deepest ambitions were never realized. Its important achievements in civil rights, environment, consumer protection, and education did not increase participatory democracy. Steeped in the rights talk popularized by FDR, it led rather to an explosion of new entitlements proclaimed by groups competing with one another for recognition and government programs to remedy the historic injustices they had suffered. Rights of women, gays and lesbians, the disabled, consumers, and welfare recipients followed logically from the New Deal idea of a just society. The New Deal promised security in the face of the uncertainties of the business cycle and the unintended hazards created by a dynamic capitalism. The rights revolution expanded on those ideas to encompass protections against the prejudices of private citizens, risks of congenital disabilities, and consequences of poverty and family decomposition. Endowing those rights with practical programmatic meaning necessarily implied the expansion of the government's administrative apparatus.

## Challenge to the New Deal

This expansion of claims on the government provoked political opposition rooted in Classic Liberal adherence to limited government. This growing hostility culminated in Ronald Reagan's 1980 election to the White House. Reagan's message as candidate and president was but a variation of the theme he first developed in a nationwide address on behalf of the 1964 Republican presidential candidate, Barry Goldwater. Reagan invoked Paine, Jefferson, and Jackson as he proclaimed that citizens must not be denied the means of exercising their right of rebelling against a despotic government.

The New Deal state, Reagan argued, gave an especially pernicious turn to government oppression, cloaking its intrusiveness in the language of the Declaration. By acting "outside of its legitimate function," Reagan insisted, "natural unalienable rights" were presumed to be a "dispensation of government," which stripped people of their self-reliance and capacity for self-government. "The real destroyer of liberties of the people," said Reagan, "is he who spreads among them bounties, donations, and benefits." In his inaugural address, the first in more than fifty years to appeal for limited government, he sounded the same theme: "In the present crisis, government is not the solution to our problem; government is the problem." Reagan promised to shrink government and restore the vitality of a democracy based on limited government and decentralized politics.

But Reagan's policies did not redefine the New Deal social contract and therefore did not amount to a conservative revolution. Despite his antigovernment rhetoric, Reagan managed only to halt the expansion of programmatic rights. He had little success in cutting back middle-class entitlements such as Social Security and *Medicare*, a healthcare program for the elderly created in 1965. Reagan's efforts to loosen regulatory standards for civil rights, environment, and consumer protection were successfully resisted by public interest groups and their allies in Congress and the courts.

In fact, the Reagan administration upheld many aspects of the New Deal, especially its commitment to liberal internationalism, which had lost much support among Democrats since the Vietnam War. Ironically, Reagan's greatest accomplishment may have involved an act of perpetuation. Finishing what Harry Truman began, Reagan prosecuted the Cold War to a successful conclusion. The demise of the Soviet Union occurred for many reasons, but Reagan's tough talk – he dubbed the Communist power an "evil empire" – steered American policy away from detente, the position of accommodation that had prevailed since the early 1970s. Reagan returned to containment as pursued by Presidents Truman, Eisenhower, Kennedy, and Johnson. This rhetorical hard line justified the extensive arms buildup that put great technological and economic pressure on the Soviet Union and contributed to its ultimate collapse.

Even when championing "conservative" causes, Reagan defended an activist presidency that belied his promise to "get the government off our backs." The conservative movement that helped bring him to power was aroused in no small part by the abortion controversy, which led Reagan and many of his supporters to defend the rights of the unborn in a way that required extending the power of government. Posed in opposition to the rights of pregnant women as championed by the women's movement, the Reagan administration contemplated prohibiting women from having abortions, or in certain cases even getting counseling from birth control clinics. For example, in early 1988, the Department of Health and Human Services issued a regulation declaring that federal funds could not go to clinics that provided abortion counseling. The merits of this position aside, it shows that in the post–New Deal era, when conservatives challenge liberal policies, they do so in the name of new rights that presuppose discretionary use of national administrative power.

## Conservative Liberalism – Compassionate Conservatism

Although the twenty years following the Reagan presidency were fraught with political conflict and controversy, they also displayed a compelling magnetic attraction toward the political center. The two Republican presidents, George Bush father and son, were far less critical of big government than Reagan had been. George W. Bush (2000–2008) coined the term "compassionate conservatism" to signal his willingness to deploy government to help people, as long as the type of help proffered was consistent with conservative values. The Democratic President Bill Clinton (1992–2000) declared himself a "New Democrat," distancing himself with what he deemed to be the excessive reliance on big spending and subsidizing of special interests characteristic of the old Democrats. The first Democrat to occupy the White House in sixteen years, he appeared to ratify the "Reagan revolution" when he proclaimed "the era of big government is over." After the Republicans, led by the militant conservative Newt Gingrich, won control of both houses of Congress in 1994 – the first time this had happened in forty years – Clinton signed a welfare reform bill that vastly reduced the number of persons receiving public assistance and constructed a bipartisan coalition in support of a balanced budget.

But Clinton was no Reaganite. Indeed, he revived his presidency and fended off the aggressive leadership of Speaker of the House Gingrich by defending New Deal and Great Society programs. Clinton was reelected in 1996, the first time a Democratic president had been returned to office by the voters since FDR. The crux of his reelection campaign was his dedication to perpetuating Medicare, Medicaid (a healthcare program for the disadvantaged), education spending, and stringent environmental regulation. Clinton – not his opponent, Kansas senator Robert Dole – was the real conservative in this campaign, because he fought to preserve the status quo, the programmatic rights that were the legacy of FDR and the New Deal, from Republican efforts to scale it back.

George W. Bush energetically used national government power and revenue in pursuit of his compassionate conservative goals. Nine days after being sworn in as president, he issued an executive order that aimed to increase the ability of religious organizations to avail themselves of federal funds in order to provide social services to those in need. He signaled the importance that he attached to this project by locating the new office responsible for implementing the program in the White House. Bush's major legislative priority during his first year in office was also aimed at achieving compassionate conservative goals. NCLB sought to create a national testing system that would make teachers more accountable for the success of their students. Although states were not compelled to participate, they risked losing federal aid if they did not. Bush also supported a new federal program that subsidized prescription drugs for the elderly. It was the most expensive new federally funded entitlement program since the passage of Medicare in 1965.

As we discussed in Chapter 1 and will discuss again in Chapter 10, the terror attacks of September 11, 2001 pressed Bush to endorse another major expansion of federal government responsibility, the addition of a new cabinet-level DHS. The department is immense; it has more than 180,000 employees. It signifies a major new consolidation of national government power because it places a whole array of domestic law enforcement and investigatory responsibility under national auspices that had previously rested with the states and localities.

## CONCLUSION: FUTURE CONSERVATIVE REVOLUTIONS?

Eighty years have passed since the onset of the nation's last conservative revolution. The critical choices regarding the adoption of new, programmatic rights, and the vast expansion of an administrative state to implement them set the American government on a path to which it continues to adhere. Never before have so many years gone by without such a profound contest over the meaning of the Constitution and the role of the national government. In the wake of the most serious challenge to New Deal principles, led by Ronald Reagan, there has been no retreat from the programmatic rights and centralized governmental administration the New Deal embodied.

Is there a conservative revolution on the horizon? It is impossible to tell. The 2008 election gave cause for optimism to modern Liberals seeking a broad expansion of programmatic rights along the lines established in most other wealthy nations. For the first time since 1964, a Democratic president was elected with large majorities in both houses of Congress. The Senate majority was large enough to overcome opposition efforts to stall legislative change by preventing a floor vote (for a discussion of this obstructive technique see Chapter 7). Indeed, the Obama administration did pass a major new health care program that went a long way to making health insurance coverage universal. It also spent billions rescuing the banking system, bailing out Chrysler and General Motors, and attempting to stimulate the depressed economy. When FDR engaged in such expansionary efforts, the voters rallied to his defense, but the public reacted negatively to Obama's policies. The Tea Party movement that arose in 2009 to fight against "big government" was the most energetic dissident force to arise in many years (see Chapter 12). In 2010, the Democrats suffered staggering losses in the congressional, gubernatorial, and state legislative elections, losing control of the House of Representatives.

Writers use the term "fog of war" to describe the extreme uncertainty and chaos that soldiers experience during battle. Often they cannot even tell if they are winning or losing. All they know for sure is that bullets are buzzing by. Likewise, when one is in the midst of a great political conflict the outcome is impossible to predict. Such a profound contest of opinion is now underway. Spurred by the Tea Party and by their 2010 victories, the Republicans not only sought to reduce spending, they called for a fundamental alteration in government, one that would shrink its size and ambition. In response, the Democrats mounted a spirited defense of government. They defended the principles underlying the New Deal as well as the expansion of programmatic rights, health safety, and natural resource regulation and protection for minorities that preceded it. Only in retrospect, years from now, will the fog of war lift sufficiently for us to tell whether or not a conservative revolution has resulted from this epic political struggle.

## CHAPTER SUMMARY

★ Each great political episode in American political development can be characterized as a conservative revolution that engaged citizens in conflict and resolution about the meaning of the Declaration and Constitution for their own time. Each was revolutionary in that it resulted in some major shift in the understanding of individual rights, the meaning of democracy and equality, and the role of government. It was conservative in its fidelity to fundamental constitutional norms and principles.

★ The first conservative revolution took place between 1800 and 1808, during Thomas Jefferson's two terms as president. It promoted democracy by endorsing and nurturing those political institutions and constitutional principles that Jefferson and his followers considered to be most democratic in character, such as free speech, legislative supremacy, and a powerful defense of states' rights. And it was inextricably connected to two new forms of political communication and conflict: a popular press and political parties.

★ The second conservative revolution, presided over by Andrew Jackson, sought to make the Constitution and its institutional arrangements servants of public opinion. Democracy did not displace liberalism in the Age of Jackson. Rather, Jacksonians sought to capture liberalism for the people. Demands for rights had to come to terms with a highly mobilized, competitive, and locally oriented democracy.

★ The third conservative revolution, ending slavery was revolutionary in the magnitude of its constitutional change but conservative in its rededication to unalienable rights and its preservation of the Union.

★ The importance that Lincoln placed on informing and rousing public opinion led him to focus on rhetoric. His speeches endowed the Union with a religious aura, incorporating the principles of the Declaration into America's political and constitutional practices.

★ The Progressive Era did not constitute a full-fledged conservative revolution, but it did generate political ideas and precedents that have remained critically influential. It began the process of national government expansion that proved to be the most crucial political development of the twentieth century.

☆    The New Deal was built on the two pillars of Progressive democracy: mass politics and national administration, but it added a new understanding of rights. FDR gave legitimacy to Progressive ideas by imbedding them in the language of constitutionalism and interpreting them as a fulfillment rather than a subversion of natural rights.

☆    New Deal political reforms were directed not just at creating presidential government but also embedding progressive programs – which were considered tantamount to rights – in a bureaucratic structure that would insulate reform and reformers from party politics, conservative presidents, and even, to a point, public opinion. The most important of these new *programmatic rights* was the right to economic security in old age as embodied in the Social Security Act of 1935.

☆    The most significant effort to go beyond the New Deal took place in the 1960s during the presidency of LBJ (1963–1968). Although it did not constitute a full-fledged conservative revolution, it did have important consequence regarding the expansion of the administrative state and American's understanding of their rights.

☆    Reagan promised to shrink government and restore the vitality of a democracy based on limited government and decentralized politics. But his policies did not redefine the New Deal social contract and therefore did not amount to a conservative revolution. Despite his antigovernment rhetoric, Reagan managed only to halt the expansion of programmatic rights. In fact, the Reagan administration upheld many aspects of the New Deal, especially its commitment to liberal internationalism, which had lost much support among Democrats since the Vietnam War.

☆    Bill Clinton used the term "New Democrat" to indicate that he was leading his party away from an excessive reliance on big government. George W. Bush called himself a "compassionate conservative" to show his willingness to use big government for what he considered to be legitimate conservative ends. Thus, despite the high level of partisan conflict that characterized the post-Reagan era, the presidential leaders of both parties achieved a high degree of convergence regarding the size and role of government.

## MAJOR CONCEPTS

| | |
|---|---|
| American Civil War | Conservative Revolutions |
| Democrats | Direct Democracy |
| Direct Primary | Empire of Liberty |
| Great Depression | Great Society |
| Initiative | Jacksonian Mass Democracy |
| Kansas-Nebraska Act of 1854 | Medicare |
| Merit System | National Labor Relations Act of 1935 |
| New Deal | The New Freedom |
| The New Nationalism | Party System |
| Patronage Politics | Popular Sovereignty |
| Programmatic Rights | Progressivism |
| Referendum | Republican Party (the original) |
| Revolution of 1800 | Second Inaugural (Lincoln) |
| Social Security | Spoils System |
| Veto of the Rechartering of the Second Bank of the United States | Voter Turnout |
| Whigs | |

## SUGGESTED READINGS

Ackerman, Bruce. *We the People: Foundations*. Cambridge, MA: Harvard University Press, 1991.

Ackerman, Bruce. *We the People: Transformations*. Cambridge, MA: Harvard University Press, 1998.

Bensel, Richard. *Yankee Leviathan: The Origins of Central State Authority in America, 1858–1877*. Cambridge: Cambridge University Press, 1990.

Burnham, Walter Dean. *Critical Elections and the Mainsprings of American Politics*. New York: W. W. Norton, 1971.

Derthick, Martha. *Policymaking for Social Security*. Washington, DC: Brookings Institution, 1979.

Eisenach, Eldon. *The Lost Promise of Progressivism*. Lawrence: Kansas University Press, 1994.

Gerstle, Gary. *American Crucible: Race and Nation in the Twentieth Century*. Princeton: Princeton University Press, 2002.

Jaffa, Harry. *Crisis of the House Divided: An Interpretation of the Issues in the Lincoln-Douglas Debates, with a new Preface*. Chicago: University of Chicago Press, 1982.

Jaffa, Harry. *A New Birth of Freedom: Abraham Lincoln and the Coming of the Civil War*. Lanham, MD: Rowman and Littlefield, 2000.

Keller, Morton. *Affairs of State: Public Life in Late Nineteenth Century America*. Cambridge, MA: Belknap Press, 1977.

Kennedy, David. *Freedom from Fear: The American People in Depression and War, 1929–1945*. New York: Oxford University Press, 1999.

Landy, Marc, and Martin Levin, eds. *The New Politics of Public Policy*. Baltimore: Johns Hopkins University Press, 1995.

Lowi, Theodore. *The End of Liberalism: The Second Republic of the United States*, 2nd ed. New York: W. W. Norton, 1979.

McConnell, Grant. *Private Power and American Democracy*. New York: Vintage Books, 1970.

McMahon, Kevin J. *Reconsidering Roosevelt on Race: How the Presidency Paved the Road to Brown*. Chicago: University of Chicago Press, 2004.

Mettler, Suzanne. *Soldiers to Citizens: The G. I. Bill and the Making of the Greatest Generation*. New York: Oxford University Press, 2005.

Milkis, Sidney M. *The President and the Parties: The Transformation of the American Party System since the New Deal*. New York: Oxford University Press, 1992.

Milkis, Sidney M., and Jerome Mileur, eds. *The New Deal and the Triumph of Liberalism*. Amherst: University of Massachusetts Press, 2002.

Morone, James. *The Democratic Wish: Popular Participation and the Limits of American Government*. New Haven, CT: Yale University Press, 1998.

Morone, James. *Hellfire Nation: The Politics of Sin in American History*. New Haven, CT: Yale University Press, 2003.

Patterson, James. *Grand Expectations: The United States, 1945–1974*. New York: Oxford University Press, 1996.

Sanders, Elizabeth. *The Roots of Reform: Farmers, Workers, and the American State, 1877–1917*. Chicago: University of Chicago Press, 1999.

Skocpol, Theda. *Protecting Soldiers and Mothers: The Political Origins of Social Policy in the United States*. Cambridge, MA: Harvard University Press, 1992.

Skowronek, Steven. *Building a New American State: The Expansion of National Administrative Capacities, 1877–1920*. New York: Cambridge University Press, 1982.

Skowronek, Steven. *The Politics Presidents Make: Leadership from John Adams to Bill Clinton*. Cambridge, MA: Harvard University Press, 1993.

Young, James Sterling. *The Washington Community: 1800–1828*. New York: Columbia University Press, 1965.

# Pivotal Relationships

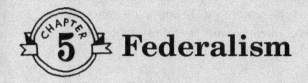

# 5 Federalism

## CHAPTER OVERVIEW

This chapter focuses on:

★   The current role of the states in making and administering public policy and influencing national politics and policy.
★   The different paths that the relationship between the national government and the states have taken.
★   How each of the historic pathways of Federalism continue to influence current American Federalism.
★   The critical choices Americans have made regarding the nature of Federalism.
★   Major new developments in American Federalism.

In 1992, a twelfth-grade student arrived at Edison High School in San Antonio, Texas, carrying a concealed .38-caliber handgun and five bullets. He was arrested and eventually charged with violating a federal law, the Gun Free School Zones Act of 1990. In 1995, in the case of *United States v. Lopez*, the U.S. Supreme Court overturned his conviction. The court did not dispute the prosecution's account. Lopez did in fact have a pistol in school. Nor did the court deny that guns in school are a bad thing deserving of punishment. Instead, the court found that the national government did not have the authority to make laws regarding guns in schools. It determined that the Constitution made this issue a state and local one, not a federal one.

In America, disputes over what the government ought to do frequently turn into disputes over where the decision should be made. The gravest crisis in all of American history, the Civil War, was fought both about the issue of slavery and whether the national government was supreme over the states. One hundred years later, when federal courts imposed crosstown busing as the remedy for racial segregation in the schools, opponents claimed that the federal government had unconstitutionally usurped the power to make education policy. The fight over what turns into a fight over where because the Constitution does not fully clarify the dividing line between state and federal power.

## FEDERALISM: A CONTEMPORARY PORTRAIT

If all one knew of the Constitution were the preamble's promise to "insure domestic tranquility and promote the general welfare," it would seem perfectly clear that the federal government had the right to put Lopez in jail. Few people would dispute that tranquility and the general welfare are better served when schools are free of guns. However, if all one knew of the Constitution was the *Tenth Amendment's* requirement that "the powers not delegated to the United States by the Constitution nor prohibited by it to the States, are reserved to the states," Lopez would be set free and a whole range of national government activity would be clearly unconstitutional. Where does the Constitution say that the federal government can set safety standards for drinking water or require colleges to provide equal funding for women's sports?

As we discussed in Chapter 3, this lack of clarity about the limits of national power exists because at the time of the founding, the country was divided between those who wanted a strong national government and those who did not. The Constitution is to some extent a compromise between those two colliding points of view. In order to obtain consent for the establishment of a strong national government, its supporters agreed to limit its powers to those that were expressly delegated to it. They also agreed to give the states a direct role in national governance via the Senate and the Electoral College, both of whose members are elected on a state-by-state basis. It is therefore not surprising that the argument about how to divide power between the states and the federal government continues.

Federalism remains an argument, but as the discussion about the ratification of the Constitution pointed out, arguments happen between friends as well as enemies. The constitutional ratification debate was a lover's quarrel because the Federalists and the Anti-Federalists shared so many important political and moral principles. The current relationship between the states and the national government would be better characterized as a partnership. Partners recognize that they need one another and must cooperate. But this does not stop them from quarreling, exerting their individuality, and trying to dominate one another. The relationships between the federal government, states, and localities likewise exhibit cooperation, conflict, autonomy, and competition for dominance.

Since the 1930s, the federal government has clearly become the senior partner. There is no longer any sphere of public policy where the localities or states enjoy such exclusive power, but each does dominate certain policy spheres. Local government dominates K-12 education, policing, firefighting, zoning of property, and construction and maintenance of local streets, sidewalks, city halls, and recreation facilities. However, the federal government retains the right to involve itself in any or all of these activities. It forces local police to abide by Supreme Court edicts regarding the searching of homes, surveillance of phone conversations, and informing of criminal suspects of the right against self-incrimination and their right to an attorney. Title 9 of the federal Equal Opportunity Education forbids sex discrimination in school athletic programs. The national NCLB law requires all schools receiving federal aid to administer achievement tests written by the states. Local zoning rules can be overturned if a federal judge finds them to be racially discriminatory. Libraries, city halls, swimming pools, and other municipal buildings must provide ramps and elevators for the handicapped as required by the federal Americans with Disabilities Act.

States are the dominant partners in the making and enforcing of both civil and criminal law. Most ordinary disputes between individuals and firms are decided in state courts on the basis of state law. With the exception of treason, terrorism, counterfeiting, kidnapping, and certain types of financial fraud, perpetrators of most other types of crime are also tried in state courts on the basis of state law. But federal courts reserve the right to hear appeals from those whom states courts have ruled against. Of the more than 2 million Americans currently imprisoned, more than half are in state correctional facilities. Local and county jails account for another third. Federal prisons housed only one-sixth of the prison population, including convicts in state prisons.

Almost all public universities, colleges, and community colleges are run by the states. Only a very few cities have their own colleges and junior colleges. The service academies are virtually the only federally run colleges. But all forms of higher education depend heavily on the federal government for student loans, graduate fellowships, and research grants. States are also responsible for regulating and licensing certain businesses and professional services. These include contractors, plumbers, electricians, doctors, and lawyers as well as banks, insurance companies, electrical generators, and hospitals.

In almost all the other important realms of public policy the federal state partnership gives the federal government the leading role in making the rules and requires the state governments to implement them. This relationship characterizes environmental regulation, unemployment assistance, welfare, healthcare for the poor, job training, and many other government programs. In some cases the federal government actually provides some or most of the money the states need to administer those programs. The federal government and the states each pay approximately half of the cost of *Medicaid*, healthcare for the poor. In other instances, it allows state agencies to perform the actual work of inspecting facilities and issuing citations if those agencies can prove that they can do so effectively.

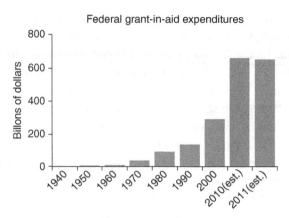

**Figure 5.1.** Federal Grant in Aid Expenditures 1940–2011.

*Source*: National Taxpayers Union. Retrieved from http://www.google.com/imgres?um=1&hl=en& tbo=d&biw=1546&bih=870&tbm=isch&tbnid=r0rEzI4dizdvrM:&imgrefurl=http://www.ntu.org/ governmentbytes/spending/growth-in-grants-in-aid.html&docid=KlnagyayncBleM&imgurl=http:// www.ntu.org/governmentbytes/spending/federal_grant-in-aid_Expenditures-1.png&w=426&h=3 20&ei=M0HjUNLgEYP48wSNIYDQDQ&zoom=1&iact=hc&vpx=829&vpy=127&dur=1462&hovh= 195&hovw=258&tx=126&ty=90&sig=109612827410253161231&page=1&tbnh=140&tbnw=18 5&start=0&ndsp=42&ved=1t:429,r:4,s:0,i:100.

For example, the federal Clean Air Act sets the standards for how clean the air should be, but the actual work of coming up with specific plans for meeting those standards including the actual inspection of factories and fining those who are not in compliance is left to the states. In other instances, the federal government simply mandates the states and localities to accomplish certain goals – such as making sure that all public buildings are fully accessible to the handicapped – and requires the states and localities to pay for these changes themselves.

States are now very dependent on the federal government to help pay their bills. Federal grants in aid to the states now constitute a very significant percentage of state budgets. Figure 5.1 shows the vast expansion in federal aid to the states that has occurred since 1940.

## State Politics

The fifty states form fifty very distinct political worlds. One might expect Vermont and New Hampshire to resemble one another politically. They border one another, neither contains a large city, and tourism and recreation are critical to their economies. Nonetheless, the two states govern themselves quite differently. Vermont has among the strictest land use regulations in the nation. State law restricts where new homes and commercial establishments can be built. It also has relatively high state taxes. New Hampshire has no state income tax and does not try to control land use to anywhere near the same degree that Vermont does. Its state motto, "Live free or die," captures its traditional aversion to intrusive government. On the other hand, Vermont Senator Bernard Sanders calls himself a socialist.

All fifty states mimic the federal government in that they have a constitution, an executive, a legislature, and a judiciary. But the forms and powers granted by their constitutions to those three branches of government differ greatly. Nebraska's legislature is unicameral; there is no upper chamber. The governors of New Hampshire and Vermont serve only two-year terms. California, Michigan, New York, and Pennsylvania have well-staffed legislatures that are frequently in session and whose members view serving in the legislature as virtually a full-time job. At the other extreme, North Dakota, South Dakota, Utah, Wyoming, Montana, and New Hampshire have legislators who are poorly paid, have little staff assistance, and must maintain other jobs to enable them to earn a living.

Finally, states differ in the degree to which they capture the loyalty and attention of their citizens. When someone from one of the five boroughs calls herself a New Yorker, she is undoubtedly referring to her identification with the city, not the state of New York. Sports fans in Massachusetts are far more likely to watch the Boston Celtics or the Boston Red Sox than the University of Massachusetts Minutemen. By contrast, on a Saturday afternoon during basketball season in Kentucky or football season in Alabama, the attention of the state is riveted on the Wildcats or the Crimson Tide. In those states, it is quite common to think of oneself as a Kentuckian or an Alabaman. This strong identification is reflected in the amount of coverage state politics and government receives in those states compared to what it receives in the *New York Times* or *Boston Globe*.

## FEDERALISM AND AMERICAN POLITICAL DEVELOPMENT

The essential federal principle enshrined by the Constitution – that the United States is a compound republic composed of state governments as well as the federal government – remains in place. But in the course of American political development that constitutionally established path has been considerably recontoured. This section describes the critical choices that have served to both reinforce and redirect Federalism's path.

### The Path of Dual Federalism

For the first 150 years of the life of the United States, the states and localities dominated. Indeed, for the first sixty years of the United States' existence, it was not clear that the Union would prevail. That question was decisively settled only by the Civil War. Even after the Civil War, local self-government, supported by the more decentralizing institutions of the Constitution – Congress and the states – remained the most prominent feature of American political life. The national idea and constitutional structure that frames it were preserved in the absence of a powerful central state. Only in the middle of the twentieth century, as a result of the New Deal and the Second World War, did Americans come to view national governance as dominant in their political lives (see Figure 5.1).

## Critical Choice: The Imposition of Dual Federalism

After the ratification of the Constitution, the next great contest in American political life was about the relative political strength of the federal government and the states. The Federalists who dominated the administrations of both Washington and Adams were unapologetically elitist. Although they accepted the idea that the people were the ultimate source of authority, they sought to make popular rule as indirect as possible. Because the central government was further removed from the citizenry than were the states and localities, Federalists were more confident that it could be made to function in a stable and reliable manner. They pressed for the establishment of a strong federal bureaucracy, a well-staffed professional army and navy, and an ambitious national bank capable of promoting national economic development.

These aggressive efforts to aggrandize the federal government sparked the growth of an opposition party, the Republicans, led by Thomas Jefferson and James Madison, which believed in majority rule. They viewed the Federalists not merely as elitists and centralists but as monarchists in the making. They saw no possibility of preserving constitutionally guaranteed liberties in the face of a strong central state. Their understanding of enumerated powers was much more severe in its limitation on government. They were deeply suspicious of the two least democratic aspects of the constitutional order, the Senate and the Supreme Court.

Jefferson's hostility to central government did not undermine his commitment to the nation. But he was convinced that the greatness of the American nation rested in the beliefs and sentiments of the people, which included a deeply felt aversion to a strong national government. Jefferson envisaged America as a vast "empire of liberty" ruled not by soldiers and bureaucrats but the shared commitment to the great governing principles of the rights to "life, liberty, and the pursuit of happiness." Jefferson's empire of liberty would be the first in all humankind not to be ruled from a single center. He was committed to preventing New York or Philadelphia from controlling this empire the way Rome,

Paris, and London had become the controlling forces of the Roman, French, and British empires.

Respect and affection between the scattered provinces of this empire would be insufficient to hold such a large entity together unless those sentiments were complemented by common material interests. If shared reverence for the principles of the Declaration of Independence was the ideological glue for holding the empire of liberty together, the practical adhesive was commerce. Trading with people in other parts of the country would enable Americans to develop ties of trust, respect, and reciprocity. Because people in different parts of the far-flung nation needed goods produced in other parts, buying and selling provided an avenue for developing a national outlook that politics, an essentially local activity, did not.

The election of 1800, pitting Thomas Jefferson and John Adams, provided a clear-cut choice between Adams's adherence to Federalist principles and Jefferson's commitment to the "Empire of Liberty." Jefferson prevailed, and his presidency set the United States on the path of *dual federalism*, which endured in crucial respects until the New Deal of the 1930s and continues to influence the dynamics of federal-state relations. Jefferson rejected the Hamiltonian spirit that had crept into the interpretation of governmental powers during the first twelve years of the new nation. He abandoned the ambitious projects that Hamilton had embarked on; he cut the federal budget; and he made clear that the initiative for domestic public policy making would reside with the individual states.

At the same time that he decentralized policy making, Jefferson spearheaded the greatest territorial expansion in American history. As a result of his purchase of the Louisiana Territory from France in 1803, the nation more than doubled in size. Although much of the newly acquired territory was thought to be uninhabitable, the sheer magnitude of the additions changed Americans' understanding of themselves from a country dominated by the eastern seaboard to a nation of truly continental proportions. As Jefferson's theory of an empire of liberty dictated, these territories would not become colonies. Each would establish its own government and quickly be absorbed into the vast nation of states, where it would essentially govern itself just as the existing states did.

After Jefferson, centralization made a comeback. The Second National Bank of the United States was chartered in 1816. The election of John Quincy Adams in 1824 promised to greatly increase the power of the central government. Adams vowed to use the national government to build roads and canals and even establish its own university. Adams failed to get much of his program adopted. Having defeated Adams in 1828, Andrew Jackson set about restoring limited, decentralized government. Lying on his sickbed in the spring of 1832, Jefferson's disciple, President Andrew Jackson, vowed, "The bank, is trying to kill me, but I will kill it."

With that, Jackson set about to veto the rechartering of the Second National Bank of the United States, an act that most vividly symbolized his determination to radically curtail the power of the national government. He objected to the bank on democratic-egalitarian grounds. Jackson was convinced that the bank granted "exclusive gratuities and privileges" that "made the rich richer and the potent more powerful."

The bank controlled the money supply and was the dominant lender in America, making 20 percent of all commercial loans. This extraordinary combination of powers enabled it to crush rival banks by manipulating their reserves and curry favor with Congress by granting legislators loans at favorable rates. Jackson was not inclined to reform the bank. He was suspicious of the very idea of a national bank, fearing that so much financial power placed in a single institution would inevitably lead to privilege and corruption. Better to abolish it and disperse its functions among state banks, believed Jackson. The best way to make the national government democratic was to give it as little to do as possible.

Jackson's actions were consonant with the growing democratic sentiment of the time and the principle that democracy could best be encouraged locally. In the 1820s and 1830s, many states rewrote their constitutions primarily in order to make them more democratic. Property qualifications for voting were eliminated, thereby expanding the size of the electorate to include virtually all white males. State offices, including judicial posts that had previously been appointed, became directly elected by the people.

Jackson's decentralist convictions were so thoroughgoing that he opposed some national government projects even though he approved of their aims. In 1830, he vetoed federal aid for construction of the Maysville Road. Although the road was supposed to be a link of the national road, it was to be built entirely within the state of Kentucky. Jackson did not believe that the federal government's interstate commerce powers encompassed a project that was essentially local in nature. The road was probably a good idea, but if the people of Kentucky wanted it, Jackson asserted, they should build it.

## Critical Choice: National Supremacy, Within Limits

Lincoln's decision to use military force to suppress the secession of southern states from the Union was the critical choice that not only enabled the Union to endure but also firmly established the supremacy of the federal government over the states. However, Lincoln and the Union would not have prevailed were it not for previous critical choices made on behalf of federal supremacy. In a series of unanimous decisions over a period of almost thirty-five years, the Supreme Court under the leadership of Chief Justice John Marshall established the principle of the supremacy of the federal government over the states and limited the states' ability to interfere with economic competition, property rights, and the sanctity of contracts.

As we discuss in Chapter 9, Marshall's opinion in *McCulloch v. Maryland* (1819) clearly established the supremacy of the federal government over the states. In that case, the Supreme Court voided a tax that the state of Maryland had imposed on the Second National Bank of the United States. Marshall asserted that the Constitution was derived from the people, not the states. Although limited to those powers specifically enumerated by the Constitution, the federal government's authority was supreme within those limits. The Constitution does not mention the chartering of a national bank, but according to Marshall, such a financial institution was obviously "necessary and proper" for carrying out the enumerated powers to tax and regulate commerce and was therefore rendered constitutional by the Necessary and Proper Clause in Article One of the Constitution. Although states also have the right to tax, they do not have the right to tax federal functions. As the Maryland example demonstrated, such taxes have the power to hamper and indeed destroy legitimate federal activities.

In *Gibbons v. Ogden* (1824), the court ruled that New York's granting of a monopoly for steamboat service violated the federal government's right to protect the freedom of interstate commerce. Marshall took a broad view of commerce, claiming that it included all aspects of trade, including shipping. He argued that the commerce affected by the New York steamboat monopoly was interstate in character even though the monopoly applied only to the New York portion of waterways. Those waterways, coastal and inland, extended beyond the borders of New York and were therefore aquatic avenues of interstate commerce. It was the constitutional responsibility of the federal government to ensure that trade remained free at all points along those interstate routes.

Marshall's success was based on the power of his reasoning and self-discipline. He knew that the combined strength of the legislative and executive branches could defeat him by passing constitutional amendments that voided the court's decisions, impeaching him and his allies, or defying the court's rulings. Therefore, he picked his opportunities carefully. The court refused to entertain any important cases regarding the two most controversial issues of the time, slavery and the tariff, because feelings about those two issues were so strong that any decision the court might choose to render would risk tearing the country apart. Marshall's court confined itself to cases in which some disagreement existed among its erstwhile opponents, the Republicans. For example, many Republicans were so deeply committed to free enterprise that they shared Marshall's opposition to New York's establishment of steamboat monopoly. Likewise, many Republicans appreciated the positive economic contribution of the Second National Bank and were therefore opposed to the efforts of specific states to hamper its activities. Thus, the rulings that the court handed down were relatively uncontroversial; their great importance lay in the precedents they established. Because his political opponents were so preoccupied by the immediate implications of the rulings, they underestimated the long-term implications.

Unlike his idol Jefferson, Jackson did not believe in the compact theory of the Constitution. He took the phrase "We the People" literally. His vision of national power was that its scope of responsibility was very limited, but within that scope it reigned supreme. While attending a dinner in honor of Jefferson's birthday, Jackson was disturbed to hear Robert Hayne, senator from South Carolina, offer a toast to "the Union of the States and the Sovereignty of the States." In his own toast, Jackson responded, "Our Federal Union, it must be preserved." Sensing that South Carolina was on the verge of passing a nullification ordinance in which it would refuse to pay federally imposed tariffs, Jackson told a South Carolina congressman: "Please give my compliments to my friends in your state, and say to them that if a single drop of blood shall be shed there in opposition to the laws of the United States, I will hang the first man I can lay my hand on engaged in such treasonable conduct, upon the first tree I can reach." When Senator Hayne asked Senator Thomas Hart Benton of Missouri whether Jackson would really do such a thing, Benton replied, "When Jackson begins to talk about hanging, they can begin to look out for ropes."

Jackson responded to South Carolina's Nullification Ordinance of 1832 with a Nullification Proclamation in which he explained his refusal to accept the ordinance and willingness to call out federal troops to quell any attempt by South Carolina to enforce it. South Carolina backed down. Although Jackson and Democrats in Congress conceded to a reduction in the tariff, the president succeeded in his objective of teaching his fellow partisans the difference between states rights and nullification of legitimate national policy. Had Jackson failed to defend federal supremacy, it would have no longer served as a premise of American constitutional government, and Lincoln's later defense of it would have proved impossible.

Presidential leadership prevented a rebellion over tariffs, but it could not do so over the expansion of slavery. As we discussed in Chapter 4, none of the compromises over the spread of slavery were able to stave off civil war. Because slavery was constitutionally protected, ending it would require constitutional change to enable the national government to impose abolition on the slave states. As we discussed in Chapter 3, The Thirteenth, Fourteenth, and Fifteenth Amendments to the Constitution committed the national government to forcing the former slave states to grant civil and political rights to African Americans. War and constitutional amendment achieved the supremacy of the national government over the states that the Supreme Court had proclaimed in *McCulloch*.

In the immediate aftermath of the war, it appeared that African-American civil and political rights would indeed be secured through the vigorous exertion of national power. The United States established, for the first and only time, a

"**ONE VOTE LESS.**"—*Richmond Whig.*

**Figure 5.2.** "One Vote Less." 1868 Cartoon depicting the cruelty of the Klu Klux Klan, wood engraving by Thomas Nast. Credit: The Granger Collection, NYC — All rights reserved.

powerful military government to rule on domestic soil. *Reconstruction* involved thousands of troops and was led by thirty-five generals. The South was divided into five military districts. Generals were empowered to void state and local elections; dismiss governors and mayors; and participate in the selection of tax collectors, sheriffs, judges, and other local officials. The military staffed and led the key Reconstruction agency, the Freedman's Bureau, which provided food and medical assistance to both blacks and whites and established schools for 500,000 children. Federal troops maintained law and order while southern states rewrote their constitutions to provide slaves with full civil and political rights. But the Reconstruction effort became increasingly halfhearted over time. The South remained unalterably opposed and the political enthusiasm for it among northerners waned. The number of troops stationed in the South declined, as did the size and ambition of the Freedman's Bureau. Resistance by white southerners took many forms, including terrorism and murder. The Ku Klux Klan was a powerful symbol and organizational weapon for this resistance (Figure 5.2).

Reconstruction ended as a result of a deal to resolve the disputed 1876 presidential election. In exchange for granting the presidency to the Republican, Rutherford B. Hayes, Democrats, the party of the white South, exacted Hayes's tacit endorsement for the end of all meaningful federal reconstruction efforts. The withdrawal of the U.S. military from the southern states allowed them to evade both the letter and spirit of the Fourteenth and Fifteenth Amendments by erecting the complex and comprehensive system of racial oppression nicknamed *Jim Crow*. State laws and administrative practices prevented African Americans from voting and other forms of political participation, forbade them from eating at restaurants or staying at hotels patronized by whites, and relegated them to inferior facilities at theaters and on streetcars. States and localities established separate schools and prisons. Mobs tortured and hung African-American suspects with no police interference or national government intervention.

## The Second Federalism Path: Cooperative Federalism

The refusal of the federal government to intervene to enforce the constitutional protections provided to former slaves did not bespeak a full-fledged return to the limited role it had occupied during the era of dual federalism. Instead, the federal government chose to widen a different path, that of *cooperative federalism*, which had been a minor side road even when dual federalism was the major thoroughfare. The father of dual federalism, Thomas Jefferson, had permitted Treasury Secretary Albert Gallatin to give grants of land to the states for the support of public schools. Jefferson did not object to this form of federal involvement in his empire of liberty because he felt that it was noncoercive. Land was preferable to cash as a form of subsidy, believed Jefferson, because the federal government owned so much land.

During the second half of the nineteenth century, cooperative Federalism became a fully accepted and critically important form of intergovernmental relations. It was the driving force in the creation of the American system of state universities. The *Morrill Act of 1862* gave land grants to states to establish colleges that taught agriculture, mechanical arts, military science, natural science, and classical studies. Only seventeen state universities existed before 1862. Over the next fifty years, the Morrill Act led to the creation of more than fifty additional universities.

Modern agricultural and transportation policy have also been framed by cooperative federalism. The Smith Lever Act, enacted in 1914, created the Department of Agriculture's Extension Service. Rather than impose technical advice on

THE PUBLIC HIGHWAY OF THE FUTURE.

**Figure 5.3.** "The Public Highway of the Future." An 1880 wood carving celebrating the great advancement of American roads and highways. Credit: The Granger Collection, NYC – All rights reserved.

wary farmers, the Extension Service functions as a partnership between the Department of Agriculture and the state land-grant colleges. Federal employees work with federally subsidized state specialists to develop programs of technical assistance geared to the specific needs and preferences of local farmers (Figure 5.3).

Road building is one of the most important but also most politically sensitive responsibilities of government. Decisions about where to put roads and locate entrances and exits to limited-access roads can determine which communities prosper and which ones die. Rather than try to make such difficult and politically potent decisions from afar, Washington has, for the most part, restricted its role to providing funds to the states to pursue highway projects. Since the 1920s, federally subsidized road building and repair have been among the most important activities of the states.

## Critical Choice – Opting for Direct Democracy

In Chapter 3 we discussed the great impact that Progressivism had on American Political Development. Because state constitutions and municipal charters were far more easily changed than the U.S. Constitution, Progressivism had a more decisive impact on state than federal politics and governance. The Progressives were able to convince many states to adopt party primary elections, and citizen-initiated referenda, initiatives, and recalls. Primary elections substituted the will of party voters for that of political leaders in determining whom the party would nominate for state and federal office. The referendum enabled voters to bypass the state legislature and vote directly for or against specific policy proposals. The recall allowed the voters to remove governors and judges from office. These Progressive-inspired changes reflected a critical choice in favor of direct democracy at the expense of representative democracy. The vast size of the national polity and key provisions of the U.S. Constitution that bolster the representative form of government have prevented the national government from moving toward direct democracy the way the states have. As a result the critical choice in favor of direct democracy altered the path of state but not federal government. Figure 5.4 shows which states have adopted the referendum and the initiative.

## "Strings Attached" Federalism: Federalism Meets the Modern Administrative State

The New Deal of the 1930s altered cooperative federalism by requiring the states to abide by federal dictates in order to receive the funds that the federal government made available. New Deal welfare grants required states to match its contributions with monies of their own and designate a single agency to be responsible for receiving and spending welfare aid. Many states had no existing agency capable of performing such a task, and were compelled to create state welfare departments. Even those that already had welfare departments were required to expand and professionalize the operations of those agencies in order to meet federally imposed standards. States were "blackmailed" into administering the federal unemployment compensation scheme because a 3 percent tax would be levied on all employers in states that did not assume this administrative burden.

States emerged from the New Deal with many more functions and far greater administrative capacity with which to perform them. But the relationship between the states and federal government was irrevocably altered. The federal government had become the senior partner. Goals and strategies for an ever-

| Statutes | Constitution | | | | |
|---|---|---|---|---|---|
| State | Initiative | Citizen Petition Referendum | Legislative Referendum | Initiative | Legislative Referendum |
| Alaska | D* | Yes | No | None | Yes |
| Arizona | D | Yes | Yes | D | Yes |
| Arkansas | D | Yes | Yes | D | Yes |
| California | D | Yes | Yes | D | Yes |
| Colorado | D | Yes | No | D | Yes |
| Florida | None | No | No | D | Yes |
| Idaho | D | Yes | Yes | None | Yes |
| Illinois | None | No | Yes | D | Yes |
| Kentucky | None | Yes | Yes | None | Yes |
| Maine | I | Yes | Yes | None | Yes |
| Maryland | None | Yes | Yes | None | Yes |
| Massachusetts | I | Yes | Yes | I | Yes |
| Michigan | I | Yes | Yes | D | Yes |
| Mississippi | None | No | No | I | Yes |
| Missouri | D | Yes | Yes | D | Yes |
| Montana | D | Yes | Yes | D | Yes |
| Nebraska | D | Yes | Yes | D | Yes |
| Nevada | I | Yes | Yes | D | Yes |
| New Mexico | None | Yes | Yes | None | Yes |
| North Dakota | D | Yes | Yes | D | Yes |
| Ohio | I | Yes | Yes | D | Yes |
| Oklahoma | D | Yes | Yes | D | Yes |
| Oregon | D | Yes | Yes | D | Yes |
| South Dakota | D | Yes | Yes | D | Yes |
| Utah | D&I | Yes | Yes | None | Yes |
| Washington | D&I | Yes | Yes | None | Yes |
| Wyoming | D* | Yes | No | None | Yes |
| U.S. Virgin Is. | I | Yes | Yes | I | Yes |

**Figure 5.4.** Shows which states have adopted the referendum and the initiative. The Initiative and Referendum States.

wider sphere of policies were set in Washington. Federal grants in aid now came with *strings attached.* The states were left with the task of implementing those policies according to rules and regulations dictated to them from above. If they failed to abide by federal guidelines, they risked losing those grants.

States responded to their roles as junior partners in different ways. Some sought to make the New Deal programs their own by vigorously endorsing and expanding them. These states created "little New Deals" in which state government took on the same expansive and experimental character that the national government did. Led by Governor Philip La Follette, Wisconsin increased taxes on the rich, expanded aid to education, and reorganized state agencies. Some states sought to resist federal encroachment. In Georgia, Governor Eugene Talmadge actually reduced state spending for highways, daring the federal government to cut highway assistance in response. He also refused to cooperate with the mandates of federal welfare and agricultural assistance programs. The fear that this approach would actually cause the federal government to stop helping Georgians led to Talmadge's defeat for reelection in 1936.

In general, the wealthier industrial states of the East and Midwest tried to cooperate with and even emulate FDR's New Deal, whereas the poorer states, primarily those in the South, resisted change to the extent they could without endangering their access to federal help. Despite the strings it imposed, the New Deal did not succeed in unifying policies across the states. Indeed, the differing state responses to it in many ways served to accentuate the political and policy differences among them.

During the New Deal the Supreme Court abandoned what had previously served as the most important brake on federal government intervention in the affairs of the states, the Commerce Clause of the Constitution, which limits the federal government's regulatory role to "interstate and foreign commerce." Prior to the New Deal the Court had interpreted the word "commerce" to exclude other related economic activities such as manufacturing. It had also interpreted "interstate" narrowly to mean the direct exchange of goods between states. The New Deal interpreted commerce far more loosely to mean almost any form of production, employment arrangements, sale, or transport of goods or services.

In 1942, in *Wickard v. Filburn*, the Supreme Court erased the distinction between intrastate and interstate commerce altogether. In order to drive up wheat prices, Congress had passed the Agriculture Adjustment Act, which imposed limits on wheat production based on acreage owned by a farmer. Roscoe Filburn claimed that the act did not apply to him because his wheat was not for sale; he was growing it exclusively to feed his own chickens. Nonetheless, the Court ruled that Filburn was subject to the Act and he was ordered to pay a fine for exceeding production limit. For the next fifty years the Supreme Court did not overturn a single federal statute on Commerce Clause grounds or for any other reason.

In *Garcia v. San Antonio Metropolitan Transit Authority* (1985), the Supreme Court appeared to give a blanket endorsement to national government intrusions into what had previously been the domain of the states and localities. It adopted a theory of federal-state relations known as *process federalism*, which argues that the meaningful constitutional protections for the states are not provided either by the Tenth Amendment or by the principle of enumerated powers, but by the structure of the national government itself. The most important of these structural protections is the U.S. Senate, whose members are chosen by the states. This opinion implied that the court would not object to any imposition by the national government on the states as long as the Senate approves it.

## CRITICAL CHOICE: REASSERTING NATIONAL SUPREMACY: CIVIL RIGHTS FOR AFRICAN AMERICANS

Although the New Deal profoundly altered the relationship between the states and the federal government by requiring the states to accept federal regulation of aid, this shift did not affect Jim Crow. The southern states remained free to deprive African Americans of voting rights and equal access to job opportunities, education, and public facilities. Starting in the 1950s and culminating in the 1960s, the federal government revived the Fourteenth and Fifteenth Amendments to overturn the state laws and administrative practices that promoted and enforced racial segregation. In the 1940s, FDR and Truman had taken steps to racially integrate federal employment practices and, most significantly, racially integrate the armed forces. But the first serious blow to state laws and practices was imposed by the Supreme Court in 1954. In *Brown v. Board of Education* it declared all state and local efforts to racially segregate schools to be unconstitutional. In 1964, Congress, aggressively prodded by President Johnson, passed the first major Civil Rights Act since Reconstruction, outlawing discrimination in public accommodations, housing, and employment. The following year it passed The Voting Rights Act, which not only overturned state laws that prevent African Americans from voting but also empowered the Justice Department to intervene to enable African Americans to freely exercise their voting rights.

These critical choices were the result of pressure from a grassroots movement, shifts in public opinion, and aggressive leadership. African Americans borrowed the tactics of *nonviolent resistance* from the Indian independence movement led by Mohandas Gandhi and the U.S. labor union struggles of the 1930s. They organized peaceful "sit ins" at segregated lunch counters, bus terminals, and other segregated public facilities in the South. Black and white protestors would refuse to give up their seats when asked to leave and would then submit peacefully to the beatings and arrests to which they were then subjected (Figure 5.5).

**Figure 5.5.** "Seated in History." 2005 Cartoon Commemorating Rosa Parks's role in initiating the Montgomery Bus Boycott. Political Cartoons.com #20710.

The civil rights struggle was the first serious political conflict to be fully televised. Americans all over the country watched southern sheriffs and police officers beat and bully well-mannered young African-American men and women for the "crime" of ordering food at a whites-only lunch counter or helping fill out voter registration papers. Americans saw southern governors blocking the schoolhouse doors that African-American children were politely trying to enter. These dramatic moments tarnished the image of state and local government in the minds of many Americans. Although they might continue to respect the leadership in their own state, they increasingly came to question whether important policy matters should be left in the hands of states whose own troopers used cattle prods to disperse peaceful civil rights demonstrators.

The initial wave of resistance to integration of school and public facilities and African-American voter-registration efforts seemed to confirm the skepticism of those Americans who doubted that racial attitudes could be changed by federal legislation. But in the face of persistent and aggressive national intervention, the resistance soon crumbled. Although racial politics would continue to roil American politics for many years, schools and facilities in the South were desegregated and African Americans achieved comparability with whites in terms of voter participation; the promise of the Fourteenth and Fifteenth Amendments was finally fulfilled.

## MANDATES AND COERCION: STRINGS-ATTACHED FEDERALISM MEETS THE RIGHTS REVOLUTION

In the late 1960s and early 1970s, the rights revolution spread beyond issues of voting to include an entire host of policy issues such as the environment, job safety, mental health, education, and the rights of people who are disabled. Although this rights revolution was inspired by the civil rights crusade, the national government's response to it was critically different. No federal marshals showed up to enforce national environmental or occupational safety and health laws. No dramatic confrontations occurred between state governors and national authorities. Instead, the national government relied, for the most part, on the states to implement the new array of federally imposed mandates. Although the states rarely disagreed with the broad purpose of the federal mandates, they often adamantly opposed the specific regulations that dictated the pace at which the mandates would be implemented. No longer did Washington simply point the states in a particular policy direction; it now provided detailed timetables for meeting specific objectives and penalties for failing to attain them in the time allotted.

To press states to comply with federal objectives, Washington also devised a new form of string to attach to its grants to the states. It now threatened to take money away from one grant category if the states failed to comply with a totally different one. For example, the Clean Air Act of 1970 requires states to bring noncompliant metropolitan areas into compliance. Failure to do so makes the states liable to lose federal highway subsidies, even though there is no direct connection between the program they are required to comply with, the Clean Air Act administered by the EPA, and the subsidy they are threatened with losing, which comes from a totally different program administered by a different federal agency, the Department of Transportation. In 2012, the Supreme Court overturned the Medicaid provision of President Obama's healthcare reform (Patient Protection and Affordable Care Act), declaring that threatening to take funds from one state subsidy program if the states failed to comply with a totally different one was an unconstitutional form of coercion of the states by the federal government. If the Court remains firm in sticking to this precedent, the federal government will no longer be able to employ this powerful weapon for coercing state compliance with federal dictates.

In addition to threatening to withhold funds, Congress has sometimes chosen to simply mandate the states to accomplish congressionally determined objectives without providing any funds to the states and localities to implement those goals. This approach is particularly appealing to Congress because it enables the central government to gain the credit for accomplishing popular policy goals without having to pay the large costs that such policies incur. Federal statutes established the goals to be accomplished and then required others to pay the cost of meeting them. For example, local school systems have to pay for the installation of federally mandated elevators that improved accessibility for disabled students. Municipalities have to install expensive new equipment at their own expense to meet more stringent federally mandated drinking water standards. In the mid-1990s, the city of Columbus, Ohio, conducted a study demonstrating that federal mandates were costing the city hundreds of millions of dollars a year.

## Contemporary Federalism: Pathways Converge

Contemporary Federalism bears the marks of all the different pathways we have described. This section highlights the continued relevance of each pathway by showing how it shapes contemporary public policy. The continued dominance of strings-attached Federalism is illustrated by its extension to a policy area that had previously hewed to the cooperative Federalism path, education. Ever since the 1960s, the states have received extensive federal aid, but that money did not come with many strings. The 2001 NCLB Act supported by President Bush and bipartisan majorities in both houses of Congress places a great many demands on states. It requires them to devise statewide standards in reading and mathematics, to test all students annually in grades three through eight, and to meet annual statewide progress objectives ensuring that all groups of students reach proficiency within twelve years. States that fail to abide by those guidelines are subject to losing federal aid.

As the strings attached to federal aid have grown tighter and more numerous, some states have sought ways to convince their federal overseers that they can accomplish the goals that the strings are intended to make them attain while avoiding much of the red tape and wasteful effort that so many specific and detailed requirements inevitably produce (see Chapter 10 for an explanation of "red tape"). The result can be termed *negotiated federalism*. States produce a comprehensive plan for accomplishing what federal law demands and the federal government gives the state a waiver from the specific guidelines it has written to accomplish those aims. These negotiations do no signal a return to a purely cooperative relationship. The federal government remains the senior partner dictating what must be accomplished. But such negotiations promise to give the states a great deal more leeway in how best to attain the goals the federal government establishes.

The most significant example of negotiated federalism regards federal welfare policy. In 1994, Wisconsin obtained the first of a series of waivers from the Department of Health and Human Services allowing it to establish an innovative statewide program called W-2. Instead of using strict income criteria to determine who was eligible for welfare payments as federal policy required,

Wisconsin was allowed to adopt a job-readiness standard. Regardless of how little income a person had, if a person was deemed to be job ready they were required to find work rather than be given welfare. To help in that process, the state greatly expanded its capacity to help job-ready people find work. Those low-income people who were not considered job ready were required not simply to train for jobs, as HHS demanded, but to actually perform community services jobs. Nor did W-2 adjust the level of assistance it offered to take account of family size. Thus, eligible mothers did not receive extra payments for having more children. W-2 proved so successful both in slashing welfare rolls and in assisting previously eligible persons find jobs that it served as the model for the federal law, The *Personal Responsibility and Work Opportunity Reconciliation Act* of 1996, popularly known as Welfare Reform.

A waiver from ordinary federal requirements was likewise essential to the most ambitious state effort at healthcare reform, embarked on by Massachusetts in 2006. The goal of the reform was to provide universal health care coverage by mandating that every resident have health insurance. Prior to the reform, Massachusetts received federal funds to reimburse hospitals and doctors for providing care to the poor. In order to find a way to enable poor people to obtain insurance, it convinced the Department of Health and Human Service to use much of that money to subsidize the purchase of health insurance by the poor. Because nearly everyone would then have insurance, hospitals and doctors would no longer have to treat patients for nothing and therefore they would no longer need to be compensated by the government for doing so. As a result of the waiver, Massachusetts was able to devise a plan that provides health coverage to 93 percent of its residents, by far the highest coverage percentage of any state.

## The Persistence of Cooperative Federalism

As the negotiated Federalism example shows, the line between strings-attached and cooperative federalism is a blurry one because so often federal and state officials share the same goals. Much of what the federal government requires the states to do they would choose to do anyway, especially if they are being given the money to do it and granted sufficient flexibility regarding how best to attain the specified ends. Thus, regardless of how many specific strings are attached, a spirit of cooperation rather than one of antagonism typifies most federal state public-policy partnerships. This cooperative spirit permeated the effort of the Obama administration to provide a stimulus to the economy in the wake of the financial collapse that began in the fall and winter of 2008. In February of 2009, Congress enacted the American Recovery and Reinvestment Act. It provided a total of $787 billion to combat the recession, with $354 billion of that money to be divided amongst the fifty states. States used that money primarily to do two things they very much wanted to do. One was prevent the layoffs of state employees. The other was to embark on road, bridge, and rail construction and repair. Thus, the states and the federal government cooperated to achieve goals near to both their hearts: stimulating the economy, retaining jobs, and improving the provision of important state services.

## The Persistence of Dual Federalism

Despite the rise of the federal government to senior-partner status, critical areas of public policy, such as marriage law, remain the province of the states. Currently, same-sex marriage is legal in seventeen states. Thirty states have amended their constitutions to specifically forbid same-sex marriage and another six have adopted laws that ban the practice.

Beginning with *Lopez* in 1995, the case discussed at the beginning of the chapter, the Supreme Court has pushed back the boundaries of federal authority to create more room for state control. Retreating from the process federalism principle of *Garcia*, the majority argued that the very principle of enumerated powers underlying the Constitution meant that the Commerce Clause was intended to exclude *something*. If interstate commerce could be used to justify all manner of congressional activity regardless of how tenuous the connection between the problem at hand and the flow of interstate commerce, then the Commerce Clause was meaningless.

In 1996 and 1997, the court issued a series of decisions that reinforced the defense of states' rights begun by *Lopez*. The Eleventh Amendment to the Constitution forbids the federal judiciary from entertaining any suit against a state by a citizen of another state. In *Seminole Tribe v. Florida* (1996), the Supreme Court interpreted the Eleventh Amendment to mean that states enjoy *sovereign immunity*, meaning that the federal courts may not hear a case against a state brought by a citizen of that state. The Supreme Court did not declare this immunity to be absolute; it is limited by the due process and equal protection guarantees of the Fourteenth Amendment. But if those civil rights protections are not at stake, the federal courts may not intrude in legal disputes between a state and its citizens. In *Printz v. United States* (1997), the Supreme Court invalidated a section of the Handgun Violence Protection Act, popularly known as the Brady Bill, which required local law enforcement officials to conduct background checks on people seeking to buy guns. The Court interpreted the Tenth Amendment to mean that local and state officials cannot be compelled to do the national government's business.

## Innovative Federalism

States are currently forging a new Federalism path by taking the lead in developing policy initiatives in areas where they consider federal policy to be inadequate. Even this new path has some precedent in the innovative policy initiatives that some states took during the Progressive Era. Both Wisconsin and New York developed old-age pension schemes before the federal government did. Louis Brandeis was so impressed by these efforts to test out policies that could later be adopted by the federal government that he referred to the states as "Laboratories of Democracy."

What distinguishes the most ambitious of the current state efforts, those related to reducing $CO_2$ emissions in an effort to reduce climate change, is that it is a coordinated effort among many states. Twelve states took the U.S. EPA to court to force the federal government to regulate climate change more aggressively. The Attorneys General of those states did not argue that the EPA's failure affected their states in particular; rather, they claimed that their role as legal guardians of their states required them to take action when the national government failed to protect the nation as a whole, of which their states are obviously a part. In April 2007, the Supreme Court ruled five to four that the EPA violated the Clean Air Act by improperly declining to regulate new-vehicle emissions standards to control the pollutants that contribute to global warming and required the agency to develop policies to reduce $CO_2$ emissions.

To reduce $CO_2$ emissions from generators of electricity, ten New England and Mid-Atlantic states have banded together to establish the Regional Greenhouse Gas Initiative(RGGI). This project is innovative both in its involvement of many states and in the manner in which it seeks to achieve reductions. To do so in the most efficient manner possible, RGGI employs a market-based "cap-and-trade" approach. Initially, each electric power generator is given an allowance equal to 90 percent of their current emissions. To achieve a 10 percent reduction they either reduce on their own or buy excess allowances from other generators who have reduced by more than 10 percent and therefore have extra allowances to sell. This system encourages efficiency because it gives an incentive to those generators that can achieve their reductions most cheaply to keep doing so beyond the 10 percent requirement because they can sell those reductions at a profit to those who cannot reduce as cheaply. As Brandeis would have hoped, this scheme, having been tested in the laboratory of a group of states, has now been incorporated in climate-change legislation currently before Congress.

## CONCLUSION

The "empire of liberty" that Jefferson envisaged has not disappeared. An American traveling abroad is struck by how much more intrusive and pervasive government is elsewhere. In many other democratic countries, citizens must carry identity cards. If they move, they must inform the government. Government permission may be required for activities, such as laying off a worker, that Americans consider to be matters of strictly private concern. Texans have a legal right to carry concealed handguns and, as we learned in *Lopez*, the federal government has no right to keep those handguns away from schools. Other countries have national police forces whose jurisdiction extends as far as the nation's borders. In this country, ordinary police work is done by local police forces whose powers cease at the city and county limits. We have all seen movies in which the police have to give up chasing the crook because he gets across the county line. The willingness to put up with this ridiculous outcome is eloquent testimony to how deeply Americans cherish the idea of local government.

France has a national education system. A fourth grader in Marseilles studies the same things and reads the same textbooks as a fourth grader in Lyon or Strasbourg. In the United States, most school systems are governed at the town or county level. A fourth grader in one school may study something far different from the fourth grader who is just across the road but on the other side of the county line.

The presidential election of 2000 that pitted Democrat Al Gore against Republican George W. Bush showed the price that Americans pay for their empire of liberty. The electoral vote was so close nationwide that the outcome of the election would be decided by Florida. Florida and many other states allow individual counties to select their own methods of ballot design and vote counting. The presidential election in Florida was, in reality, a series of local elections with different ballot designs, tabulation methods, and recount procedures. In Palm Beach County in particular, the ballot design was sufficiently confusing that many elderly voters who intended to vote for Gore voted for Patrick Buchanan instead. In other counties, failure to fully poke a hole next to the name of the candidate one favored resulted in so-called hanging chads, which made it impossible to tell for sure who the voter had voted for. As initially tallied, the vote was so close that the loser, Gore, refused to acknowledge Bush as the winner. The resulting chaos and confusion encouraged each party to suspect the other of "stealing" the election. Ultimately, the outcome in Florida, and thus in the election as a whole, was decided by the U.S. Supreme Court, who declared Bush the winner.

However, state and local discretion also enables Americans to enjoy enormous freedom to pick the style of government that suits them. If they do not like the way things are being done where they live, they have the option of moving. As our earlier comparison showed, a New Hampshire resident wanting more state services and protection of rural open space has only to move across the Connecticut River and live in Vermont.

American Federalism is no longer of interest only to Americans. As the European countries struggle to determine how best to strengthen and expand the European Union, they have increasingly come to look to American Federalism as a source of inspiration. America's form of government organization, which in the wake of the New Deal and rights revolution seemed destined to disappear, now serves as a model for emulation. Seen through European eyes, it is Federalism's overall success, not its many specific failures, that is most impressive.

America invented republican government on a continental scale. Now, as the Europeans try to form a union of comparable size and even greater diversity, they recognize Federalism as the key device for reconciling the governance of immense territory and population with meaningful liberty and democracy. Federalism enabled the United States to become the most powerful nation-state in the world, allowing its component parts the liberty to express meaningful political differences. It has helped Americans possess the security that only great size and strength can provide and still enjoy the democratic participatory opportunities that only small-scale government can offer. As Jefferson recognized, Federalism is what saves the empire of liberty from being a contradiction in terms.

## CHAPTER SUMMARY

☆ The Constitution is a compromise between those who wanted a strong national government and those who did not. In order to obtain consent for the establishment of a strong national government, its supporters made concessions to those who feared a strong national government. They agreed to limit its powers to those that were expressly delegated to it, reserving all other powers to the states. They also agreed to give the states a direct role in national governance via the Senate and the Electoral College.

☆ Path dependency and critical choice are important concepts for understanding the political development of American Federalism. Contemporary Federalism bears the marks of all the different pathways previously established.

☆ States and the national government have formed a partnership. Partners recognize that they need one another and must cooperate. But this does not stop them from quarreling, exerting their individuality, and trying to dominate one another. Over the course of American political development, the federal government has emerged as the senior partner.

★ The fifty states form fifty very distinct political worlds. They differ in the degree to which they capture the loyalty and attention of their citizens and the structure and content of their constitutions.

★ Dual federalism was imposed by the Jefferson administration, reinforced by the Jackson administration, and remained the dominant Federalism pathway until the Civil War.

★ Lincoln's decision to use military force to suppress the secession of southern states from the Union was *the* critical choice that not only enabled the Union to endure but also firmly established the supremacy of the federal government over the states.

★ The bargain resolving the 1876 presidential election stalemate was the critical choice that enabled the southern states to impose the Jim Crow regime of racial oppression and segregation.

★ Influenced by Progressivism, many states chose to incorporate forms of direct democracy into their constitutions.

★ The New Deal of the 1930s altered cooperative federalism by attaching strings to federal grants, thus requiring the states to abide by federal dictates in order to receive the funds that the federal government made available.

★ During the New Deal, the Supreme Court abandoned what had previously served as the most important brake on federal government intervention in the affairs of the states, the Commerce Clause of the Constitution.

★ The high tide of process federalism was reached in the 1980s.

★ Beginning in the 1970s, the federal government imposed unfunded mandates on the states and localities as a means of accomplishing federal government goals with the costs borne by the states and localities.

★ Current Federalism represents an amalgam of all the Federalism pathways previously established as well as a new pathway in which states coordinate policy efforts and efforts to alter national policy.

★ Federalism enabled the United States to become the most powerful nation-state in the world while allowing its component parts the liberty to express meaningful political differences. It has helped Americans possess the security that only great size and strength can provide and still enjoy the democratic participatory opportunities that only small-scale government can offer.

## MAJOR CONCEPTS

| | |
|---|---|
| Block Grants | Brown v Board of Education |
| Centralization | Commerce Clause |
| Cap-and-Trade | Cooperative Federalism |
| Dual Federalism | Empire of Liberty |
| *Garcia v. San Antonio Metropolitan Transit Authority* | Gibbons v. Ogden |
| Innovative Federalism | Jim Crow |
| McCulloch v. Maryland | Medicaid |
| Missouri Compromise of 1820 | Morrill Act of 1862 |
| National Supremacy | Negotiated Federalism |
| No Child Left Behind (NCLB) Act | Nonviolent Resistance |
| Nullification | Personal Responsibility and Work Opportunity Reconciliation Act (Welfare Reform) |
| Printz v. United States | Process Federalism |
| Progressive Movement | Reconstruction |
| Seminole Tribe v. Florida | Sovereign Immunity |
| Strings-Attached Federalism | Sovereign Immunity |
| Tenth Amendment | Unfunded Mandates |
| United States v. Lopez | Wickard v. Filburn |

## SUGGESTED READINGS

Beer, Samuel. *To Make a Nation: The Rediscovery of American Federalism*, rev. ed. Cambridge, MA: Belknap Press, 1998.

Conlan, Timothy. *From New Federalism to Devolution: Twenty-Five Years of Intergovernmental Reform*. Washington, DC: Brookings Institution, 1998.

Derthick, Martha, ed. *Dilemmas of Scale in America's Federal Democracy*. New York: Cambridge University Press, 1999.

Derthick, Martha. *Keeping the Compound Republic: Essays on American Federalism*. Washington, DC: Brookings Institution, 2001.

Diamond, Martin. *As Far as Republican Principles Will Admit: Essays by Martin Diamond*. Washington, DC: AEI Press, 1992.

Donahue, John D. *Disunited States*. New York: Basic Books, 1998.

Ehrenhalt, Alan. *Democracy in the Mirror: Politics, Reform, and Reality in Grassroots America*. Washington, DC: CQ Press, 1998.

Elazar, Daniel. *American Federalism: A View from the States*, 3rd ed. New York: Harper and Row, 1984.

Feeley, Malcolm, and Rubin Edward, *Federalism: Political Identity and Tragic Compromise*. Ann Arbor, MI: University of Michigan Press, 2008.

Greve, Michael. *The Upside-Down Constitution*, Cambridge, MA: Harvard University Press, 2012.

McDonald, Forrest. *States Rights and the Union: Imperium in Imperio, 1776–1876*. Lawrence, KS: Kansas University Press, 2000.

Nugent, John. *Safeguarding Federalism: How States Protect Their Interests in National Policymaking*, Norman OK: University of Oklahoma Press, 2009.

Peterson, Paul E. *The Price of Federalism*. Washington, DC: Brookings Institution, 1995.

Walker, David B. *The Rebirth of Federalism: Slouching toward Washington*. New York: Chatham House, 2000.

# 6 Political Economy

## CHAPTER OVERVIEW

This chapter focuses on:

★ The essentials of contemporary economic policy.
★ The path of economic liberalism that American political economy has followed.
★ The critical choices made both to keep the economy on that path and allow for various forms of government intrusion into the economy.
★ The shifts that have taken place in the arguments made in favor of government intrusion.

The economic collapse that began in 2008 posed the greatest threat to economic well-being since the Great Depression. It began with a fall in housing prices that forced many homeowners into defaulting on their mortgages, which in turn set off a chain reaction of huge losses for the banks, investment firms, and insurance companies that were placed at risk when the mortgages and mortgage-backed securities they owned declined steeply in value. The stock market lost almost half its total value; unemployment soared.

The great debate sparked by the collapse was whether or not the government should intervene to bailout the large banks, insurance companies, and industrial giants whose very existence was now in jeopardy. Those who opposed government intervention did so because they considered such a *bailout* was unfair and would promote inefficiency and irresponsibility. In a market system, the penalty for being unable to pay one's debts is to fail. The government does not intervene to prevent the local dry cleaner from going out of business when too many of its customers decide that the new one down the street does a better job getting the spots out of their clothes. Nor does it allow people to keep their jobs if the boss is dissatisfied with their work performance. It is unfair to make ordinary people pay the price for a competitive loss when the wealthy and powerful do not have to pay such a price. Market efficiency rests on the freedom to fail. Markets create a competition in which the more efficient producers drive out the less-efficient ones. Government intervention promotes irresponsibility because it creates what economists call a *moral hazard*. Firms that expect the government to bail them out will take risks that they would not take if they expected to actually bear the full brunt of those risks. The taxpayers will be stuck paying for their losses. But if they win, they alone reap the gain.

Supporters of a bailout argued that the banks, the mortgage insurer for those banks, and America's leading auto company, General Motors (GM), were simply too big to be allowed to fail. The world economic system functions on the basis of credit. These institutions were major providers of credit, and they also owed huge sums to other providers of credit. If they failed, they would bring the other credit providers down with them, and the whole credit and lending system would implode. The failure of GM would also set off a negative chain reaction. GM relies on thousands of different parts suppliers and provides product for thousands of dealers. If it failed, so would they. Thousands of workers employed by GM, its suppliers, and its dealers would be put out of work. These workers are also consumers. The failure of GM would also threaten the survival of the stores where they shopped, the restaurants where they ate, and all the other businesses that relied on their purchases.

The bailout supporters won. As we will discuss toward the end of this chapter, Congress passed legislation providing huge loans to several of the nation's largest banks, investment houses, and the largest mortgage insurance company, American Insurance Group. It also took over control of General Motors, investing billions to keep the company from going out of business.

This conflict over the proper role of government in the economy is simply the latest in a debate that is as old as the Union itself. This chapter focuses on the most important historical moments in this debate to show how critical choices between the relative merits of free markets and government intervention have shaped the character of America's political economy. It also shows how each of these choices has forged paths along which the American political economy continues to travel, paths that continue to intersect and collide.

## A SKETCH OF THE CONTEMPORARY AMERICAN POLITICAL ECONOMY

### Insurance

Even during less trying economic times, the government is deeply involved in the world of industry, commerce, and finance. It insures against risk; subsidizes favored economic activities; and punishes misbehavior. Its insurance efforts are geared to fight fear. One of the greatest enemies of economic prosperity is fear. People fear putting money in banks if they are concerned that the banks might not give them back their money when they ask for it. At the more 8,000 banks that pay premiums to it, the *Federal Deposit Insurance Corporation (FDIC)* insures deposits of up to $250,000 per depositor. Therefore, depositors can feel good about leaving their money in the bank. Banks need not worry that too many depositors will withdraw their money at one time and therefore they can be more aggressive in lending money.

The federal government also provides insurance to workers who lose their jobs. Currently, workers who are laid off or fired from their jobs receive a stipend from the government. The program is administered by the states so that benefits differ somewhat state by state. Typically, unemployed workers will receive half their normal weekly paycheck tax free. The length of the payment period varies according to state law, but depending on overall economic conditions might extend six months, a year, or even longer. The effect of this insurance is to lessen the fears that inevitably strike when one loses a job. How will I pay the mortgage? How will I buy groceries? In addition to the psychological damage instilled by such fears, they also have a negative economic impact. They impel unemployed workers to take the first available job, even if that job is a poor match for their skills and ambitions. Unemployment insurance allows them to take the chance to hunt for jobs that are more challenging and make fuller use of their talents. As a result, the economy enjoys a more talented and motivated work force.

The largest government insurance programs of all are aimed at the elderly. Social Security old-age pensions provide income to older Americans who have worked for a specified number of years in the course of their lives. Social Security is the single largest federal government outlay. In 2010 it accounted for 20 percent of all federal spending. Medicare provides health insurance for older Americans. In 2010 it accounted for 15 percent of all federal spending, placing it third on the list of most-expensive federal outlays, exceeded only by Social Security and Defense.

## Subsidies

The federal government provides huge subsidies to encourage economic behavior that it deems to be in the public interest. These subsidies are either paid directly to the recipient or provided indirectly in the form of lower tax payments. The largest direct subsidy the government provides is to the farmers of certain specified crops. The governments spends more than $13 billion a year on farm subsidies, most of which goes to corn, wheat, rice, and cotton farmers. They receive a specified amount per bushel and an additional subsidy based on a price level that the government guarantees them. Thus, if the government guarantees a price of $2 a bushel for corn but the price falls to $1.90, the corn farmer receives an extra ten cents per bushel. If the price remains above $2, no extra subsidy is paid. These subsidies keep food prices low because they encourage farmers to grow more crops than they would if they were just paying attention to the market price. It also helps farmers survive market downturns.

The largest indirect subsidies, provided via the tax code and therefore known as *tax expenditures*, are for employee health benefits, home ownership, and retirement savings. Homeowners may deduct the interest they pay on their mortgages from their taxable income. If one makes $50,000 a year and pays $4,000 a year in mortgage interest, one will be taxed as if one only made $46,000 a year. If one is in the 25 percent tax bracket, meaning one pays a quarter of one's taxable income in tax, one saves $1,000. In 2011 this subsidy cost the federal government more than $100 billion a year in tax revenue sacrificed.

Workers do not pay tax on the money they and their employers place in retirement plans or health insurance plans. Indeed, tax expenditures for employee health benefits constituted the single greatest source of tax expenditure. In 2011 it amounted to $177 billion. When the social benefits – mostly in the form of health insurance and old-age pensions – that these tax expenditures provide are added to publicly provided Social Security, health care, veterans benefits, and welfare, it turns out that the United States spends roughly the same amount on social programs (as a percentage of *Gross Domestic Product*) that Europeans spend. In 2011, total U.S. tax expenditures exceeded a trillion dollars (see Figure 6.1).

Retirement plans are not only important because of the income security they provide, they also constitute the chief source of investment capital for the U.S. economy. These plans use the contributions that workers and employers make to invest in stocks, bonds, and real estate. The profits these investments earn enable the plans to accumulate wealth that greatly exceeds the value of the contributions made by those workers and their employers. In 2010, U.S. retirement plans had assets totaling more than $6 trillion even though they received contributions of only $446 billion that year.

The tax code provides thousands of other specific subsidies for various forms of business investment. For example, producers of wind energy receive a corporate income tax credit of .019 cents for every kilowatt hour of energy they produce during the first ten years that a particular wind-energy facility is in production. A credit is more valuable than a deduction because it is subtracted not from taxable income but rather from the actual tax one would otherwise pay. If the facility produces a million kilowatt hours a year it would save $19,000 in taxes.

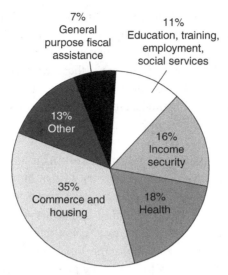

**Figure 6.1.** Tax Expenditure Budget, 2008.

*Note*: a. The three largest expenditure categories included in "Other" are Social Security (3.3 percent), International Affairs (5.2 percent), and General Science, Space, and Technology (1.4 percent).

*Source*: Budget of U.S. Government, FY 2010, Analytical Perspectives, Table 19–1.

## Regulation

The federal government polices many aspects of the behavior of industry, transport, communications, advertising, banking, and securities. This function of government is called *regulation*. Most of this policing is done through regulatory agencies. These regulators are either lodged in federal departments, including Labor, Justice, and Transportation, or in independent agencies such as the EPA, Consumer Product Safety Commission, Federal Trade Commission (FTC), and Securities and Exchange Commission (SEC). The aim of such regulation is to improve market performance by ensuring the provision of adequate information, forcing producers to bear the full social cost of production, punishing efforts to restrict competition, and protecting civil rights. For example, the SEC requires the issuers of stocks and bonds to provide a full and accurate statement of what their companies are worth so that prospective buyers have sufficient information to make an informed decision about whether or not to purchase securities in that company. The Food and Drug Administration (FDA) requires food manufacturers to list the ingredients in their produce so consumers know what they are getting. Pharmaceutical manufacturers must list the most frequent side effects of the medications they sell so that doctors and patients can have a fuller picture of the risks specific drugs pose.

Environmental regulation is largely devoted to forcing producers to bear the full costs of production. Producers choose to pollute because it is cheaper for them to do so than to employ cleaner techniques. But pollution is not really cheap, its actual costs are paid by others – those who breathe the dirty air or drink the poisoned water the polluters have emitted. By requiring producers to employ cleaner production methods, environmental regulators diminish the gap between the costs the polluters pay for and the full social costs imposed by their production practices.

The FTC and the Department of Justice work to protect free and fair market competition by punishing those who try to use unfair practices to eliminate competition or monopolize a market. The Equal Employment Opportunity Commission protects civil rights by suing employers who engage in discriminatory hiring or firing on the basis of race, color, religion, sex, national origin, age, disability, or genetic information. The Fish and Wildlife Service protects the rights of endangered species to survive by preventing land development that threatens the habitats of those species.

## Macroeconomic Policy

These regulatory efforts are aimed at the micro level, the functioning of specific markets and the behavior of firms engaged in those markets, and are referred to as microeconomic *policy*. Through its powers to tax, spend, and manage the currency, the federal government also intervenes at the macroeconomic level, the economy as a whole, in order to encourage price stability, full employment prosperity, and growth. Such efforts are referred to as *macroeconomic policy*. The Federal Reserve, whose members are appointed by the president, is in charge of monetary policy. It tries to manage the money supply primarily through selling government securities to banks and buying them from banks. When it sells, it reduces the amount of money the banks have. Because banks are required by law to keep a certain portion of their money in reserve, the Federal Reserve Board (the Fed) has lessened the amount of money they have available to lend. Because they have less money to lend, they will charge more by raising the interest rate on their loans. When the Fed buys securities, it pours more money into the banking system and therefore increases the amount banks can lend, thereby lowering the interest rate.

The government can also try to control overall economic activity by means of its taxing and spending policies. This is called *fiscal policy*. If it spends more than it takes in through taxes it runs a deficit. Advocates of deficit spending believe that it spurs economic activity because it raises *aggregate demand*, meaning the total demand for goods and services of the economy as a whole. Government demand stays high because the tax cuts do not produce commensurate cuts in government spending. Private demand rises because tax cuts raise taxpayers' incomes, which encourages them to consume more. If government chooses to run a surplus by taxing more than it spends, the opposite result is supposed to come about. Government buys less than it takes in and consumers spend less because their incomes have declined. Fiscal policy is controversial; some economists doubt whether it works, and it is rarely used as a vehicle for reigning in demand. Politicians find it too politically risky to raise taxes or cut spending for any reason, let alone as a speculative attempt to cool down the economy.

The United States is not unique in performing the micro and macro political-economic activities described. The other nations of the world that are both democratic and rich also engage in most if not all of them. The greatest difference between the United States and the rich countries of Europe and Asia is the degree of government intervention in the labor market. In addition to enforcing fair employment practices, the United States intervenes in the labor market to regulate worker pension programs; limit child labor; protect worker safety and health; set a minimum wage; and enable workers to join labor unions. But most rich countries do much more. They specify how many vacation days an employee must receive, and place restrictions on the number of hours the employee can work that are much stricter than those imposed by the U.S. government. The International Labor Organization reports that Americans work 137 more hours per year than Japanese workers, 260 more than British workers, and 499 more than French workers.

These other countries also make it extremely difficult to fire workers. This has the perverse effect of making firms in those countries more reluctant to hire new workers because once they hire them it is virtually impossible to lay them off. As a result, workers in other countries enjoy much greater job security than in the United States, but their unemployment rate is much higher. In some of these countries government involves itself directly in negotiations between unions and employers. In the U.S., government's role is limited to sometimes requiring "cooling off" periods before strikes are called. In general, private employers and unions negotiate on their own.

## Path Dependency: Economic Liberalism

Acknowledging the many ways that government intervenes in the economy should not obscure the fact that the central path followed by American political economy has been one of private property and free markets as set out by the Classic Liberal philosophers discussed in Chapter 2. When Thomas Jefferson drafted the Declaration of Independence, he borrowed from John Locke's *Second Treatise*, which argued that government could only be legitimate if it rested in the consent of the governed and protected the "natural rights" of "life, liberty, and estate." But Jefferson changed "estate," by which Locke meant "property," into "the pursuit of happiness." This wonderfully enigmatic phrase captures the essence of the liberal political economic system the Founders envisioned. The phrase is based on rights, not results. It does not promise happiness, but rather, a fair chance to pursue that dream; equal opportunity rather than equal results. It hints at the complex amalgam of striving, optimism, and uncertainty that form the distinctively American economic quest.

The *liberal economy* that embodies this understanding of the pursuit of happiness has three essential aspects: private property, competition, and promise keeping. Jefferson did not want to list property among the three most essential inalienable rights, but he did not intend to deny its importance. Government protects private property against theft and refrains from taking private property itself. Thus, persons are enabled to keep what possessions they have and to know that if they make investments or do work, they can keep the fruits of those risks and labors.

The liberal economy is inherently competitive; it depends on producers vying with one another for the patronage of consumers by offering better goods and cheaper prices. It is like a track meet in which everyone is given an opportunity to run the race. The competition is not entirely fair, because some runners are better trained, coached, and equipped. But once at the starting line, everyone must obey the same rules or face disqualification. In the economic version of the race, contracts are kept, debts are paid, thieves and counterfeiters are caught and punished, and the list of ingredients printed on the package is accurate. Government officiates; it writes the rules and enforces them. A liberal economy requires people to keep their word as well as do their work. Such trust cannot develop in an atmosphere of deceit. I lend to you only if I believe your pledge to repay me. If we sign a contract together, it is because we trust each other to live up to the bargain.

## A CRITICAL CHOICE: THE CONSTITUTION AND THE LIBERAL ECONOMY

The adoption of the Constitution, including the Bill of Rights, was the critical choice that set the United States firmly on the path of economic liberalism. It commits the U.S. government to sustaining the essentials of a liberal economy: the sanctity of private property, contracts, and free and open competition, Article VI holds the federal government responsible for debts that the previous government under the Articles of Confederation was obligated to pay. Article One Section Ten forbids states from "impairing the Obligation of Contracts" or grant any Title of Nobility." The Fifth Amendment forbids government from taking a person's property without just compensation. Article I authorizes Congress to tax, borrow money, coin currency, issue patents and copyrights, and regulate interstate and foreign commerce. Indeed, in the minds of many Framers, federal oversight of interstate and foreign commerce was the most compelling reason for creating the Union in the first place. Lack of such authority under the Articles of Confederation raised such dangerous possibilities as coastal states blackmailing landlocked ones into paying for permission to ship products overseas, or downstream states imposing tariffs on goods shipped from states upstream. But even more important than any of these specific clauses were the overarching constitutional principles of limited government and enumerated powers. These principles kept government from interfering with Americans' freedom to do what they liked with their property and conduct their business as they pleased as long as contracts were kept and laws were obeyed.

The United States has remained on this constitutionally prescribed path, but several critical questions regarding the nature of political economy were not determined by the Constitution. Most critical of all was how best to promote the pursuit of happiness. Those who favored active government intervention argued that it was necessary to maximize both economic progress and protect national security. Those opposed claimed that government could never be trusted to intervene fairly and equitably. It would always use its great power to help those in power and their friends. Therefore, it had to be kept out of economic life in order to maintain equality of opportunity. Those who sought to keep government out of the economy argued that such abstention was the only way to prevent the rise of a privileged class. The clash between these two point of view dominated American economic policy in the nineteenth century. In the twentieth century the nature of that debate shifted, with those who opposed greater government intervention arguing that such intervention would stifle economic progress, whereas the other claimed that government intervention was necessary to protect free and open competition and rather than threatening equality had become necessary to protect it.

## Hamilton versus Jefferson

During the early years of the life of the United States, the chief advocate of greater government involvement in the economy was Secretary of Treasury Alexander Hamilton. His interventionist strategy was composed of four essential elements. First, he sought to have the new central government assume the debts incurred by the states during the Revolution. Even though the states had promised to repay bondholders many had not done so. Hamilton argued that the United States would be able to borrow in the future only if it maintained an unsullied record of paying off the debts it had already incurred. He also recognized that if the national government took over state debt it would cement itself as the dominant force in financial affairs and thereby increase its power and prestige.

Second, Hamilton proposed that the debts be repaid through the issuance of new federal government bonds, an approach called *funding the debt.* In addition to simply providing a mechanism for paying off the state debts the federal government had assumed it had a great political advantage. Rich Americans would buy bonds because they paid a decent interest and looked like a good investment opportunity. Therefore, it was for the nation to remain permanently indebted. Hamilton mistrusted the rich, fearing that they would always put their private interests above their patriotic obligations. Funding the debt was a means to bind their public and private interests together. For if the nation floundered, the bonds held by the rich might not be redeemed.

The third element of Hamilton's strategy was intimately connected to the first two. He argued that managing the debt, when added to the many other critical financial tasks to perform, required the government to create a national bank. He admitted that the Constitution did not provide for a national bank, but it did grant Congress the power "to make all Laws which shall be necessary and proper for carrying into Execution the foregoing Powers, and all other Powers vested by the Constitution in the Government of the United States." Surely a bank was a necessary and proper means for carrying out such diverse financial responsibilities as raising revenue, borrowing money, and coining currency. Congress chartered the *First National Bank of the United States* in 1791.

The final element of Hamilton's plan was to use federal banking and tariff policy to promote U.S. manufactures. Congress had asked Hamilton to investigate manufactures as a way "to render the United States independent of foreign nations for military and other essential supplies." Hamilton argued in his *Report on Manufactures* that even more than providing essential military supplies, manufactures would help forge the strong sense of national identity that makes a country feel secure. He encouraged trade between South and North as a way to develop closer ties between the two regions and promote a common sense of nationality. But southern states would sell their products in the North instead of Europe only if the North could replace Europe as the South's source of manufactured goods. Therefore, argued Hamilton, national security required federal support for manufactures. To promote manufacturing, Hamilton supported not only a national bank to supply capital to manufacturing enterprises but also subsidies to manufacturers in the form of high tariffs on imported manufactures, and a government commission to award bounties for the establishment of new industries and prizes for the encouragement of inventions, particularly of labor-saving machinery.

The key opponent of Hamilton's scheme was Secretary of State Thomas Jefferson. He opposed federal assumption of state debt because he believed it rewarded greed. Many people who bought state bonds to finance the war had come to doubt that the bonds would ever be repaid, so they sold them at a loss to those who could afford to wait and see what the government would eventually do. Jefferson sympathized with the original bondholders who would now lose money twice, first by selling the bonds at a loss and then by paying additional taxes in order to pay off the bonds in full.

Jefferson opposed the national bank on constitutional and political grounds. He interpreted the term "necessary" in the *Necessary and Proper Clause* to mean "essential" not merely "helpful." A bank would indeed facilitate the implementation of financial policies, but it was not essential for doing so and therefore it was unconstitutional. Jefferson was a staunch defender of the states and he was therefore hostile to allowing the central government to so greatly enhance its power. He was also convinced that such a bank would not operate fairly but would make loans at favorable rates to Hamilton and his friends

Jefferson did not agree that the nation would benefit by promoting manufactures. He believed that a free republic needed to be based on agriculture. Farmers owned their own property and worked for themselves. Unlike manufacturing laborers, they did not develop the servile and resentful attitudes that come about when one has to work for a boss. Farmers also developed a wide range of skills and talents and learned to be stewards of the land. Workers forced to live in crowded decadent cities enjoyed no such opportunities. Therefore, Jefferson bitterly opposed Hamilton's scheme for privileging manufactures.

Hamilton plans achieved mixed results. He succeeded in convincing Congress to assume state debts, fund the debt, and establish a national bank. Jefferson dropped his opposition to debt assumption in exchange for obtaining Hamilton's support for Jefferson's plan to site the nation's capital on the Virginia-Maryland border rather than in either of the nation's two most populous and commercial cities – New York or Philadelphia. Congress created a national bank, but when Jefferson became president he convinced it not to renew the bank's charter. Then, in the aftermath of the War of 1812, it chartered the *Second Bank of the United States*. Twenty years later, President Andrew Jackson vetoed the Second Bank and no successor was brought into being during the nineteenth century. Congress failed to implement Hamilton's financial subsidy schemes for manufacture. However, it did agree to raise tariffs periodically during the following decades and such tariff rises did indeed favor certain manufacturing sectors.

The assumption and funding of the debt were critical choices for American political economy. They ensured that the national government would be able to function as a creditworthy entity and therefore have the financial strength to act as a great nation, should it choose to do so. The debt policies also created a creditor class whose own economic well-being was now tied to the fiscal and monetary stability and economic prosperity of the nation as a whole. The destruction of the Bank was equally critical because it put limits on the extent of special access and privileged treatment that the creditor class would receive from the government. President Andrew Jackson declared war on the "monster" Second Bank of the United States. Like Jefferson, Jackson's bitter opposition was rooted in the liberal principle of equal opportunity and resentment against speculators and influence peddlers. The small farmer and the westerner did not enjoy access to the bank's loans, which went to those Hamilton had hoped they would go to, eastern commercial and industrial bigwigs. Also, the bank threatened democracy by lavishing money on its political allies and subverting democratic essentials – honest toil and social solidarity. Its credit manipulation created an artificial economy of phony paper assets and speculation that threatened the health of the real economy, the one based on hard work, honest exchange, and neighborliness.

Jackson vetoed the bank's recharter. By supporting his subsequent reelection, a majority of voters voiced their own qualms about economic privilege. Like Jackson they preferred a tangible, manageable economy in which profit and competition blended with affection for customers, confidence in partners, respect for rivals, and trust in coworkers. Jackson called the people who live this kind of economic life – "the farmer, the mechanic, and the laborer" – the "bone and sinew of the country." This decisive tilt in the direction of unfettered competition did not come free of charge. Credit and currency controls remained very weak until after the turn of the twentieth century. The federal government lacked the tools to cope with rampant speculation and the periodic financial crises it sparked.

## The Modern Economy Takes Shape

The Civil War and post–Civil War periods witnessed the realization of Hamilton's dream of using government to promote economic progress in general and manufacturing in particular. The war accelerated demand for manufacturing production and labor. Armies need uniforms, weapons, ammunition, wagons, cooking utensils, and more. At the same time, taking so many young men away from their jobs drastically reduced the industrial labor supply. To produce more with less, industry invented new labor-saving techniques, including steam-powered equipment and other forms of mechanization.

To ensure the security of war supplies, in 1861 Congress enacted a very high tariff on imported goods. Prior to seceding, southern states, fearing that European countries would revenge themselves by imposing similarly high tariffs on their cotton exports, had opposed it. But during the war and its aftermath, the South was unable to influence Congress to protect its economic interest. Therefore, high tariffs survived long into the postwar period, increasing the profitability of American manufacturing and greatly accelerating its growth. National security likewise provided a strong rationale for the building of the transcontinental railway. Because it would take years for sufficient freight traffic to develop to make the railway profitable, Congress provided enormous subsidies in the form of land grants to the two railroads that were partners in the project.

By the 1880s, as Hamilton had hoped, the U.S. economy had expanded phenomenally and had become a major manufacturing power. But no longer was it an economy dominated by individuals and small companies. Whole sectors of the economy – oil, steel, sugar refining, and others – came to be dominated by one or few huge corporations. To some extent the shrinking number of individual firms in a given industry was the result of the superior efficiency of the firms that came to dominate. But the creation of huge economic entities capable of controlling entire industries was also greatly facilitated by government.

Perhaps the most important changes in government policy toward business firms were the revisions of state incorporation laws that adopted the principle of *limited liability*. Unlike an ordinary firm, the owners of a limited liability corporation, its shareholders, could not be held responsible for paying its debts. If the corporation failed, the liability of its shareholders was limited to the amount they had invested. Limited liability meant limited risk. Potential investors could calculate how much money they could afford to lose and limit their stock purchase to that amount.

Limited liability was defended on democratic grounds. The great Massachusetts senator Daniel Webster gave the following explanation as to why limited liability served vital democratic purposes. Industrial expansion provided more jobs and cheaper products, but it was hindered by lack of capital. America lacked a large class of very wealthy people who could afford to take great investment risks. To encourage ordinary people to invest, the system needed to limit their risk by enabling them to calculate in advance how much they could possibly lose. Thereby, limited liability democratized the investment process.

But this vast expansion in the capacity to raise money also permitted corporations to grow to previously unimaginable size. And because their potential loss was limited, investors had less cause to pay attention to what corporate management was actually doing and therefore became more tolerant of the ruthless practices that were often required to dominate an industry. Not only were these corporations large and powerful, but because their liability was limited, no actual person could be held accountable for the promises they made. At the stroke of a pen, a corporation could go out of business and leave suppliers, customers, and creditors with nobody to hold responsible for what was owed to them.

The U.S. Supreme Court likewise fostered the growth of corporate power and economic concentration. In *Wabash, St. Louis, and Pacific Railroad Company v. Illinois (1886)* it forbade states from regulating railroads. The Court decreed that corporations were legally "persons" entitled to the Fourteenth Amendment's guarantees of equal protection and due process of law, protections that would

**Figure 6.2.** Swallowing Free Enterprise: Railroad Tycoon Edward Harriman swallowing the American railroads. Drawing, 1907, by Luther Daniels Bradley. Credit: The Granger Collection, NYC – All rights reserved.

be violated if different states adopted different rules for governing railroad fares, taxes and labor standards (Figure 6.2).

In 1890 Congress attempted to prevent monopolies from forming by passing the *Sherman Antitrust Act*, which made it a crime for companies to attempt to do so. The constitutional basis for this statute was the commerce clause of the Constitution granting Congress the right to regulate interstate and foreign commerce. But the Supreme Court interpreted the commerce clause so narrowly as to render the law virtually impotent. In *United States v. E. C. Knight Co. (1895)* the Court said that the interstate commerce only referred to the buying and selling of products across state lines and did not include the manufacturing of products. EC Knight was a manufacturer, a sugar refiner, and therefore it was not covered by the Sherman Act.

## CRITICAL CHOICE: THE REGULATORY STATE

Starting in the late nineteenth century and continuing in the early twentieth, the terms of economic policy debate underwent a major shift. Those who led the fight for greater economic equality and more fair and open competition went from opposing greater government intervention in the economy to embracing it. The growing political and economic dominance of large corporations convinced them that the only way to countervail such concentrated economic power was to bring the force of government to bear on the other side. This outlook was given political momentum by the Populists and then by the Progressives. The path of free enterprise now changed course as a result of a critical choice in favor of granting the federal government broad regulatory power over various aspects of the economy.

Railroads were the lightning rods for popular discontent with the new corporate order. Railroads needed government help to acquire property along proposed routes and subsidize construction costs. To obtain such assistance, they bribed state legislatures and other government officials. Railroads' tentacles crossed state lines, which thwarted a state's ability to discipline them. Thus, the states had failed to exercise meaningful discipline of the railroads even before the Supreme Court's *Wabash* decision deprived them of the legal right to do so. The great expense of building railroads made the companies quasi-monopolies. Farmers were lucky to have even one railroad nearby; therefore, they could not credibly threaten to ship their crops on a rival line. Farmers might be charged different prices for the same service depending on whether they had alternative transportation options. Such *price discrimination* made economic sense, but it fed the farmers' fear of being held hostage to the whim of the "monster." Ignoring the extent to which they relied on government, railroads tried to evade government regulation and control by arguing that such interference was a violation of their economic freedom.

In the late 1870s a grassroots effort arose among farmers in such Great Plains states as South Dakota, Kansas, and Iowa to demand that the federal government intervene to protect them from the railroads. This movement called itself the People's Party, but it soon became known as the *Populists*. The Populists demanded that the federal government take over the railroads because of the monopoly power these leviathans were exercising, but generally speaking, they were not socialists. They did not challenge the essential principles of economic liberalism but rather sought to rid it of its antidemocratic and anti-Christian tendencies. In 1887, Populist agitation provoked Congress to create the first significant federal regulatory initiative, the Interstate Commerce Commission (ICC). The ICC was granted the power to prevent railroads from setting rates that discriminated against small farmers in favor of large shippers and investigate charges of illegal railroad practices.

In 1896, Populist leader William Jennings Bryan was nominated by the Democrats for president (see Chapter 11). At the nominating convention, Bryan defended free enterprise, claiming that the measure of a businessman was not money or property but productiveness, like a farmer who "by the application of brain and muscle to the natural resources of the country creates wealth." Bryan scolded adherents of laissez faire for undemocratically depriving most hard-working Americans of the status they had earned:

> We say to you that you have made the definition of a businessman too limited in its appli-
> cation. The man who is employed for wages is as much a businessman as his employer; the
> attorney in a country town is as much a businessman as the corporation counsel in a great
> metropolis; the merchant at the crossroads is as much a businessman as the merchant in
> New York.... We come to speak for this broader class of businessmen.

Bryan recognized that "the broader class of businessmen" were mostly debtors. Therefore, in addition to calling for regulation of the railroads, he also sought to ease the plight of debtors by inflating the currency, taking the United States off a currency standard that was strictly gold and onto a standard that would include silver, as well. Because silver was more plentiful than gold, this change would increase the money supply, making money cheaper and debts easier to pay. Bryan transformed this seemingly technical question about currency into a titanic religious struggle by denouncing his opponents in starkly religious terms: "You shall not press down upon the brow of labor this crown of thorns, you shall not crucify mankind upon a cross of gold."

In defending the Gold Standard, Bryan's opponents made a similar argu-ment to that made by Alexander Hamilton in favor of the federal government's assumption of the Revolutionary War debt. They invoked the principle of prom-ise keeping. If borrowers cheapen the value of money when their debt comes due, Gold Democrats claimed, they are cheating on their promise to pay back their debt in full, an action that is both immoral and economically destructive. If creditors doubt that their loans will be fully repaid, they will be less likely to make loans and economic activity will decline. Bryan and the Silver Democrats did not dispute the importance of promise keeping. Rather, they stressed other virtues that the liberal emphasis on promise keeping ignored – justice, forgive-ness, and charity. They believed that the farmer who could not pay his loan because his crops failed was not a sinner, but that the banker who called in the loan was, because he ignored the Christian duty to be charitable and the demo-cratic duty to help a neighbor.

## Progressivism

Bryan lost the 1896 election and the political strength of Populism waned. But its efforts to reign in big business were sustained by a more widespread and successful political movement, discussed in Chapters 4 and 5 and later in Chapter 12, Progressivism. Under the leadership of presidents Theodore Roosevelt and Woodrow Wilson the federal government embarked on extensive regulation of the economy. The Hepburn Act greatly increased the regulatory power of the Interstate Commerce Commission by allowing it to set ceilings on the freight rates that railroads could charge their customers. In 1906 Congress passed legislation establishing the *FDA* to protect consumers from rotten food and impure pharmaceuticals. In 1914, it created the *FTC* to provide more effective regulation of unfair business competition by supplementing judicial enforcement with the active intervention of an executive agency.

The shift in attitude toward government intervention extended to banking, as well. In 1907, the third-largest New York bank failed. In response to the ensuing panic, Republicans proposed a banking federation resembling a European central bank. The Democrats were opposed, but once they regained control of the House of Representatives in 1910, they felt obliged to come up with an alternative. In 1913 Congress passed the Federal Reserve Act that created a decentralized federation of twelve regional reserve banks, each a private institution owned and operated by its member banks. Each regional reserve bank acquired capital by requiring its members to spend 3 percent of their own capital to buy its stock.

Regional reserve banks had three tools with which to regulate the money supply. First, they could change the *discount rate*, the interest rate that member banks paid to borrow money from them. The higher the discount rate, the more expensive it was for members to borrow money and the higher the rate was that members would charge to lend money to customers. Raising the discount rate made money more expensive, thereby lowering demand for it. Second, regional reserve banks could change the reserve requirements imposed on members. If banks had to keep more assets in reserve, they could make fewer loans, thereby shrinking the amount of money in circulation. Third, reserve banks could engage in open market operations, buying and selling government bonds and notes. When the reserve banks sold notes and bonds, the money used to pay for them was taken out of circulation, thereby reducing the money supply. During a panic, a reserve bank might use all three tools – buying bonds and notes, lowering the discount rate, and reducing reserve requirements – to rapidly expand the money supply and make more funds available to threatened banks. The Federal Reserve was a distinctively American solution to the problems posed by an inflexible money supply. It created institutions for manipulating money and credit but did not cede control to either Washington or Wall Street. The twelve regional banks were responsive to their members and to the *Fed*, whose members were appointed by the president but had staggered terms so that no single president could appoint a majority.

## The New Deal

FDR's New Deal was both an extension of Progressive regulatory principles to other branches of the economy – securities, chain stores, trucking; airlines, and coal mining – and a critical choice in favor of a vastly more ambitious view of government economic involvement. As we discussed in Chapter 4, it went far beyond Progressive principles by instilling a new concept of *federally* guaranteed economic security. The new programmatic rights aimed at protecting economic security were embodied in the Social Security Act and the National Labor Relations Act, both passed in 1935 and discussed in Chapter 4. In addition, The *FDIC*, discussed earlier in this chapter, provided a government guarantee that depositors could reclaim their bank deposits, up to a certain limit, if a bank failed. This government-supported flexibility improved labor-market efficiency by emboldening workers to find the best outlet for their talents.

To pay for this vastly more expansive notion of government the New Deal imposed far greater tax burdens on the wealthier segments of the populace than had previously been in place. The Constitution had imposed strict limits on federal taxing power. Those limits were not eased until 1913, when the Sixteenth Amendment to the Constitution was adopted, which permitted the imposition of an income tax. Over time Congress turned the income tax into a *progressive tax*, meaning that as a person's income increased, so did the percentage of tax paid by that person. The 1935 Revenue Act raised taxes on those making more than $5 million a year to 75 percent of all income in excess of $5 million (Figure 6.3).

In practice, the degree of progressivity was lessened because the government allowed many income deductions, including the deduction for interest paid on home mortgages and for gifts made to charity. Nonetheless, the progressive tax did force the rich to pay a larger share of their income in taxes than those less well off, and it did raise an enormous amount of revenue. Because those in the high tax brackets paid such a high percentage of their income in tax, the value of tax deductions was greatly increased. Ever since tax deductions have become a major tool of government economic policy because they provide such a strong incentive for the wealthy to invest in tax-deductible endeavors.

## MACROECONOMICS

As we discussed earlier, much of contemporary economic policy is devoted to trying to stabilize and improve the economy as a whole, the macro-economy. The founder of the study of macroeconomics was an Englishman, John Maynard Keynes. He recognized that the overall performance of an economy was not just

**Figure 6.3.** No Egg on His Face: A 1938 Cartoon by Quincy Scott depicting FDR's supposed hatred of the wealthy. Credit: The Granger Collection, NYC – All rights reserved.

the sum of its parts. It depended on the expectations of businesspeople about the future performance of the economy. If expectations were high, businesses would invest in new equipment, add supplies, and hire more workers. If expectations were low – even if business was good at the time – they would reduce inventory, eliminate new investment, and fire workers. Keynes saw that worldwide economic depression made businesspeople pessimistic about the future, which created a self-fulfilling prophecy. To create business optimism, the government needed to put more money into the hands of the non-rich. If the wealthy were given more money, they might save some of it. The non-wealthy would spend a higher proportion because they had more pressing material wants. Giving the non-rich money, regardless of how, was therefore the most efficient way to stimulate a rise in consumer demand that would encourage businesses to purchase new resources and equipment and hire more workers to satisfy it. As unemployment declined, purchasing power would increase and consumer demand would continue to grow. A new, optimistic, self-fulfilling prophecy would be established.

FDR was reluctant to embrace *Keynesianism* because it required government to spend money it did not have and therefore to operate at a deficit. Government had engaged in *deficit spending* in the past, but only in wartime. Purposely going into debt in peacetime seemed immoral. Initially, FDR allowed for deficit spending only as an emergency measure. When the economy showed signs of recovery, he cut federal spending to reduce the deficit. The economy declined. When spending was increased because of the imminent threat of World War II, the economy rebounded.

The New Deal also deepened government involvement in macroeconomics by centralizing monetary policy making. The 1935 Banking Act shifted decision-making power from the regional reserve banks to the Federal Reserve Board and its chairman, Mariner Eccles. This change was accompanied by a new understanding of the Fed's mission. It was no longer merely an instrument for adjusting seasonal changes in credit demands and averting bank panics; it was now a full-fledged partner in manipulating the economy to stimulate economic growth. Eccles invoked the Fed's credit-expanding authority because he realized that the simulative effect of deficit spending would be blunted unless interest rates were kept low. Low interest rates allowed businesses to borrow money in order to expand their production in response to the increased demand for their goods brought on by increased government spending.

## The Postwar Political Economy: Path Dependency

### Free Trade

Economic policy has gone through many changes, but it has remained on the path that was established at the founding as modified by the Progressives and the New Deal. It is still a liberal, free-market economy, albeit one subject to considerable government regulation, insurance provision, and subsidy. Indeed, the single most important set of choices made since WWII has been to further liberalize the economy by reducing tariff and other barriers to international trade.

Although the United States has been involved in world markets from its beginnings, it had also erected significant barriers to international trade. From the Civil War until the end of World War II, high tariffs were in place on many manufacturing products. In 1930, the average tariff on imported goods was 50 percent of their price. But the United States was the only major industrial economy left intact by World War II. As a consequence it had a great opportunity to increase its manufacturing exports and little to fear from foreign manufacturing competition. By lowering its tariffs it hoped to induce other nations to lower theirs. By 1951, average tariffs had fallen to 12.5 percent, and by the end of the 1990s to approximately 5 percent. The lowering of U.S. tariffs and other forms of trade barriers has continued even as other nations restored and expanded their industrial capacity and specific sectors of the U.S. economy, such as steel, textiles, garments, and toys, have been decimated by foreign-import competition.

U.S. commitment to free trade has national security as well as strictly economic roots. As the Cold War intensified, the United States sought to enlist other countries as allies in that worldwide struggle. It recognized that efforts to induce those nations into military and mutual security agreements would be greatly hampered if, at the same time, the United States was limiting importation of those nations' goods. Therefore, it coupled its international alliance-building initiatives with policy proposals to expand world trade. In 1994 the United States joined the *World Trade Organization*, a new international body with extensive powers to settle trade disputes, and endorsed the most recent *General Agreement on Tariffs and Trade (GATT)*. GATT reduced tariffs by 40 percent by phasing out quotas on textiles and apparel and extending copyright and other forms of protection to intellectual property, including recordings and books. Although the Cold War has ended, the United States still considers the expansion of worldwide free trade and the increased prosperity it brings to be a crucial tool for enhancing peaceful international relations.

The United States has been especially active in promoting free trade among its hemispheric neighbors in North, Central, and South America. In 1993, President Clinton signed the *North American Free Trade Agreement*, which eliminated tariff barriers and other trade constraints between the United States, Mexico, and Canada. This free-trade zone encompassed a $6.5 trillion market containing 350 million consumers. The following year, in 2005, the U.S. Congress approved the Dominican Republic-Central American Free Trade Agreement (DR-CAFTA). DR-CAFTA eliminated all tariffs imposed by the United States on manufactured goods from the other DR-CAFTA signatories – Costa Rica, the Dominican Republic, El Salvador, Guatemala, Honduras, and Nicaragua. The long-term goal of U.S. policy is to merge these agreements to form a free trade zone that would extend from the southern tip of South America all the way to Canada.

## Economic Security

The path of providing greater economic security pioneered by the New Deal's Social Security Act was extended to include medical care as well as old-age pensions. In 1965 Congress passed Medicare (see Chapter 4), which provides all Americans over the age of sixty-five with government-funded health care. It also established Medicaid (see Chapter 5), a program for providing health care to the poor. The cost of Medicaid was shared with the states. Old-age and medical benefits were also greatly expanded via the tax code. Normally, workers might be expected to prefer higher wages to fringe benefits such as health insurance or old-age pension. But changes in the federal tax codes enacted during World War II exempted benefits from taxes. Because wages were taxed and benefits were not, workers preferred receiving the same amount of additional money in the form of benefits. Employers, with the support of labor leaders, could buy more worker loyalty and contentment per dollar by expanding benefits. Therefore, many workers came to enjoy low-cost health care as well as pensions that were far larger than what Social Security provided.

Ever since the Revolutionary War, the U.S. government had paid various forms of pensions and bonuses to war veterans. This tradition was continued in the wake of World War II, but with a novel twist. The *1944 GI Bill of Rights* did not simply provide veterans with cash. Rather, it entitled them to attend universities and specialized training programs of all sorts at government expense. It thus served to benefit not only the veterans themselves but the economy as a whole. The skills of the American workforce were greatly improved at no cost to employers. The pool of well-educated workers expanded dramatically, raising labor productivity and increasing the proportion of workers in high-paying jobs. Just as the United States was the first nation in history to enable most young people to go to school, it was also the first to provide mass higher education. Thanks in part to the GI Bill, the number of students enrolled in college jumped from less than 1.5 million in 1941, representing just 16 percent of high school graduates, to almost 2.5 million in 1949, representing 40 percent of high school graduates. Enrollment dipped somewhat in the later 1950s as the number of new veterans declined, but it never again dropped below 25 percent of high school graduates. In 2001, more than 15 million students were enrolled in college, representing 47 percent of high school graduates.

### Macroeconomics

The government also extended the New Deal practice of trying to maintain prosperity and economic growth by manipulating the macro-economy. Keynesianism did not become official government doctrine until 1946, when President Harry Truman signed the Full Employment Act, committing government to maintain a growing economy using all available means, including Keynesian tactics. The act created a *Council of Economic Advisors*, professional economists who would provide the president with technical expertise in maintaining high levels of employment and steady economic growth. The Keynesian approach to the macro-economy has been adopted by presidents such as Kennedy and Obama.

They sought to stimulate economic growth and prosperity by increasing govern-ment spending while holding taxes steady or even reducing them.

Ronald Reagan also made use of the macroeconomic tools of taxes, govern-ment spending, and control of the money supply, but not entirely in the manner prescribed by Keynes. He hoped to stimulate the economy not by encouraging greater consumption but by increasing the supply of capital available for invest-ment. This approach came to be known as *Supply Side Economics.* More invest-ment would create more business activity and employment, which in turn would lead to greater prosperity. He convinced Congress to adopt massive tax cuts, primarily for business and the wealthy. Reagan's policies did indeed enliven a sluggish economy, but it is unclear whether or not this was a result of the sup-ply-side theory. In the absence of compensating budget cuts his tax reductions led to unprecedented peacetime budget deficits. Deficit spending to increase demand is the classic Keynesian solution for addressing economic recession. Thus, the boom that took place starting in 1983 could have been the result of either a supply-side stimulus resulting from tax cuts on businesses and the wealthy or a demand-side stimulus resulting from deficit spending, or both.

## Regulation

As the contemporary economic portrait showed, regulation of industry remains an important component of current economic policy. The most important types of regulation pioneered during the Progressive era and expanded during the New Deal remain in place, including: regulation of securities, wages and hours, monopolistic practices, food safety, and the safety and effectiveness of prescrip-tion drugs. But the regulatory path has also displayed several important twists and turns. New regulatory domains have been entered. Some Progressive and New Deal regulations have been repealed or loosened. Some of those were sub-sequently restored and even expanded.

The most important new realms of regulation involve the environment, con-sumer protection, and occupational safety and health. The Clean Air Act of 1970, the Clean Water Act of 1972, and the Resource Conservation and Recovery Act of 1976 required firms to reduce the amounts of chemicals and other pol-lutants they were emitting into the air and water and burying in the land. The OSHA of 1970 required employers to make sure that they provided a safe and healthy workplace for their employees. The Consumer Product Safety Act of 1972 established a commission charged with making sure that the toys, elec-tronic equipment, clothing, appliances, and other products purchased by con-sumers were safe.

These new controls used the same regulatory tools adopted by their Progressive predecessors – commands to regulated firms to change their practices, inspec-tions to make sure those commands were obeyed, penalties imposed on those who disobeyed – however, an additional rationale for imposing regulation was added. Environmental and occupational health regulations were defended *both* on the grounds that they corrected imperfections in the market *and* that they protected fundamental rights.

Just as FDR had justified the Social Security Act by proclaiming Americans' right to economic security, the leading congressional environmental spokesman, Senator Edmund Muskie, declared that clean air and water laws were necessary to protect Americans' right to a safe and healthy environment. The right of workers to enjoy a safe and healthy workplace underpinned the passage of OSHA. Rights claims have dominated every subsequent debate over environmental policy. The current debate over the regulation of $CO_2$ and Methane in order to reduce the greenhouse gases implicated in global warming actually extends the rights rationale to a global scale. Advocates of stringent regulation propound a universal human right to protection from the threats posed by climate change.

At more or less the same time that regulation was expanding into new areas, it was being selectively cut back in others. The deregulation of trucking, telephone, and airlines that took place during the 1970s was designed to foster competition in those businesses. As a result of government policy only one company, American Telephone and Telegraph Company, enjoyed a virtual monopoly in providing telephone service. Federal price regulation of airline fares discouraged new competitors from providing air passenger service. Regulatory restrictions on routes and loads hampered trucking competition. These deregulatory efforts were a tacit admission that the New Deal regulations they were undoing had actually worked against the interests of consumers by discouraging competition. Because these regulatory barriers to new entry benefited the existing companies and their workers, deregulation had been considered politically impossible. However, the defensive advantage enjoyed by these employer-employee coalitions was overcome by the ability of the president, congressional leaders, and professional economists to convince ordinary Americans that they had something at stake in the outcome, namely lower prices.

## New Regulation

Both the financial collapse of 2008 and a wave of fraud induced corporate failure at the turn of the millennium led to major new initiatives to regulate financial activity. As a result of the widespread participation of ordinary workers in stock-owning pension funds and the great increase of mass participation in buying and selling stocks that occurred during the 1980s and 1990s, most Americans had become stockholders. Therefore, the health of the stock market had become of much more widespread public concern. That health was threatened beginning in the late 1990s by the discovery of massive financial fraud at such major corporations as Tyco, WorldCom, Global Crossing, Adelphia, and Enron, all of whom went out of business as a result. By July of 2002, the Dow Jones Industrial Average, a major stock market index, had dropped 25 percent from its historic high in March of 2000. It has been estimated that in this period the stock market lost $7 trillion. This collapse riveted public attention on the variety of accounting techniques that these corporations had used to overstate profits, minimize losses, and otherwise exaggerate how economically healthy they were. There were also disturbing revelations about the extent to which the outside accountants hired by corporations to audit the company books had abetted these fraudulent practices. Likewise, these companies had bribed stock analysts to encourage their clients to buy the companies' stock.

In 2002 Congress passed a major new regulatory initiative aimed at curbing such abuses. It was named the *Sarbanes-Oxley Act* in honor of its sponsors, Congressman Michael Oxley (R-OH) and Senator Paul Sarbanes (D-MD). The act imposed federal rules regarding the composition, structure, and operation of corporate governing boards. Formerly, such matters had been dealt with by state corporation law, and dealt with very loosely. Sarbanes-Oxley required public corporations to appoint an Audit Committee and Compensation Committee composed entirely of independent directors, thus excluding the corporation's own management. The audit committee was granted sole responsibility for hiring and approving the work of the outside auditors. The compensation committee determined how much management was to be paid.

Sarbanes-Oxley also required the Chief Executive Officer (CEO) and the Chief Financial Officer to personally attest that the corporation's financial statements were accurate and complied with the accounting rules the new law set in place. The CEO also had to certify that the company's own accounting practices were capable of detecting and preventing fraud. Making top corporate CEO executives personally liable for the quality and accuracy of their companies' financial statements inspired a massive reorganization and reform of internal accounting and reporting procedures. The Act also established the Public Company Accounting Oversight Board to devise and enforce federal accounting rules that auditors must abide by.

As we discussed in the beginning of the chapter, the essential rationale for using taxpayer money to save major banks, investment firms, and insurance companies from bankruptcy was that they were too big to fail. These mega corporations played such a dominant role in the overall banking and investment system that the failure of any one of them could cause the entire system to unravel. In 2010 Congress passed the *Dodd-Frank Wall Street Reform and Consumer Protection Act*, named for its sponsors Congressman Barney Frank (D-MA) and Senator Thomas Dodd (D-CT). The Act created the Financial Stability Oversight Council chaired by the Treasury Secretary to monitor threats to financial stability, especially those caused by those giant firms too big to fail. If the Council concludes that such a firm was in danger of failing it could order a government takeover of the company in order to dismantle the company in a deliberate and orderly manner so as not to endanger the overall financial system. Thus, it would enable the market to punish companies that made bad risks, but exert government control over the process of liquidation to make sure that the failure of a too-big firm did not set off a destructive chain reaction involving other large financial companies. It also attempted to reduce the likelihood of failures by forcing big banks to adopt more conservative loan practices, requiring them to keep more of their assets in reserve against the possibility of loan defaults.

## CONCLUSION

This chapter has shown how both those who favor and those who oppose government intervention in the economy draw on the same cherished political principles – liberty, equality, and rights. Those who have argued against government intrusions, whether they are the 2nd National Bank or the bailout of General Motors, maintain that such efforts promote privilege and reward irresponsible behavior. Those who act prudently and keep their promises do not get government aid, whereas those who enjoy special access to policy makers, even if they take foolish risks and break their promises, are rewarded with government largesse. As we have seen, there have been important changes in the nature of the argument in favor of government intervention. At first the argument was based on the need to create a strong and dependable financial system that would give the government the resources necessary for national security and to promote economic growth. Later, as the economy grew more concentrated and became dominated by massive corporations, the pro-government argument expanded to include securing of economic rights and protecting of liberty and democracy by deploying greater public power to check and countervail ever-increasing private power.

The United States has indeed benefited from the opportunity to pursue the happiness that a free economy provides and the necessity of taking care of oneself that a free economy demands. But it has also benefited from the government's capacity to regulate private excesses, provide a modicum of financial security for the sick and the old, and promote great national enterprises such as the transcontinental railroad and the exploration of outer space. Because both arguments are so persuasive, even as economic circumstances change and new crises develop, conflict over the relative merits of unfettered private enterprise and government discipline and direction is likely to persist.

## CHAPTER SUMMARY

★ Current American economic policy ensures against risk; subsidizes favored economic activities; punishes misbehavior; and intervenes at the macroeconomic level, the economy as a whole, in order to encourage price stability, full employment prosperity, and growth.

★ The greatest difference between the United States and the rich countries of Europe and Asia is that the United States does less to control the labor market.

★ The essential aspects of economic liberals are: private property, competition, and promise keeping.

★ The adoption of the Constitution, including the Bill of Rights, was the critical choice that set the United States firmly on the path of economic liberalism.

★ American political development has been pervaded by the conflict between those who favor and those who oppose greater government intervention in the economy. But, for the most part, those who favor greater government intervention do not want to stray far from the economic liberal path.

★ The argument in favor of government intervention shifted ground between the nineteenth and twentieth centuries.

★ Federal government regulation of economic activity took hold during the Progressive Era and was expanded during the New Deal.

★ The principle of economic rights was introduced during the New Deal. Initially, this principle was limited to providing economic security for the elderly. Later, during the 1960s, it was extended to providing health care for the elderly.

★ The single greatest economic policy change since the New Deal has been the liberalization of international trade accomplished by tariff reduction and the elimination of other import and export barriers.

## MAJOR CONCEPTS

| | |
|---|---|
| Aggregate Demand | Bailout |
| Council of Economic Advisors | Deficit Spending |
| Discount Rate | Dodd-Frank Wall Street Reform and Consumer Protection Act |
| Federal Deposit Insurance Corporation | Federal Reserve Board |
| First National Bank of the United States | Food and Drug Administration |
| Federal Trade Commission | Funding the Debt |
| General Agreement on Tariffs and Trade (GATT) | GI Bill of Rights |
| Keynesianism | Liberal Economy |
| Macroeconomic Policy | Microeconomic Policy |
| Moral Hazard | Necessary and Proper Clause |
| North American Free Trade Agreement | Progressive Taxation |
| Price Discrimination | Populists |
| Report on Manufactures (Hamilton) | Regulation |
| Sarbanes-Oxley Act | Second Bank of the United States |
| Sherman Antitrust Act | Supply-Side Economics |
| Tax Subsidies | *United States v. E. C. Knight Co* |
| *Wabash, St. Louis, and Pacific Railroad Company v. Illinois* | World Trade Organization |

## SUGGESTED READINGS

Chandler, Alfred Dupont. *Scale and Scope: The Dynamics of Industrial Capitalism.* Cambridge, MA: Belknap Press, 1990.

Chandler, Alfred Dupont. *The Visible Hand: The Managerial Revolution in American Business.* Cambridge, MA: Belknap Press, 1977.

Derthick, Martha, and Paul J. Quirk. *The Politics of Deregulation.* Washington, DC: Brookings Institution, 1985.

Friedman, Milton. *Capitalism and Freedom.* Chicago: University of Chicago Press, 1963.

Hacker, Jacob. *The Divided Welfare State: The Battle over Public and Private Social Benefits in the United States.* New York: Cambridge University Press, 2002.

Harris, Richard, and Sidney M. Milkis. *The Politics of Regulatory Change: A Tale of Two Agencies*, 2nd ed. New York: Oxford University Press, 1996.

Hawley, Ellis. *The New Deal and the Problem of Monopoly: A Study in Economic Ambivalence.* New York: Fordam University Press, 1995.

Howard, Christopher. *The Hidden Welfare State: Tax Expenditures and Social Policy in the United States.* Princeton, NJ: Princeton University Press, 1997.

McCoy, Drew R. *The Elusive Republic: Political Economy in Jeffersonian America.* Chapel Hill: University of North Carolina Press, 1996.

McCraw, Thomas K. *Prophets of Regulation: Charles Francis Adams, Louis D. Brandeis, James M. Landis, Alfred E. Kahn.* Cambridge, MA: Belknap Press, 1984.

Samuelson, Robert. *The Great Inflation and Its Aftermath: The Past and Future of American Affluence.* New York: Random House, 2008.

Sellers, Charles. *The Market Revolution: Jacksonian America, 1815–1846.* New York: Oxford University Press, 1991.

Skidelsky, Robert. *Keynes: The Return of the Master.* Philadelphia: Public Affairs, 2009.

Stein, Herbert. *Presidential Economics: The Making of Economic Policy from Roosevelt to Clinton*, 3rd rev. ed. Washington, DC: AEI Press, 1994.

Stiglitz, Joseph E. *Freefall: America, Free Markets, and the Sinking of the World Economy.* New York: W. W. Norton, 2010.

PART THREE

# Governing Institutions

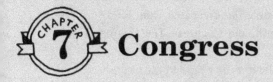

# 7 Congress

## CHAPTER OVERVIEW

This chapter focuses on:

☆ The crucial questions the Framers confronted when they set out to create an independent legislature.

☆ The critical choices that have forged its unique political character and the role of leadership during those episodes.

☆ Three remarkable midterm congressional elections that took place between 1994 and 2010, each of which altered the course of American politics.

In 2001, President Bush proposed and Congress passed major tax cuts. They reduced tax rates for people in all income brackets, reduced the tax on capital gains held for five years or more, and gradually raised the amount of inherited wealth that could be excluded from estate tax, abolishing the entire tax in 2010. Because the rich pay the most tax they were also the greatest beneficiaries of the tax cuts. In the 2008 presidential campaign, Democratic candidate Barack Obama promised to raise additional revenues in order to reduce the budget deficit by ending those Bush tax cuts that benefited those making $250,000 a year. In office he continued to denounce the tax cuts for the wealthy.

The Bush tax cuts were due to expire at the end of 2010, and therefore congressional failure to act on them would have led to major tax hikes for both middle-class and wealthy individuals. As the recession brought on by the financial collapse of 2008 deepened, the Republican argument that raising taxes on the rich would be counterproductive because it would lower the amount of money the rich had to invest gained support among moderate Democrats. Because the Democrats in Congress were no longer united behind Obama's plan to increase taxes only on the rich, efforts to pass the Obama plan stalled. The impasse continued until after the 2010 Congressional elections, in which the

Republicans regained control of the House of Representatives and diminished the Democratic margin in the Senate. But the Congress that went back into session immediately after the elections was the old Congress. The new one would not convene until January 2011.

The session of Congress that meets in the interim between the election and the New Year has the nickname Lame Duck, signifying its weak political position. Lame Duck or not, the Democrats still retained their large preelection majorities in both houses. Democratic members could not predict when they would return to power, and many were determined to approve Obama's plan so as to take the issue off the table before the new Republican-dominated Congress was installed. The Republicans continue to refuse to go along with the Obama Plan, but they denounced the Democratic leadership as antidemocratic for refusing to yield to the will of the people as expressed in the 2010 vote.

Despite his previous opposition to retention of the Bush tax cuts for the rich, President Obama chose to side with the Republicans. He chose to accept the logic of the 2010 vote rather than make use of the temporary Lame Duck Democratic majority to try to enact his preferred plan. Not only would he have to face the Republican-dominated Congress in less than a month, but his own reelection was now less than two years away. Obama reached a compromise with congressional Republicans in which he agreed to continue all the Bush tax cuts in exchange for their agreement to an extension of unemployment compensation for the long-term unemployed. The president's change of heart sapped the morale of congressional Democrats to continue the fight. Most of them grudgingly agreed to support Obama's deal with the Republicans.

As this story shows, congressional elections can prove politically decisive. Rather than try to enforce his will, Obama acknowledged the significance of midterm congressional elections as a device for enforcing democratic accountability. He realized that for at least the next two years the Congress would be his coequal in governing. Such a concession by the chief executive would not, could not, occur in any other contemporary democratic republic. There is no other nation in the world where the legislature enjoys this high level of political power and independence. So-called parliamentary systems fuse the executive and legislature with the result that the legislature is controlled by the executive. The executive, the prime minister, is chosen by the legislature. Except under very rare circumstances, the prime minister is the leader of the majority party in the parliament. There is no equivalent of a midterm election in which voters can force the executive to alter course by depriving the executive of a legislative majority.

This chapter examines how Congress functions and how it has managed to retain its independence and authority despite the rising power and prestige of the presidency. After sketching a contemporary portrait of Congress, it examines the crucial questions the Framers confronted when they set out to create

" SIR, I DEMAND THAT I BE TREATED WITH THE RESPECT DUE ME."

" SIR, I GLADLY OBEY."

**Figure 7.1.** The Contemporary Congress – A Portrait. Punch Line: A 1916 Cartoon by AB Walker depicting the people's lack of respect for the United States Congress. Credit: The Granger Collection, NYC – All rights reserved.

an independent legislature. Then it looks at each crucial phase of congressional development: Congress' emergence as the dominant branch of government in the nineteenth century; its transformation in response to the rise of activist national government in the twentieth century and its resurgence, accompanied by intensified institutional combat with the president that began in the late 1960s. The final section focuses on the last twenty years of congressional politics and the remarkable political impact of three extraordinary midterm elections – 1994, 2006, and 2010 (Figure 7.1).

The Constitution grants the legislative power to Congress. No law can be established unless passed by Congress. In principle, the Constitution restricts the legislative power to those specific matters "here in granted" in Article One. As we discussed in Chapter 3, these specific grants of authority, known as enumerated powers, are the critical tools by which the Constitution establishes a limited government. However, in modern times the courts have greatly expanded the meaning of some of those enumerated powers, especially the power to regulate commerce (see Chapter 9), and the limitations on what Congress can pass laws about have greatly eased. In the second session of the 111th Congress, which met in 2010, Congress deliberated on such diverse matters as the creation of an Algal Bloom Reduction Program to develop a strategy to reduce marine and freshwater algal blooms; the declaration of Cervical Health Awareness Month; establishment of a pilot program within the Department of Labor to encourage the employment of veterans of the armed forces in energy-related jobs; and creation of a $3.6 billion package of tax incentives for small business.

Recent sessions of Congress have varied greatly in terms of the quantity and importance of the legislation they produced. The eminent American historian Alan Brinkley called the 111th Congress, whose first session met during 2009 and second during 2010, "probably the most productive session of Congress since at least the '60s." It passed the most significant expansion of health care coverage since the Medicaid Act of 1965, providing access to insurance to 32 million previously uninsured Americans. It created the most important overhaul of the regulation of banks and other financial institutions since the New Deal. It spent more than $1.67 trillion to stimulate the stagnant American economy, and it banned discrimination against gays and lesbians serving in the military. By contrast, the 112th Congress, whose first session met during 2011 and second during 2012, passed very little significant legislation. The 2010 congressional elections handed control of the House of Representatives to the Republicans, whereas the Senate and the presidency remained in the hands of the Democrats. Differences between the parties about how best to reduce the federal budget deficit dominated both sessions of the 112th Congress. It was only after weeks of deadlock in the summer of 2011 that the House and Senate were able to agree to increase the federal government's debt limit, barely avoiding tumbling the federal government into a severe financial crisis.

As the Constitution provides, Congress checks the power of the executive through its *power of the purse*. It can reward or punish executive agencies by either increasing or reducing their budgets. For example, if influential congresspersons believe that the EPA is being too aggressive in closing down dry cleaners that violate clean air regulations, they can threaten to reduce the EPA's enforcement budget unless the agency adopts a less aggressive policy. In this manner, Congress uses its legislative power to obtain executive influence. Its budgetary power is so great that it rarely has to carry out a budgetary threat. Instead, the committee and subcommittee staffs conduct extensive investigations of the agencies that fall within their jurisdiction. Those investigations are often followed by committee or subcommittee oversight hearings at which the members subject agency officials to extensive cross-examination about agency activities. Based on what they learn from staff reports and hearings testimony, the committees may choose to direct the agency to make changes. In order to avoid even the whisper of budgetary retribution, agency officials are highly responsive to those congressional directives.

For similar reasons, agency officials are receptive to requests from well-placed congresspersons to give special consideration to constituents or other persons whom those representatives wish to help. Often, congressmen ask nothing more than that an agency official search for and retrieve a license application, social security check, or visa request that has somehow gotten lost in the bureaucratic maze. Indeed, the members employ staffers who do nothing but work with the bureaucracy on these sorts of issues. This function is known as *constituency service*. But there is no clear line separating this type of problem solving and the exertion of undue pressure on agencies to show favoritism. For example, in 2009 Congresswoman Maxine Waters (D-CA), a member of the House Banking Committee, arranged a meeting between government officials and a group of bankers to discuss applications made by the banks for financial assistance under the bank bailout program that Congress had passed. Among the banks represented was One United, in which her husband was an investor. When she was accused of using her power over the banking industry to help her husband she denied the charge. All the banks at the meeting were experiencing serious financial difficulties and were owned by racial minorities. She claimed that she had pushed for the meeting to help all those minority-owned banks, not One United in particular. The Office of Congressional Ethics determined that she was guilty of a conflict of interest and recommended that she be disciplined by the House Ethics Committee.

Article One requires the Senate to confirm the appointments that the president makes to the federal courts and high-level executive positions. Among the major judicial and executive nominations confirmed by the Senate in 2010 were those of Sonia Sotomajor and Elena Kagan to the Supreme Court, and General David H. Petraeus to commander of U.S. and coalition forces in Afghanistan. The Senate can use its appointment power as a bargaining chip. It can delay confirming presidential appointments to particular agencies and departments and then demand changes in how those agencies and departments function as the price for granting confirmation.

The Senate must approve all treaties that the president enters into with foreign governments. The most recent major treaty approved by the Senate was in 2010 when it ratified a new Strategic Arms Reduction Treaty with Russia. The treaty reduced the number of both nations' nuclear missile launchers by half and created a new set of procedures for verifying that the treaty was being adhered to. It also put limits on the number of intercontinental and submarine-based intercontinental ballistic missile launchers as well as manned nuclear-equipped bombers.

## THE LEGISLATIVE PROCESS

When a proposal for a new law is introduced into Congress, it is referred to as a *bill* and assigned a number. If it is first introduced by a senator, the number is given the prefix "S." For example, the Energy Policy and Conservation Act of 1975 was first introduced in the Senate labeled S622. If a bill is first introduced by a House member, the number is given the prefix "HR." For example, a 1990 bill overhauling federal aid for vocational education was first introduced into the House labeled HR7. Executive departments also draft bills, as do various lobbying organizations. But no bill becomes a law unless it is introduced by a congressperson, passed by both houses of Congress, and signed by the president. If the president vetoes the bill, it must be repassed by a two-thirds majority in each house of Congress in order to become a law, a move that is known as a *veto override*.

Each bill is first assigned to the *committee* or committees that have jurisdiction over the issues the bill deals with. The more complex the bill the more likely it will be assigned to more than one committee. Most senators and congressmen keep their same committee assignments from session to session. They become expert in the matters their committees deal with. When a bill is reported out of committee and onto the House or Senate floor, non-committee members often depend heavily on the views and opinions of the committee members they most trust in deciding how to cast their votes. It is usually the case that the most important decisions regarding the shape and scope of a particular bill are made in committee, not on the floor. Figure 7.2 provides a list of all congressional committees.

| **Senate Committees** |
| --- |
| Senate Committee on Agriculture, Nutrition, and Forestry |
| Senate Committee on Appropriations |
| Senate Committee on Armed Services |
| Senate Committee on Banking, Housing, and Urban Affairs |
| Senate Committee on the Budget |
| Senate Committee on Commerce, Science, and Transportation |
| Senate Committee on Energy and Natural Resources |
| Senate Committee on Environment and Public Works |
| Senate Committee on Finance |
| Senate Committee on Foreign Relations |
| Senate Committee on Health, Education, Labor, and Pensions |
| Senate Committee on Homeland Security and Governmental Affairs |
| Senate Committee on Indian Affairs |
| Senate Committee on the Judiciary |
| Senate Committee on Rules and Administration |
| Senate Committee on Small Business and Entrepreneurship |
| Senate Committee on Veterans' Affairs |
| Senate Select Committee on Ethics |

**Figure 7.2.** List of Committees of Congress (House and Senate).

*Source*: http://www.govtrack.us/congress/committees/.

| |
|---|
| Senate Select Committee on Intelligence |
| Senate Special Committee on Aging |
| United States Senate Caucus on International Narcotics Control |
| **Joint Committees** |
| Commission on Security and Cooperation in Europe |
| Joint Committee on the Library |
| Joint Committee on Printing |
| Joint Committee on Taxation |
| Joint Economic Committee |
| Joint Select Committee on Deficit Reduction |
| **House Committees** |
| House Committee on Agriculture |
| House Committee on Appropriations |
| House Committee on Armed Services |
| House Committee on the Budget |
| House Committee on Education and the Workforce |
| House Committee on Energy and Commerce |
| House Committee on Ethics (Select) |
| House Committee on Financial Services |
| House Committee on Foreign Affairs |
| House Committee on Homeland Security |
| House Committee on House Administration |
| House Committee on the Judiciary |
| House Committee on Natural Resources |
| House Committee on Oversight and Government Reform |
| House Committee on Rules |
| House Committee on Science, Space, and Technology |
| House Committee on Small Business |
| House Committee on Transportation and Infrastructure |
| House Committee on Veterans' Affairs |
| House Committee on Ways and Means |
| House Permanent Select Committee on Intelligence |
| House Select Committee on Energy Independence and Global Warming |

**Figure 7.2** (*cont.*)

In recent decades it has become common for bills to be assigned to more than one committee. Usually such *multiple referrals involve* only two committees, but if committee chairs consider it important to give a bill scrutiny by their committee, a bill may be sent to many committees. Political scientist Barbara Sinclair points out that President Clinton's initiative to significantly alter the organization and behavior of federal agencies was referred to seventeen different committees. Multiple referrals can vastly complicate congressional deliberations if the committees considering the bill produce draft bills that differ from one another in significant ways. There is no formal procedure for resolving such differences, but in practice the *Speaker of the House* and the Speaker's staff have taken on the job of brokering compromise. Because this task is so critical and difficult, the power and importance of the Speaker has expanded considerably. Nancy Pelosi, House Speaker from 2006 to 2010, played a critical role in the passage of the health care reform legislation that became law in 2010. Repeatedly, she found ways to compromise deep differences that surfaced among members of the House and between House committees and pressure members whose support for the legislation was wavering.

The various committees responsible for writing laws are known as authorizing committees. But one House and one Senate committee do not write laws. They spend money. Those committees are known as the House and Senate *Appropriations Committees.* Their various subcommittees decide how much of the money that the authorization committees allow for should actually be spent in a given year. This process of appropriating is necessary in order to bring total congressional spending in line with the total amount of money that the annual budget has available. The appropriations process does not guarantee that revenue and spending will balance. Often, the federal government runs a deficit. But without the work of the appropriations committee and its subcommittees there would no means for disciplining congressional spending.

Committee assignments, and the appointment of committee chairs, are chosen by the members of the party that controls the House or Senate, the majority *party caucus.* This caucus is much more unwieldy in the House, where it must consist of least 218 members (half of 435 plus one) than in the Senate, where it could be as small as 51. In order to enable the House majority caucus to function effectively, it grants a great deal of control over its procedures to its leader, the Speaker of the House. As a result of the Speaker's critical role in choosing the people who control the crafting legislation, the Speaker enjoys great power. A critical avenue for exerting that power is the *House Rules Committee.* Because there is not enough time in a session of Congress to deal with all the bills that the committees approve and the leadership may have additional reasons for keeping a bill from coming to a floor vote, the Rules Committee decides which bills will indeed reach the floor and the specific rules governing how it will be considered. Because the Speaker controls the appointment of the Rules Committee and its chair, the Speaker of the House determines which bills will be voted on and which will not.

If a proposal deals with revenue, the Constitution requires that the proposal first be considered by the House. If the proposal covers any other topic, the Senate is free to consider it first. Because the Senate has fewer members, however, it cannot scrutinize as many proposals as the House can. Therefore, the Senate often allows the House to act first, using the lower chamber as a filter to determine which issues really merit further attention. Like the House, initial Senate consideration of a bill takes place in committee, but multiple committee referrals are far less common.

Unlike the House, the Senate does not adopt time limits for the consideration of statutes, treaties, or presidential nominees. Therefore, a senator or group of senators can prevent the Senate from voting on a statute or nominee simply by engaging in a *filibuster*, continuing to talk and refusing to yield for a vote. It takes sixty votes to end a filibuster. Therefore, controversial legislation that comes before the Senate needs more than the support of a majority. If the majority is less than sixty the minority may well succeed in blocking the legislation by filibustering. The mere threat of filibuster is often enough to force the majority to make significant concessions to the majority regarding the content of the legislation.

Often, each chamber will pass a significantly different version of a bill. To reconcile these differences, the House and Senate leadership each appoint members to a *joint conference committee*. The conference committee tries to achieve compromises regarding the major issues in dispute. If it succeeds, the conference version goes back to each house to be ratified or defeated. If both houses approve of the compromise bill, it is sent to the president's desk for a signature.

A good example of how the legislative process operates is provided by the landmark financial regulatory statute, the 2010 Dodd-Frank Wall Street Reform and Consumer Financial Protection Act. It is named for its Senate and House sponsors Christopher Dodd (D-CT) and Barney Frank (D-MA). After extensive discussion with the Department of the Treasury, Congressman Barney Frank introduced his financial regulatory proposal to the House as HR4173 on December 2, 2009. The bill was then referred to the Houses Financial Services Committee chaired by Frank, as well as to several other committees whose jurisdictions encompassed some particular aspect of what Frank was proposing. On December 8, 2009, the Rules Committee proposed a rule that would bring the bill to the floor. The rule provided three hours of general debate. The House passed the rule and then proceeded to debate the bill. It considered a number of amendments offered by various House members, some of which passed and some of which failed. On December 11, a vote was taken and HR4173 passed by a vote of 223 to 202.

On January 12, 2010, HR4172 was received by the Senate and referred to the Committee on Banking, Housing, and Urban Affairs, chaired by Senator Dodd. On May 20, 2010, that committee discharged it and it was taken up for debate on the Senate floor. The Senate then voted to substitute the version of the bill written by Dodd's Committee. The Senate Banking Committee version passed the Senate by a vote of fifty-nine to thirty-nine. The Senate then requested a conference with the House to reconcile the differences between the two versions. The leaders of both Houses selected the members for the conference. The conference held nine sessions to hammer out a compromise, which was then reported to both houses on June 29, 2010. The following day the House agreed to accept the conference compromise by a vote of 237 to 192. The Senate followed suit two weeks later, passing the conference version by a vote of sixty to thirty-nine.

## The Supporting Cast

The sheer amount of work that Congress must undertake pursuant to its legislative, oversight, and constituency services is far more than 435 representatives and 100 Senators can handle on their own. In response to this ever-growing workload, Congress has transformed itself into a large, complex organization. It now employs more than 17,000 people. Congressmen are heavily dependent on the personal staffs, committee staffs, and research organizations that compose a large part of this workforce.

House members are limited to a *personal staff* of eighteen. The size of Senate staff varies according to the size of the state the senator represents. A typical senator from a large state employs between forty-five and fifty staffers. A congressperson's staff conducts research, writes speeches, drafts bills, fields requests and complaints from constituents, and badgers the bureaucracy. Representatives reserve their own work time for the public and politically delicate aspects of the job. Staffers cannot substitute for the representative when it comes to making speeches, attending campaign events and committee meetings, giving press interviews, or negotiating with other members or prominent White House officials and constituents.

Each congressional committee and subcommittee has a staff of its own. These staffs are responsible for keeping committee members informed about the specialized policy questions about which the committee legislates and activities of the executive agencies over which it has oversight. *Committee staff* drafts the specific language that transforms the decisions the committee makes into actual legislation. It also plans and schedules committee hearings and writes committee reports. The average number of committee staff is sixty-eight in the House and forty-six in the Senate.

Congress has also established research organizations of its own to serve the informational needs of the individual members, the committees, and staffers. The three most important of these are: The *Congressional Budget Office* (CBO), *General Accountability Office*, and *Congressional Research Service*. The CBO's mandate is to provide the Congress with "objective, nonpartisan, and timely analyses to aid in economic and budgetary decisions on the wide array of programs covered by the federal budget." Later on in the chapter we will see how important the CBO has become in the policy-making process. The Speaker of the House of Representatives and the president pro tempore of the Senate jointly appoint the CBO director, after considering recommendations from the two budget committees. The term of office is four years, with no limit on the number of terms a director may serve. CBO currently employs about 250 people.

The Government Accountability Office (GAO) is the chief investigative agency supporting congressional efforts to oversee the executive branch. It audits the spending of every part of the federal government and performs other types of analyses and investigations designed to measure agency performance and unearth agency misdeeds. The head of the GAO, the Comptroller General of the United States, is appointed to a fifteen-year term by the president from a slate of candidates Congress proposes. The GAO has 3,350 employees.

The Congressional Research Service (CRS) is an all-purpose research agency performing whatever type of information gathering a member or committee requests of it. It provides policy analyses briefings and seminars as well as con-fidential memoranda and expert testimony at congressional hearings. The CRS is part of the Library of Congress, the head of which is the Librarian of Congress, who is appointed by the president and confirmed by the Senate. It has 450 pro-fessional employees.

## The Size and Shape of Congress

Because the Constitution grants every state two senators, the size of the Senate only changes when new states are added to the Union. This last hap-pened when Alaska and Hawaii became states in 1958 and 1959, respectively, increasing the total number of states from 48 to 50 and the size of the Senate from 96 to 100 members. The Constitution does not set the size of the House of Representatives. It merely guarantees that each state will have at least one representative; each congressional district will have at least 30,000 persons, and that the districts will be apportioned among the states on the basis of population. In 1790, each member of the House of Representatives represented about 34,000 residents. Today, the House has more than quadrupled in size, and each member represents about nineteen times as many constituents. In 2000, each member of the House of Representatives represented a population of about 647,000. The 2010 census showed a 9.7 percent increase in the size of the U.S. population and therefore each congressional district grew by approximately that same percentage. The current size of 435 representatives was established in 1911.

In order to ensure that each congressional district has more or less the same number of people, congressional seats are *reapportioned* in response to the population shifts discovered by the census, which is conducted every ten years. The 2012 House elections were the first ones conducted according to the 2010 census, which requires that eleven seats be reapportioned among the states.

The states gaining seats were: Texas (4), Florida (2), Arizona (1), Georgia (1), South Carolina (1), Nevada (1), and Utah (1). The states losing seats were: New York (2), Ohio (2), Massachusetts Pennsylvania (1), Michigan (1), Illinois (1), Iowa (1), Missouri (1), and Louisiana (1). Notice that all the gainers are in the South and West and all the losers, except Louisiana, are in the North and Midwest. Louisiana's population loss is due to very special circumstances – the devastating effect of Hurricane Katrina in 2005. This shift of population from the North and East to the South and West was also detectable in the 2000 Census when twelve seats were reapportioned.

Because population growth and decline happens unevenly within as well as between states, states are also obligated to redraw their congressional boundaries even if they do not gain or lose seats. In most states redistricting is the responsibility of the state legislature. How those districts are drawn has a huge impact on who wins and loses. Every incumbent and likely challenger wants their district to be dominated by voters favorable to them. This goal may well put them at odds with leaders of their own party. Each political party wants the districts drawn to maximize the number of seats they are likely to win. Whereas incumbents want to stack their district with likely supporters, party leaders do not want any one district to have so many favorable voters that it deprives the party of the ability to win in the other districts. They would rather spread their partisan supporters around, giving them an ability to win more seats by slimmer margins rather than a smaller number of seats by large margins. Thus, the redistricting process is highly politically charged. The parties fight between themselves, but even within each party, incumbents battle to retain or gain favorable voters and party leaders battle with incumbents to spread favorable voters around. Seventeen states have attempted to depoliticize this process by removing it from the legislature and assigning it to an independent commission. It is very hard to evaluate whether or not these commissions do a better and fairer redistricting job than partisan legislators do because it is so difficult to determine what it means to be fair when drawing district lines.

## POLITICAL DEVELOPMENT

### The Constitutional Path

Article I of the Constitution established Congress as the preeminent branch of government, granting it seventeen legislative powers, including the most important of all governmental powers: taxation, regulation of commerce, and declaration of war. These enumerated powers are followed by the "necessary and proper clause," which grants Congress whatever additional powers are required to exercise its specific responsibilities, assuming those powers do not expressly violate the Constitution. Article I, Section 2 designates the speaker as the principal officer of the House of Representatives; the president of the Senate, who is the vice president, as the presiding officer of the Senate; and a president pro tempore who presides in the absence of the vice president.

Having granted so much power to the legislature, the Convention delegates sought to avoid the intemperate and irresponsible behavior of their own state legislatures during the currency crisis of 1785. Americans went on such a buying spree after the Revolutionary War – importing such luxuries as clocks, glassware, and furniture from Great Britain – that gold and silver became scarce and the value of money was driven up. Indebted farmers were able to convince several state legislatures to loosen the money supply by printing vast sums of money. The price inflation that followed proved economically disastrous.

This irresponsible behavior of state legislatures was aggravated by the impotence of the central government under the Articles of Confederation. The national legislature lacked authority to regulate interstate commerce or compel states to the funds the Congress requisitioned from them. Members of Congress were chosen by the state legislatures, which paid their salaries and had the power to remove them at any time. Therefore, congressional representatives were afraid to take actions that their state legislatures disapproved of for fear of losing their positions or having their pay reduced. To craft a Congress capable of more enlightened statesmanship and better public policy making than could be found in the state legislatures, the Framers carefully considered how best to select representatives, how many should be chosen, and what checks to establish between House and Senate; Congress and the states; and Congress and the other two branches of the federal government.

## Selection and Size

To select better representatives, the Framers determined to draw them from a bigger pool. House districts would be large; senators would be chosen by entire states. State legislators were often elected for periods of six months or even a year. By creating longer congressional terms – two years for the House, six for the Senate – the Framers hoped to insulate representatives from volatile changes in public opinion.

To promote deliberation, Congress was to be a relatively small body. The House of Representatives would initially have only sixty-five members and the Senate twenty-six. By contrast, the legislature of Massachusetts had more than 300 members. Anti-Federalists protested that the small size of the legislature made it insufficiently representative. So intent were the Framers on maintaining distance between House members and their constituents that until the very last day of the Constitutional Convention, they fought to maintain a ratio of 1 member per 40,000 citizens. Fearing that such a high ratio would offend democratic sentiments, George Washington stepped down from the chair – the only time he did so – to defend reducing the minimum from 40,000 to 30,000. The Convention had debated and rejected this proposition several times in the preceding weeks, but once Washington endorsed it, debate ceased and it passed unanimously.

## Bicameralism

The Framers feared the democratic character of the House, which, if left to its own devices, would become all too responsive to popular whims and passions. They sought, as Madison put it, to refine popular passions by "successive filtrations." The first line of defense was bicameralism, the creation of two separate houses of Congress with all laws having to be passed by both. The House's state delegations were based on population and its members elected directly by the people every two years, thus making it a national representative body. By contrast, each state, regardless of size, would have two senators selected by the state legislatures for six-year terms, thus establishing the Senate as an important ingredient of federalism.

All revenue bills had to originate in the House. This concession to the House shows the Framers' commitment to giving the primary power over the operations of the federal government to its most democratic element. But the House would be moderated by the more discerning attention of the Senate. The Senate's smaller size, its longer terms, the staggering of members' terms (only one-third of the body would be up for reelection every two years), and their selection by state legislatures, not the people, encouraged prudence. Therefore, the Senate was given a privileged part in foreign affairs and government staffing. It was granted sole authority to ratify foreign treaties, confirm presidential nominations to the executive branch and judiciary, and try public officials impeached by the House.

## Midterm Elections

Even as it was checking excessive democratic responsiveness by creating a bicameral legislature, the Framers were promoting democratic responsiveness by providing for *midterm congressional elections.* In the midst of the president's four-year term, the Constitution requires the entire House of Representatives as well as one-third of the Senate to stand for reelection. Thus, the Congress can change its political character in between presidential elections. No other republican democracy has midterm parliamentary elections. As we shall see in the last section of this chapter, congressional midterm elections have proven themselves to be critical devices for ensuring democratic accountability. By shifting control of Congress to the minority party they have forced both the president and Congress to alter course in a direction more in line with the public will.

## Congressional Dominance

For the first half of the United States' political development, Congress served as the chief national policy-making body. As we shall see in Chapter 8, the president did not dominate the legislative process in the nineteenth century as he would later. Nor had he yet become the single focal point of national political attention. The scope and reach of federal departments and agencies were far narrower and more limited than they would become in the twentieth century and, therefore, administrative policy making was far less important than congressional law making. In the course of the nineteenth century, Congress developed the strong internal organization and leadership necessary for maintaining its political dominance.

### Organizing Congress: The Emergence of the Party Caucus

Chapter 11 describes the Framers' fear of political parties as factions that would incite class, religious, or racial conflict and thereby endanger liberty. The Constitution's system of separation of powers, operating in a large and diverse society, was intended to inhibit the emergence of a strong two-party system. Ironically, it was that very party system that enabled Congress to more fully perform its constitutional responsibilities.

In 1800, the Republicans triumphed over the Federalists and installed Thomas Jefferson as the nation's third president. The most important result of this critical election was to empower a party dedicated to constraining the president and strengthening Congress and the states. In order to perform its democratic function of passing laws that reflect majority sentiment and its republican function of holding executive power in check, Congress needed a unifying force that, as Jefferson saw, could only be provided by political parties. Presidents can be strong and appear "above party." Congress, however, is a large collection of individuals. Although members of Congress may achieve celebrity and popularity outside of parties, Congress as an institution can rival the president's claim to public confidence only if it can be held collectively accountable. Accountability requires that parties reward and punish members based on their adherence not only to collective decisions of the party but also to the tactics adopted by the party leadership implementing those decisions.

Unlike Washington and Adams, therefore, Jefferson deemphasized his formal powers and governed instead through his extra-constitutional role as party leader. He helped build a disciplined party organization in Congress and relied on *party leaders* in the House and Senate to advance his program. Jefferson himself sometimes presided over the meetings of the congressional Republican representatives, known as *party caucuses.*

### The Rise of the Power of the House Speaker

The Constitution establishes the post of Speaker of the House of Representatives, but it does not enumerate the Speaker's responsibilities and powers. Nor was there any significant discussion of these questions at the Constitutional Convention. Until Henry Clay of Kentucky was elected Speaker in 1811, party leadership in the House was shared by several floor leaders. The Speaker acted as merely a moderator. A strong president such as Jefferson could dominate such diffuse congressional leadership. Clay displaced the president as the leader of the majority party in the House. He extended party control over congressional committees, which became, in Woodrow Wilson's celebrated phrase, "little legislatures," meaning that the committees performed the real work of formulating legislation.

Like most great legislative leaders, Clay derived his success in large part from his extraordinary personality. John C. Calhoun, a fierce rival, said, "I don't like Henry Clay, he is a bad man, an imposter, a creator of wicked schemes. I wouldn't speak to him, but, by God, I love him." The leadership strength of the House Speaker has ebbed and flowed over the course of American political development. But many speakers, including recent ones such as Newt Gingrich, Speaker from 1994 to 1998, and Nancy Pelosi, Speaker from 2006 to 2010, have exerted powerful control over the House.

Clay emerged as the dominant national political leader during the controversy with Britain that led to the War of 1812. Clay was one of the most influential of the "Warhawks," a congressional faction that favored making aggressive demands on Britain and going to war if those demands were not met. Unifying the Republican caucus behind him, Clay strengthened the House's capacity to meet its broader legislative obligations by expanding the number and influence of its committees, which enabled each representative to specialize in a specific policy area such as finance or foreign policy. Clay was especially careful to appoint Warhawks to key posts, including the chairmanship of the foreign affairs committee. Clay and his allies forced a reluctant Madison to deliver a war message to Congress. On June 18, 1812, President Madison signed the first war declaration in American history.

Unfortunately, Congress proved far more eager to declare war than prepare for it. Traditional Republican hostility to centralized power caused Congress to slash tax revenues and military appropriations, leaving the military both understaffed and undersupplied. Legislative dominance deprived the country of the solid benefits that the Framers expected from a unified and energetic executive. The inability of Congress to match its talent for deliberation and debate with administrative competence would continue to bedevil national governance throughout the nineteenth century.

## A Citizen Legislature

Building on Clay's inspired organizational and leadership talents, Congress continued to be the dominant branch of government until the election of Andrew Jackson in 1828 (see Chapters 4 and 8). And, despite Jackson's strengthening of the presidency, Congress remained at the center of American politics and government. It benefited greatly from the rise of the mass-based, decentralized party system that we discussed in Chapter 4 and will elaborate on in Chapter 10. The parties knitted congressional representatives closely to their constituents. Congress became a more vibrant institution, one that registered competing democratic voices. Unlike the contemporary Congress, viewed as the keystone of an unresponsive government establishment, the nineteenth-century Congress became a "citizen legislature."

The most striking feature of this citizen legislature was the very rapid *turnover* of its members. For much of the twentieth century, power in the Congress was acquired through *seniority*, which encourages long congressional careers. But in the nineteenth century, the House had 30–60 percent turnover at every election. The Senate's longer and overlapping terms gives it a more stable membership than the House, but it, too, saw far more turnover in the nineteenth century than it does today. Before the Civil War, members rarely made the Senate a career. Until the end of the century, the average senator did not even finish one term, completing only three to four years of service (see Figure 7.1). By contrast, the turnover in 2010, which was quite high by modern standards, was only 20 percent in the House and 17 percent in the Senate.

One cause of the high turnover was the unpleasantness of life in Washington. Unlike the first two capital sites, New York and Philadelphia, Washington lacked culture and creature comforts. Members of Congress felt stranded in this primitive new city, described by the historian Merrill Peterson as "a village pretending to be a capitol, a place with a few bad houses, extensive swamps, hanging on the skirts of a too thinly peopled, weak and barren country." Another disincentive to long congressional service was the limited role that the national government played in the political life of the country. The triumph of the Jacksonians over the Whigs had restored the primacy of state and local government.

Another key characteristic of the citizen legislature was a high level of partisan competition. The two political parties were evenly balanced during most of the nineteenth century, and therefore House elections tended to be close, which threatened reelection prospects. State legislative elections were also close. Because the Senate was chosen by the state legislatures, senatorial elections were likewise highly competitive. State legislative candidates would often run for office pledged to a particular senatorial candidate. This is why the famous 1858 Lincoln-Douglas debates took place all over the state of Illinois. Each candidate was trying to help elect legislative candidates pledged to vote for him.

Partisan competition and member turnover combined to create a lively Congress. It became the great national theater in which passionate and lively debate over such critical issues as slavery, tariff policy, the bank, and the money supply took place. Congressional drama reached a fever pitch in May of 1856. Senator Charles Sumner (R-MA) delivered a two-day speech entitled "The Crime against Kansas" that accused the South of conspiring to admit Kansas to the Union as a slave state. Among those members of Congress singled out for insult and ridicule was Andrew P. Butler (D-SC), who Sumner described as "Don Quixote who had chosen a mistress to whom he has made his vows, and who ... though polluted in the sight of the world, is chaste in his sight – I mean the harlot slavery."

Congressman Preston Brooks (D-SC), a kinsman of Butler's, decided to avenge his family's honor. Brooks approached Sumner, who was seated at his desk mailing copies of the offending speech to his constituents. Calling the speech a "libel on South Carolina, and Mr. Butler, who is a relative of mine," Brooks brought his cane down on Sumner's head, neck, and shoulders, repeatedly and with increasing force, until the cane shattered. Sumner tried to rise from his desk, ripping up the heavy screws that bolted it to the floor. Blinded by blood, he staggered down the center aisle of the Senate chamber (Figure 7.3).

The South declared Brooks a hero. The North viewed Sumner as a martyr. Southern opposition prevented the two-thirds majority necessary to expel Brooks from the House, but he resigned anyway. South Carolinians immediately sent him back to Washington with triumphant unanimity. Sumner stayed away from the Senate for three years – recuperating, his supporters said; hiding, claimed his enemies. During that time the Massachusetts legislature reelected him as a symbolic rebuke to the "barbarism of slavery." His empty seat in the Senate chamber remained a visible symbol of the deepening sectional divide.

The Sumner-Brooks incident was hardly part of the deliberative process that the Founders of the Constitution prescribed for the Congress, but it shows how

SOUTHERN CHIVALRY — ARGUMENT versus CLUB'S.

**Figure 7.3.** "Southern Chivalry – Argument vs. Club's": An 1856 cartoon depicting Congressman Preston S. Brooks attacking Charles Sumner on the floor of the Senate chamber. Credit: The Granger Collection, NYC – All rights reserved.

the national legislature had become the center of American democratic life, a forum that helped draw Americans into struggles about the most fundamental political issues. John Quincy Adams (when he was in the House), Henry Clay, Daniel Webster, John C. Calhoun, and Charles Sumner shaped the debate over slavery, making Congress, as the historian Henry Jones Ford observed, "a school of political education for the nation."

## The Height of Congressional Government

In the post–Civil War period, Congress achieved an even greater political dominance than it had enjoyed prior to the presidency of Andrew Jackson. This dominance was achieved by combining strong congressional leadership with greater political party control of the congressional nomination and election process.

Leadership control was far stronger in the House of Representatives than in the Senate. It reached its peak late in the nineteenth century due to the leadership of Thomas B. Reed of Maine. Unlike previous celebrated legislators such as Adams, Clay, Webster, and Calhoun, Reed was single-mindedly concerned with the process of governing. He defined a statesman as "a politician who is dead," and he displayed a wit and cynicism that animated a ruthless insistence on streamlining the House's chaotic proceedings in order to eliminate obstruction and delay.

House rules required that a majority of members, a *quorum*, be present in order for the House to meet. In an effort to thwart Reed's authority, the minority Democrats sat mute during attendance call, preventing a quorum. Reed counted them present anyway. Reed appointed himself chair of the Rules Committee, enabling him to determine when and how a bill would be considered. In 1891, the Supreme Court sanctioned the transformation of the House into a more disciplined legislative body by upholding the constitutionality of these and other "Reed rules" aimed at controlling members' behavior.

The Democrats opposed the increase in discipline, contending that the Constitution intended Congress to be a body of individuals representing various localities. Reed countered that "a majority under the Constitution was entitled to legislate, and that, if a contrary practice has grown up, such practice is unrepublican, undemocratic, against sound policy, and contrary to the Constitution." He was expressing the Jacksonian principle that political parties were a critical agent of popular rule and that grassroots party control of Congress upheld the democratic character of American republican government. Before becoming speaker, Reed had written in a national magazine, "Our government is founded on the doctrine that if one hundred citizens think one way and one hundred and one think the other, the one hundred one are right."

Democrats nicknamed him "Czar" Reed and made his "tyranny of the House" a major campaign theme in the 1890 congressional elections. After winning an overwhelming victory, they repealed most of Reed's rules. But Reed, now in the minority, launched a retaliatory campaign of obstruction designed to persuade Democrats to acknowledge that his procedural innovations had been necessary to allow the House to function. Although many Democrats remained unhappy with the quorum rule and other procedures that centralized power in the House, they grudgingly reinstituted similar procedural tools for maintaining majority party control. By the end of the nineteenth century, the House was a highly centralized institution, dominated by a powerful speaker who could restrict obstructionist tactics on the floor, control committee assignments, and, through the Rules Committee, exercise influence over the legislative agenda (Figure 7.4).

The Senate did not achieve a similar degree of leadership control. Its party leaders were less likely to remove a committee member for disloyalty. The Senate rules allowed "legislative holdups" by which a member could prevent a bill from coming to the floor for full debate. Also, individual senators could filibuster. Still, by the late nineteenth century it, too, had become far less tolerant of obstruction and delay. Finance Committee chairman Nelson Aldrich (R-RI) and other influential Republican senators succeeded in imposing a previously unknown degree of partisan and procedural discipline in the Senate. These efforts were reinforced in 1917 when the Senate, at the suggestion of President

**Figure 7.4.** "Senatorial Courtesy": An 1893 cartoon of the Senate filibuster.

*Source*: http://www.senate.gov/artandhistory/art/common/image/Ga_cartoon_38_00652.htm. Cat. no. 38.00652.001.

Woodrow Wilson, adopted a rule (Rule XXII) allowing it to end debate with a two-thirds majority vote – a motion known as *cloture* (cloture now only requires sixty votes).

Although party control was justified on the basis of majority rule, critics charged that it worked against the interests of the many. The close identification of the Republican Party with business made the Congress vulnerable to control by the great corporations that were coming to dominate American politics in the late nineteenth century. The *protective tariff* became the party's signature policy (see Chapter 6). Laws such as the McKinley Tariff of 1890 strengthened the Republican Party's business connections. The identification with business would later become a liability, but during the prosperous times of the late nineteenth century, it was politically advantageous. Congress, under the tight grip of party leadership, did not engage in vital debate over industrial capitalism as it had over slavery. Party organization existed to pass legislation, not discuss it.

## THE EMERGENCE OF CONGRESSIONAL PROFESSIONALISM

The party model of congressional government soon became obsolete. Acquisition of the Philippines and greater influence over Cuba, brought about by victory in the Spanish-American War in 1898, broadened America's international obligations and muted partisan differences. William McKinley, a former member of the House elected president in 1896, noted how the emergence of the United States as a world power freed the president from collective party responsibility: "I can no longer be called the President of a party; I am now the President of the whole people." Greater attention to foreign affairs expanded executive discretion and diminished the role of lawmaking. In Chapter 8, we examine additional sources of the rise of presidential power and popularity in the early twentieth century, particularly the impact of Progressivism. Through these combined factors, the presidency threatened to displace Congress as the principal agent of popular rule.

Congress's reaction to this executive challenge gave rise to changes that would define legislative politics and governance for most of the twentieth century. It transformed Congress's organization and practices to make legislators policy specialists. Party organization gave way to narrowly focused autonomous committees, which enabled representatives to acquire expertise in programs that served their ambition. They made Congress their career as they functioned as "policy entrepreneurs," that is, formulators and stewards of new policies and programs for their constituencies and the organized interests with whom they were allied. These changes improved Congress's ability to oversee the activities of the executive branch and serve local districts and states. But they sapped its vitality as a representative institution capable of forging consensus among the nation's diverse voices.

Making a career in Congress also required legislators to have more control over their personal electoral fortunes. Therefore, they supported progressive reforms such as the direct primary, which replaced partisan campaigns with candidate-centered campaigns (see Chapters 11 and 12). They also sought changes in the power structure of Congress to better enable them to influence public policy in ways that would serve their districts and states and thus enhance their prospects for reelection.

## A Revolution in the House

The attack on congressional party leadership began in 1910 with a revolt against third-term Speaker of the House Joseph Cannon (R-IL). A disciple of Czar Reed, "Uncle Joe" Cannon managed the House with an iron fist.

Cannon was a *standpat* Republican, meaning that he resisted popular economic and political reforms. Like Henry Clay, Cannon prevailed over a weak president. He opposed President William Howard Taft's tariff reduction efforts and pushed the Paine Aldrich tariff, which raised rates on many items, through the House in 1910. But unlike Clay's command during Madison's occupation of the executive mansion, Cannon's dominance of Taft incited a rebellion that stripped the office of much of its influence.

Cannon retaliated against three Republicans who voted against the Paine Aldrich Tariff by removing them as committee chairmen. Incensed by this and other dictatorial acts, Progressive Republicans joined with the Democrats to strip the speaker of his powers to appoint committee chairs and members and control the Rules Committee as well as many of his other means for controlling the business of the House.

The Progressive revolt spread rapidly to the Senate, where it was led by Robert La Follette (R-WI), elected in 1906. He was so despised by the leadership that he was denied the minimal courtesies extended to a freshman senator. Instead of being granted a seat on the Committee on Interstate Commerce, a fine vantage point for taking on the railroads, which reformers viewed as the most egregious of the Trusts, La Follette was appointed chair of the Committee to Investigate the Condition of the Potomac River Front, which never had a bill referred to it or even held a meeting.

But this effort to humiliate La Follette backfired. With the help of the press, he took his case for railroad regulation as embodied in the Hepburn Bill directly to the people, arousing popular opposition to corporate power and the Senate leadership that served it. Only President Theodore Roosevelt, who also stumped for the bill (see Chapter 8), played a more important part in mobilizing support for it. The Hepburn Bill was enacted despite the efforts of Senate leaders to kill it.

La Follette's successful insurgency signaled the emergence of a new kind of senator, one who stood apart, who resolutely attacked parties and private interests, who was celebrated by the press. La Follette's celebrity contributed not only to economic reform but also to the downfall of the most powerful Republican senator, Nelson Aldrich, who like Speaker Cannon was deprived of legislative control by a coalition of Progressive Republicans and Democrats. The Progressive attack also aroused public sentiment for the direct election of senators. Enacted in 1913, the Seventeenth Amendment provided that senators be elected by voters, not state legislatures. This change further undermined *party discipline* because candidates now had to depend on their own electioneering ability rather than party control of state legislatures.

## The Emergence of Committee Government

After the downfall of Cannon and Aldrich, and continuing well into the twentieth century, committees dominated Congress. They held hearings and wrote legislation in the privacy of their chambers. Committee chairs were virtually legislative barons, controlling committee agendas, hiring staff, and scheduling hearings. Party strength remained important because it determined the relative number of Democrats and Republicans on each committee and whether the senior Democrat or Republican would be chair. But party leaders did not choose chairs. Instead, a seniority system allocated leadership positions and committee assignments based on length of congressional service.

The *seniority system* remained in place until 1974. It enabled members of Congress to plan long careers on a particular committee without fear of being removed by party leaders. Individual members, no longer subject to collective partisan responsibility, became policy makers in their own right. They used this influence to benefit constituents, thereby improving their reelection prospects. Thus, committee government reduced the number of competitive districts, and turnover of both House and Senate seats declined.

Committee government made Congress a less representative institution. In the party-dominated system, members of Congress could be disciplined by party leaders and lose cherished committee assignments. The new seniority system ensured that committee chairs would remain in office even if they thwarted congressional majorities, held meetings in secret, and denied access to dissenting groups. Because many Southern Democrats were especially good at holding onto their seats, they rose to be chairs of several key committees. The used their power as chairs to keep Congress from deliberating over and passing civil rights legislation. In the face of Congress' increasing insulation from public opinion, the task of popular representation fell increasingly to the president (see Chapter 8). The two branches traded constitutional roles. The people looked to the president for democratic innovation, whereas the House and Senate applied restraint.

The primary responsibility for Congress in this revised constitutional order was to oversee administration of public policy. It used committee hearings, investigations, and individual member or staff interrogations to try to hold the executive accountable. Individual legislators developed policy expertise to match the bureaucrats who staffed the burgeoning executive branch. Committee organization mirrored that of departments and agencies. Thus, for example, the Senate Foreign Relations Committee oversaw the State Department; the Labor and Human Resources Committee oversaw the Department of Health and Human Services.

The 1946 Legislative Reorganization Act codified and rationalized congressional oversight. It reduced the number of committees and subcommittees and clarified their jurisdictions. It made Congress's oversight responsibility explicit and called on it to engage in "continual watchfulness" over the activities of administrative agencies. It provided individual representatives and committees with large staffs, which enhanced Congress's capacity to oversee the bureaucracy. Committee staff grew from 103 in 1891 (41 in the Senate and 62 in the House) to 483 in 1947 (290 in the House and 193 in the Senate) As congressional staff continued to expand in the post–World War II era, staff members came to perform a variety of crucial roles. The greatest prestige went to committee, and later subcommittee, staff. They were, and still are, policy specialists. But even they cannot master all the issues that come before their committee, so they reach out to experts from universities, think tanks, and lobbying organizations. The staff's job is largely to synthesize those expert opinions in a manner that makes them comprehensible to the members. Once a subcommittee reaches agreement on specific issues, its staffers produce a draft that is sent up to the full committee. Committee staff performs similar tasks for the committee as a whole and also become involved in negotiating with the staffs of other committees, particularly the Rules Committee, to resolve issues of jurisdiction and scheduling.

This shift toward *oversight* brought with it a new set of constitutional difficulties. In the late 1940s and early 1950s the most publicized and controversial use of congressional investigations was for the purpose of uncovering domestic subversion. In the late 1940s, as the power of the Soviet Union grew, Americans began to worry about threats to national security posed by communist espionage. Several different members of the House and Senate made use of their leadership positions on committees or subcommittees to launch investigations into domestic communist subversion. The most prominent of these investigators was Senator Joseph McCarthy (R-WI). His inquisitorial methods and blatant disregard for the civil liberties of the subjects of his investigations became so notorious that the term "McCarthyism" entered the language as a synonym for unfair and obnoxious intrusion into the private lives and political views of citizens. Despite his highly publicized and extensive investigations, McCarthy unearthed few if any serious instances of security breaches. Such breaches did occur and spies were caught and convicted, but not by McCarthy or his committee's most influential House counterpart, the House Committee on Un-American Activities.

The witch hunt wilted by overreaching itself. Beginning in April of 1954, Senator McCarthy's Subcommittee on Investigations of the Committee on Government Operations began televised hearings on charges of communist subversion in the U.S. Army. Such sustained exposure to McCarthy's bullying tactics, rude behavior, and the weakness of his evidence eroded popular support. A critical moment in McCarthy's political demise occurred when he implied that a young lawyer named Fred Fischer who worked for the law firm of the Army's special counsel, Robert Welch, had communist leanings. Welch replied: "Until this moment, Senator, I think I never gauged your cruelty or recklessness.... Have you no sense of decency, sir?" Welch's calm and measured response to McCarthy's brutalities struck a responsive chord. The audience in the gallery burst into applause. McCarthy's day as a popular leader was done. McCarthy's ignominious political demise served as a salutary cautionary tale. His successors have only rarely wielded congressional investigatory power in ways that threaten civil liberties.

## THE RESURGENCE OF CONGRESS AND THE RISE OF INSTITUTIONAL COMBAT

Starting in the late 1960s, the relationship between the president and Congress began to change, leading over the course of the decade to a significant resurgence of congressional power and a major increase in institutional combat between the two branches. Much of this resurgence was due to growing fears that the presidency was becoming too powerful. The failure of the United States to achieve "peace with honor" in Vietnam, discussed in more detail in Chapter 8, fostered public cynicism about the merits of presidential policies and a greater inclination by the press to challenge the wisdom and veracity of presidential statements and proposals. Even champions of a strong presidency became concerned about presidential imperialism and more appreciative of Congress's constitutional responsibility to represent public views and refine and imbed them in settled, standing law.

Concerns about presidential excess were greatly aggravated by the presidency of Richard Nixon. Nixon was the first new president since Zachary Taylor in 1848 to be elected without a party majority in either house of Congress. Nonetheless, he unilaterally extended the Vietnam War and bombed Cambodia. In further disregard of Congress, Nixon *impounded*, refused to spend, funds appropriated by Congress. Presidential impoundments had previously been exercised only for reasons of economy and efficiency, but Nixon's were an attempt to undermine the legislative process. In an effort to curtail his predecessor Lyndon Johnson's "War on Poverty," he impounded funds that Congress had appropriated to one of its signature policies, the Community Action Program (see Chapter 8). The impoundment was subjected to judicial challenge and ultimately overturned. In 1974 Congress would pass legislation curbing the president's ability to impound funds.

The Watergate scandal caused Congress to go beyond curbing the president to actively seeking his removal. For the first time in history, a president resigned from office, a direct consequence of the House Judiciary Committee's recommendation that the full House vote to impeach him. The *Watergate* scandal was named for the building that housed the Democratic National Committee headquarters, which was broken into by operatives of the Republican Committee to Re-Elect the President during the 1972 presidential campaign. The key issue was whether Nixon knew about the break-in and tried to cover up his connection to it. The Senate Select Committee on Presidential Campaign Activities, known as the Watergate Committee, ordered Nixon to hand over tapes that he had made of his Oval Office conversations and sued him when he refused to do so.

Nixon claimed *executive privilege*, a president's right to withhold information from Congress. Committee chairman Senator Sam Ervin (D-NC) countered that executive privilege could be defended under some circumstances, such as those dealing with national security, but could not be invoked when dealing with possible criminal activities. Nixon argued that "inseparably interspersed in the tapes are a great many very frank and very private comments wholly extraneous to the committee's inquiry."

Partisanship gave way to institutional loyalty, as even Nixon's staunchest congressional defenders demanded that he produce the tapes. Senator Howard Baker (R-TN), committee vice chairman, who had long been a friend and advisor to the president, contended that the tapes contained material "essential if not vital, to the full inquiry mandated and required by this committee." Baker and Ervin's engagingly telegenic presences did much to reassure the nation that the confrontation between the president and Congress could be resolved through regular constitutional procedures. Ervin's country lawyer image and his passionate but calm invocations of the separation of powers made him a folk hero. His judicious committee leadership served to remind the American people of Congress's critical constitutional responsibility to hold the president accountable.

On July 24, 1974, in *U.S. v. Nixon*, the Supreme Court unanimously ruled against the president. Chief Justice Warren Burger, a Nixon appointee, stated that: "To read the Article II powers of the President as providing an absolute privilege against a subpoena essential to enforcement of criminal statutes ... would upset the constitutional balance of a 'workable government' ... and cut deeply into the guarantee of due process of law." On the heels of the court's decision, the House Judiciary Committee voted to impeach Nixon on August 4, 1974. His chances of surviving a Senate trial suffered when he admitted that the tapes did implicate him in the Watergate cover-up. Also, a gap was discovered in one of the tapes during what appeared to be a crucial conversation about the break-in between Nixon and key aides. Even Nixon's Republican supporters on the Judiciary Committee conceded that the president had virtually confessed to obstruction of justice. On August 8, 1974, Nixon announced to the nation his decision to resign, becoming the first president forced from office. Whatever the president's actual guilt, the public was left with the impression that he had been involved in something foul, and the scandal further jeopardized confidence in the integrity of the office.

Asked in 1959 whether the president or Congress should have "the most say in government," a representative sample of Americans favored the president 61 percent to 17 percent. Watergate shattered that virtual consensus. A similar survey in 1977 showed that 58 percent of Americans believed Congress should have the most say; only 26 percent supported presidential primacy. For the first time since the heady days of Czar Reed and Nelson Aldrich, Congress seemed poised to assume its place as the primary representative institution.

The Watergate scandal provoked Congress to pass a multitude of laws curbing the president's powers, including the Congressional Budget and Impoundment Control Act of 1974, which required the president to obtain Congress's approval before impounding any funds. The act also created budget committees in both houses to coordinate and strengthen legislative involvement in fiscal policy making, and it established the CBO to provide Congress with the same level of fiscal expertise that the Office of Management and Budget provides the executive branch (see Chapter 8).

The CBO has proven to be an especially important tool for reestablishing congressional influence. Prior to its existence the Congress had to rely on the revenue and spending projections provided to it by the executive branch when making budget and tax policy. Because the CBO had its own staff of economists and budget analysts it was able to offer the Congress an independent appraisal of the budgetary consequences of alternative taxing and spending decisions. Over time the CBO has acquired a reputation for technical excellence and impartiality, enabling Congress to exert effective influence in the making of budgetary policy. For example, President Obama's health care reform policy would not have passed Congress had the CBO not confirmed the president's claim that the plan would not have long-term negative budgetary consequences.

Congress also reasserted itself in foreign affairs. The 1972 Case Act reduced the president's ability to conduct personal diplomacy by requiring that all *executive agreements*, which are agreements made between heads of state, be reported to Congress. The War Powers Resolution, enacted over Nixon's veto in 1973, sought to reestablish Congress's war powers by requiring the president to consult with Congress, when possible, before committing troops to combat and submit a report to Congress within forty-eight hours after doing so. The

Resolution demands that after sixty days troops be removed unless Congress votes to declare war or approve their continued deployment.

In a further effort to reestablish itself as an equal governing partner, Congress reformed its own internal procedures. Both chambers took action to reduce the committee chairs' near dictatorial control over the legislative process. A coalition of liberal Democrats and junior members of both parties enacted the Legislative Reorganization Act of 1970, which required committees to adopt written rules and promoted open meetings. The most important provision of the act provided for recorded votes on floor amendments in the House. This prevented committee chairs from quietly killing amendments. Now that constituents would know how their representative voted on an amendment, committee chairs would no longer be inoculated from public pressure and floor assaults on their legislation.

The attack on the seniority system and the committee chairs it protected shifted power upward to party leaders and downward to subcommittees and individual members. The majority Democratic caucus in the House, in particular, was revitalized as conservative southerners began to decline in number and liberals gained a clear majority in the party. The caucus enacted a "subcommittee bill of rights" in 1973 that removed from committee chairs the power to select subcommittee chairs and instead allowed that power to be shared by all Democratic members of each committee. Each member of a committee was also given the right to serve on at least one "choice" related subcommittee. Subcommittees were given fixed areas of responsibility, authorization to meet and hold their own hearings, and larger budgets and staffs. Subcommittees replaced committees as the little legislatures that dominated the work of Congress.

More dramatic devolution occurred in the Senate. The Senate adopted a new staffing policy in 1975 that provided each senator on a committee with additional staff who were independent of the chairmen. In addition, the filibuster, which had been used rather rarely for much of American history, became a routine tool used by individual senators to influence or entirely block pending bills.

This reform movement came to fruition in 1975 with the arrival of the huge freshman class of seventy-four "Watergate babies," elected in the wake of Nixon's resignation. These reform-minded newcomers spearheaded successful efforts in both houses to ensure that chairs of committees would no longer be chosen on the basis of seniority but instead would be elected by secret ballot of the majority party caucus. They pressed the House Democratic caucus to remove three aging southern committee chairs, the first exception to the seniority rule since 1920. Committee chairs were put on notice that they likewise faced being deposed if they did not share power with their committee colleagues and become more responsive to party members. House Republicans also challenged seniority by providing for individual votes on the party's ranking committee members. Although no Senate chairmen or ranking committee members were deposed, the new rules, adopted by both Democrats and Republicans, served notice that chairmen were expected to be more responsive to party members.

This legislative rebellion in the House and Senate was carried out by insurgents whose target was as much the president as it was their more stolid and conservative congressional adversaries. It resulted in a severe challenge to the modern president's preeminence in legislative and administrative matters. As political scientist R. Shep Melnick has written:

> No longer would Congress respond to calls for action by passing vague legislation telling the executive to do something. Now Congress was writing detailed statutes, which not infrequently deviated from the president's program. Subcommittees were also using oversight hearings to make sure that administrators paid heed not just to the letter of legislation but to its spirit as well.

The new vitality that was created by *subcommittee government* is best illustrated by the outpouring of congressionally initiated environmental, consumer protection, worker safety, and civil rights laws that took place during the 1970s. These initiatives were not the sort of measures one would expect from the keystone of a conservative Washington establishment.

Greater party caucus influence in organizing the House and Senate did not return the speaker and Senate majority leader to the preeminence they lost during the Progressive insurgency, but the two positions did acquire more power to control the federal budget, make committee assignments, and control the flow of legislation. The new budgetary process, in particular, increased centralization in both the House and Senate. It gave the majority party dominant influence over the budget committees and enabled the speaker, in consultation with the Senate's president pro tempore, to appoint the director of the Congressional Budget Office.

## Divided Government – Institutional Combat

Congress's resurgence was accompanied by a rise in the level and bitterness of institutional combat with the president. From 1968 to 1992, Republicans held the presidency for all but four years. By contrast, Democrats controlled the House of Representatives for that entire twenty-six-year period and the Senate for all but six. This recurring partisan divide, the longest period of almost continual *divided government* in the nation's history, greatly aggravated relations between the executive and the legislature. Republican efforts to enhance the unilateral powers of the executive and circumvent legislative restrictions on presidential conduct were matched by Democratic initiatives to burden the executive with smothering oversight by congressional committees and statutory limits on presidential power.

The main forum for partisan conflict was a series of investigations in which the Democrats and Republicans sought to discredit one another. From the early 1970s to the mid-1980s, there was a tenfold increase in the number of indictments brought by federal prosecutors against national, state, and local officials, including more than a dozen members of Congress, several federal judges, and a number of high-ranking executive officials. This heightened legal scrutiny was partly a response to the Watergate scandal. In what became known as the "Saturday night massacre," Nixon fired special prosecutor Archibald Cox, who had been charged with investigating the scandal.

To prevent future "massacres," Congress passed the 1978 Ethics in Government Act. It provided for the appointment of *independent counsels* to investigate allegations of criminal activity by executive officials. Not surprisingly, divided government encouraged the exploitation of the act for partisan purposes. In the 1980s, congressional Democrats were able to demand criminal investigations and possible jail sentences for their political opponents. When Bill Clinton became president in 1992, congressional Republicans turned the table with a vengeance. Political disagreements were readily transformed into criminal charges, culminating in the impeachment of the president.

## The Midterm Rebellions

In the beginning of this chapter we emphasized the importance of midterm elections as devices for enabling the public to register its disapproval with the political direction in which the president was leading the country. Between 1994 and 2010 overwhelming midterm election victories by the party out of power dramatically served that purpose. Remarkably, however, none of these spectacular changes in voter preference led to a sustained period of undivided government. A mere two years after gaining control of both houses of Congress for the first time in a half-century, the Republicans were defeated in the presidential election of 1996. Only four years after regaining control of Congress in 2006, the Democrats suffered the worst loss of seats in the House of Representatives since 1938, losing control of that body, and lost seats in the Senate, as well. As we shall see, these landslide midterm victories excessively emboldened the victors, causing them to overreach and then be punished by the voters.

In 1994 Republicans gained control of both houses of Congress for the first time since the 1952 election. Sensing that Bill Clinton's efforts to expand government and raise taxes had become highly unpopular, the second-ranking House Republican, Minority Whip Newt Gingrich, persuaded more than 300 House candidates to sign a *Republican Contract with America* that promised to restore limited government by eliminating programs, lightening regulatory burdens, and cutting taxes. Although *exit polls* - surveys of voters after they voted – suggested that few voters had actually heard of the Republican manifesto, Clinton's attack on the contract during the campaign unwittingly served the Republican objective of turning the congressional elections into a national referendum on his presidency and the Democratic party. The president's assault backfired, serving only to abet Republicans in their effort to highlight his failure to move Democrats toward the center and mute partisan division in Washington.

The new House Republican majority chose Gingrich to be Speaker. Gingrich viewed Congress as a key part of the corrupt Washington establishment. He set out to reform House rules, promising to restore its constitutional responsibility to foster democratic debate and resolution. The number and size of committees were reduced, as were their staffs. Term limits were imposed on the speaker and committee and subcommittee chairs. Closed-door hearings and unrecorded votes were prohibited. Gingrich pledged a renewed emphasis on legislative debate that would "promote competition between different political philosophies." Yet the basic thrust of the Republican reforms was to centralize power in the hands of the party leadership. Party leaders strengthened their hold over committee chairmen, who in turn were empowered over subcommittee leaders. For the first time since Cannon was shorn of his powers, the Speaker of the House presumed to command the counsels of government, restoring Congress as the first branch of government. As Gingrich seized control of the legislative initiative during the early months of the 104th Congress, Clinton issued a plaintive reminder that "the President is relevant here."

The House Republicans provoked a fierce battle over the budget by advancing a bold plan to balance it by 2002. Clinton rejected key specifics of the plan; especially an effort to scale back the growth of Medicare by encouraging beneficiaries to enroll in health maintenance organizations and other privately managed health care systems. To pressure Clinton into accepting its budget-cutting priorities, Congress refused to extend government borrowing privileges, thereby shutting down government offices and threatening to put the U.S. treasury into default. These tactics backfired. Clinton's December 1995 veto of a sweeping budget bill that overhauled Medicare and revised decades of federal social policy roused popular support. Neither the Contract with America nor Speaker Gingrich's bravado had prepared the country for such a fundamental assault on the welfare state. In attacking Medicare and popular educational and environmental programs, Republicans went beyond their 1994 campaign promises. They, not Clinton, appeared to be the radicals in this budgetary brinkmanship. Clinton's triumph paved the way for his reelection victory a year later.

Clinton's reelection did not serve to dampen the House Republicans' partisan zeal. Rather, it goaded them into overreaching once again by impeaching him. In 1994 President Clinton asked the Justice Department to appoint a special prosecutor to investigate allegations against both him and his wife, Hillary Rodham

Clinton, stemming from their involvement in a failed real estate development scheme called Whitewater. In January 1998, Congress authorized independent counsel Kenneth Starr to expand the Whitewater inquiry to pursue allegations that the president had had an affair with White House intern Monica Lewinsky, and that he and his friend Vernon Jordan had encouraged her to lie about it under oath. Clinton not only denied the affair with Lewinsky but accused Starr, a prominent Republican, and his supporters in Congress of orchestrating a slanderous, partisan campaign to weaken the president.

Starr's relentless investigation uncovered evidence that forced Clinton to admit he had had an "improper relationship" with Lewinsky. In September 1998, Starr issued a report compiling a devastating chronicle of the president's adulterous affair and his months of subsequent lies. The House of Representatives, voting largely along party lines, approved a resolution calling for a full inquiry into possible grounds for impeachment. But the public continued to express overwhelming approval of Clinton's performance in office. Americans appreciated his successful management of the economy; disapproved of Starr's prosecutorial tactics, and were disgusted by the Republicans' sensationalization of the prosecutor's findings. Defying opinion polls, the House voted to *impeach* Clinton on charges of perjury and obstruction of justice. The vote split along partisan lines with only six Democrats voting for any of the articles of impeachment and only one Republican voting against them. After a five-week trial, on February 12, 1999, the Senate failed to produce the 2-3 vote needed to convict Clinton on any of the charges. It rejected the charge of perjury by a vote of fifty-five to forty-five, with ten Republicans voting against conviction; then, with five Republicans breaking ranks, the Senate split fifty-fifty on a second article accusing the president of obstruction of justice.

In 2006, Democrats scored massive gains in the House of Representatives and impressive gains in the Senate to regained full control of Congress for the first time since 1994. Because the Democrats lacked a veto-proof majority in the Senate their landslide victory did not immediately result in any major legislative victories. The 1994 Republicans were much more fortunate because much of their ambition lay in preventing the passage of Clinton Administration initiatives, whereas the 2006 Democrats sought new policy reforms, which President Bush could still prevent by exercising his veto. The most important short-term consequence of the Democratic victory was the election of Nancy Pelosi (D-CA) as Speaker of the House. Pelosi proved to be the most powerful Speaker since Gingrich. Like Gingrich, she came from the liberal, not the moderate, wing of her party. Her great influence would not be felt until the 2008 election put a Democrat, Barack Obama, in the White House.

With control of Congress and the presidency in Democratic hands, the period 2008–2010 would witness the greatest outpouring of new and ambitious policy changes since the heyday of LBJ's Great Society, 1964–1966. In order to

cultivate close ties to the House leadership and ensure passage of his top legislative priority, healthcare reform, the president put the chief responsibility for
crafting the legislation in the hands of Congress. Pelosi showed extraordinary
leadership ability as she kept her fractious supporters in line behind a truly
ambitious pathbreaking bill. However, she paid an enormous price for this sin-
gleness of purpose. She failed to obtain the vote of a single Republican support
for the measure. By contrast, Republicans supported the Social Security Act
of 1935 by a margin of better than three to one in the Senate and better than
five to one in the House. A majority of House Republicans supported Medicare.
Thirteen Senate Republicans also voted for it, whereas seventeen were opposed.
Each of these landmark pieces of legislation could make a credible claim to having been passed on a bipartisan basis. The Healthcare Reform Law of 2010 could
make no such claim.

Final passage of the Healthcare Act was only achieved because the House and
Senate Democratic leaders resorted to an irregular and highly controversial procedural maneuver. On November 7, 2009, the House passed its version of health
reform 220 to 215. On December 24, 2009, the Senate cut off a filibuster and
passed its own version of health reform by a vote of sixty to thirty-nine. But
before a conference committee could forge a compromise and obtain passage
from both houses, the Senate lost their sixty-member majority needed for cloture
against the filibuster the Republicans had promised to mount against a compromise bill. Senator Edward Kennedy (D-MA) died, leaving the Democrats with a
Senate majority of only fifty-nine. A special election held to replace him was
won by a Republican, Scott Brown, who had pledged to support a Republican
filibuster. To thwart the Republicans, the House and Senate leadership found a
way to avoid the need for a cloture vote. They adapted a procedure designed for
dealing with strictly budgetary issues called *reconciliation* to enable the Senate
to pass the measure by majority vote. No piece of legislation as important as the
health care bill had ever been adopted by the Senate in this manner. The Senate
Parliamentarian ruled that using reconciliation for this purpose did not violate
Senate rules. Nonetheless, Republicans called it a violation of Senate tradition,
likening it to the "nuclear option" for circumventing the Democrats' filibuster
of Bush's judicial nominees that they had refrained from invoking when they
were in the majority. Because the health care measure proved to be unpopular
with the public, the Republicans benefited politically from their unqualified
opposition to it. Another major Democratic initiative, the nearly $800 billion
stimulus package aimed at resuscitating the economy in the wake of the financial collapse of 2008, likewise received no Republican votes in the House and
only three in the Senate.

If public opinion had been strongly in support of these initiatives, the lack
of minority party support might not have proven so politically damaging. But
opinion polls revealed a majority of the public opposed both of them. The

Democrats gambled that once the bills passed, their popularity would improve, but this was not the case. The unambiguous opposition to these measures shown by the Republicans established a clear choice in the voters mind. If one opposed these new laws one should vote for the Republicans, and in the 2010 congressional elections a great majority of voters did just that. In 2012, despite President Obama's reelection, the Republicans retained their strong grip on the House of Representatives but lost two seats in the Senate.

## CONCLUSION

As we have seen, the greatest source of Congress's strength is the powers provided for it in the Constitution. But those powers alone would not have sufficed to preserve its viability were it not for its remarkable adaptive capacity. Inspired by Henry Clay, the House developed an internal organizational structure and modes of leadership that enabled it to effectively carry out its constitutional duties. A strong Speaker of the House and the allocation of the House workload among a group of specialized committees remain critical attributes of the current Congress. Later in the nineteenth century the party system served to further guide and discipline congressional performance, as it still does today. In the twentieth century the rise of the personalized presidency did indeed put an end to congressional preeminence. Contrary to the Founders' expectations Congress is no longer the first branch of government. As Chapter 8 discusses, the public regards the president, not Congress, as the embodiment of government, the chief organ for exercising democratic rule.

Nonetheless, Congress has managed to retain its critical role in the constitutional system of checks and balances. The constitutional requirement of midterm elections has preserved its legislative independence. Those elections limit the president's ability to dominate Congress to his first two years in office. Then the voters have the chance to vote in a hostile Congress, one capable of minimizing his legislative influence. As the 2010 election so vividly demonstrated, midterm congressional elections serve as one of the most valuable means for ensuring democratic accountability. Furthermore, the Congress has also developed its own novel adaptive devices for maintaining its power and influence. The critical role of the Congressional Budget Office in providing independent revenue and spending estimates and the procedural reforms that restored power to the House leadership are powerful examples of Congress's ability to successfully adapt to the challenge posed by a powerful executive, and the inherent difficulty of turning such a large and diverse body into an effective legislative instrument. The modern Congress is not the Congress of "Czar" Reed, but thanks to Article One of the Constitution and its remarkable ability to recover from adversity, it remains the world's most powerful legislative body.

## CHAPTER SUMMARY

☆ The Framers designed the Congress both to provide for democratic accountability and limit the threat to liberty and stability resulting from an excess of democracy.

☆ In order to perform its democratic function of passing laws that reflect majority sentiment and republican function of holding executive power in check, Congress needed a unifying force. Political parties provided that force.

☆ During the mid-nineteenth century, Congress became the great national theater in which passionate and lively debate over such critical issues as slavery, tariff policy, the bank, and the money supply took place, helping draw the public into struggles about the most fundamental political issues.

☆ In the post–Civil War period, Congress achieved its highest level of dominance by combining strong congressional leadership with even greater political party control of the congressional nomination and election process.

☆ The tight grip of party leadership deprived Congress of its ability to serve as the primary arena for debating the great issue of the time, as it had done before the Civil War.

☆ Congress's reaction to the rise of the presidency, beginning in the early twentieth century, transformed Congress's organization and practices to make legislators policy specialists. Party organization gave way to narrowly focused autonomous committees, which enabled representatives to acquire expertise in programs that served their ambition and encouraged them to make Congress their career.

☆ Enacted in 1913, the Seventeenth Amendment provided that senators be elected by voters, not state legislatures.

☆ The Progressive revolt of the early twentieth century deprived party leaders of the power to choose chairs. Instead, committee assignments and chairmanships were based on seniority.

☆ Starting in the late 1960s a significant resurgence of congressional power occurred spurred both by dissatisfaction with presidential leadership of the war in Vietnam and President Nixon's abuses of executive power.

☆ The longest period of almost continual divided government in the nation's history, lasting from 1968 to 1992, greatly aggravated relations between the executive and legislature. Republican efforts to enhance the unilateral powers of the executive and circumvent legislative restrictions on presidential conduct were matched by Democratic initiatives to burden the executive with smothering oversight by congressional committees and statutory limits on presidential power.

☆ Between 1994 and 2010, the party out of power won three overwhelming midterm-election victories. These results vividly demonstrate the importance of midterm elections as devices for enabling the public to register disapproval with the political direction in which the president was leading the country. Remarkably, however, none of these spectacular changes in voter preference led to a sustained period of undivided government. Rather, these landslide midterm victories excessively emboldened the victors, causing them to overreach and then be punished by the voters.

## MAJOR TERMS AND CONCEPTS

| | |
|---|---|
| Appropriations Committees | Bicameralism |
| Cloture | Committee and Subcommittee Staff |
| Congressional Budget Office | Congressional Committee |
| Congressional Research Service | Divided Government |
| Executive Privilege | Filibuster |
| General Accountability Office | House Rules Committee |
| Impeachment | Impoundment |
| Independent Counsels | Joint Conference Committee |
| Midterm Congressional Elections | Multiple Committee Referrals |
| Oversight | Party Caucus |
| Personal Staff | Power of the Purse |
| Protective Tariff | Quorum |
| Reapportionment | Reconciliation |
| Republican Contract with America | Seniority |
| Seniority System | Speaker of the House |
| Subcommittee Government | Turnover |
| *U.S. v. Nixon* | Watergate |

## SUGGESTED READINGS

Binder, Sarah. *Stalemate: Causes and Consequences of Legislative Gridlock*. Washington, DC: Brookings Institution Press, 2003.

Cooper, Joseph, ed. *Congress and the Decline of Public Trust*. Boulder, CO: Westview Press, 1999.

Dodd, Lawrence C., and Bruce Ian Oppenheimer, eds. *Congress Reconsidered*, 7th ed. Washington, DC: CQ Press, 2000.

Dodd, Lawrence C., and Richard Schott, eds. *Congress and the Administrative State*. New York: John Wiley, 1979.

Fenno, Richard E. *Congressmen in Committees*. Boston: Little, Brown, 1973.

Fenno, Richard E. *Home Style: House Members in Their Districts*. Boston: Little, Brown, 1978.

Fiorina, Morris. *Congress: Keystone of the Washington Establishment*, 2nd ed. New Haven, CT: Yale University Press, 1989.

Ginsberg, Benjamin, and Martin Shefter. *Politics by Other Means: Politicians, Prosecutors, and the Press from Watergate to Whitewater*, 3rd ed. New York: W. W. Norton, 2003.

Hibbing, John R., and Elizabeth Theiss-Morse. *Congress as Public Enemy: Public Attitudes toward American Political Institutions*. New York: Cambridge University Press, 1996.

Jacobson, Gary. *The Politics of Congressional Elections*, 5th ed. New York: Addison-Wesley, 2000.

Lee, Frances. *Beyond Ideology: Politics, Principles, and Partisanship in the U. S. Senate*. Chicago: Chicago University Press, 2009.

Mayhew, David. *Congress: The Electoral Connection*. New Haven, CT: Yale University Press, 1986.

Peters, Ronald M., Jr. *The American Speakership: The Office in Historical Perspective*, 2nd ed. Baltimore, MD: Johns Hopkins University Press, 1997.

Polsby, Nelson W. *How Congress Evolves: Social Bases of Institutional Change*. New York: Oxford University Press, 2003.

Rohde, David W. *Parties and Leaders in the Postreform House*. Chicago: University of Chicago Press, 1991.

Schickler, Eric. *Disjointed Pluralism: Institutional Innovation and the Development of the U.S. Congress*. Princeton, NJ: Princeton University Press, 2001.

Sundquist, James L. *The Decline and Resurgence of Congress*. Washington, DC: Brookings Institution, 2002.

Theriault, Sean. *Party Polarization in Congress*. New York: Cambridge University Press, 2008.

Wawro, Gregory, and Schickler, *Filibuster: Obstruction and Lawmaking in the U.S. Senate*. Princeton, NJ: Princeton University Press, 2006.

# CHAPTER 8 ☆ The Presidency

## CHAPTER OVERVIEW

This chapter focuses on:

☆ A contemporary portrait of the Obama presidency.

☆ George Washington's role as precedent setter for the presidency.

☆ The critical roles of Jefferson, Jackson, and Lincoln in shaping the presidency.

☆ The role of Theodore Roosevelt, Woodrow Wilson, and FDR in transforming the office.

☆ The growing personalization of the presidency since FDR.

On September 22, 1993, in the midst of his battle to overhaul the U.S. health care system, President Bill Clinton gave a critical speech to a joint session of Congress. The president considered this speech the most important one of his life, the moment at which he would launch a titanic struggle to enact a program that would affect the lives of every citizen and one-seventh of the U.S. economy. Understandably, Clinton felt great pressure as he looked out on the assembled dignitaries, but tension nearly dissolved into panic when he found the wrong speech displayed in the TelePrompTer. He furtively signaled to Vice President Al Gore, sitting behind him on the dais, and then proceeded to improvise. After seven harrowing minutes, the president's aides, notified by the vice president of the mishap, managed to insert the right speech.

Clinton's prepared remarks called for government to "guarantee all Americans a comprehensive package of [health care] benefits over an entire lifetime." He brandished a red, white, and blue "health security card" – similar to the Social Security card Americans carry – to symbolize that this plan would be the greatest extension of the welfare state since enactment of Social Security in 1935. The program would mandate employer-paid insurance, provide benefits to nonworkers, and create federal purchasing alliances to regulate managed care and control costs.

The president's speech was very well received in the hall. Clinton's pollster, Stanley Greenberg, reported that the Dayton, Ohio, focus group he had convened to provide instantaneous public reaction was also highly favorable to both Clinton's impromptu and planned remarks. The president and his aides would have been shocked to discover that this spine-tingling oratorical episode would prove to be the high point of their battle for health care reform. The TelePrompTer gaffe foreshadowed more serious and irremediable problems. Ensuring that no American will go without health care was a popular idea, but the complexity of the 1,342-page plan and the prospect of government controls on such a large and pervasive industry eventually turned the public and Congress against it. In September 1994, almost a year to the day after Clinton introduced the Health Security Act with such fanfare, Senate majority leader George Mitchell declared the president's bill dead.

Clinton's healthcare debacle illustrates that surveys and focus groups can be a very unreliable basis of support for presidential causes. A president, particularly one as politically gifted as Clinton, can dominate the national political agenda. But as both of his successors, George W. Bush and Barack Obama, would also discover, the president's powerful public presence does not necessarily enable him to achieve his policy goals. This case also illustrates an uneasy relationship between the people, the president, and the welfare state. Since the Great Depression of the 1930s, Americans have tended to view the national government – and its steward, the president – as the guarantor of economic and social security. They view government entitlements favorably but reject the centralized power necessary to implement those policies. This contradiction poses a profound challenge for public officials, especially for the president.

This chapter begins with a contemporary portrait of the presidency. Then it analyzes how the presidency was intended to fit into the overall constitutional order and how the first, precedent-setting president interpreted his constitutional mandate. Next, the chapter looks at the democratization of the office, especially as it was accomplished by Thomas Jefferson and Andrew Jackson. It discusses how Abraham Lincoln harnessed the democratic energy that was now attached to the office to produce a new public philosophy, a "new birth of freedom" that ended slavery and revised the Constitution to guarantee civil rights. Then the chapter charts the rise of the modern presidency after its post-Lincoln decline, with special attention to the role of the Progressive movement. The focus shifts to Franklin D. Roosevelt and the New Deal to show the flowering of the modern presidency. The rest of the chapter describes the presidency as it has developed since FDR. The focus here is on the growing personalization of the presidency, how it has come increasingly to serve as the very personification of government, and the opportunities and pitfalls that this shift in the stature and prominence of the office has created.

## THE PRESIDENT: A CONTEMPORARY PORTRAIT

Article Two of the Constitution vests the *executive power* in the president and assigns the president specific duties to perform. As president, Barack Obama has performed the duties specified, but those amount to only a part of the many critical roles he, like his modern predecessors, has adopted and the myriad other activities he engages in. This portrait of the Obama presidency first looks at the constitutional duties he has performed continues with the constitutional duties that he, and his modern predecessors, has expanded on, and finishes by discussing those of the presidency with no clear constitutional basis.

The President shall be Commander in Chief of the Army and Navy of the United States, and of the Militia of the several States, when called into the actual Service of the United States.

As commander in chief, President Obama has made many critical military decisions. In September 2009, he rescinded an agreement President Bush had reached with Czechoslovakia and Poland to install missile systems in those two countries designed to defend against a future Iranian missile attack. On December 1, 2009, in a speech delivered at West Point, he announced that he would send an additional 30,000 troops to Afghanistan. He also approved of the Central Intelligence Agency's (CIA) plan to fire unmanned drones at targets in Pakistan. In March of 2011 he committed U.S. warplanes to take part in the United Nations-sponsored military mission in Libya. In May of 2011 he authorized a raid by Navy SEALS on a compound of houses in Abbottabad, Pakistan, in order to kill Osama Bin Laden, the leader of Al Queda. In December of 2011 he completed the withdrawal of U.S. troops from Iraq.

The President's commander in chief authority can also have domestic ramifications. As part of the government's response to the worst oil spill in American history, he ordered National Guardsmen from four states to join in combating the spill.

He shall have Power, by and with the Advice and Consent of the Senate, to make Treaties.

In April of 2010 President Obama and President Medvedev of Russia signed a treaty pledging both nations to reduce their stockpile of nuclear weapons. The treaty requires the United States and Russia to diminish their strategic nuclear warheads by approximately one-third over a period of seven years from the present limit of 2,200 to 1,550. Both nations also agreed to limit their land-, sea-, and air-based missile launchers to 800 each. Congress did not consider the

Treaty until after the 2010 elections that returned control of the House to the Republicans. Although many Republicans voiced displeasure with aspects of the Treaty, it passed.

He shall nominate, and by and with the Advice and Consent of the Senate, shall appoint Ambassadors, other public Ministers and Consuls, Judges of the Supreme Court, and all other Officers of the United States, whose Appointments are not herein otherwise provided for, and which shall be established by Law.

As of October 2010 Obama had appointed and the Senate had confirmed 119 ambassadors and 86 federal judges, including two Supreme Court nominees. As of 2008 7,996 positions were available to be chosen by the president rather than be filled through the civil service (see Chapter 10). Of those, only 1,141 required senatorial confirmation. Considering that there are almost 3 million federal employees, the number subject to presidential appointment is quite small.

The president's cabinet includes the vice president and the heads of fifteen executive departments. These departments are listed in Figure 8.1. Unlike in a parliamentary system, the cabinet is not an official policy-making body. The president is not obligated to ask it for its collective opinion or to go along with those opinions. The president's vary in how frequently they call the cabinet into session. Reagan held thirty-six cabinet meetings, whereas Clinton held only six. President's often find it far more useful to speak informally to those few cabinet members who have deep knowledge of a particular problem he is facing than to call the entire group into session for a formal meeting.

Every Bill which shall have passed the House of Representatives and the Senate, shall, before it become a law, be presented to the President of the United States: If he approve he shall sign it, but if not he shall return it, with his Objections to that House in which it shall have originated.

If any Bill shall not be returned by the President within ten Days (Sundays excepted) after it shall have been presented to him, the Same shall be a Law, in like Manner as if he had signed it, unless the Congress by their Adjournment prevent its Return, in which Case it shall not be a Law.

The president's party enjoyed substantial majorities in both Houses of Congress during his first two years in office, and therefore Obama made minimal use of his *veto* power. He did not cast his first veto until he had been in office for practically a year, and he did so with regard to a matter of trivial importance. His one significant veto was cast against a bill that would have facilitated home foreclosures by requiring federal and state courts to accept and recognize mortgage-related documents signed in other states. Because Congress was no longer in session when the bill reached his desk, Obama chose the option of simply not signing the bill, which had the effect of terminating it. This option, available only under the conditions described in the above quote from the Constitution, is

- Department of Agriculture (USDA)
- Department of Commerce (DOC)
- Department of Defense (DOD)
- Department of Education (ED)
- Department of Energy (DOE)
- Department of Health and Human Services (HHS)
- Department of Homeland Security (DHS)
- Department of Housing and Urban Development (HUD)
- Department of Justice (DOJ)
- Department of Labor (DOL)
- Department of State (DOS)
- Department of the Interior (DOI)
- Department of the Treasury
- Department of Transportation (DOT)
- Department of Veterans Affairs (VA)

**Figure 8.1.** Executive departments.

called a *pocket veto*. Despite the return of Republican control to the House of Representatives in 2010, Obama did not cast a single veto in 2011.

## Expansive Powers

The Constitution gives the president legislative responsibilities and some power to oversee the activities of his subordinates in the executive branch. But the text of Article Two is quite modest when compared to the very extensive legislative and managerial leadership President Obama and all his modern predecessors have displayed.

He shall from time to time give to the Congress Information on the State of the Union, and recommend to their Consideration such Measures as he shall judge necessary and expedient.

President Obama has delivered state of the union addresses in February of each year of his presidency, but he has done far more than make recommendations to Congress. He has been the dominant force in setting the congressional legislative agenda and serving as the chief advocate for the matters he has placed onto that agenda. The health care plan that became law in 2010 is one of the most ambitious new social programs adopted in modern times. Congress passed it, but the president was its champion. He performed his role as chief salesmen by mobilizing public opinion to pressure Congress to act. President Obama launched his health care campaign by hosting The White House Forum on Healthcare Reform, attended by senior members of Congress and leaders of such prestigious and powerful lobbying organizations as the Teamsters, The American Association of Retired People, the U.S. Chamber of Congress, and the Children's Defense Fund. The only other speaker to address the entire gathering besides the president was not a health care expert or a prominent politician, but rather an ordinary citizen, a firefighter and emergency medical technician from Dublin, Indiana, Travis Ulerick. Ulerick had served as a host at one of the hundreds of health care community discussions that the White House had sponsored and that were attended by 30,000 people. The reason for featuring Ulerick was to demonstrate to members of Congress that Obama's health care plan had the strong support of people who were just like the voters in their home districts.

The energy and effort that President Obama put into galvanizing public opinion for health care reform exceeded what any previous president had expended on a single legislative proposal. In June of 2009 ABC News televised "Questions for the President: Prescription for America." On a Wednesday night, during the coveted prime time hour between 10:00 and 11:00 PM, President Obama answered questions about his health care proposal from an audience chosen by ABC to represent a cross section of ordinary people. The White House organized nine events with a similar format that it called "Town Meetings" in towns and cities in various parts of the country. In addition, President Obama gave fifty-four speeches and public statements on health care reform and devoted thirteen of his Saturday radio and Internet addresses to the topic.

He may require the Opinion, in writing, of the principal Officer in each of the executive Departments, upon any Subject relating to the Duties of their respective Offices.

This is the only clause in the Constitution that describes how presidential appointees relate to the president. It gives no indication of the breadth and depth of executive-branch responsibilities or the president's deep immersion in the attempt to direct and manage executive-branch activities. Federal judges and many members of independent regulatory commissions are appointed by the president but cannot be fired by him, thus, he exerts direct control over an even smaller number of federal employees than his appointments power would seem to indicate. Nor does he have automatic authority to rearrange the bureaus, agencies, commissions, and departments that comprise the executive branch. Under current law, such reorganizations must pass Congress. President Bush undertook two major reorganizations: the creation of the DHS as authorized by the *Homeland Security Act of 2002* and the reorganization of the intelligence services as authorized by the *Intelligence Reform and Terrorism Prevention Act of 2004*.

President Obama has not chosen to embark on any reorganization. Instead, he has relied on executive orders to make major shifts in how the executive branch operates. An executive order is a legally binding instruction to a federal agency. It can only be used regarding matters within the proper scope of the president's power and therefore cannot usurp matters that require congressional approval. Obama has used executive orders for a wide variety of purposes. His order to the CIA regarding prisoner interrogation was his signal to Congress, the American public, and the world of a major change in how the War on Terror would be conducted. The order required the CIA to abandon the harsh methods the Bush Administration had permitted and follow the same guidelines, detailed in the Army Field Manual, which the military was required to abide by. Obama also ordered the agency to close any secret detention facilities overseas.

Executive orders can also serve as a means for negotiating with Congress. Several Democratic congressmen were refusing to support the health care reform bill because they believed that it opened the door to federal funding of abortion. To win their support, Obama issued an executive order proclaiming that nothing in the new health care law would alter the congressionally imposed abortion funding ban. Of the sixty-five executive orders Obama issued during his first twenty months in office, almost half of them were designed to create organizations – taskforces, commissions, boards or committees – whose purpose was to conduct investigations and/or provide information and advice either directly to him or some part of the executive branch. Because such bodies lack decision-making and enforcement authority they do not require congressional approval. Among the advisory bodies Obama ordered into being were: the National Ocean Council; the President's Management Advisory Board; National Commission on Fiscal Responsibility and Reform; and Interagency Task Force on Veterans Small Business Development.

As the size, complexity, and scope of the executive branch has grown, the challenge of controlling it has grown apace. As we shall see later on in this chapter, it was only in the late 1930s that Congress created an executive office of the president providing him with staff to help him manage the federal bureaucracy. In Chapter 10 we will discuss two of its most important managerial tools, the Office of Management and Budget and the National Security Staff. Figure 8.2 lists the specific components of the Executive Office of the President.

The EOP is now so large that most of it is housed outside the White House. But because the president needs a great deal of staff assistance on a minute-to-minute basis there is also a White House Office situated in the West Wing of the building and made famous by the television series entitled "The West Wing." Presidents each have their own distinctive approach to governing, therefore the precise nature and composition of the West Wing changes with each presidential administration. However, certain key aspects remain constant. The West Wing always includes a press secretary and a staff of speech writers to manage the president's relations with the media and produce drafts of speeches and

- Council of Economic Advisers
- Council on Environmental Quality
- Domestic Policy Council
- National Economic Council
- National Security Council (NSC)
- Office of Administration
- Office of Management and Budget (OMB)
- Office of National AIDS Policy
- Office of National Drug Control Policy
- Office of Science and Technology Policy
- Office of the United States Trade Representative
- Serve.gov Volunteer Network
- White House Military Office

**Figure 8.2.** The executive office of the President.

messages. It also includes a person, sometimes referred to as the White House chief of staff and sometimes by another name, which supervises and coordinates the West Wing as a whole. That person may also serve as the president's personal chief of staff, working closely with him to plan political and legislative strategy and how best to manage the president's time. However, the closest and most trusted aide to the president may hold some other post in the West Wing. Valerie Jarrett was widely considered to be the advisor whom Obama most relied on. Her official title was Senior Advisor to the President and Assistant to the President for Intergovernmental Relations and Public Engagement.

### The Contemporary Presidency: Beyond the Constitution

The duties assigned to Congress in Article One of the Constitution dwarf this short list assigned to the president. And yet the president is the political figure that looms largest in American political life. The public is kept informed of all his activities, even those that would normally be considered private. We know that the Obamas have a dog. Furthermore, we know that it is a male, neutered Portuguese Water Dog named Bo. We are kept informed about the activities of his children, his difficulties quitting smoking, and his reluctance to give up his Blackberry. He has a large staff devoted to making sure that the messages and image he wants to convey reach the public via all the key forms of mass communications – print, internet, radio, and television. His face is regularly on the cover of the news magazines and the front pages of the newspapers. His activities are regularly the lead on national television and radio news. E-mails from him go out to millions of his supporters. He and his wife Michelle have their own Facebook pages and Twitter accounts.

This exposure extends worldwide. As the president of the most economically and militarily powerful country in the world, President Obama's words and deeds carry far more weight abroad than the words and deeds of foreign leaders carry in the United States. More than most presidents, Obama has sought to use his fame and prestige to improve relations with other countries. During his 2008 campaign, he promised to speak to Muslims worldwide from the capital of a prominent Muslim nation. On June 4, 2009, he fulfilled that promise. He gave a speech in Cairo, Egypt, that was broadcast live throughout the Middle East and South Asia via satellite. The speech emphasized reconciliation with Muslim countries and a sense of mutual respect between the West and Islam.

As a further demonstration of his aim to improve the United States' image and prestige, Obama traveled to more countries than any previous president. During his first year in office, Obama made nine trips overseas. Among the countries he visited were: China, Japan, Korea, Egypt, Norway, Denmark, Ghana, and Russia. His first trip to Denmark was especially noteworthy because it involved none of the activities traditionally engaged in by a visiting head of state – meetings with leaders of the host nation, attending conferences of heads of state, dealing with international security or economic issues. Rather, it was for the sole purpose of meeting with the International Olympic Committee in order to urge it to choose Chicago as the venue for the 2016 Olympic Games. Obama was in Denmark for three hours. He learned during his flight back to the United States that Chicago's bid had been rejected.

A major preoccupation of the president regards a political entity not even mentioned in the constitution: his political party. President Obama is the *party leader* of the Democrats. He is its most effective fund-raiser and he dominates its national committee. Most importantly, he campaigns for Democratic candidates. In 2009 the election contests of national significance were the gubernatorial elections in New Jersey and Virginia. President Obama made campaign appearances in support of the Democratic candidates in both those states. In February of 2010 a special election for U.S. senator was held in Massachusetts to fill the seat left vacant by the death of Senator Edward Kennedy. Obama came to Massachusetts to campaign for the Democratic candidate. Each of the Democrats lost.

The 2010 midterm elections were an even grimmer reminder of how fragile the president's grip is on power. It was the worst defeat suffered by the majority party and its leader, the president, in many decades. The Democrats relinquished control of the House of Representatives, losing sixty-one seats. They also lost 6 governorships and close to 700 seats more in state legislatures around the country. Like Bill Clinton, President Obama's command of the airwaves and his great attractiveness as a public figure could not prevent him from suffering a devastating political defeat a mere two years after his own electoral triumph. Figure 8.3 provides a list of the presidents and vice presidents of the United States in chronological order. It also shows how long they served and what political party each belonged to.

| # | PRESIDENT | VICE PRESIDENT | TERM | PARTY |
|---|-----------|----------------|------|-------|
| 1 | George Washington | John Adams | 1789–1793 | None |
|   |   | John Adams | 1793–1797 |   |
| 2 | John Adams | Thomas Jefferson | 1797–1801 | Federalist |
| 3 | Thomas Jefferson | Aaron Burr | 1801–1805 | Republican |
|   |   | George Clinton | 1805–1809 |   |
| 4 | James Madison | George Clinton | 1809–1813 | Republican |
|   |   | Elbridge Gerry | 1813–1817 |   |
| 5 | James Monroe | Daniel D. Tompkins | 1817–1821 | Republican |
|   |   |   | 1821–1825 |   |
| 6 | John Quincy Adams | John C. Calhoun | 1825–1829 | Republican |
| 7 | Andrew Jackson | John C. Calhoun | 1829–1833 | Democrat |
|   |   | Martin Van Buren | 1833–1837 |   |
| 8 | Martin Van Buren | Richard M. Johnson | 1837–1841 | Democrat |
| 9 | William Henry Harrison | John Tyler | 1841 | Whig |
| 10 | John Tyler | None | 1841–1845 | Whig |
| 11 | James K. Polk | George M. Dallas | 1845–1849 | Democrat |
| 12 | Zachary Taylor | Millard Fillmore | 1849–1850 | Whig |
| 13 | Millard Fillmore | None | 1850–1853 | Whig |
| 14 | Franklin Pierce | William R. King | 1853–1857 | Democrat |
| 15 | James Buchanan | John C. Breckinridge | 1857–1861 | Democrat |
| 16 | Abraham Lincoln | Hannibal Hamlin | 1861–1865 | Republican |
|   |   | Andrew Johnson | 1865 |   |
| 17 | Andrew Johnson | None | 1865–1869 | Democrat |
| 18 | Ulysses S. Grant | Schuyler Colfax | 1869–1873 | Republican |
|   |   | Henry Wilson | 1873–1877 |   |
| 19 | Rutherford B. Hayes | William A. Wheeler | 1877–1881 | Republican |
| 20 | James Garfield | Chester A. Arthur | 1881–1881 | Republican |
| 21 | Chester A. Arthur | None | 1881–1885 | Republican |
| 22 | Grover Cleveland | Thomas A. Hendricks | 1885–1889 | Democratic |
| 23 | Benjamin Harrison | Levi P. Morton | 1889–1893 | Republican |
| 24 | Grover Cleveland | Adlai E. Stevenson | 1893–1897 | Democratic |
| 25 | William McKinley | Garret A. Hobart | 1897–1901 | Republican |
|   |   | Theodore Roosevelt | 1901 |   |

**Figure 8.3.** The presidents of the United States.

| #  | PRESIDENT | VICE PRESIDENT | TERM | PARTY |
|----|-----------|----------------|------|-------|
| 26 | Theodore Roosevelt | Charles W. Fairbanks | 1901–1905<br>1905–1909 | Republican |
| 27 | William H. Taft | James S. Sherman | 1909–1913 | Republican |
| 28 | Woodrow Wilson | Thomas R. Marshall | 1913–1917<br>1917–1921 | Democrat |
| 29 | Warren G. Harding | Calvin Coolidge | 1921–1923 | Republican |
| 30 | Calvin Coolidge | Charles G. Dawes | 1923–1925<br>1925–1929 | Republican |
| 31 | Herbert C. Hoover | Charles Curtis | 1929–1933 | Republican |
| 32 | Franklin D. Roosevelt | John N. Garner<br>Henry A. Wallace<br>Harry S. Truman | 1933–1937<br>1937–1941<br>1941–1945<br>1945 | Democrat |
| 33 | Harry S. Truman | Alben Barkley | 1945–1949<br>1949–1953 | Democrat |
| 34 | Dwight D. Eisenhower | Richard M. Nixon | 1953–1961 | Republican |
| 35 | John F. Kennedy | Lyndon B. Johnson | 1961–1963 | Democrat |
| 36 | Lyndon B. Johnson | None<br>Hubert H. Humphrey | 1963–1965<br>1965–1968 | Democrat |
| 37 | Richard M. Nixon | Spiro T. Agnew<br>Gerald R. Ford | 1969–1973<br>1973–1974 | Republican |
| 38 | Gerald R. Ford | Nelson A. Rockefeller | 1974–1977 | Republican |
| 39 | Jimmy Carter | Walter F. Mondale | 1977–1981 | Democrat |
| 40 | Ronald W. Reagan | George H.W. Bush<br>George H.W. Bush | 1981–1985<br>1985–1989 | Republican |
| 41 | George Herbert Walker Bush | Dan Quayle | 1989–1993 | Republican |
| 42 | William J. Clinton | Albert Gore Jr. | 1993–1997<br>1997–2001 | Democrat |
| 43 | George Walker Bush | Richard B. Cheney | 2001–2005<br>2005–2009 | Republican |
| 44 | Barack H. Obama | Joseph Robinette Biden, Jr. | 2009- | Democrat |

**Figure 8.3** (*cont.*)

## POLITICAL DEVELOPMENT

### Washington: President as Precedent Maker

As we discussed in Chapter 3, the decision to establish a president and grant him significant powers was made grudgingly. The only reason that many doubters about the wisdom of granting a single man so much power was their certainty that the first president would by George Washington. He was the most respected and beloved American and he had already proven that he could be trusted not to make himself a tyrant. In 1783 he had refused to join the so-called Newburgh Mutiny staged by some of his senior officers in the hopes of toppling the Continental Congress and installing him as king. As the doubters hoped, Washington firmly established the republican character of the office. But as the proponents of a strong executive hoped, he also showed that the president was no mere clerk. He asserted the president's right to create a link directly to the people. And, as the president's oath of office demanded, he also proved that the president could respond swiftly and decisively to threats to the nation's security, thereby "preserving and protecting the Constitution."

Washington's determination to maintain the republican character of the office was evident in the very first controversy that arose regarding the president: what to call him? A committee of the House of Representatives wanted to address him simply as "the President of the United States." But the Senate, at the behest of Vice President John Adams, rejected the House committee's report. Because "titles and politically inspired elegance were essential aspects of strong government," Adams insisted he be addressed as "His Highness the President of the United States and Protector of Their Liberties." Madison led House opposition to what he took to be antirepublican terminology. He was supported by President Washington, who made known his annoyance at Adam's efforts "to bedizen [him] with a superb but spurious title." The Senate proposal was defeated. The chief executive would have no more august title than the President of the United States. Adams's efforts to give the presidency aristocratic airs led him to be nicknamed "His Rotundity."

Washington rejected the substance as well as the trappings of monarchy. Hamilton had argued in *Federalist Paper* No. 73 that the president should veto bad laws, but Washington disagreed. He cast only two vetoes, both on constitutional grounds. One was in response to a measure he considered unconstitutional. The other was in response to a bill that undermined national security and therefore, as commander in chief, required his veto. Most importantly, Washington voluntarily stepped down after completing his second term, although the Constitution did not require him to do so, thereby establishing an enduring precedent for peacefully and lawfully relinquishing presidential power.

Washington strengthened the presidency even as he preserved its republican character. The Constitution does not empower the president to address the people. Indeed, his duty to preserve the presidency in the face of popular intemperance might be understood to preclude such direct address. Nonetheless, early in his term Washington issued a proclamation honoring Thanksgiving Day. This seemingly innocuous gesture established the tradition of direct popular communication that provides much of the president's power and prestige. Although far more circumspect than Clinton or Obama's pleadings for healthcare reform, Washington's proclamation supported his conviction that communication between the nation's first citizen and its people was a vital form of civic education.

Washington also defended the president's capacity to manage the executive branch. As we have seen, the Constitution grants the president extensive appointment powers as well as the right to obtain in writing the views of the principal executive officers. But it does not declare the president to be in control of those departments, nor does it give the executive a clear directive to treat employees as subordinates. If Washington had not insisted that all members of the executive branch were in fact his "deputies," the president might have become, as the name suggests, a mere "presider" who ceded actual control over executive affairs to individual department heads acting in conjunction with their senior associates and powerful members of Congress.

The Constitution requires the president to obtain the advice and consent of the Senate when appointing department heads. Many representatives assumed that, by implication, Senate confirmation was also necessary for the president to fire an executive official. Washington disagreed. In a bill establishing the Department of State, Congress decided to allow the president to fire executive officials on his own, to grant him *removal power,* but only after Vice President Adams broke a tie in the Senate. From then on, Congress passed laws to establish the major departments of government that were carefully designed to minimize the legislature's influence in the executive branch. If the president had been a less universally admired and trusted figure than Washington, at least one more senator would probably have voted no, and the deputy theory would not have become part of the unofficial Constitution.

Washington asserted presidential authority regarding both domestic insurrection and foreign threat. Several western Pennsylvania towns resisted a federal whiskey excise tax and drove away the tax collectors. Washington summoned troops to quell the uprising, commanding them himself. He risked his prestige to enforce the principle of national supremacy. In the face of a Washington-led army, the rebellion dissolved (Figure 8.4).

The Constitution gave the president no authority to dissolve treaties or to declare peace, a power that seemed intimately related to Congress' power to declare war. Washington determined that the mutual defense treaty with France threatened war with Britain, so he broke it, issuing the Neutrality *Proclamation of*

**Figure 8.4.** Commander in chief: President Washington sends troops to put down the Whiskey Rebellion of 1794. Credit: The Granger Collection, NYC – All rights reserved.

*1793* (see Chapter 4). Alexander Hamilton aggressively defended Washington's right to issue the proclamation in a series of newspaper articles under the pseudonym Pacificus. He distinguished between the *vesting clause* in Article I, which states that "all legislative Powers herein granted shall be vested in a Congress of the United States," and the vesting clause in Article II which states that "the executive Power shall be vested in a President of the United States of America" (see Appendix 2 for the full Constitution). The absence in Article II of the words "herein granted," Hamilton argued, clearly indicated that the executive power of the nation was lodged exclusively in the president, "subject only to the exceptions and qualifications which are expressed in the Constitution." In foreign affairs, wrote Hamilton, explicit constitutional restrictions on presidential power extended no further than the right of the Senate to ratify treaties and Congress to declare war and did not hinder the executive in other foreign policy matters that were "naturally" his domain.

Madison, writing under the name Helvidius – a Roman patriot who had been the victim of tyranny – replied to Hamilton. He denied that foreign policy was "naturally" an executive power. The tasks of foreign policy – to declare war, conclude peace, and form alliances – were among "the highest acts of sovereignty;

of which the legislative power must at least be an integral and preeminent part." In foreign as in domestic affairs, wrote Madison, republican government confined presidential power to the execution of the laws; otherwise, the executive would acquire legislative power. Madison lost the argument. The Neutrality Proclamation established the precedent that the president can act unilaterally in foreign affairs except where the Constitution provides specific exceptions and limitations.

The precedents Washington established set the presidency on a path that, for the most part, it continues to follow today. With some key exceptions, the president retains the power to remove members of the executive branch and can thus be rendered accountable for their actions. He is not limited to being head of government but has the freedom to speak directly to the people. He exerts broad authority over foreign policy and national security matters. And, as republican humility demands, he is addressed simply as Mr. President, the President of the United States.

## DEMOCRATIZING THE PRESIDENCY I – THOMAS JEFFERSON

Washington had asserted the presidents' right to communicate with the people; this did not imply that he felt himself reliant on their support. Thomas Jefferson was the first president to argue that the strength of the executive office depended not only on its constitutional authority but also on "the affections of the people." He claimed a popular mandate to make the presidency more democratic and more subordinate to Congress, and he celebrated "the state governments in all their rights, as the most competent administrations for our domestic concerns and the surest bulwarks against anti-republican tendencies."

Jefferson also made the president look like a democrat. He jettisoned the presidential coach and rode his own horse. At presidential dinners, he flouted distinctions in rank and purposely ignored diplomatic protocol in the reception of foreign envoys. He believed that a presidential appearance before Congress resembled too much a speech from the throne, which would threaten to interfere with the deliberations of the people's representatives. He began the century-long practice of sending the president's annual State of the Union message to Congress in writing to be read aloud by the clerk of the House.

Jefferson also democratized the presidency by connecting it to a political party. The Republican Party linked the president and the people. Nomination and election by a mass political party made the president both a popular spokesman and accountable to a collective organization that enlarged even as it restrained presidential ambition. It restrained the president because he was as beholden to the party leaders of the various states as they were to him. The Revolution of

1800 could not have occurred without Jefferson and Madison's sustained party-building efforts during the 1790s. As the beloved author of the Declaration of Independence, Jefferson might well have been elected in 1800 in the absence of a party. But without its support and discipline, he would have either become a prisoner of the status quo or prey to schismatic pressures. He initiated the replacement of incumbent federal officials with party loyalists that would later acquire the title the spoils system (see Chapter 4). Federal appointments would become the staple of party organization in the nineteenth and early twentieth centuries, thereby adding a practical underpinning to principled loyalties.

The president now derived power directly from the people through a party program. Washington's dream of an executive who stood apart from factions had proved unrealistic. Ironically, Jefferson shared Washington's antipathy to party politics. Once the Republican Party triumphed over the Federalists, he expected it to dissolve and nonpartisan constitutional government to be restored. But Jefferson was a better politician than a prophet. As president, he continued to function as a party leader. He encouraged party discipline in Congress and relied on House and Senate floor leaders to advance his programs. He made extensive use of *party caucuses* – meetings of leaders from the executive and legislative branches – to formulate policy and encourage party unity. Jefferson constructed a highly centralized partisan system within the government.

## DEMOCRATIZING THE PRESIDENCY II – ANDREW JACKSON

Andrew Jackson, a disciple of Jefferson, was even bolder in his assertion of the democratic character of the presidency. Because he was the only official elected by the whole people, he considered himself to be uniquely responsible for their welfare. He was the tribune of the people, devoted to shrinking the federal government to prevent it from becoming excessively powerful and threatening the people's economic and political independence. He stopped federal funding of internal improvements – the building of roads and canals – because he saw no constitutional basis for them. The army was reduced. Expenditures shrank. The Bank of the United States, which Jeffersonians had grudgingly accepted, was dismantled, and its deposits were reinvested in selected state banks. In carrying out these reductions, Jackson exercised presidential power more aggressively than Jefferson. Federalist and Republican presidents had abided by Washington's view that a veto should be cast only if the president believed that a piece of legislation was unconstitutional. But in 1832, Jackson justified vetoing the bank partly on the grounds that the recharter was bad policy.

Jackson combined his support for limited government with an abiding commitment to the Union. When South Carolina threatened to refuse to abide by a new tariff law passed by Congress, Jackson made clear that he himself would lead the military force that would invade the state and force it to abide by its constitutional obligation to obey federal law (see Chapters 5). It is inconceivable that Lincoln could have defeated the much more potent secession threat he faced if Jackson had succumbed to South Carolina.

No president between Jackson and Lincoln was able to emulate Jackson's close identification with the people. Even Jackson did no personify government to the extent that modern presidents do. For all his personal popularity, he did not shift governmental authority toward the executive branch nor even toward the federal government. Like his idol Jefferson, Jackson wielded presidential power in the cause of a government of limited power in which the states and localities were preeminent.

## THE PRESIDENT AS AGENT OF CONSTITUTIONAL CHANGE: ABRAHAM LINCOLN

Abraham Lincoln was not a folk hero like Jackson, but he, too, sought to establish a strong link to the common man. He cultivated the image of himself as a rail splitter who was born on the frontier in a log cabin. But as president he aimed not merely to serve the people but to educate them about the very meaning of constitutional rights. He provided new and provocative answers to fundamental political questions about the proper role of executive power and how to reconcile the Constitution as a legal document with democratic principles and practice (Figure 8.5).

Lincoln argued that the Constitution embodied the American democratic tradition because it was inextricably connected to the Declaration of Independence. Stephen Douglas's concept of popular sovereignty (see Chapter 4) deviated from the Declaration and the spirit of the Constitution because it tolerated the expansion of slavery. This error was compounded by the Supreme Court's 1857 *Dred Scott* decision, authored by the militant Jacksonian Roger Taney, which declared unconstitutional any act of Congress or the territorial legislatures that abolished slavery. Lincoln feared that Douglas and Taney's doctrines would transform slavery from a necessary evil into a positive good, a moral right, producing "a gradual and steady debauching of public opinion." The consequences of such a change in the public mind would be devastating.

The Republican indictment of slavery and the constitutional changes stemming from it brought forth a new, more positive view of liberty that obliged government to ensure equality under the law. Thus, Lincoln and his party lessened the inherent tension between liberalism and democracy. They incorporated the Declaration of Independence into the Constitution by abolishing slavery, promising that American citizens could not be denied the right to vote "on account of

**Figure 8.5.** Abraham Lincoln (1809–1865), 16th President of the United States., reading with a bust of George Washington peering at him from the window sill. Steel engraving, 1866. Credit: The Granger Collection, NYC – All rights reserved.

race, color, or previous condition of servitude" (the Fifteenth Amendment), and guaranteeing all Americans the "privileges or immunities" of citizenship, "due process," and "equal protection of the laws" (the Fourteenth Amendment). These amendments altered the course of constitutional development. Eleven of the first twelve constitutional amendments limited national government powers;

six of the next seven expanded those powers at the expense of the states and localities.

At Lincoln's insistence, the Republicans made the Thirteenth Amendment, which emancipated the slaves, "the keystone of its 1864 platform." His Emancipation Proclamation only freed slaves held on enemy territory. Lincoln claimed that it was strictly a measure to aid the war effort and therefore something he could order using his war powers. But he had no right to abolish slavery altogether. Because the Constitution protected slavery, it could only be ended by constitutional amendment.

Reelected by large majorities, Lincoln and congressional Republican leaders pushed the amendment through a reluctant Congress. The Constitution does not require a presidential signature on constitutional amendments, but Congress sent it to the president to sign anyway. This oversight, deliberate or not, testifies to Lincoln's importance as a popular and a party leader. The Thirteenth Amendment was self-consciously based on the Northwest Ordinance, supporting Lincoln's claim that the Northwest Ordinance symbolized the Framers' hostility to slavery (see Chapter 2). Its passage further vindicated Lincoln's position that the Republicans, not the Democrats, were the true heirs of Jeffersonian democracy.

The magnitude of Lincoln's conservative revolution was limited by his identification with Jeffersonian principles. His view of the limits of federal government powers was quite narrow compared with the twentieth-century presidents we are about to discuss – Theodore Roosevelt (1901–1909), Woodrow Wilson (1913–1921), FDR (1931–1945), and Lyndon Johnson (1963–1969). Like the Whigs before them, Lincoln's Republicans favored a stronger national government than the Democrats did. But by modern standards their view of the federal government remained quite limited. They remained tightly bound by the Classic Liberal commitment to private property, limited government, and administrative decentralization. They demonstrated their commitment to what Lincoln called "a fair race of life" by ending slavery and enhancing "free labor" through policies such as the 1862 Homestead Act (see Chapter 6). With these principles firmly in place, there was no longer a need for the dynamic and aggressive presidential leadership that had secured them. The obscurity of the presidents who served between Lincoln and Theodore Roosevelt is a testimony to the limits that congressional party leadership placed on presidential power and therefore on the prestige and popularity of those who held the office.

## THE PERSONALIZED PRESIDENCY

In the twentieth century a critical change took place in the public's perception of the presidency. He came to personify government. The older understanding of America as a decentralized political order in which the drama of politics was played out primarily in the states and localities was replaced by a sense that grand political theater took place only in the nation's capital with the president cast in the leading role. We call this transformation of the presidency the *personalized presidency.* By tracing its birth during the Progressive Era and its development through the rest of the twentieth and into the twenty-first centuries, we will come to appreciate both the enhanced power and prestige it has brought to the presidential office and the enormous difficulties and dangers it poses.

This transformation began to take shape during the Progressive Era, the period of reform spanning the last decade of the nineteenth century and the first two decades of the twentieth century (see Chapter 4). In response to massive economic, cultural, and social changes that occurred during this period, pressures mounted for a more expansive national government and a more systematic administration of public policy. The late nineteenth-century polity, which could accommodate decentralized party organizations, political patronage, and a dominant Congress, began to give way to a new order that depended on consistent and forceful presidential leadership.

The vigorous expansion of presidential power began with Theodore Roosevelt TR).TR proclaimed that the president was "a *steward of the people*," bound actively and affirmatively to do all he could for the people, and not content himself with the negative merit of keeping his talents undamaged in a napkin." TR's conviction that the president possessed a special mandate from the people made him a self-conscious disciple of Jackson. Unlike Jackson, however, TR wanted to join popular leadership to a greater sense of national purpose. He trumpeted a New Nationalism that foretold an unprecedented expansion of government's responsibility to secure the nation's social and economic welfare. The New Nationalism was indebted to Hamilton's original understanding of a great American nation. TR also relied on the defense of a broad discretionary authority for the president that Hamilton articulated to justify Washington's Neutrality Proclamation. Washington, Jackson, and Lincoln had all taken a broad view of presidential authority in times of national crisis. But TR was the first president to apply the Hamiltonian principle to the day-to-day administration of government. But TR turned Hamilton on his head. Hamilton supported an energetic executive because he thought it would curb popular influence and implement policies geared toward aiding the commercial and business elite to foster economic development. TR devoted his energy to social and economic reform dedicated to helping ordinary people. As a self-proclaimed disciple of Lincoln he asserted that "men who understand and practice the Lincoln school of American political thought are necessarily Hamiltonian in their belief in a strong and efficient National Government and Jeffersonian in their belief in the people as the end of government" (Figure 8.6).

**Figure 8.6.** Astride the World: A 1905 cartoon depicting the "Big Stick Policy" of President Theodore Roosevelt. Credit: The Granger Collection, NYC – All rights reserved.

Jefferson and especially Jackson had sought to establish closer ties between the presidency and the public, but they had worked through their party organizations to do so. Similarly, Lincoln had relied heavily on the Republican Party to mobilize support for the war and his Reconstruction policies. But TR's Republican Party was badly divided regarding a bill to regulate railroad rates that he considered vital to public well-being. When the bill stalled in the Senate, TR toured the country to stir up support for it. The public pressure that his rhetoric stimulated overcame Senate resistance. The president of the Rock Island Railroad confided to Secretary of War William Howard Taft that senators he had counted on for "allegiance," although privately opposed to the Hepburn bill, so named after its Senate sponsor, yielded because the president had "so roused the people that it was impossible for the Senate to stand against the popular demand." The Hepburn Act marked not only the first significant strengthening of national administrative power to regulate the economy since Washington but also the first time a president successfully forced the hand of Congress through a direct appeal to the people. TR thus advanced the Progressive cause by establishing the president as the principal agent of popular rule.

TR not only spoke directly to the public in support of policies he favored, he also exploited the newly emerging mass circulation newspapers and magazines to go over the heads of party leaders and establish direct links with the people.

He ushered in what has been called the "rhetorical presidency," an approach to presidential leadership that relied primarily on direct communication with the public. He described the presidency as a *"bully pulpit"* from which he could and should vigorously promote himself as the leader of public opinion.

TR's successor, Woodrow Wilson, expanded the concept of the rhetorical presidency, announcing in his first inaugural address that presidential rhetoric was the "high enterprise of the new day." In his 1913 address to Congress on tariff reform, he revived the practice, abandoned by Jefferson, of addressing Congress in person. Even TR had not dared to abandon this precedent, which, like the two-term tradition, was viewed as a bulwark against despotism. But Wilson believed that Progressive democracy required the president to take advantage of congressional messages to influence public opinion. The rise of the mass media increased public attention to such events and enabled the president to use them to bring public pressure to bear on Congress. Although die-hard Jeffersonian Democrats resented it, the speech was well received by Congress and the public, aiding Wilson to launch the first successful campaign for tariff reform since before the Civil War. By 1914 Wilson had won congressional approval for a series of other Progressive reforms including the establishment of the Federal Trade Commission and the Federal Reserve banking system.

## The Personalized Presidency Matures: Franklin Delano Roosevelt

FDR further expanded the personalized presidency by creating a new and more intimate mode of public communication and attempting to increase the personal power of the president at the expense of the Court, rival party leaders, and the two-term tradition that Washington and Jefferson had established. In an effort to allay public anxiety about such massive new government programs as Social Security, FDR invented a new rhetorical form, the "Fireside Chat." By the early 1930s radios were widely available, and most homes had one. FDR realized that radio demanded a very different speaking style than did large public rallies. Over radio he was not speaking to vast crowds but rather to families sitting comfortably and quietly in their own living rooms or kitchens. Such an audience would respond far better to a calm conversational speaking style than to a formal passionate speech. Therefore FDR spoke to them as if he was seated in their midst, warming himself by the fireside. He explained complex new policies to them in simple terms using homey examples. These "chats" proved to be greatly successful in reassuring the public that the president knew what he was doing and fears these major departures had instilled in them were groundless.

The Supreme Court also helped expand presidential power as a result of a key decision it issued in 1936. In *U.S. v. Curtiss-Wright Export Corporation* (1936), the court upheld a 1934 law authorizing the president to forbid the sale of weapons to countries engaged in armed conflict. This law had been passed with the so-called Chaco War between Bolivia and Paraguay in mind, and FDR quickly forbade arms sales to both countries. Weapons merchants challenged the measure as an unconstitutional delegation of legislative authority to the president. A federal district court agreed, but a near-unanimous Supreme Court held that the president is the government's "sole organ" in international relations, and therefore his actions do not require a specific grant of power from either the Constitution or Congress.

The *Curtiss-Wright* case established as constitutional doctrine the sweeping defense of the executive's prerogative in foreign affairs that Hamilton had offered in 1793 to defend Washington's Neutrality Proclamation. This principle was reinforced by *U.S. v. Belmont* (1937), which approved the president's right to reach executive agreements with other countries without Senate ratification. These court decisions made it virtually impossible to challenge FDR's increasingly internationalist policies on constitutional grounds.

### The Limits of Presidential Expansion

During his second term, FDR launched four major initiatives aimed at expanding presidential power: "court packing," the purge campaign, a plan for reorganizing the executive branch, and a campaign to win an unprecedented third term in office. He did get elected to a third and even a fourth term, and each of the other initiatives also had a measure of success. But each also ended up setting enduring limits on the expansion of executive power.

### Court Packing

Shortly after he was sworn in for his second term, FDR announced his court-packing plan, enabling the president to appoint an additional Supreme Court justice for every existing one who failed to retire within six months of reaching the age of seventy. Six of the nine current justices were seventy or older, which meant that FDR could enlarge the court to fifteen justices, thereby overcoming the court's resistance to New Deal policies.

Jefferson, Jackson, and Lincoln had each fought with the court, but the intensity of the opposition to FDR's plan was unprecedented. Although the new rights that FDR championed had broad popular support, the public was hostile to the plan's audacious aggrandizement of executive power. By controlling the judiciary, the final constitutional barrier to expansion of government and of the presidency would be eliminated.

*Humphrey's Executor v. United States* and *Schechter Poultry Corp. v. United States* both handed down on "Black Monday," May 27, 1935, severely constrained presidential authority. *Humphrey* forbade the president from firing members of independent regulatory commissions, a power the court had affirmed in 1926. *Schechter* declared the National Recovery Administration's discretionary powers to regulate prices, wages, and other business conditions to be an unconstitutional delegation of legislative authority. Thus, FDR's effort to extend power over the judiciary was more than simply a ploy to amplify his own power or win disputes over particular policies. It was an effort to regain the powers that he felt the president needed to create and maintain the new economic constitutional order.

Much to FDR's surprise the court-packing plan provoked an outpouring of public and congressional opposition. Although literally constitutional, critics recognized that it represented an effort of the president to control the court and therefore was a frontal assault on two of the deepest principles underlying the Constitution, checks and balances and separation of powers.

As we shall see with regard to each of the four initiatives, court packing was not an unmitigated failure. Shortly after FDR introduced it, the Supreme Court abruptly ceased overturning New Deal initiatives. Since 1937, it has not invalidated any significant federal statute regulating the economy. The expansion of federal government power the New Deal ushered in survived the court-packing campaign intact, but so did the existence of the Supreme Court as an independent branch of government that has on several important occasions reigned in presidential power.

To provide the president with the managerial tools needed to run the enlarged federal bureaucracy, FDR asked Congress to approve a major executive-branch reorganization and provide him with greater staff resources. The most ambitious part of the proposal called for taking the vast number of independent commissions, bureaus, and agencies that had been created during the Progressive Era and the New Deal and integrating them into the existing cabinet departments. This reorganization would have enabled the president, through the cabinet secretaries that he appointed, to direct and control such key activities as food and drug, securities, communications, and railroad regulation that remained largely outside his span of authority. Congress refused to grant him such powers. It preferred to retain the greater degree of influence it enjoyed with such agencies precisely because they were not within the president's grip. Congress did however recognize that the president lacked sufficient managerial resources. Therefore it did enable him to hire additional staff and created the *Executive Office of the President* (EOP), which contains the White House Office (the so-called West Wing), the nerve center of the modern executive establishment. It enhanced his budgetary control by moving the Bureau of the Budget, later the *Office of Management and Budget* (OMB), from the Treasury to the Department to the EOP (for a detailed discussion of OMB see Chapter 10).

The third initiative was FDR's purge campaign. As the New Deal wore on, many southern Democrats, and some northern Democrats, as well, became increasingly hostile to the great increase in federal government power that it entailed. The southerners were especially worried that the New Dealers might decide to try using these new powers to end the discrimination against African Americans that pervaded southern life. During the 1938 midterm elections, FDR intervened in one gubernatorial and several Senate and House primaries in a bold effort to replace conservative Democrats with 100 percent New Dealers. Although Wilson and Jefferson had dabbled with the idea, no president had ever challenged his own party on such a scale. The press nicknamed FDR's effort the "purge," evoking Adolph Hitler's murder of Nazi dissenters and Joseph Stalin's elimination of suspected opponents within the Soviet Communist party. Although bloodless, FDR's aggressive intervention challenged the very foundation of the party system as a check on presidential ambition. FDR won only two of his twelve purge attempts. This largely failed effort showed that even a president as popular as FDR could not succeed in dominating his party. No subsequent president has launched such an ambitious effort to challenge intraparty rivals and opponents.

Only FDR himself knew why he chose to break with tradition and run for a third term. Certainly, his inability to purge conservatives from his party as well as the growing threat emanating from Nazi Germany entered into his calculations. Whatever his motives, his election to a third, and then to a fourth, term set a new precedent with the potential to vastly enhance presidential power. But the precedent proved short-lived. The Twenty-Second Amendment to the Constitution, which limited presidents to two terms, was ratified in 1951. It made mandatory what Washington and all his predecessors prior to FDR had done voluntarily.

## The Impact of the Personalized Presidency

The personalized presidency that FDR did so much to create had a variety of critical consequence for the office. Aides to the president displaced party leaders as formulators of policy, organizers of campaigns, liaisons with interest groups, and communicators with the public. Party was no longer the controlling element in presidential elections and governance. Presidents campaigned and governed as the heads of their own personal organizations. Increasingly, the public came to hold the president responsible for government action, even for economic and social developments beyond the executive's authority. America's emergence as a world power during and after WWII further widened the scope of responsibilities and increased his prominence and visibility. But, as the opening story of Bill Clinton and health care reform demonstrated, placing the president on such a pedestal has not necessarily served to enhance presidential authority or ensure the adoption of his policies.

At critical moments the public has turned on incumbent presidents, using midterm elections to hamstring their initiatives by electing a hostile congressional majority. Distrust of their motives and disgust at their behavior impelled the House of Representatives to impeach a president, Clinton, and to force another from office because it was on the verge of impeaching him, Nixon. In the entire previous history of the Republic it had impeached only one and never forced one from office. Even where presidential power had come to seem most sacrosanct, war making, the Congress tried curtailed the ability of the president to initiate hostilities in 1973 when it passed the War Powers Resolution, and the Supreme Court issued a series of rulings aimed at forcing the president to alter his conduct of the war on terror. The ever-present image of the president and the public's preoccupation with him has also made him more subject to public rebuke and efforts by the other branches to curtail his powers.

## The Personalized Presidency Post-FDR

Two critical postwar events, the Cold War and television, served to further increase the personalization of the presidency. The advent of the Cold War meant that the United States did not return to peacetime in the aftermath of WWII. Therefore, the president retained much of the power and dominance he had only previously enjoyed during peacetime. After the advent of nuclear weapons, his personal role was greatly enhanced, at least in the popular mind, because he and he alone had his "finger on the button." Only the president could make the decision to drop "the bomb." To calm public fears of nuclear holocaust, the Soviet and American governments installed a special telephone, called the "hotline," that would permit the U.S. president and Soviet premier to communicate directly in the event that either suspected the other of provoking a war. During the periods of greatest tension the Soviet and U.S. leaders met in what were billed as "summit meetings" to try to find ways to ease tensions between the two superpowers. The intense publicity that surrounded summit meetings and the installation of the hotline promoted the image of the Cold War as a personal duel between the president and his Soviet counterpart

### The Impact of Television

The advent of television meant that the face as well as the voice of the president entered the nation's living rooms. Dwight Eisenhower (1953–1961) was the first president to appear on television regularly, but John F. Kennedy (1961–1963) was the first to master the new medium. Convinced that viewers were bored by formal speech making, Kennedy relied more on press conferences. Previous presidents, notably TR and FDR, had used press conferences to cultivate the journalistic fraternity. Kennedy used television to turn them into the visual equivalents of FDR's fireside chats: informal, intimate means for going over the heads of Congress and journalists to reach the public directly. Public-opinion surveys gave Kennedy a 91 percent approval rating for his press-conference performances. The key was his careful preparation and an ability to appear comfortable and in command on television.

Kennedy's very success compounded the modern president's problems. Because they were such effective communicators, Reagan and Clinton were tempted to promise more than they could deliver. As they became increasingly cut off from Congress and party, modern presidents had great difficulty satisfying the very reform demands they helped stimulate. Kennedy's personalization of the presidency greatly accentuated its separation from the other centers of political power.

## The Vice Presidency

The personalization of the presidency had a major impact on the vice presidency, as well. Because presidents perform on such a large and prominent stage, they have come to rely on vice presidents to play a more prominent supporting role. This role had shrunk to virtual insignificance during the nineteenth century. Martin Van Buren (1837–1841) was the last incumbent vice president elected president until George H. W. Bush (1989–1993). Other nineteenth-century vice presidents – chosen to provide geographical balance to the presidential ticket – succeeded to the presidency because of the death of the president, but not one of these "accidental presidents" was elected to a full term. It was not until the election of 1904 that an accidental president, TR, was elected on his own.

When FDR died, it was obvious that he had failed to fully prepare Vice President Harry Truman to take over. This dilemma created sufficient public anxiety to encourage future presidents to confide more fully in their vice presidents and provide more extensive briefings, particularly about national security. Eisenhower initiated this new relationship by giving Vice President Richard Nixon extensive diplomatic responsibilities. Reagan made Vice President George H. W. Bush head of a task force to provide regulatory relief for business. Clinton put Vice President Al Gore in charge of a major initiative to reform the federal bureaucracy. George W. Bush relied on Vice President Dick Cheney with regard to a whole raft of domestic and national security matters. Cheney is widely believed to be the most powerful vice president ever.

President Obama has also chosen to give his vice president, Joseph Biden, very important and visible responsibilities. In 2009 he put Biden in charge of implementing the $787 billion stimulus package passed by Congress to bring the economy out of the doldrums created by the 2008 financial crisis. Obama has also called on the foreign policy expertise Biden garnered as Chairman of the Senate Foreign Relations Committee. Biden was a major participant in President Obama's extended deliberations regarding the decision to send 30,000 additional troops to Afghanistan. He also served as the lead administration official in dealing with Iraq.

## The Hazards of the Personalized Presidency: LBJ

Of all the post-FDR presidents, LBJ most clearly exemplified both the extraordinary prospects and the fragile authority of the personalized presidency. His greatest achievement came in the struggle for civil rights. More than any of his predecessors, he identified himself with that struggle and enlisted the full force of his rhetorical and legislative gifts in its service. By persuading Congress to enact the 1964 and 1965 civil rights laws, LBJ accomplished what Lincoln could not – statutory protection for African-American political participation, employment opportunity, and access to public accommodations.

Like the Social Security Act and the Wagner Act, the 1960s civil rights acts became endowed with quasi-constitutional status. Although racial issues remain controversial, the specific rights that these two landmark statutes propound have become as unexceptional as free speech, assembly, or practice of religion. Obviously, the enactment of these laws was not all LBJ's doing. He was responding to powerful political and moral pressures exerted by the civil rights movement under the unofficial but inspired leadership of Martin Luther King, Jr. LBJ also built on Kennedy's initiatives, who, after a period of indecision, had decided to support the civil rights struggle. But LBJ aggressively exploited the political opportunity provided by Kennedy's assassination to press a reluctant Congress to pass the 1964 bill and then availed himself of the huge congressional majority obtained in the 1964 election to pass the 1965 Voting Rights Act.

Taking further advantage of this immense electoral victory, Johnson expanded the New Deal vision of programmatic rights by winning passage of Medicare, which provided the elderly with a right to healthcare. He also obtained congressional approval of a program to give health care to the poor, Medicaid (1965), and a law providing educational opportunities for the disadvantaged, the Elementary and Secondary Education Act (1965).

But LBJ was not content to deliver on promises made by Lincoln and FDR. He heralded a Great Society that went beyond the "pursuit of happiness" – as propounded in the Declaration of Independence – to the promise of happiness itself (see Chapter 4). At its most grandiose, the Great Society sought not to enlarge the liberal tradition but to transcend it. LBJ's vision gave rise to a legislative program of remarkable breadth. Policies dedicated to enhancing the quality of American life included pollution reduction, urban redevelopment, consumer protection, and preschool education. These policies of the "spirit rather than the flesh" were also expected to restore a sense of citizenship to political life that had been sapped by bureaucratic indifference and the crass consumerism of mass society.

The Johnson administration launched new social initiatives to foster "participatory democracy." Those people affected by government programs were to be directly involved in policy formulation and implementation. This promise of political self-determination marked a renewal and intensification of the

Progressive principle of direct democracy. Participatory democracy was central to LBJ's War on Poverty, which was administered by local community action programs and was required to involve the "maximum feasible participation of residents of the areas and the groups served."

The Great Society did not fulfill its ambitions to supersede the New Deal. Local elected officials threatened by the support given to grassroots movements in their cities and towns appealed to Congress to rein in participatory democracy. The Great Society's hallmarks, those programs that went beyond providing civil and programmatic rights, were killed or gutted. Indeed, by failing in its most grandiose ambitions to restore direct democracy, the Great Society served to increase public skepticism about both the sincerity of governmental intentions and the capacity of government to act effectively. As the personal embodiment of these great ambitions, the prestige of the presidency suffered accordingly.

Although rhetorically committed to grassroots democracy, LBJ's early years in power were the apex of "presidential government." Major policy departures were conceived in the White House, hastened through Congress by the legislative skill of LBJ and his sophisticated congressional liaison team, and administered by new or refurbished executive agencies highly responsive to the president's directives. LBJ also established a personal governing coalition that reached beyond his party. This personalized presidency proved his undoing. His domination of the political process ensured that he, not Congress, would be blamed when his Great Society programs failed, victims of hasty packaging and unrealistic goals.

The war in Vietnam demonstrated even more starkly both LBJ's personal shortcomings and the more troubling aspects of modern presidential government itself. He extended the American commitment in Vietnam because, as a progressive internationalist in the tradition of TR, FDR, and Kennedy, he believed that the righteous use of force was necessary in foreign affairs to make the world safe for democracy. In Korea, Harry Truman could claim to be carrying out the United Nations' dictate. In Vietnam, however, no treaty or other obligations required the United States to intervene. Nor did Congress authorize a "police action" of a magnitude justifying the commitment of 500,000 troops (the size of the American force fighting in Vietnam by the end of 1967). The Johnson administration's claim that such action was authorized by the 1964 Gulf of Tonkin Resolution was dubious. In truth, LBJ believed and stated publicly that he had constitutional authority to deploy troops in Vietnam without congressional authorization.

By early 1968, LBJ was trapped, unable to withdraw troops for fear of being damned as the first American president to lose a war, yet lacking the popular support to undertake more aggressive military action. Attacked by left and right, he shocked the nation by announcing in a televised address on March 31, 1968, that he would not seek reelection (Figure 8.7).

**Figure 8.7.** The Arrows of Outrageous Fortune: A 1960s caricature by Cy Hungerford of President Lyndon Johnson. Credit: The Granger Collection, NYC – All rights reserved.

### Curbing the Personalized Presidency: Disciplining Richard Nixon

Despite growing mistrust of the presidency, the welfare state continued to expand. During the 1970s Congress passed a host of new environmental, special education, and consumer protection initiatives as well as a major expansion of the Social Security Act that pegged Social Security payments to the consumer price index, thereby insulating millions of old-age pensioners from the risk of inflation. But these popular new initiatives did not serve to increase trust in the president.

Public mistrust grew in response to LBJ and Nixon's conduct of the war and the evidence of presidential misconduct revealed in the Watergate Scandal (see Chapter 7). As we discussed in Chapter 7, Congress sought to curb presidential abuse of power by impeaching President Nixon and passing the War Powers Resolution over Nixon's veto. As we also discussed in Chapter 7, the courts also acted to curb presidential power by ruling against Nixon's impoundments of funds appropriated by Congress and his assertion of executive privilege as a rationale for withholding the Watergate tapes from Congress.

### The Personalized Presidency Curbs the Welfare State: Ronald Reagan

Although all the Republican presidents of the postwar period considered themselves conservatives, only Ronald Reagan mounted a serious effort to halt the expansion of the federal government. He convinced Congress to make major tax cuts. There were no commensurate reductions in spending; nonetheless, the sheer size of the reductions in revenue resulting from the tax cuts put a severe damper on Congress' programmatic ambitions. However, except for the tax cut, all of Reagan's efforts to cut government were accomplished through acts of presidential discretion that short-circuited the legislative process. Although done in the name of limited government, Reagan's approach to reform was as president-centered as that of FDR and LBJ. Even reductions in environmental and consumer protection were done by administrative action, not legislative change.

To obtain a Republican congressional majority required mounting a full-scale assault on the New Deal. Reagan would have needed to put his popularity and rhetorical ability in the service of winning votes for Republican congressional candidates. Forging such partisan loyalty was precisely what FDR accomplished in 1936. Confident of his own reelection, FDR risked alienating voters by demanding that they support Democratic congressional candidates, as well. Instead of defusing partisan conflict, FDR crystalized it. He did not take the safe road of simply rehearsing his administration's accomplishments and taking credit for economic recovery. Instead, he castigated New Deal opponents in harsh, provocative terms as "economic royalists" and "privileged princes of the economic dynasty." He turned the election from a personal contest into a partisan conflict, which, given the popularity of the New Deal, he knew he could win.

Reagan did just the opposite. His 1984 reelection campaign was geared to maximize his personal appeal at the price of draining the election of broader political meaning. Its theme, "Morning in America," provided a soft focus that failed to clarify the choice between Democrats and Republicans. Campaign advertising stressed the virtues and charms of Reagan the man rather than pressing voters to elect Congress members who supported his programs. The result was a stunning victory for the president. He defeated Walter Mondale by a larger popular-vote margin than any presidential victor has been able to accomplish since. He carried every state except Minnesota, Mondale's home state. But this personal victory was bought at the price of foreswearing partisan advantage. Republicans gained just fourteen House seats, leaving Democrats still in control, and lost two seats in the Senate, retaining a very slim majority. In 1986, Democrats took the upper chamber, as well. Failing to gain control of Congress, Reagan had no hope of advancing his agenda during his second term.

### Winning the Cold War

Although Reagan opposed many of the domestic policies of his Democratic predecessors, on the foreign policy front, he steadfastly continued the policy of containing the Soviet Union begun by Democrat Harry Truman (1946–1952) and brought them to fruition by winning the Cold War. He expanded the military buildup begun by his immediate Democratic predecessor, Jimmy Carter (1977–1981), in response to the Soviet Union's war in Afghanistan. *Containment* was the policy of exerting continuing pressure on the Soviet Union by stationing troops on its borders and actively preventing its efforts to expand militarily. Containment required vast expenditures on defense, much of which was devoted to remaining technologically superior. Even before Reagan began his offensive, the Soviets were experiencing severe internal difficulties. But to bring them down, he capitalized on what otherwise might have proved only a temporary setback. The enormity of the economic and technological challenge posed by his military buildup and the staunchness of his rhetoric may have sapped the Soviets of the vigor that otherwise might have proved sufficient for them to stage a comeback.

Unfortunately, Reagan's foreign policy also confirmed the personalized presidency's extraordinary isolation and its tendency to ignore constitutional limits. In November 1986, the nation learned that with the president's approval, National Security Council staffers had sold weapons to Iran and that, with or without the president's knowledge, some of the proceeds had been used to assist the Contras, opponents of the socialist Nicaraguan government. Congress had passed the Boland Amendment, which expressly forbade arming the Contras, and it would have prohibited selling arms to Iran if it had any inkling such sales were being contemplated. In reaction to the scandal, Reagan's approval rating fell from 67 percent to 46 percent in one month. Although Reagan later reclaimed some of his popularity, his administration never recovered from the institutional estrangement that the Iran-Contra affair instigated.

## *Personal Victories, Political Defeats: Bill Clinton*

The presidency of Bill Clinton also displayed both the problems and opportunities created by the increased personalization of the office. In the words of the great presidential scholar Richard Neustadt, Clinton's greatest mistake was to think that he won the 1992 election. Of course he got elected, but he only received 43.3 percent of the popular vote, beating George W. Bush by slightly less than 6 percent. It is impossible to tell how the election would have turned out were it not for the enormous impact of third-party candidate Ross Perot, who relentlessly attacked Bush, not Clinton, and who received 19 percent of the vote, the best showing by a third-party candidate since Theodore Roosevelt in 1912. Neustadt's point is that Clinton misinterpreted the election results. He had not won over a majority of voters, and that should have given him cause for caution. He should have realized that the fame and adulation that go along with winning a presidential election are not in themselves sufficient to push Congress to adopt major new initiatives.

In the manner of the personalized presidency, Clinton did not involve his congressional allies in the formulation of the massive new health care proposal whose demise we discussed at the beginning of this chapter. Instead, he entrusted the task to a nonelected individual who had no appointive position in the administration and therefore had never undergone Senatorial confirmation, his wife Hilary Clinton. She in turn appointed a taskforce of health care experts who met in secret and handed Congress a fully articulated program package for its consideration. This lack of prior consultation offended senior Democratic congressmen on whom the administration had to rely to obtain congressional passage. Because it had received no political vetting, Republican congressional leaders suspected that the public could be turned against it. Thus, they chose to oppose it in its entirety rather than seek to modify it. This decision was critical to their success in winning both houses of Congress in 1994.

Remarkably, this political humiliation did not foreclose Clinton's reelection in 1996. He also withstood his impeachment, provoked by the Monica Lewinsky sex scandal, and served out his second term (see Chapter 7). Both these victories were due to Clinton's personal political skills. He regained strength with the voters by shrewdly cooperating with the Republicans on initiatives he knew to be popular with the voters. Despite protests from fellow Democrats, he signed the Republican-sponsored Welfare Reform. But he staunchly opposed Republican initiatives he knew to be unpopular, such as revamping Medicare and Social Security.

Clinton survived impeachment by convincing the majority of the public that special prosecutor Kenneth Starr's vendetta against him was a greater evil than his own immoral sexual behavior. In the face of such staunch public support, the Senate vote fell far short of the two-thirds majority required to oust the president from office. Clinton faced two separate charges: perjury and obstruction of justice. Ten Republican Senators joined all forty-five of the Senate Democrats to acquit Clinton of the charge of perjury by a vote of 55 to 45. Five Republicans joined the Democrats to acquit him of the obstruction of justice charge by a 50–50 vote. Thus, Clinton combined three great personal victories – two presidential electoral victories and impeachment acquittal – with major policy defeats and the loss of control of both houses of Congress for six of his eight years in office.

### A Reassertion of Party Leadership: George W. Bush

George W. Bush was the first president since FDR to actively and successfully reassert the president's role as party leader. During the Clinton era, Republicans not only took control of Congress, they also captured the governorships of all the most heavily populated states except California – Texas, New York, Florida, Pennsylvania, Illinois, Michigan, Ohio, New Jersey, and Massachusetts. Recognizing that a defeat of Democratic nominee Al Gore would require them to promote a moderate candidate, these large-state Republican governors united behind Governor George W. Bush of Texas. This display of solidarity shows that even though candidate-centered politics and declining party cohesion emerged as powerful trends after the New Deal, it was still possible, at least for Republicans, to put party well-being above personal ambition.

As president, Bush built on the party effort that had won him nomination. As we discussed in Chapter 7, his active and energetic campaigning on behalf of Republican congressional candidates in 2002 was critical to the party's success in regaining control of the Senate and garnering additional seats in the House. In preparation for 2004, Bush and his advisors launched what could be called the first "national party machine" in American history. It was an elaborate network of campaign volunteers concentrated in the sixteen most competitive states. Instead of focusing on so-called "*swing*" voters, voters who were still on the fence between the two candidates, the 2004 Bush-Cheney grassroots organization reached out to "*lazy Republicans.*" These were people predisposed to vote for Republicans at all levels but who needed to be prodded to go to the polls.

Bush reaped enormous benefits from his reinvigoration of presidential party leadership. He was the first president since FDR to be reelected and also have his party gain seats in both the House and Senate, and the first Republican President to do so since Calvin Coolidge in 1924. Bush's four most recent Republican predecessors – Dwight Eisenhower in 1956, Richard Nixon in 1972, Ronald Reagan in 1984, and Bill Clinton in 1996 – won reelection by much larger margins than he did. But theirs were "lonely landslides" in which the president did well but his party suffered in the congressional elections. In contrast, Bush's 2004 reelection spearheaded a partisan victory.

It is unclear whether Bush's success in restoring presidential party leadership will have any long-term impact. In 2006, his personal unpopularity rendered him helpless to assist his congressional allies as Democrats swept into control of both houses of Congress. In 2010 President Obama was unable to mobilize the same impressive volunteer network on behalf of Democratic congressional candidates that had operated so energetically and successfully for his own election. Because he had become unpopular in much of the country, he confined his campaigning on behalf of congressional and gubernatorial candidates to college campuses, African-American neighborhoods, and other places where he retained popularity. He rebounded impressively to gain reelection in 2012, and the Democrats did win two additional seats in the Senate and seven more in the House. However, the Republicans maintained solid control of the House and most governorships and houses of the state legislatures.

### Personalizing a War: Bush and Iraq

In contrast to his successful party leadership, Bush's conduct during the War on Terror revealed him to be a victim of the personalized presidency. Like LBJ, he was unable to maintain public support for his war policies. Like Richard Nixon, his unilateral efforts caused him to run afoul of the Supreme Court.

Bush's initial response to 9/11 gave no indication of the political difficulties to come. Like a true Progressive, Bush emphasized that the War on Terror was not only an effort to protect American lives and property but also a "crusade" to protect liberal and democratic values. In words reminiscent of FDR, Bush told a joint session of Congress on September 20, 2001, "Freedom and fear are at war.... The advance of human freedom, the great achievement of our time, now depends on us. Our nation, this generation, will lift a dark threat of violence from our people and our future. We will not tire, we will not falter, and we will not fail."

Bush's estrangement from public opinion is traceable to his decision to invade Iraq. He did obtain Congressional endorsement, an Authorization for the Use of Military Force in Iraq. But the rationale for the invasion was based in large measure on the threat Iraq posed by virtue of its possession of weapons of mass destruction. Post-invasion, no such weapons were found. This failure fed the cynicism of Bush's critics, who claimed that Bush was aware that Iraq had no such weapons. Although the invasion itself went smoothly, the United States was unsuccessful in establishing a new government capable of suppressing armed resistance. As American casualties mounted the war became ever more unpopular with the American public. Like LBJ, Bush was unable to make a persuasive case to the American people that the gains from pacifying Iraq were worth the loss of life, hence the 2006 electoral defeat, in which the Democrats recaptured control of both houses of Congress.

Bush also faced rebuke from the Supreme Court. In June 2006, the Supreme Court ruled in *Hamdan v. Rumsfeld* that the Bush policy of holding illegal enemy combatants at Guantanamo Bay, Cuba, and having them tried by military tribunals with no right of habeas corpus was illegal because it had not been authorized by Congress. The right of *habeas corpus* is a hallowed legal protection that compels the government to bring anyone charged with a crime before a civilian judge. In response, Bush obtained congressional passage of the Military Commissions Act authorizing the use of military tribunals and the denial of habeas corpus. Then the Supreme Court shifted its grounds for opposing military tribunals. In *Boumediene v. Bush* it ruled that regardless of congressional approval, the denial of habeas corpus to illegal enemy combatants was unconstitutional. The practical meaning of this seemingly far-reaching decision is hard to evaluate. Although President Obama promised to close the Guantanamo Bay detention facility, as of September 2012 it was still open. Military tribunals were still in place. Although the Justice Department announced its intention to try the alleged mastermind of the 9/11 attacks in civilian court, the outcry against this decision caused it to delay the trial indefinitely.

## CONCLUSION

Because the president has come to personify government in the public mind, many commentators have come to view him as a threat to the constitutional order. FDR's four-term reign so frightened Republican political leaders that they spearheaded the ultimately successful campaign to pass a constitutional amendment limiting the president to two terms. President Nixon's efforts to centralize power in the White House and cover up the Watergate scandal led to a liberal outcry against the "imperial presidency" and a spate of Congressional initiatives designed to restrict presidential discretion. As we have discussed, the Supreme Court also moved against the president, demanding that he release his secret White House tapes. The Court continued to curb presidential power by depriving him of the line-item veto. All modern presidents have sought to acquire the power to not only veto congressional statues but to veto particular parts of bills that they otherwise support. In *Clinton v. New York City* (1998) the Supreme Court ruled that the Constitution does not give the president such a power. Most recently, as we have already discussed, the Court ruled that the executive could not restrict the right to habeas corpus of illegal enemy combatants.

This pushback from the Court and Congress shows the continuing strength of the checks and balances enshrined in the Constitution. For all its glamor and attention-getting capacity, the American president continues to be subject to effective institutional constraint. The president is certainly a celebrity, a media star who performs on a worldwide stage. But the institutionally imposed restraints on his power have so far succeeded in staving off the threat of his becoming a tyrant.

## CHAPTER SUMMARY

☆   President Obama and all his modern predecessors have displayed
    legislative and managerial authority far beyond what the Constitution
    explicitly grants them.

☆   The vesting clause in Article Two of the Constitution grants all
    executive power to the president, leaving considerable room for
    controversy about just how broad the president's powers really are.

☆   George Washington established critical precedents for presidential
    conduct.

☆   Thomas Jefferson and Andrew Jackson both acted to democratize the
    presidency.

☆   Abraham Lincoln demonstrated that the president could serve as an
    agent of constitutional change. He provided new and provocative
    answers to fundamental political questions about the proper role
    of executive power and how to reconcile the Constitution as a legal
    document with democratic principles and practice.

☆   In the twentieth century the president came to personify government.
    The older understanding of America as a decentralized political order,
    in which the drama of politics was played out primarily in the states
    and localities, was replaced by a sense that grand political theater
    took place only in the nation's capital, with the president cast in
    the leading role. We call this transformation of the presidency the
    personalized presidency.

☆   TR and Woodrow Wilson pioneered the personalized presidency
    and Franklin Delano Roosevelt added further critical rhetorical and
    political dimensions to it.

☆   Two of the most critical factors that further personalized the
    presidency after World War II were the Cold War and television.

☆   Of all the post-FDR presidents, LBJ most clearly exemplified both the
    extraordinary prospects and the fragile authority of the personalized
    presidency.

☆   Although all the Republican presidents of the postwar period
    considered themselves conservatives, only Ronald Reagan mounted
    a serious effort to halt the expansion of the federal government.
    Although done in the name of limited government, Reagan's
    approach to reform was as president-centered as that of FDR and LBJ.

☆    The presidency of George W. Bush (2000–2008) marked both an expansion of the personalized presidency via his approach to fighting terrorism and an effort to reduce presidential isolation through his reassertion of party leadership.

☆    The Supreme Court and Congress have both taken important steps to reign in the expansion of presidential power, demonstrating the continued viability of constitutionally imposed mutual checks and balances among the three branches.

## MAJOR CONCEPTS

| | |
|---|---|
| *Boumediene v. Bush* | Cabinet |
| *Clinton v. New York City* | Cold War |
| Commander in Chief | Containment |
| Executive Office of the President (EOP) | Great Society |
| *Humphrey's Executor v. United States* | National Security Council (NSC) |
| Neutrality Proclamation of 1793 | Office of Management and Budget (OMB) |
| Party Leader | Personalized Presidency |
| Pocket Veto | Removal Power |
| Rhetorical Presidency | *Schechter Poultry Corp. v. United States* |
| Steward of the People | The Great Society |
| *U.S. v. Curtiss-Wright Export Corporation* | Vesting Clause |
| Veto | |

## SUGGESTED READINGS

Arnold, Peri. *Making the Managerial Presidency*, 2nd rev. ed. Lawrence: University Press of Kansas, 1998.

Binkley, Wilfred E. *The President and Congress*. New York: Knopf, 1947.

Ceaser, James. *Presidential Selection: Theory and Development*. Princeton, NJ: Princeton University Press, 1979.

Cornwell, Elmer, Jr. *Presidential Leadership of Public Opinion*. Bloomington: Indiana University Press, 1965.

Corwin, Edward. *The President: Office and Powers, 1787–1984*, 5th rev. ed. New York: New York University Press, 1989.

Crenson, Matthew, and Benjamin Ginsberg. *Presidential Power: Unchecked and Unbalanced*. New York: W. W. Norton, 2007.

Karl, Barry D. *The Uneasy State: The United States from 1915 to 1945*. Chicago: University of Chicago Press, 1983.

Landy, Marc, and Sidney M. Milkis. *Presidential Greatness*. Lawrence: University Press of Kansas, 2000.

Lowi, Theodore. *The Personal President*. Ithaca, NY: Cornell University Press, 1995.

Milkis, Sidney M., and Michael Nelson. *The American Presidency: Origins and Development, 1776–2007*, 5th ed. Washington, DC: CQ Press, 2007.

Nelson, Michael, ed. *The Presidency and the Political System*, 8th ed. Washington, DC: CQ Press, 2005.

Neustadt, Richard. *Presidential Power and the Modern Presidents: The Politics of Leadership from Roosevelt to Reagan*. New York: Free Press, 1991.

Paludan, Phillip S. *The Presidency of Abraham Lincoln*. Lawrence: University Press of Kansas, 1994.

Rudalevige, Andrew. *The New Imperial Presidency: Renewing Presidential Power after Watergate*. Ann Arbor: University of Michigan Press, 2005.

Skowronek, Stephen. *The Politics Presidents Make: Leadership from John Adams to Bill Clinton*. Cambridge, MA: Harvard University Press, 1997.

Tulis, Jeffrey. *The Rhetorical Presidency*. Princeton, NJ: Princeton University Press, 1987.

# The Judiciary

## CHAPTER 9

## CHAPTER OVERVIEW

This chapter focuses on:

- ★ A contemporary portrait of the federal judiciary, particularly the Supreme Court.
- ★ Forging the path of judicial review.
- ★ Critical choices make by the Court that have altered the path of constitutional interpretation.
- ★ The failed efforts of the Supreme Court to impose its will on two great national controversies – slavery and government regulation of the economy.
- ★ The redefinition of the meaning of rights brought about by the Warren and Burger Courts and the political consequences of that redefinition.
- ★ The complex web of retrenchment, extension, and reaffirmation of rights that have characterized the Rehnquist and Roberts Courts.

At about 10:00 PM on Tuesday, December 12, 2000, more than a month after Election Day, the Supreme Court issued a dramatic decision that ended the historic dispute over the presidential election and enabled Republican governor George W. Bush of Texas to become president of the United States. The court's decision was the last act in a legal drama that began the day after the election when Americans awoke to discover that the contest between Bush and his Democratic opponent, Vice President Al Gore, was still undecided. Gore defeated Bush in the popular vote by almost a half-million votes, but in the Electoral College (see Chapter 3) Gore led Bush by 266 votes to 246 votes, short of the majority needed to win. The outcome would be determined by the vote in Florida, where Bush held a popular vote margin of less than 2,000 of the nearly

6 million votes cast. If Florida's 25 electoral votes went to Bush, he would have 271 electoral votes, a bare majority of the 538 total, and would become president despite losing the popular vote.

A discrepancy between the popular and electoral vote had not occurred since 1888, when Republican Benjamin Harrison won despite receiving fewer popular votes than Democrat Grover Cleveland. The 2000 election was a reminder that the Constitution does not provide for majority rule but for republican government, which moderates, or frustrates, majorities in the name of minority rights and local self-government. But the import of this discrepancy was largely disregarded amid the dispute over Florida's votes.

Claiming that machines had failed to count all his votes, Gore called for a hand recount in four counties with high Democratic totals that were controlled by Democratic election commissions. The crux of Gore's legal challenge, supported by the Florida Supreme Court, was that voting machines, and therefore official ballots, were flawed, especially in Democratic counties. A hand count would show the true intent of voters and, in all likelihood, overcome Bush's lead, which had shrunk to 327 votes after the November 10 statewide machine recount required by Florida law for such close elections. As a complex and bitter legal process played out, Americans sought comic relief in stories of how chads, cardboard dots that Florida's voters punched out in casting their ballots, clung stubbornly to ballots, disguising the real intention of voters.

Discerning voter intent was the subject of the Supreme Court decision in *Bush v. Gore*. The Court ruled that the Florida Supreme Court order requiring manual recounts of every under vote in Florida (that is, every ballot in the state for which a machine failed to register a vote for president) was unconstitutional. By failing to establish a standard by which counties across the states would judge voter intention, the Florida court violated the Fourteenth Amendment's requirement that states protect the right of individuals to equal protection and due process of the law. Seven of the nine justices agreed that the Florida court had violated basic Fourteenth Amendment rights (Figure 9.1).

But the Supreme Court divided more closely and bitterly on the second, decisive part of its ruling. By a 5-4 vote, the court ruled that the Florida court had also violated the Constitution in overruling the state legislature. The legislature had invoked a federal law that insulates a state's electors from challenge as long as they are certified by December 12. A proper recount simply could not be conducted by that date, and an attempt to do so violated "the constitutional prerogative of the state legislature to determine how electors are chosen."

Gore conceded. But this surrender did not take place without considerable protest. Justice John Stevens criticized the Court's majority for emphasizing the need to certify votes by December 12 rather than enforcing Florida's obligation to determine voter intent. In the interest of "finality," Stevens charged, "the majority effectively orders the disenfranchisement of an unknown number

**Figure 9.1.** An Imperfect Balance: A 2005 cartoon by Hanson and Dagbladt depicting the judicial contest between Bush and Gore for the United States Presidency.

*Source*: Political Cartoons.com #17286. Retrieved from http://www.politicalcartoons.com/cartoon/9294b230-f4c8-412d-aa0c-7f53004c668c.html.

of voters whose ballots reveal their intent – and are therefore legal votes under state law – but were for some reason rejected by ballot-counting machines."

Chief Justice William Rehnquist's majority opinion replied that the Supreme Court's first obligation was to the Constitution, not the voters: "The individual citizen has no federal constitutional right to vote for electors for the President of the United States"; that privilege, according to Article II of the Constitution, exists at the pleasure of the state legislatures. The Florida state legislature had a constitutional right to resolve any controversy over the final selection of electors in order to meet the December 12 deadline imposed by Congress.

In his concession speech, Gore congratulated Bush on "becoming," not "being elected," the forty-third president of the United States. Gore's distinction hinted at the daunting challenge Bush faced of ruling without a popular mandate. But Bush benefited greatly from the people's faith in the Supreme Court as the proper interpreter, the guardian, of the Constitution. Although many militant Democrats viewed the decision as a crude conservative power play, surveys indicated that most people wanted the courts to decide the contest. They accepted Bush as the legitimate president.

It is hard to imagine public officials and citizens in other representative democracies allowing judges to decide the outcome of a national election. Americans' acceptance of *Bush v. Gore* speaks to the extraordinary power of the independent judiciary to influence virtually every aspect of American political life. How is it that a people with a strong democratic tradition have given so much authority to nine unelected judges? This chapter explores the fundamental constitutional debate about the judiciary in relation to the elected branches. It traces the development of that relationship and the strains it has caused. After painting a contemporary portrait of the judiciary, this chapter considers the origins and growth of the judiciary's role in protecting America's liberal tradition against the tide of public opinion. It then examines the failed efforts of the court to impose its will on two great national controversies – slavery and government regulation of the economy. Next, it examines the court's role in the redefinition of the meaning of rights that has occurred since the New Deal and the political consequences of that redefinition. Finally it looks at the Court during the last three decades to understand the complex web of retrenchment, extension, and reaffirmation of rights that have taken place.

## THE JUDICIARY: A CONTEMPORARY PORTRAIT

The contemporary judiciary deals with several different kinds of law. *Civil law* establishes a framework for overseeing the rules that govern the relationships between private parties, individuals, associations, and firms. When one party believes itself aggrieved by another, it brings a civil action that petitions the judiciary to rule against the other party and provide relief. The party bringing a civil action is called a *plaintiff*. The other party is the *defendant*. The most common forms of civil actions involve contracts and torts. A *contract* is a binding agreement between those who sign it, its signatories. A signatory sues when he or she believes that another signatory has violated the terms of the contract. For example, if a sawmill promises to deliver 1,000 two-by-fours to a lumberyard and only delivers 900, the lumberyard might sue the sawmill for breach of contract. A *tort* is a harm done to one party by another. If one believes that someone else has done damage to one's property or person, one brings a tort action seeking compensation for that injury. For example, if someone slips on a banana peel in the supermarket and breaks an ankle, if that person sues the supermarket claiming the market bore responsibility for the fall, the case would be considered a tort.

Whereas civil actions involve disputes among persons or organizations, criminal actions involve offenses against the people as a whole. The criminal law enumerates and describes what constitutes such public offenses. Offenses are ranked in terms of their severity. *Misdemeanors* are composed of petty crimes such as vandalism and the theft of inexpensive objects. *Felonies* are composed of more serious offenses such as murder, rape, assault, robbery, and theft of expensive objects. Because a crime is an offense against all of us, the government, not the person or persons directly harmed, acts as the plaintiff.

As we discussed in Chapter 2, one of the most serious grievances brought by the American colonists against the British Crown concerned restrictions placed on trial by jury. To guard against such a threat in the future, the Constitution grants criminal defendants a right to a jury trial and the Seventh Amendment extends that right to civil cases, as well. Likewise, state constitutions guarantee this right in criminal trials and every state except Louisiana also guarantees it in civil trials. Relatively few Americans can expect to serve as public executives, legislators, or judges, but most can expect to be called for jury duty. The difficult judgments regarding guilt and responsibility jurors are called on to make may well be the most important and demanding forms of public service that citizens are ever called on to perform.

*Public law* concerns those cases in which the government or the constitutional rights of citizens are involved. *Constitutional law* is that form of public law that involves judicial scrutiny of government or private action in terms of whether it violates the Constitution. Most of the cases discussed in this chapter relate to constitutional law. *Administrative law* is the form of public law that relates to the conduct and rulings of administrative agencies in determining whether they are in conformity with the will of Congress and the rights accorded to those subject to administrative rulings are being protected. For example, if OSHA issues a regulation requiring all metal workers to wear safety glasses and the owner of a metalworking factory thinks that some metalworking machines are so safe that the owner should not have to provide glasses to the operators of those machines, the owner can sue OSHA in federal court claiming that the regulation is arbitrary and capricious and therefore it needs to be modified.

A key difference between a court and legislature regards the matter of standing. Anyone can petition a legislature to request that it take up an issue. But to be heard in court one must have standing. One must show that one has been directly harmed by the entity one is suing; one cannot sue simply to make a political point or because one is sympathetic to the problems of others. Later on, we will see that with regard to a whole host of federal laws and regulations, Congress has chosen to relax the rules of standing and made it far easier to claim that one has been harmed by a polluter or a destroyer of natural resources.

The American judicial system is made up of two parallel systems: state courts and federal courts. *State courts* vary enormously, as befits the differences in state constitutions. Some states elect their judges, including their state Supreme Court justices. In other states, the system of district, appeal, and supreme courts are appointed. Most ordinary civil and criminal matters are handled, under state law, by state courts.

Generally speaking, a case goes to *federal court* rather than state court if the federal government is directly involved, if a federal statute is at issue, if a claim of a violation of the U.S. Constitution is made, or if a civil suit is brought that involves citizens from more than one state. The federal system is composed of three tiers: district courts, appeals courts, and the Supreme Court. *District courts* are where ordinary civil and criminal federal trials take place. Nationwide, there are ninety-four district courts handling in excess of 200,000 civil cases and 45,000 criminal cases a year. Each state has at least one federal district court. The nation is carved up into eleven separate courts of appeals. There is a twelfth one for the District of Columbia, and the thirteenth is the U.S. Court of Appeals for the Federal Circuit, which specializes in patents and financial claims against the government. *Appeals courts* deal only with cases brought to them on appeal either from the district courts or federal administrative agencies. The latter type of appeal goes to the DC circuit, which has thus acquired a particular expertise in administrative law.

The *Supreme Court* takes cases that arise on appeal from the federal appeals courts; the highest court of a state; or that the Constitution specifically assigns to it, its sphere of original jurisdiction. That sphere includes disputes between: citizens from different states; a state and the federal government; two or more states; or cases involving foreign diplomats. Unlike the lower courts, the Supreme Court is free to decide which cases it wants to hear and which it does not.

For a case to be accepted by the Supreme Court at least four justices must agree that it involves "a substantial federal question"; if so, the court issues a writ of *certiorari* – Latin for "made more certain" – which brings the case before the court. The court refuses to hear far more appeals than it accepts. It tends to accept those cases that raise issues about which different lower courts have issued contradictory opinions. In such an instance it attempts to establish a clear-cut set of principles and standards in order to provide guidance to the lower courts to encourage them to arrive at a consistent set of decisions regarding those issues. But it may also choose to accept other sorts of cases in which at least four of the justices believe that a ruling by the Court is useful and important for the well-being of the nation.

In 2010, 361,323 were tried by U.S. district courts. Of those, 282,895 were civil cases and 78,428 were criminal. Federal courts of appeals reviewed 55,992 cases. Seven hundred and thirty-eight cases were filed with the Supreme Court during its 2009–2010 term (which ended in October of 2010). Of those, the Court chose to consider only eighty-two. Among the important and controversial questions raised by cases the Court accepted for 2010–2011 were: can a state restrict the sale of violent video games to minors; can a federal court order California to release 46,000 inmates to relieve prison overcrowding; can a state take away the business licenses of employers who knowingly hire illegal immigrants; and can the government require employees to reveal personal details such as past drug use?

Federal judges are chosen by the president, who relies heavily on the advice of the attorney general and other members of the president's political inner circle. These designees are almost always from the same party as the president. Judicial nominees come from a variety of legal backgrounds. Many have had previous careers as state judges and prosecutors. Others have been law professors or prominent attorneys. Because these selections must be confirmed by a majority vote in the Senate, its members have a great deal of influence in the selection process. The president, before making a judicial nomination, asks for the support of the senators from the prospective nominee's state, if they are of the president's party. This custom is known as *senatorial courtesy*. The Senate will normally reject a candidate if those senators object (Figure 9.2).

Once the president nominates a federal judge, the Senate Judiciary Committee conducts hearings during which its members interrogate the nominee and also hear from a wide variety of interest groups who seek to influence the Senate vote. The committee then votes on whether or not to recommend the nominee to the full Senate. Then the Senate debates the nomination and votes to either approve or disapprove the nomination.

Currently, the Supreme Court has nine members, the chief justice and eight associate justices. The number is not set in the Constitution but by Congress, and has varied over time. However, Congress has left the number at nine since 1869. Scholars of the court divide its history into distinct eras named in honor of the chief justice. John Roberts is the current chief justice, so the contemporary court is called The Roberts Court. Later on this chapter will discuss especially the Marshall, Warren, Burger, and Rehnquist Courts. Figure 9.3 lists all the current members of the Supreme Court, the each was appointed and the president who appointed them.

President Obama has appointed two associate justices to the Supreme Court. In May 2009, he nominated Sonia Sotomayor to replace retired Justice David Souter. She was the first person of Hispanic descent to be chosen for the court. Sotomayor had considerable federal judicial experience prior to her nomination. From 1991 to 1997 she served on the U.S. District Court for the Southern District

**Figure 9.2.** No Pleading the Fifth: A 2009 cartoon by Joseph Heller depicting the Supreme Court nomination process.

*Source*: Political Cartoons.com #64945. Retrieved from http://www.politicalcartoons.com/cartoon/10b23c1e-8269-48d0-9045-0aab45fea78b.html.

| Name | Year Appointed | Nominated by |
| --- | --- | --- |
| Antonin Scalia | 1986 | Reagan |
| Anthony Kennedy | 1988 | Reagan |
| Clarence Thomas | 1991 | George H. W. Bush |
| Ruth Bader Ginsburg | 1993 | Clinton |
| Stephen Breyer | 1994 | Clinton |
| John Roberts* | 2005 | George W. Bush |
| Samuel Alito | 2006 | George W. Bush |
| Sonia Sotomayor | 2009 | Obama |
| Elena Kagan | 2010 | Obama |

**Figure 9.3.** Justices of the Supreme Court.

of New York, having been nominated by a Republican president, George H. W. Bush. In 1997, Sotomayor was nominated by a Democrat, President Bill Clinton, to a seat on the U.S. Court of Appeals for the Second Circuit. In July of 2009, Sotomayor appeared before the Senate Judiciary Committee, which conducted hearings on her confirmation. The committee approved her nomination by a vote of 13-6. Only one Republican Senator, Lindsay Graham of South Carolina, supported her. Her nomination was confirmed by the United States Senate in August 2009 by a vote of 68-31. No Democrats opposed her and only nine Republicans supported her.

In May of 2010, Obama chose Elena Kagan to replace retiring Justice John Paul Stevens. Unlike Sotomayor, Kagan had never been a judge. Her career had been spent in law schools and the executive branch of the federal government. She began her career as a law professor at the University of Chicago. President Clinton appointed her Associate White House Counsel and Deputy Assistant to the President for Domestic Policy and Deputy Director of the Domestic Policy Council. Then she returned to academia as a professor at Harvard Law School and, later, as its first woman dean. President Obama chose her to be solicitor general. She was the first woman to serve in that post.

The Senate Judiciary Committee voted 13-6 to recommend Kagan's confirmation to the full Senate. Again, Lindsay Graham was the only Republican committee member to support the nomination. On August 5 the full Senate confirmed her nomination by a vote of 63-37. In addition to Graham, four other Republicans (Richard Lugar, Judd Gregg, Susan Collins, and Olympia Snowe) voted for Kagan, along with the Senate's two independents. One Democrat, Ben Nelson of Nebraska, opposed her.

In the time period between the two nominations, a crucial change occurred in the makeup of the Senate. As a result of the election of a Republican, Scott Brown, to fill the vacancy created by the death of Senator Edward Kennedy of Massachusetts, the Democratic Senate majority (including the two independents who caucus with the Democrats) was reduced to 59-41. It only takes a majority of the Senate, fifty-one votes, to confirm a Supreme Court nominee. But, as Chapter 7 discussed, sixty votes are needed to end a filibuster. The Republicans could not block Sotomayor because the Democrats had a sixty-vote majority and remained united in support of her. But, with the Democratic majority reduced to fifty-nine, had the Republicans remained united, they would have been able to block Kagan. Thus, Republican support for Kagan was critical to the success of her nomination.

When the Supreme Court agrees to hear a case, it accepts briefs from the contending parties and outside groups whom the litigants ask to submit *amicus curiae*, or "friend of the court," briefs. A *brief* is a written explanation of the legal reasons why the court should rule in a particular way. Then the court schedules oral arguments, during which the two sides present their case directly to the justices and the justices question the presenting attorneys. Afterward, the justices meet in secret conference to discuss the case and vote on it. After the case has been decided, the chief justice assigns an associate justice to write the majority opinion, unless the chief justice is on the losing side, in which case the assignment is made by the most senior justice voting with the majority. Every justice is free to write a *dissenting opinion*, that is, an opinion that opposes the majority, or justices can write opinions that concur with the majority but that either offer different reasons for their vote or take up issues not addressed in the majority opinion.

At every stage of a case's consideration except the conference, the court is assisted by its clerks. As of 2001, there were thirty-four clerks, each assigned to a specific justice. Because clerking for the Supreme Court is a highly prestigious post, these clerks, who are all law school graduates, usually have outstanding academic records and come from top-ranked law schools. They scrutinize petitions for certiorari and make recommendations to the justices they work for. They also do the bulk of the research and help draft the justices' opinions.

As this chapter will explore, two of the most significant functions the Supreme Court performs are to interpret the meaning of the rights mentioned in the Bill of Rights and rule on the constitutionality of laws enacted by Congress. This latter function is known as *judicial review*. In recent years the Court has exercised both these vital functions.

Three significant recent Bill of Rights cases were *McDonald v. Chicago*, which dealt with the Second Amendment right to bear arms; *Citizens United v. Federal Election Commission*, which dealt with the free speech provision of the First Amendment; and *Hosanna-Tabor Church v. Equal Employment Opportunity Commission*, which involved the religious liberty provision of the First Amendment.

The Second Amendment states, "A well-regulated militia, being necessary to the security of a free state, the right of the people to keep and bear arms, shall not be infringed." In 2008 the Court ruled in *District of Columbia v. Heller* that this language meant that government could not infringe on the right of citizens to self-defense, and therefore Washington DC's law that banned the possession of handguns in the home was unconstitutional. The majority opinion in that case claimed that the intentions of the Framers made clear that the right to keep and bear arms is fundamental to the American system of ordered liberty and that therefore citizens enjoyed the right to defend themselves.

The question in *McDonald* was whether the Second Amendment applied to the states. The City of Chicago had adopted a ban on handguns in the home similar to that in Washington DC. As we shall see later, the Supreme Court has decided to extend to states and localities an ever-expanding list of Bill of Rights protections that were originally intended to apply only to the federal government. It interpreted the Fourteenth Amendment's assertion that no state can deny equal protection and due process of law to mean that many critical Bill of Rights protections must extend to states and localities, as well. In the majority opinion, Justice Samuel Alito noted that self-defense is a fundamental right, recognized by many legal systems from ancient times to the present day: "In *Heller*, we held that individual self-defense is 'the central component' of the

Second Amendment. The right to keep and bear arms was considered no less fundamental by those who drafted and ratified the Bill of Rights." Therefore, he concluded the right to bear arms was as fundamental as the other rights enumerated in the Bill of Rights that the Court had previously determined deserved to be incorporated with regard to the states. Alito admitted that allowing people to keep handguns in their homes might have negative public safety implications. However, he pointed out that "the right to keep and bear arms ... is not the only constitutional right that has controversial public safety implications." Restricting the power of the police to conduct searches, eavesdrop, and interrogate criminals may likewise threaten public safety, and yet the Court had determined that in the protection of individual liberty such risks be borne. If a fundamental right exists it cannot be denied because its exercise will sometimes cause harm. In his dissent, Justice Stevens denied that the Chicago law constituted the denial of a fundamental right. The Chicago ordinance did not deny the right of citizens to own weapons, even handguns. It simply said they could not keep them in the house:

The notion that a right of self-defense implies an auxiliary right to own a certain type of firearm presupposes not only controversial judgments about the strength and scope of the (posited) self-defense right, but also controversial assumptions about the likely effects of making that type of firearm more broadly available. It is a very long way from the proposition that the Fourteenth Amendment protects a basic individual right of self-defense to the conclusion that a city may not ban handguns.

The issue of free speech emerged in relation to the provision of the Campaign Finance Act, prohibiting corporations and unions from spending their own money on "electioneering communication" within thirty days of a primary or general election. In January 2008, Citizens United, a nonprofit corporation, released a documentary criticizing then-Senator Hillary Clinton, who had become a Democratic presidential candidate. To promote this documentary, Citizens United produced television advertisements to run on broadcast and cable television. Because its promotion efforts would occur while presidential primaries were taking place, Citizens United feared that they would be considered electioneering communications and therefore kept off the air. Citizens United sought relief in federal court seeking to prevent the Federal Elections Commission from enforcing the applicable provision of the Campaign Finance Act because it was an unconstitutional limit on free speech. The lower courts dismissed the Citizens United petition and the case went to the Supreme Court.

Justice Kennedy, writing for the five-justice majority, agreed with Citizens United. He noted that the First Amendment categorically declared that the Congress "shall make no law ... prohibiting or abridging the freedom of speech." The Amendment did not limit who had the right to exercise such speech and therefore the Congress could not exempt corporations, unions, or any other entity from exercising free speech. He did not claim that freedom of speech was absolute. He did not deny Justice Holmes's famous dictum that freedom of speech did not allow someone to "shout fire in a crowded theatre." But he insisted that there had to be a "sufficient governmental interest" to justify "limits on the political speech of nonprofit or for-profit corporations." He denied that any such interest had been demonstrated in this case. In his dissent, Justice Stevens denied that the First Amendment

required that corporations must be treated identically to natural persons in the political sphere.... Although they make enormous contributions to our society, corporations are not actually members of it. They cannot vote or run for office. Because they may be managed and controlled by nonresidents, their interests may conflict in fundamental respects with the interests of eligible voters.

Because corporations pose a serious threat to the holding of free elections, they constituted just the sort of sufficient government interest that the majority said was lacking as a rationale for limiting speech in this instance: "The financial resources, legal structure, and instrumental orientation of corporations raise legitimate concerns about their role in the electoral process. Our lawmakers have a compelling constitutional basis, if not also a democratic duty, to take measures designed to guard against the potentially deleterious effects of corporate spending in local and national races."

The First Amendment also forbids Congress from making any law respecting the establishment of religion (the Establishment Clause, or prohibiting the free exercise of religion [the Free Exercise Clause]). In *Hosanna-Tabor Church v. Equal Employment Opportunity Commission*, the Court declared, based on those two clauses, there existed a "ministerial exemption" preventing the government from enforcing federal employment discrimination law against a religious body.

Cheryl Perich was a teacher at a school in Redford, Michigan, run by the Hosanna-Tabor Church, which belonged to the Lutheran Church-Missouri Synod, the second-largest Lutheran denomination in the United States. She suffered from narcolepsy, a disease that caused her to unpredictably fall into sudden and deep sleeps from which she could not awakened. She began the 2004–2005 school year on disability leave but sought to return to work midyear. The school had already hired a replacement and refused her request. She was asked to resign in exchange for the school continuing to pay part of her health insurance premiums. Perich refused to resign, and after persisting in trying to return to work she was warned that she risked being fired. She then informed the school that she had spoken to a lawyer and was planning to sue for reinstatement. The church then fired her, stating that her threat to take legal action violated church policy. She reported her firing to the U.S. Equal Employment Opportunity Commission (EEOC), which then sued the church on her behalf, claiming that her firing violated the Americans with Disabilities Act.

In ruling against the EEOC, the Court did not address the question of whether, indeed, the firing violated the act. Rather, it determined that the language of the First Amendment prevented the government from interfering in the hiring and firing of anyone who could plausibly be viewed as a minister of a church. Although Ms. Perich mostly taught secular subjects, she did devote forty-five minutes of her workday to religious subjects. She was trained as a teacher of religion and was considered by the church to be a minister. Therefore, the church was entitled to treat her as a minister and the government could not consider whether or not she was the victim of discrimination based on her disability. The importance of the decision was reinforced by the fact that it was unanimous. Writing for the united Court, Justice Roberts declared: "The Establishment Clause prevents the government from appointing ministers ... the Free Exercise Clause prevents it from interfering with the freedom of religious groups to select their own."

The most significant recent exercise of judicial review came in the Court's 2012 decision upholding the individual mandate provision of President Obama's signature health care reform plan, the Patient Protection and Affordable Care Act (PPACA) passed by Congress in 2010. The mandate provision required most Americans who did not have healthcare coverage to purchase it by 2014. Those who did not would be required to pay a specified amount of money to the federal government. Although it would be paid to the government's tax-collecting agency, the Internal Revenue Service, PPACA stated that it was a penalty not a tax. The plaintiffs, led by the National Federation of Independent Business, claimed the mandate was unconstitutional. They pointed out that no provision of Article One of the Constitution gave the federal government the power to force individuals to buy something. The commerce power had never been interpreted by either Congress or the Court as granting Washington such a power. They did not deny that Congress has the power to tax individuals, but, since PPACA created a penalty not a tax, the taxing power was inapplicable.

Chief Justice John Roberts's majority opinion upheld the mandate provision but did so in such a way as to serve as a warning to the national government regarding the limits of its legislative authority. He agreed with the plaintiffs that the commerce clause could not be invoked as a rationale for the mandate: "The power to regulate commerce presupposes the existence of commercial activity to be regulated." He did not read the word "regulate" as including to power to create. Such an expansive reading would rob the commerce clause of virtually any capacity to restrict what the federal government did. For example, the obesity that stems from poor eating habits imposes far greater costs on the health care system than the failure of some to buy health insurance: "Under the Government's theory, Congress could address the diet problem by ordering everyone to buy vegetables" and impose a penalty on those who did not obey that mandate.

Nonetheless, Roberts ruled for the defendants on the grounds that regardless of the language of the law, the fee imposed for not buying insurance was a tax not a penalty and therefore fell under the taxing power granted in Article One. Roberts saved the mandate by demonstrating that the administration's claim on its behalf was mistaken:

If the concept of penalty means anything, it means *punishment for an unlawful act or omission*. While the individual mandate clearly aims to induce the purchase of health insurance ... *neither the Act nor any other law attaches negative legal consequences to not buying health insurance.* (If) someone chooses to pay rather than obtain health insurance, they have fully complied with the law. Indeed, it is estimated that four million people each year will choose to pay the IRS rather than buy insurance. We would expect Congress to be troubled by that prospect if such conduct were unlawful (my emphasis).

In Roberts's mind, the job of the Court was not to rule on public statements by the president, or even on rationales stated in the law, but rather to evaluate whether the Constitution permitted the exercise of the specific activity under challenge. Because this activity functioned like a tax, not a penalty, it *was* a tax and therefore it was constitutional. The Court upheld PPACA by a 5-4 vote. The dissenters, all Republican appointees, agreed with Roberts's effort to reign in the commerce clause but claimed that the mandate was a penalty not a tax. The rest of the majority, all Democratic appointees, disagreed with Roberts's narrow reading of the commerce clause.

## The Development of Judicial Power

The power of the judiciary is one of the most distinctive characteristics of the American constitutional order. It was often the first thing a foreign visitor noticed about American government. As early as the 1830s, Alexis de Tocqueville observed, "There is hardly a political question in the United States which does not sooner or later turn into a judicial one." American judges, he noted, did not simply interpret an existing body of law, as they did in France or Great Britain; nor were they limited to arbitrating legal disputes. They played a very large part in the development of law and public policy itself.

As we just saw, the Supreme Court determines the constitutionality of laws passed by Congress. But the Constitution does not expressly give it the power of judicial review. Those Framers who favored this principle claimed that it was granted implicitly on the basis of the special status that federal judges are accorded in the document. They are chosen by the executive with the advice and consent of the Senate. They serve for life unless they commit an impeachable offense. These conditions endowed the judiciary with a unique capacity to protect individual rights and the rule of law. George Mason of Virginia voiced the view of many Framers that the judiciary could be a "restraining power," protecting the fundamental law against the designs of unruly majorities and popular demagogues. But many other framers disagreed. They denied that judges had any special wisdom to offer and feared giving too much power to unelected officials. They echoed the sentiments of The Anti-Federalists who believed that if judges decided important moral questions, representative government would become a farce.

The Constitutional Convention defeated every attempt to endow the Supreme Court with powers to overturn the decisions of other branches. As we shall soon see, the power of judicial review came into being only after a bitter struggle between the Court and President Thomas Jefferson. Before the adoption of the Constitution, Americans viewed the protectors of their rights to be local governments and elected assemblies, not a nonelected judiciary. Even after the Constitution's adoption, the courts did not immediately obtain authority to interpret the Constitution. The Court's refusal to challenge the constitutionality of the 1798 Sedition Act, which made it a crime to publish anything that could be taken as derogatory about the government, raised doubts about the Court's willingness to protect fundamental constitutional rights. As we pointed out in Chapter 4, the act blurred the distinction between conspiracy and legitimate political opposition and seemed to violate the First Amendment prohibition against any law abridging freedom of speech or press. Its enforcement was marred by partisan intolerance. Most sedition cases were tried in 1800 and were tied directly to that year's presidential election between incumbent Federalist John Adams and Republican Thomas Jefferson. Federal judges, most of them Federalists, were enthusiastic in their prosecution of Republicans who dared to criticize the Adams administration.

Republican concerns about the judiciary were reinforced by the Judiciary Act of 1801, enacted just before Jefferson was inaugurated. It created many new federal judgeships that were hurriedly filled via "midnight" appointments by the outgoing Adams administration. The Federalists, having lost control of the other two branches of government, hoped to maintain some governmental control by entrenching a pro-Federalist judiciary protected by life tenure. Among these last-minute appointments was that of staunch Federalist John Marshall as chief justice. This final insult convinced the Republicans to plan a campaign against the judiciary, lest the peoples' will, as expressed in the 1800 election, be denied.

Jefferson's faith in majority rule animated his war with the judiciary. He insisted that each branch of government and state governments, as well, share equally in deciding matters of constitutionality. The court's constitutional rulings would hold only for specific cases in question and would not obligate the executive or Congress to treat them as legal precedents. The Sedition Act had expired the day before Jefferson took office, but to underscore his fierce opposition to it, he pardoned everyone (mostly Republican newspaper publishers) whom it had convicted. He declared that the law had been unconstitutional, underscoring his conviction that the president as well as the courts had the right to make such a determination.

## ESTABLISHING THE PATH OF JUDICIAL REVIEW: *MARBURY V. MADISON*

These issues of power and principle came to a head in the 1803 case of *Marbury v. Madison*. Adams's secretary of state, John Marshall, in his rush to assume his new duties as chief justice of the Supreme Court, had failed to deliver commissions to seventeen of Adams's last-minute judicial appointments, including one for William Marbury as justice of the peace in the District of Columbia. Marbury's appointment now rested with the new secretary of state, James Madison, who, seeking to prevent it, withheld delivery of the commission. Jefferson supported Madison on the grounds that the previous administration had not fully executed Marbury's commission and the new administration was under no obligation to do so. Marbury and three others who had been denied their offices petitioned the Supreme Court for a writ of *mandamus* – a court order to a cabinet official to comply with a legal obligation – that would require Madison to deliver the commission. The court was authorized to issue such a writ by the Judiciary Act of 1789. Jefferson made clear he would order Madison not to comply.

The court lacked the prestige to stand up to a popular president. To order Madison to deliver Marbury's appointment would expose not only the court's inability to enforce its own rulings but also its fragile standing in the country. Yet, to deny Marburg's petition would confirm the president and Congress's freedom from judicial oversight. Writing for a unanimous court, Marshall declared that Jefferson and Madison had abused their offices by refusing to deliver an appointment signed by a president, confirmed by the Senate, and sealed by a secretary of state. Jefferson was abrogating a lifetime appointment and thus violating the principal foundation of the judiciary's constitutional independence. Marshall insisted that the protection of constitutional rights required such independence.

But after scolding the president, Marshall sidestepped a direct political confrontation by denying Marbury his writ. He ruled that Section 13 of the Judiciary Act of 1789, under which Marbury had brought suit, was unconstitutional. The section gave the Supreme Court original jurisdiction in the matter; even though the Constitution insists that the court's jurisdiction is appellate in all but a few kinds of cases. In adding to the court's original jurisdiction, the Judiciary Act violated the Constitution.

Marshall's opinion avoided a bitter political controversy that he could not win. He gave Jefferson a free hand to bar Federalist appointees from office, but only if the president accepted the Court's power to interpret the Constitution. Like Hamilton, Marshall argued that a Constitution embodying the rights and privileges of the American people required an independent judiciary that could only fully guard those rights and privileges if it had the final say in deciding if a law was or was not constitutional. Marshall's decision in *Marbury v. Madison* was the first successful effort by the Supreme Court to exercise judicial review.

Jefferson did not accept this argument, but Marshall's ruling was so adroit that the president had no way to disobey it. After all, the court had refused Marbury his appointment. In the final analysis, Jefferson's attack on the courts failed because the Republicans were not sufficiently aroused against the judiciary to destroy its independence. Marshall had disarmed them by holding his partisan fire in the service of the court as an institution. By doing so, he displayed just the sort of impartiality the judiciary's special constitutional status called for.

## Critical Choice: Establishing National Supremacy

Jefferson's Revolution of 1800 (see Chapters 4 and 8) placed the presidency in the service of democratic rather than liberal principles, which invited a struggle between Republicans and Federalists. Marshall's statecraft preserved the Court's impartiality in the face of this great party contest and thereby strengthened its authority and prestige. The Court was raised from third-rate power to coequal branch of government and obtained the special constitutional status its champions had sought. With both president and Congress enmeshed in a party struggle, only the judiciary remained above the partisan fray. As Hamilton anticipated, because the Court was an independent, small, cohesive body whose members enjoyed life tenure, it could maintain a long-term view, which gave it a decided advantage over a scattered and divided opposition. Marshall fulfilled Hamilton's hopes; under his leadership the court successfully defended the Hamiltonian principles of national supremacy and judicial review.

To defend Hamiltonian principles, it was first necessary to enhance the prestige and authority of the court itself. Marshall took advantage of his position as chief justice to cultivate the distinctive qualities of the Court and gave it institutional identity and standardized its procedures. He led discussion and directed the order of business in private conferences. He either wrote the Court's opinions or assigned that task to another justice. Getting the Supreme Court to speak with one voice would enhance its prestige. Marshall worked skillfully to forge consensus and persuade those in the majority not to write their own opinions but to sign on to the "opinion of the court." He wrote an overwhelming number of opinions himself, even when he disagreed with the ruling.

As Jefferson and his Republican successors made appointments to the bench, achieving unanimity became more difficult. But the Court did not return to the fractious practices that preceded Marshall's arrival. Jefferson's first appointment, Justice William Johnson of South Carolina, persuaded Marshall to appoint someone to deliver the opinion of the Court, but to leave the rest of the judges free to voice their dissents. The Court still adheres to that procedure. Still, Marshall's firm yet deft hand kept the Court from dividing along partisan lines. The example of judicial restraint that he set during his long tenure, which lasted until his death in 1835, enabled the Court to fully grasp the role of interpreter of the Constitution.

Marshall interpreted the Constitution in a more centralizing direction than the Jeffersonians and their successors, the Jacksonians, were comfortable with. He thereby moderated their inclination toward local self-government and left a nationalist legacy for future generations. His most important defense of national supremacy related to the national bank controversy that we discussed in Chapters 4 and 6. With Washington's support, the government chartered the Bank of the United States in 1791. The Republicans let it expire in 1811, but some of them, including Jefferson and Madison, had second thoughts after the War of 1812, in which the American military effort was hampered by the national government's reliance on state banks. Consequently, Congress created a second Bank of the United States in 1816 with another twenty-year charter. Continued state-level opposition gave the Marshall court its opportunity to address the constitutional issues raised by the bank controversy in the landmark 1819 case *McCulloch v. Maryland* (see Chapter 5). Maryland retaliated by enacting a law that imposed a $15,000 tax ($229,000 in 2006 currency) on any bank not chartered by the state. The Bank of the United States, the only financial institution operating in Maryland that was not chartered by the state, and thus clearly the target of the law, refused to pay the tax, and Maryland filed suit against James McCulloch, the cashier of the Baltimore branch of the national bank.

The federal government argued in *McCulloch* that Maryland's tax on the bank was unconstitutional. Maryland replied that Congress had no power to incorporate a bank, and in any event, states could tax as they willed within their own borders. Speaking for a unanimous court, Marshall upheld the bank's constitutionality and gave the classic statement of the doctrine of national authority. His argument was not new, but he added his own memorable rhetoric and lent the now-considerable prestige of the Court to a sweeping concept of nationalism.

Challenging the Jeffersonian notion that the states were the repositories of popular rule, the chief justice responded that the Constitution belonged, as the preamble made clear, to "We, the People": "In form and in substance it emanates from them. Its powers are granted by them, and are to be exercised directly on them, and for their benefit." Although the Constitution limited the powers of the national government, it also clearly established the central authority as "supreme law of the land." Therefore, the national government must retain sufficient powers to carry out the great responsibilities vested in it. And those means must be understood flexibly, lest the Constitution be laden with the sort of policy detail that would bog down a great experiment in self-rule. "We must never forget it is a constitution we are expounding ... intended to endure for ages to come," wrote Marshall.

Marshall admitted that the Constitution did not list a bank as one of the enumerated powers. But a bank was a useful tool for powers that the Constitution did enumerate: collecting taxes, borrowing money, regulating commerce, and supporting armies and navies. Therefore, as the Constitution provides, the bank was "necessary and proper" for implementing those powers. The final part of Marshall's opinion followed from this generous interpretation of national sovereignty. Maryland's tax was unconstitutional because the "power to tax involves the power to destroy." To uphold the tax would empower an inferior to destroy a superior.

Jefferson and Madison had come to accept the bank as a necessary evil, so they accepted the Court's holding. But, they abhorred Marshall's expansive interpretation of national power and the pressure toward governmental consolidation that it created. In 1819, Jefferson said, "After twenty years' confirmation of the federal system by the voice of the people, declared through the medium of elections, we find the judiciary on every occasion, still driving us into consolidation." Marshall saw no reason why the court should be bound by Jefferson's vision of states' rights; he claimed a "mandate" to uphold the nationalist principles that "We the People" had established in 1787. In deftly positioning itself as the guardian of the people's Constitution, the Marshall Court established a tradition of judicial independence and elevated the position of chief justice to a status that would rival the power and prestige of the executive.

## A FALSE PATH: SETTLING ON SLAVERY

Limits on the Supreme Court's power to chart a course for the country were set in response to the Court's attempt to impose a settlement of the slavery controversy that was wracking the nation during the 1850s. Fearing they would eventually lose if the slavery issue were decided by Congress, proslavery politicians – including President James Buchanan, a Democrat from Pennsylvania who had been elected in 1856 – yearned to have the Court set a clear proslavery path for the country. The case the Court chose to "settle" the matter of slavery was *Dred Scott v. Sandford* (1857). Buchanan's wish to defer to the Court stemmed from his prior knowledge of how the case would be decided. A majority of the justices were from the South. Buchanan knew that they would take a proslavery position. But Buchanan believed that the decision would lack

DRED SCOTT.
HARRIET, WIFE OF DRED SCOTT.

**Figure 9.4.** No Legal Escape: An 1887 wood engraving of Dred Scott and his wife Harriet.
Credit: The Granger Collection, NYC – All rights reserved.

credibility in the North unless a northern justice voted with the southerners. He privately lobbied a fellow Pennsylvanian, Justice Robert Grier, to side with those who wanted to deny both Congress and the territorial legislatures the right to prohibit slavery. Greer succumbed, giving the Court false hope that its opinion would have the appearance of a national, not a sectional, ruling.

Dred Scott (Figure 9.4) had been taken as a slave into Illinois and the northern part of the Louisiana Purchase. Illinois law forbade slavery. Congress had prohibited slavery in the northern part of the Louisiana Territory in the Missouri Compromise of 1820. Scott, now living in the slave state of Missouri, sued his present owner, arguing that prolonged visits to a free state and territory made him a free man. The case came to the Supreme Court on appeal from the Missouri Supreme Court and the federal appeals court, both of which had ruled against Scott.

Chief Justice Roger Taney's majority opinion supported Missouri's contention that Scott was a slave and that the Supreme Court was bound by Missouri law in this case. But, as Buchanan had hoped, the opinion went much further in that it denied that African Americans were citizens in the eyes of the Constitution and stated that they therefore could not sue in federal court. It also declared that Scott's journey to a free territory was meaningless in any case because Congress did not have authority to prohibit slavery in the territories. The Missouri Compromise itself was therefore unconstitutional.

But the "cult of the robe" could not resolve the slavery controversy. The Supreme Court's claim to authoritatively interpret constitutional disputes rested on public perception that its judgments were impartial. In attempting to judge a profound political issue, the Court forfeited that claim. The Court's diminished influence was confirmed by the triumph of Abraham Lincoln and the Republicans in the 1860 election. Lincoln refused to accept *Dred Scott* as a binding precedent. He insisted that the great issues raised in the case had to be resolved by the American people. Chief Justice Taney had denied African Americans citizenship on the grounds that the grand words of the Declaration of Independence that "all men are created equal" did not include "the enslaved African race." But Lincoln insisted that the Declaration's meaning, and its relationship to the Constitution, was not a narrow legal issue. It raised the most basic questions about the nature of American rights and responsibilities. Lincoln granted that the *Dred Scott* decision was binding on the parties to the suit, but he would not allow it to determine the future course of slavery policy. If the Supreme Court were going to settle vital political questions, "the people will have ceased to be their own rulers, to that extent, practically resigned their government, into the hands of that eminent tribunal." Lincoln and the Union's triumph in the Civil War ensured that *Dred Scott* would not stand and the court would not rule the nation.

## Another False Path: Blocking Economic Regulation

Less than a decade elapsed between the *Dred Scott* decision and its political reversal. The second failure of the court to settle a profound national controversy, its effort to prevent meaningful government regulation of the economy, took decades to play out. As it had done during the Marshall era, the post–Civil War judiciary served as the "aristocratic" anchor on America's democratic sail, this time as the protector of property rights. It successfully blocked state and federal efforts to regulate the economy, fearing that such efforts would destroy the free-enterprise system. Its success in these efforts rest on the ability of the Republican Party to dominate presidential and congressional politics from the 1870s to the 1930s and thus to control Supreme Court appointments during this long period (see Chapters 4 and 11).

The Supreme Court based its opposition to most forms of economic regulation on its reading of two critical constitutional provisions: the commerce clause in Article One and the due process clause found in both The First and Fourteenth Amendments. In *United States v. E. C. Knight Co.* (1895), the court rested its gutting of the Sherman Antitrust Act (see Chapter 6) on its interpretation of the commerce clause. The Sherman Act made it illegal for business to contract, combine, or conspire to create a trust or monopoly for the purpose of restraining free trade and monopolizing interstate or foreign commerce. *E. C. Knight* involved the American Sugar Refining Company, which already controlled a majority of American sugar-refining companies. It sought to purchase control of four additional ones, including E. C. Knight, and thus acquire 98 percent of refining capacity. The Department of Justice asked for a Court order that forbade the purchase, contending that the companies were combining in restraint of trade. The Court disagreed, holding that the Sherman Act did not apply to monopolies in manufacturing, because *manufacturing*, no matter how large the companies were or how widely distributed their goods were, and was not part of interstate *commerce*. The court confined the term "commerce" to its most literal meaning, "trade." Manufacturing had only an indirect impact on trade, and regulating it was a matter for the states.

The Due Process Clause had traditionally been interpreted to mean that government action, national or state, was beyond judicial review as long as fair procedures had been followed. But lawyers and judges who opposed economic regulation fastened on the idea of *substantive due process*. This concept declared that intruding on a fundamental right, such as the right of contract, was a violation of due process of law no matter what procedural niceties had been observed. A New York law required bakery employees to work no more than ten hours per day or sixty hours per week. In *Lochner v. New York* (1905) the Supreme Court declared that this use of New York's police power violated "the right of contract between employer and employees" and was therefore a violation of the Due Process Clause.

The Court's suppression of economic regulation was not complete. Both TR and Woodrow Wilson succeeded in championing railroad regulation, food and drug safety, and some other forms of government intrusions into economic life (see Chapter 6). But the full-scale defeat of the Court's efforts to constrain government economic intervention did not occur until the New Deal. New Deal efforts to lift the Great Depression and promote economic security caused it to intrude into virtually all realms of economic endeavor including banking, stock and bond trading, labor practices, and food supply. The Court – *Dred Scott* excepted – had usually restrained itself during national emergencies. But by 1935, a majority of justices resolved to make a stand against what they took to be a massive assault on economic liberty.

The four justices who anchored that resistance – James McReynolds, Willis Van Devanter, George Sutherland, and Pierce Butler – were determined to protect the Constitution, no matter how great the public clamor for change. For a time, they were joined by two others, Owen Roberts and Chief Justice Charles Evans Hughes. The result was that during the term spanning 1935 and 1936, the court struck down more important national laws than in any comparable period in American history, and a number of important state laws, as well.

In *Schechter Poultry Corporation v. United States* (1935), the court declared the National Industrial Recovery Act (NIRA) unconstitutional. Schechter operated slaughterhouses in New York City. The company received live chickens from outside the state, slaughtered them, and then sold them to local stores.

It was convicted in federal court of violating a number of standards set under NIRA, including hours and wage regulations. The court used E. C. Knight as a precedent to claim that such regulation of hours and wages exceeded the national government's commerce power. Moreover, the court claimed NIRA to be an unconstitutional delegation of authority to the executive branch, violating the separation of powers.

The court had never before declared an act of Congress unconstitutional for delegating legislative power to the executive. As such, *Schecter* was a direct challenge to the modern administrative state, whose expansion, in the face of terrifying economic insecurity, seemed inevitable. The decision was unanimous. Even Justice Louis Brandeis, whose righteous anger against big business led his political friends to call him Isaiah, voted with the majority. In *Morehead v. New York, ex rel. Tipaldo* (1936), the court voted 5-4 to overrule a New York law that set a women's minimum wage, reaffirming the Due Process Clause of the Fourteenth Amendment as a barrier to assaults on the liberty of contract. Justice Butler announced an unyielding rule of substantive due process, arguing "the state is without power by any form of legislation to prohibit, change or nullify contracts between employers and adult women workers as to the amount of wages to be paid." This case created, FDR explained, a "no man's land": it showed that the court majority was opposed to all economic reform regardless of whether it was federal or state.

As we discussed in Chapter 8, FDR responded to these threats to the New Deal by launching his court-packing plan. Although the plan failed, the Hughes Court chose not to emulate the Taney Court and to shift ground in the direction of self-restraint.

Justices Hughes and Roberts adopted pro-New Deal positions in a series of critical cases. In *West Coast Hotel v. Parrish* (1937), issued less than two months after FDR's court plan (see Chapter 8) appeared, the Court retreated from substantive due process, ruling 5-4 that a Washington state minimum-wage law was constitutional. Justice Roberts switched from the position he had taken in *Tipaldo* just ten months earlier. Because the Washington law protected women, Chief Justice Hughes, writing for the majority, could have resorted to the specific women's exemption the court had established in a previous case. Instead, he defended the general authority of state government to protect all vulnerable citizens against the uncertainties of the market (Figure 9.5).

Only two weeks later, in *The National Labor Relations Board v. Jones and Laughlin Steel Corporation*, the Court upheld the National Labor Relations Act. In so doing, the Court extended the notion of commerce to include manufacturing and also declared that the federal government could regulate intrastate commerce if it had a "close and substantial relation to interstate commerce." Just how loosely the majority of justices were willing to define "close and substantial" was revealed in *National Labor Relations Board v. Friedman–Harry*

THE RETREAT FROM MOSCOW.

**Figure 9.5.** "The Retreat from Moscow": A 1937 cartoon by James Berryman comparing President Franklin D. Roosevelt's failure to "pack" the Supreme Court with Napoleon's retreat from Moscow. Credit: The Granger Collection, NYC – All rights reserved.

*Marks Clothing Co.* (1937). In this case, the Court ruled against a Richmond, Virginia, clothing company whose production, unlike the Jones and Laughlin steel empire, had only a minimal effect on interstate commerce.

In *Steward Machine Co. v. Davis* (1937), the Supreme Court upheld the New Deal's centerpiece, the Social Security Act. Justices Roberts and Hughes once again cast the deciding votes in a 5-4 opinion, delivered by Justice Benjamin Cardozo, that sustained the unemployment compensation system despite the act's requirement that state laws meet national standards to be eligible for federal funds. Speaking for six justices, Cardozo also upheld the old-age pension system in *Helvering v. Davis* (1937) even though the pensions were funded by a special tax. A year earlier, the Court had ruled that using taxes to promote public welfare intruded on the reserved powers of the states and violated the Tenth Amendment, which reserves to the states and the people those powers not delegated to the national government. By upholding the Social Security Act, the Court apparently had given up its commitment to so-called *dual federalism*, an interpretation of the Tenth Amendment that strictly limited the powers of the national government to constitutionally enumerated powers and viewed the national and state governments as sovereign and equal in their respective spheres of influence (see Chapter 4).

FDR solidified the court's transformation. As a result of retirements and deaths, he was able to appoint eight justices in the next six years, all of whom were selected less for their distinguished jurisprudence than for their devout loyalty to the New Deal. Thus, despite his plan's defeat, FDR eventually "packed" the court. After winning a third term, he even had the pleasure of replacing his archenemy, Justice McReynolds, who between 1937 and 1941 had dissented from pro-New Deal opinions 119 times. These new appointments caused what historian William Leuchtenburg has called "the constitutional revolution of 1937," a full acceptance of the New Deal constitutional order. Since then, the Court has not struck down a single piece of significant economic legislation. Nor has it judged any law (with the exception of the Line Item Veto Act passed in 1996) to be an unconstitutional delegation of authority to the executive.

## CRITICAL CHOICE: DEFENDING PROGRAMMATIC RIGHTS

FDR used the term "liberalism" to describe his philosophy of government. By using this term, FDR meant that the New Deal and the modern presidency were to be a liberal as well as a democratic phenomenon, "supplementing," as he put it, the traditional American understanding of rights with a new one (see Chapter 4). FDR was astute enough to recognize that if the court became sympathetic to the new idea of rights he championed, it could help protect liberal programs from inevitable future political attack.

FDR differed from his Progressive predecessors, especially TR, who had called for formal constitutional changes to weaken the court's institutional authority. Theodore Roosevelt's Progressive party campaign in 1912 favored submitting court decisions to voter referenda and making it easier to amend the Constitution and thus override judicial interpretations of it. As FDR foresaw, when the Democrats lost the presidency to Republican Dwight Eisenhower in 1952, liberals became increasingly dependent on the court. Although Democrats had a majority in both houses of Congress for most of the 1950s, actual control was exercised by a coalition of Republicans and southern Democrats. With conservatives commanding the presidency and Congress, the judiciary, remade by the constitutional revolution of 1937, became the agent of national political reform.

For the next several decades, much of the court's reform effort focused not on restraining government but on demanding that government secure rights for people that they were unable to secure for themselves. We term these new forms of entitlement *programmatic rights*, to emphasize that they cannot be realized simply by restraining government but require positive governmental action to be secured. Thus, they differ from those rights enumerated in the Bill of Rights, all of which limit the scope of governmental activity:

As political scientist R. Shep Melnick says, contemporary liberalism promises a broader security against the vagaries of the business cycle; against the multiple unintended hazards created by a dynamic capitalism; against the prejudices of private citizens and the consequences of three centuries of racism; against the risks of congenital handicaps and inevitable old age; and against the consequences of poverty and of family decomposition.

This new understanding of security forms the basis for many of the Court's novel constitutional interpretations, especially with respect to the Fourteenth Amendment. Many of these new claims on government have also been written into law. The judiciary does not hesitate to supervise wide swaths of the economy and society based on these statutory provisions.

Since the New Deal, the Supreme Court has gone through two distinct phases. During the first phase, from 1953 to 1986, the Warren and Burger Courts were in the forefront of what Shep Melnick has deemed "the Rights Revolution." They not only spearheaded the effort to end racial discrimination but also led crusading efforts to end voting inequality and established a right to privacy. The second period that began with the appointment of William Rehnquist as chief justice in 1986 and continues today with John Roberts as Chief Justice is more difficult to characterize. The Rehnquist and Roberts Courts have embodied three distinct and at times conflicting themes: a reaffirmation of most critical aspects of the prior rights revolution; a conservative reaction against some aspects of the rights revolution; and a push to establish rights dearer to the hearts of conservatives than liberals.

## The Rights Revolution

The Fourteenth Amendment's promise that no state could deprive American citizens of the "equal protection of the laws" appeared to offer African Americans full citizenship, but, as of the 1950s, that promise had not been fulfilled. The nineteenth-century Court upheld the notorious Jim Crow laws in the southern states that forcibly separated the races and deprived African Americans of equal treatment.

In *Plessy v. Ferguson* (1896), the court invoked the doctrine of "separate but equal," meaning that as long as accommodations of the same quality were provided, it was permissible to segregate according to race. Homer Plessy, a Louisiana resident, boarded a train in New Orleans, having bought a first-class ticket, and took a vacant seat after refusing the conductor's order to sit in the "Colored Only" section. He was arrested and convicted for violating Louisiana's segregation statute. The Supreme Court upheld the conviction, denying that racial segregation was discriminatory. It did not choose to address the obvious reality that accommodations for African Americans were almost never of the same quality as those provided to Whites. An 8-1 majority insisted that the Louisiana statute did not imply racial inferiority but was a reasonable exercise of state police power to promote the public good.

Justice Harlan's dissent challenged this tortured interpretation of the Fourteenth Amendment. He insisted that the "constitution is color-blind" and that therefore it was unconstitutional for a state to base laws on race. He noted that the purpose of the Louisiana law was not to exclude whites from black railroad cars but solely to exclude blacks from white cars, which made a mockery of the state's claim that the law was not racially discriminatory.

Justice Harlan's solitary protest was finally vindicated in *Brown v. Board of Education of Topeka* (1954). Brown revitalized the Fourteenth Amendment Equal Protection Clause as a weapon to uphold civil rather than economic rights. This case, which involved segregated elementary schools in Topeka, Kansas, had come to the court in 1951. But in recognition of its great historical importance, the justices delayed their decision until after the 1952 presidential election and until they could achieve unanimity. Chief Justice Earl Warren's opinion was crafted less to convince legal scholars than to gain public support for a decision that would inevitably engender resistance. Hoping to see the entire *Brown* decision printed in every newspaper, he insisted that "the opinion should be short, readable by the lay public, non-rhetorical, unemotional, and, above all, not accusatory." In order to avoid accusations, the justices admitted that the historical intent of the Fourteenth Amendment's framers was inconclusive regarding segregation. Nor did they argue that the amendment justified school desegregation as a remedy for a century of government neglect and oppression. Rather, *Brown* was rendered on sociological and psychological grounds. It claimed that education had become critical to American democracy, "the foundation of good citizenship." No child could be expected to succeed in life if denied an education, and therefore education had to be provided on equal terms.

The court then moved to consider the deleterious psychological effects that legal separation of the races had on black children's motivation to learn. It found that segregation generated "a feeling of inferiority as to their status in the community that may affect the hearts and minds." Therefore, *de jure segregation* (segregation enforced by law) was a form of discrimination, and therefore, regarding public education at least, "separate but equal has no place." The Court's reliance on sociological and psychological grounds rather than textured constitutional interpretation made it vulnerable to the charge that it was engaged in judicial legislation. Indeed, the *Brown* decision signaled a new era of court activism.

## A Right to Fair Representation

In the 1960's the Warren Court began to move aggressively beyond racial justice to insist that government protect other neglected rights. Beginning with *Baker v. Carr* (1962), the court took up voter apportionment in order to determine whether various sizes and shapes of state, local, and national election districts were ensuring that every voter had an equal right to determine electoral outcomes. The Tennessee legislature had not reapportioned its legislative districts since 1901, even as the state's population shifted from rural to urban and suburban areas. Charles Baker and several other Tennessee residents sued, claiming that as urban dwellers they were being denied equal protection of the laws. In previous cases, the Court had defined the formation of electoral districts as a political question poorly suited to judicial resolution and best solved by the political branches. It recognized that in the American constitutional order representation was a means for moderating majority opinion as well as for articulating it. The very existence of the Senate, said the Court, shows that the framers of the Constitution considered state boundaries, not simply population, in designing the nation's legislative branch.

Justice William Brennan's majority opinion in the *Baker* case abandoned this restrained position. He understood the Equal Protection Clause of the Fourteenth Amendment as protecting the right of all voters to have their votes count equally. Justice Felix Frankfurter, a militant New Dealer appointed by FDR, dissented. He warned his progressive colleagues that they were committing the same constitutional crime they had once accused their conservative predecessors of perpetrating. Just as the Court had previously misused the Fourteenth Amendment to uphold the right of contract and usurp policy responsibility best left to political representatives, it was now improperly using the same amendment to enter a "political thicket." Denial of franchise because of race, color, religion, or sex was an appropriate matter for intervention by the courts, said Frankfurter, but not the relationship between population and legislative representation, which was never a straightforward matter under the Constitution. The judiciary could not reliably adjudicate such disputes impartially because no clear constitutional standard existed. To involve the courts implied that judges were "omnicompetent" and risked "enthroning the judiciary." Appeals for fairer apportionment should be addressed to "an informed, civically minded electorate." Frankfurter wrote, "There is not under our Constitution a judicial remedy for every political mischief. In a democratic society like ours, relief must come through an aroused popular conscience that sears the conscience of people's representatives."

Critics of Frankfurter might argue that malapportioned districts prevent deprived citizens from finding adequate political avenues for registering their grievances. Even some of the Warren Court's critics conceded that malapportionment was severe enough in many states, as well as in some congressional districts, to warrant a federal judiciary remedy. But they would have preferred the court to rest its opinion on different constitutional grounds. The political scientist Martha Derthick would have chosen Article IV Section 4 of the Constitution, which guarantees "every State in the Union a Republican Form of Government." That clause, which had not been invoked since the mid-nineteenth century, could have been applied to cases in which a state legislature's failure to reapportion violated its state constitution and thereby undermined the federal constitution's guarantee. Derthick argued that relying on the Equal Protection Clause of the Fourteenth Amendment "catapulted the federal judiciary" into a "mathematical quagmire" in which the states would be held to a standard of equality that had no place in American constitutional history.

Two years later, the court struck down the apportionment system used by most state legislatures for their upper houses. Like the U.S. Senate, they typically represented smaller units of government, usually counties, of unequal population size. In *Reynolds v. Sims* (1964), the court declared this non-population method of apportionment unconstitutional. It rejected comparison to the Senate because the Senate had merely been a political compromise struck at the Constitutional Convention. It did not explain why the Senate's status as a compromise made it irrelevant as a model for the design of state legislatures. It also pointed out that counties, cities, and other local subdivisions, unlike states, had no claim to being sovereign entities. Chief Justice Warren's majority opinion stated, "Legislators represent people, not trees or acres. Legislators are elected by voters, not farms or cities or economic interests." The only acceptable constitutional standard was one person, one vote. a principle the court extended to almost all popularly elected, multimember, state decision-making bodies as well as congressional districts.

## CRITICAL CHOICE: INFERRING A RIGHT TO PRIVACY

In addition to defending programmatic rights, the Court also established a new right against government intrusion, a right of privacy. In *Griswold v. Connecticut* (1965), the Warren Court overturned a Connecticut law that made it a crime to sell, use, or counsel the use of contraceptives for birth control. As Justice Potter Stewart put it, this law appeared to be an "uncommonly silly law"; it grated against most Americans' sense of privacy. No language in the Constitution clearly prohibited such a law. Nevertheless, when Planned Parenthood members were charged with breaking it, the Supreme Court struck down their convictions.

In his majority opinion, Justice William Douglas granted that the Constitution did not explicitly provide a right of privacy. But the spirit of such a right pervaded the whole document. Specific Bill of Rights guarantees created "zones of privacy" that prohibited the peacetime quartering of soldiers in private houses, unreasonable searches and seizures, and self-incrimination. These specific privacy guarantees cast a broader shadow that created a penumbra, a shadow's outer reach, and protected additional privacy rights, including marital privacy.

The Burger Court extended the concept of privacy rights to abortion. *Roe v. Wade* (1973) involved an unmarried pregnant woman who sought an abortion in Texas, where abortions were prohibited by law except when the life of the mother was at stake. Justice Harry Blackmun's decision, for a 7-2 majority, found Texas's antiabortion law unconstitutional because it violated the Fourteenth Amendment, which he claimed, guaranteed that the states cannot restrict "personal liberty" including a right to privacy. Blackmun did not claim that this right was absolute: "A State may properly assert important interests in safeguarding health, in maintaining medical standards, and in protecting potential life." He sought to balance the right to an abortion with the state's legitimate regulatory interests by distinguishing between different stages of pregnancy. Early in pregnancy, he denied the states any power to regulate abortion. Later in the pregnancy, he found that the states' "interests become sufficiently compelling to sustain regulation of the factors that govern the abortion decision." He set the dividing line between early and late at the end of the first three months of pregnancy (the first trimester) because until that time the mother is under less risk from abortion than from childbirth. After that time "a state may regulate the abortion procedure to the extent that the regulation reasonably relates to the preservation and protection of maternal health." Because the Texas statute did not distinguish between early and late abortions it violated womens' right to an abortion during the first trimester. The Roe decision had profound political and policy consequences. It invalidated abortion statutes in forty-six states and gave rise to a pro-life movement that was animated by intense resentment of the court's claim that a fetus was not a person.

## Implementing Programmatic Rights

As we note in this chapter, the judiciary controls neither purse nor sword. When it was protecting rights such as liberty of contract, the judiciary had only to restrain government. But so many of the Warren and Burger Courts rulings were about securing rights that could only be provided by government, that it made the Court increasingly dependent on other agents of government – lower courts, Congress, and the executive – to implement its will.

Chapter 7 shows that Congress's response to the expansion of national administrative power has been to intervene in the details of administration. By doing so, it has become more like the very bureaucracies it seeks to control. Likewise as the federal judiciary has involved itself in the detailed behavior of administrative agencies, it, too, has come to assume tasks and responsibilities more typical of a federal agency than of a court. This transformation began with the *Brown* decision. The Warren Court was left with the practical problem of how to end forced school segregation. It waited a year before issuing the so-called Brown 2 case, *Brown v. Board of Education* (1955), which called for "all deliberate speed" to desegregate schools. Because it felt it could not rely on the very local governments that were resisting desegregation to fashion adequate desegregation plans, the Supreme Court assigned that responsibility to the federal district court.

In September 1957, the Democratic governor of Arkansas, Orval Faubus, called up the state National Guard to obstruct a federal court order to desegregate all-white Central High School in Little Rock. President Eisenhower, who privately opposed the *Brown* decision and refused to publicly endorse it, now found himself faced with the most serious state challenge to federal authority since the end of Reconstruction. His meeting with Faubus on September 14 only seemed to encourage the Arkansas governor's resistance to desegregation. On September 23, nine African-American students were turned away from the school by a howling mob. Eisenhower still did not come out in support of the *Brown* decision. Yet, fearing that to do nothing in the face of Faubus's resistance would encourage every segregationist governor to defy the law, he finally took action to enforce the court order. His delay enabled resistance to grow so great as to require the largest domestic military deployment in decades. On September 24, a contingent of regular army paratroopers was dispatched to Little Rock. The next day Americans saw shocking photographs of troops wielding bayonets in an American city.

The Little Rock incident dramatically underscored the need for presidential and congressional support in order to achieve desegregation. Until 1964, when President Lyndon Johnson and his congressional supporters made that support reliably available, very little actual desegregation took place. Resistant local governments emphasized "deliberate" rather than "speed" in responding to the court's school desegregation edict. After 1964, when the combined authority of all three federal government branches was deployed against the South and its system of Jim Crow, desegregation progress came quickly. Within four years, more southern schools desegregated than in the previous fourteen years.

Progress in desegregation was far slower when the objective shifted from simply eliminating legally mandated segregation to remedying the ill effects of past segregation by purposely mixing whites and blacks together. This goal was particularly hard to achieve in locales in which the two races no longer lived in the same neighborhoods. The most controversial remedy that the courts attempted was busing. In *Swann v. Charlotte-Mecklenburg Board of Education* (1971), the court approved massive busing of students as well as a system of attendance zones that was marked by sometimes drastic redrawing of traditional school boundaries. Acknowledging the difficulties that judges faced in designing practical integration plans, the court claimed that the goal was so important that "administratively awkward, inconvenient and even bizarre" solutions could not be avoided.

In a 1974 Denver, Colorado, case, the court determined that unofficial, de facto segregation patterns were unconstitutional if the school board "intended" to separate the races. Such discriminatory intent was shown in other cities including Detroit, Cleveland, and Boston. Remedying de facto segregation in places such as Boston proved very difficult. The Boston metropolitan area encompassed many separate school districts, but the Court could prove discriminatory intent only with regard to the city school district. Therefore, busing was confined to the city, which encouraged whites to flee to adjacent suburbs. African Americans were bused to white poor and working-class Boston neighborhoods. As Martha Derthick notes, "The spectacle of federal judges deciding the most mundane details of local school administration ... while ethnic neighborhoods turned into battle zones caused even the most ardent liberals to ponder whether the power of national judges was being appropriately employed." Because so many whites transferred their children to suburban or private schools, few whites remained in the Boston school system, making racial integration impossible.

During the 1970s and early 1980s, the courts, Congress, and administrative agencies reinforced each other's activism. The 1964 Civil Rights Act seemed to disallow any form of racial preference, but the courts frequently interpreted it to allow *affirmative action*, the use of racial classifications to improve access of racial minorities to education, jobs, and other important social goods. In *Griggs v. Duke Power Co.* (1972), the court struck down certain employment criteria used by the Duke Power Company because those practices excluded a disproportionate number of African Americans from the employment pool. Chief Justice Burger's majority opinion held employers responsible for justifying practices that were seemingly fair but had an "adverse impact" on women and minorities.

Griggs stopped just short of interpreting the civil rights law as requiring quotas. Congress did not endorse quotas, but it made no effort to stop courts and agencies from inferring the existence of discrimination based on "non-proportional outcomes." Faced with the difficult choice between merely punishing overt discrimination and requiring racial quotas, Congress made no choice at all, delegating this difficult decision to the courts and the bureaucracy.

The importance of the civil rights acts lay not just in their extensive reach but also in the model they established for other legislation. Emulating them, Lyndon Johnson's Great Society legislation and many laws enacted during the 1970s embodied *statutory rights*, meaning rights proclaimed by Congress in statute with no direct reference to the Constitution. Statutory rights included *procedural rights*, in which the court held administrative agencies to exacting standards for ensuring "fair representation for all affected interests" (especially those representing "discrete and insular minorities") in the exercise of the discretion Congress had delegated to them. The judiciary's strict scrutiny of administrative procedures and regulations helped convert welfare, consumer protection, and environmental measures into programmatic rights that codified, in many important respects, the New Deal vision of a good society. Once a critical veto point that restrained the growth of government, by the end of the 1970s the judiciary had become an unexpected source of political energy for an expansive welfare and regulatory state.

## Path Dependency: Reaffirming the Rights Revolution

Over the past twenty years, the Supreme Court, presided over by William Rehnquist and later by John Roberts, has, for the most part, reaffirmed the landmark decisions made by its New Deal and Post New Deal predecessors. The Warren Court had ruled in *Miranda v. Arizona* that the Fifth Amendment right against self-incrimination requires that a criminal suspect be warned of that right before he is interrogated by the police or prosecutors. Because law enforcers had bitterly complained about this restriction, Congress passed a law overturning Miranda. *In Dickerson v. United States* the court threw out the law and reaffirmed *Miranda*. Even more surprising was the court's reaffirmation of the right to an abortion.

*Roe v. Wade*, the landmark abortion ruling discussed earlier in this chapter, was perhaps the single greatest cause for conservative condemnation of the Burger Court. The 1980 Republican platform singled it out for criticism and promised to appoint justices who would overturn it. The Reagan and Bush administrations tried five times to overturn it and failed. A sixth, more promising opportunity came in 1992 when the Supreme Court heard *Planned Parenthood of Southeastern Pennsylvania v. Casey*. Only one justice who had endorsed *Roe* – Harry Blackmun, author of the original decision – remained on the bench. He had the firm support of one other justice, John Stevens. It seemed that Reagan and Bush had made enough conservative appointments to overrule the controversial abortion decision.

*Planned Parenthood* concerned a state law that limited the free exercise of abortion, by requiring the informed consent of the woman, waiting twenty-four hours after obtaining consent, notifying the husband in advance, and requiring minors to gain consent from at least one parent. The plaintiff argued that upholding the Pennsylvania restrictions amounted to overturning *Roe*.

The court upheld the Pennsylvania law, except for the part requiring notification of the husband, but did so on the grounds that the law did not unduly interfere with the right to an abortion. A five-member majority, including Reagan appointees Sandra Day O'Connor and Anthony Kennedy and Bush appointee David Souter, reaffirmed Roe's guarantee of "the right of women to choose to have an abortion before viability and to obtain it without undue interference from the state." Justice O'Connor's opinion, joined by Justices Kennedy and Souter, provided an alternative to the polarized positions on abortion and has since been the controlling view of the Court. It did not confirm that Roe had been correctly decided, but it upheld the right to choose on the basis that Roe had become settled, standing law, which must be respected by the Supreme Court. The right to privacy, Justice O'Connor argued, should be upheld under the principle of *stare decisis*, meaning, "let the decision stand."

The Rehnquist and Roberts courts also emulated their predecessors in their expansive reading of the Bill of Rights and the wide degree of protection it grants individuals against government intrusion. The Court's expansion of the meaning of free speech arose in a series of cases involving whether private groups could express religious views on public school grounds. Stephen and Darleen Fournier lived in Milford, New York, and were the adult leaders of the local Good News Club, a private Christian organization for children aged six to twelve. In September of 1996 the Fourniers asked Dr. Robert McGruder, interim superintendent of the district, for permission to use a school cafeteria after school for the club's weekly meetings. McGruder said no because the club's meetings involved bible readings, religious lessons, and hymn singing and therefore amounted to religious worship. Such worship violated the school district's policy prohibiting use "by any individual or organization for religious purposes." The Fourniers sued, claiming that the school district's action violated their First Amendment rights of free speech and free exercise of religion. A New York district court ruled for the district on the grounds that because the district excluded all religious activities it was not discriminating against the Good News Club. A federal Court of Appeals upheld the lower court ruling.

The Supreme Court agreed to hear the case of *Good News Club v. Milford Central School* because "there is a conflict among the Courts of Appeals on the question whether speech can be excluded from a limited public forum on the basis of the religious nature of the speech." The Milford District had interpreted the establishment clause to mean that it had the right, indeed the duty, to exclude all religious activity from school property. However, in two prior decisions the Rehnquist Court had resolved this tension between free speech and the establishment of religion in favor of free speech. In *Lamb's Chapel,* it ruled that a school district could not exclude a private group from presenting films in school solely because the films defended family values on religious grounds. Likewise, in *Rosenberger,* it held that a university that funded student publications could not refuse to fund one that adopted a religious perspective.

Justice Clarence Thomas's majority opinion in *Good News Club* noted the Milford ban did not extend to all efforts to encourage morality and character development: "For example, this policy would allow someone to use Aesop's Fables to teach children moral values." The sole reason for banning the Good News Club was because its efforts to develop morality and character adopted a Christian approach, and such a basis for discrimination was unconstitutional: "What matters for purposes of the Free Speech Clause is that we can see no logical difference in kind between the invocation of Christianity by the Club and the invocation of teamwork, loyalty, or patriotism by other associations to provide a foundation for their lessons." The protection against an establishment of religion should not be understood as a reason for prohibiting religious speech as long as other points of view, both religious and secular, also had an equal opportunity to be heard.

Justice David Souter's dissenting opinion denied that the Good News Club was merely engaged in moral and character development from a religious perspective. He likened its activity more to a religious worship service in which children as young as six were "to commit themselves in an act of Christian conversion." If the Good News Club could hold religious services than "any public school opened for civic meetings must be opened for use as a church, synagogue, or mosque." Therefore, he concluded that the school district was within its rights to discriminate between an act of religious indoctrination, which it could exclude, and other types of activities and discussion, which it could not. He did not however provide standards by which to distinguish indoctrination from more benign activities nor did he consider how school districts should evaluate whether or not secular groups were engaging in indoctrination and should likewise be excluded.

This chapter has already discussed the other key example of the Rehnquist and Roberts Courts' extension of their power to protect rights, their overruling of Chicago's ban on handguns in the home in *McDonald v Chicago.* Neither the Burger nor the Warren Courts had seen fit to incorporate the Second Amendment into the rights protections the Supreme Court would guard against state and local invasion. As was the case with the broad protection offered to religious expression, the Court chose to protect a right beloved of many conservatives, the right to bear arms.

## Deviating from the Path: Federalism

The only major reversal of previous rulings has come in the area of Federalism. Federalism (Chapter 5) began with a discussion of the conflict between Texas and the federal government regarding whether the federal government had a right to ban handguns near schools. Texas claimed that handgun regulation was a local matter and the federal government claimed that the Commerce Clause of the Constitution enabled it to intervene because school violence threatened interstate commerce. In *United States v. Lopez*, the Rehnquist Court sided with Texas on the grounds that the commerce clause should not be read so broadly as to encompass issues that were essentially local in character. This decision represented the first effort by the Supreme Court to place limits on the commerce clause since the New Deal. In *United States v. Morrison* (2000) it reinforced its earlier decision ruling that the commerce clause did not give the federal government the latitude to make violence against women a federal crime when other forms of violence remained the province of state criminal law. The message of these two decisions was that the federal government could no longer expect the court to allow it to use the commerce clause as an all-purpose rationale justifying legislation. The relationship between the matter being legislated and commerce had to be reasonably clear and direct; otherwise the matter at hand remained the province of the states and localities.

In *Printz v. United States* (1997) the Court provided additional rationales for defending the states against government intrusion: the principle of dual sovereignty and the Tenth Amendment. The Brady Handgun Violence Prevention Act (1993) popularly known as the Brady Bill required local law enforcement officials to conduct background checks on would-be handgun purchasers. Two county sheriffs, from Montana and Arizona, challenged the constitutionality of this provision. In overturning this aspect of the law the majority declared that "it is incontestable that the Constitution established a system of "'dual sovereignty.'" Although the states surrendered many of their powers to the new federal government, they retained "a residuary and inviolable sovereignty." This is reflected throughout the Constitution's text. Among the examples it cited were: the prohibition on any involuntary reduction or combination of a State's territory; the Judicial Power Clause, which speaks of the "Citizens" of the states; the amendment provision, which requires the votes of three-fourths of the states to amend the Constitution; and the Guarantee Clause, Art. IV, §4, which "presupposes the continued existence of the states and ... those means and instrumentalities which are the creation of their sovereign and reserved rights." It also cited the Tenth Amendment's assertion that "the powers not delegated to the United States by the Constitution, nor prohibited by it to the States, are reserved to the States respectively, or to the people." Despite the powerful language of the Tenth Amendment, the Court had rarely made reference to it. The majority opinion's assertion of its importance might well give the court a powerful new weapon for overturning federal efforts to coerce the states. In the same vein, refer back to Chapter 5 for a discussion of the Supreme Court's decision to over-rule the Medicaid provision of President Obama's health care reform.

## CONCLUSION

As this chapter demonstrates, the United States has an extraordinarily powerful and independent federal judiciary headed by a supreme court that can declare actions of the other branches and states unconstitutional. One might expect the public to resent this highly undemocratic exercise of power, and yet the Court has become increasingly prestigious and popular over time. This chapter shows why this is the case. On several important occasions the Court has acted uni-laterally, making decisions in the absence of clear-cut public support and the presence of vehement opposition from particular segments of the public. The critical examples discussed in this chapter were its defense of slavery in *Dred Scott;* its opposition to government regulation of the economy as typified by its ruling in *Lochner*; its support of racial integration in *Brown*; and its declara-tion of a right to an abortion in *Roe*. But in those cases where political leaders were able to rouse the public in opposition to the court's position, as Lincoln did regarding slavery and FDR with regard to economic regulation, the Court's efforts to decide great matters of national controversy did not stand. Inspired by their president and the sacrifice of their soldiers, the citizens of the United States voted overwhelmingly to support the Thirteenth Amendment to the Constitution banning slavery. Grateful for FDR's efforts to combat the Great Depression, vot-ers gave him a resounding victory in his 1936 reelection bid. In the face of such an overwhelming popular mandate, the Supreme Court abandoned its efforts to oppose government intervention in the economy.

When public opinion has rallied around the Court's decisions, its efforts to decide matters of great national controversy have succeeded. Prior to *Brown*, public opinion outside the South had been essentially passive regarding racial desegregation. However, when various southern cities and states defied the ruling, national public opinion rallied in support of civil rights for African Americans. Prior to *Roe,* abortion had not been a major national issue. But in the wake of *Roe*, majority opinion came to support the right to an abortion, although it also supported limits on how that right was exercised. In these instances the Court's willingness to put itself in advance of public opinion has proved successful. Thus, leadership by the Court triumphs when the public is eventually convinced of the wisdom of its decisions and fails when the public concludes it is in the wrong. The modern Court has amassed enormous prestige and public support because it is the court of *Brown* and *Roe*, not *Lochner* and *Dred Scott*.

## CHAPTER SUMMARY

☆ The two most significant decisions the Court rendered during 2009–2010 both involved constitutional law, and more specifically, the Bill of Rights. *McDonald v. Chicago* dealt with the meaning of the Second Amendment right to bear arms. *Citizens United v. Federal Election Commission* dealt with the free speech provision of the First Amendment.

☆ The Constitution does not expressly give the judiciary power to determine the power of judicial review. That power was successfully asserted by the Marshall Court beginning with its decision in *Marbury v. Madison*.

☆ By means of skillful leadership and carefully reasoned and worded opinions, John Marshall enabled the Supreme Court to provide a centralizing, restraining counterweight to the decentralist and democratic tendencies of the Jefferson and Jackson presidencies.

☆ Limits on the Supreme Court's power to chart a course for the country were set in response to the Court's attempt in *Dred Scott* to impose a settlement of the slavery controversy that was wracking the nation during the 1850s.

☆ After 1936, the Supreme Court retreated from its previously successful efforts to prevent meaningful government regulation of the economy and became highly supportive of such efforts.

☆ The Supreme Court's decision in *Brown v. Board of Education of Topeka* (1954) revitalized the Fourteenth Amendment Equal Protection Clause as a weapon to uphold civil rather than economic rights.

☆ In the 1960s the Warren Court began to move aggressively beyond racial justice to insist that government protect other neglected rights, including the right of each vote to count equally and the right to privacy.

☆ Because many Warren and Burger Courts rulings were about securing rights that could only be provided by government, the Court became increasingly dependent on other agents of government – lower courts, Congress, and the executive – to implement its will. As it involved itself ever more in the detailed behavior of administrative agencies it, too, came to assume tasks and responsibilities more typical of a federal agency than of a court.

☆    The only major reversal by the Rehnquist Court of rulings by previous courts came in the area of Federalism. The greatest innovation of the Rehnquist and Roberts Courts has been to broaden the interpretation of the rights the federal government needs to protect against the intrusion of the states and localities, most notably with respect to the free exercise of religion and gun ownership. For the rest, the Rehnquist and Roberts Courts have reaffirmed the expanded interpretations of rights initiated by its two predecessors.

## MAJOR CONCEPTS

| | |
|---|---|
| Administrative Law | Amicus Curiae Brief |
| *Baker v. Carr* | *Brown v. Board of Education of Topeka* |
| *Bush v. Gore* | *Citizens United v. Federal Election Commission* |
| Civil Law | Constitutional Law |
| Contract | Court of Appeals |
| Criminal Law | Defendant |
| *Dred Scott v. Sandford* | Federal Court |
| *Good News Club v. Milford Central School* | *Griswold v. Connecticut* |
| Judicial Review | *Lochner v. New York* |
| *Marbury v. Madison* | *McDonald v. Chicago* |
| *Miranda v. Arizona* | Plaintiff |
| *Plessy v. Ferguson* | Public Law |
| *Reynolds v. Sims* | *Roe v. Wade* |
| *Schechter Poultry Corporation v. United States* | Standing |
| State Courts | *Substantive Due Process* |
| Tort | *United States v. Lopez* |

## SUGGESTED READINGS

Abraham, Henry. *The Judicial Process*, 7th ed. New York: Oxford University Press, 1998.

Ackerman, Bruce. *We the People: Volume I, Foundations*. Cambridge, MA: Harvard University Press, 1991.

Bickel, Alexander. *The Least Dangerous Branch: The Supreme Court and the Bar of Politics*. New York: Bobbs-Merrill, 1963.

Burke, Thomas F. *Lawyers, Lawsuits, and Legal Rights: The Battle over Litigation in American Society*: Berkeley, CA: University of California Press, 2004.

Fallon, Richard. *The Dynamic Constitution: An Introduction to American Constitutional Law*. New York: Cambridge University Press, 2004.

Ginsberg, Benjamin, and Martin Shefter. *Politics by Other Means*, 3rd ed. New York: W. W. Norton, 2003.

Jacobsohn, Gary Jeffrey. *Constitutional Identity*, Cambridge, MA: Harvard University Press, 2010.

Kahn, Ronald, and Ken I. Kersch. *The Supreme Court and American Political Development*. Lawrence, KS: University Press of Kansas, 2006.

Kersch, Ken I. *Constructing Civil Liberties: Discontinuities in the Development of American Constitutional Law*. New York: Cambridge University Press, 2004.

Melnick, R. Shep. *Between the Lines*. Washington, DC: Brookings Institution, 1994.

O'Brien, David. *Storm Center: The Supreme Court in American Politics*, 9th ed. New York: W. W. Norton, 2011.

Perry, H. W., Jr. *Deciding to Decide: Agenda Setting in the United States Supreme Court*. Cambridge, MA: Harvard University Press, 1991.

Powe, Lucas, Jr. *The Warren Court and American Politics*. Cambridge, MA: Harvard University Press, 2002.

Shapiro, Martin. *Who Guards the Guardians?* Athens, GA: University of Georgia Press, 1988.

# Bureaucracy

## CHAPTER OVERVIEW

This chapter focuses on:

☆ The struggles that have taken place to make the bureaucracy democratically accountable while preserving its ability to perform the functions for which it was intended.

☆ What the federal bureaucracy does, how it is organized and what tools are available to the president to coordinate its activities and exercise control.

☆ The path the bureaucracy has followed and the critical choices that have shaped its nature and functioning.

The Pure Food and Drug Act of 1906 established the *Food and Drug Administration* and gave it the authority to protect the public from unsafe food and unsafe and ineffective drugs. But the law does not clearly define what is and is not a drug. No statute could possibly provide a definitive list of all the substances that should be defined as drugs, and the Act does not even try. After the surgeon general of the United States declared that tobacco smoking was causally related to cancer, Congress decided to treat tobacco as a public health problem. It passed the Cigarette Labeling and Advertising Act requiring the statement "Cigarettes May be Harmful to your Health" appear on all cigarette packages. In 1970 it passed a law banning cigarette and cigar advertising on television. But it never declared tobacco to be a drug, nor did it repeal an earlier law designed to promote the sale of tobacco products that declared the "marketing of tobacco to be necessary to the general welfare." Indeed, prior to 1996 the FDA had stated that it did not consider tobacco to be a drug. However, in 1996 the FDA Commissioner, David Kessler, announced that the FDA had changed its mind. In his message declaring tobacco to be a drug he noted that "more than 400,000 people die each year from tobacco-related illnesses, such as cancer, respiratory illnesses, and heart disease, often suffering long and painful deaths," and that "tobacco kills more people each year in the United States than acquired immunodeficiency syndrome (AIDS), car accidents, alcohol, homicides, illegal drugs, suicides, and fires, combined." Congress had not explicitly prohibited the FDA from regulating tobacco and therefore he assumed that he had the discretion to declare it a drug. Based on this finding, the FDA banned tobacco sales to minors; ordered cigarette vending machines removed from locations frequented by children such as supermarkets; forbade tobacco advertising on billboards near schools and playgrounds; and required tobacco companies to refrain from any marketing activities aimed at young people.

In 2000 the Supreme Court ruled that the FDA had exceeded its authority by declaring tobacco to be a drug. Ten years later Congress explicitly granted FDA such authority. But what if neither the Court nor Congress had intervened? Did David Kessler abuse his authority? The function of federal bureaucrats such as Dr. Kessler is to turn the directives that come from Congress, the President, and the federal courts into concrete actions. They implement statutes, executive orders, and judicial decisions. But as the tobacco case demonstrates, it is often very hard to tell whether or not bureaucrats are actually doing Congress's bidding or taking the law into their own hands. Neither the president nor Congress nor the courts has the time or the expertise to specify in detail what their directives mean and how they are to be carried out. Therefore, bureaucrats must exercise their own discretion. But how much? Dr. Kessler was a highly trained and respected scientist, as were key members of the FDA staff. Should elected officials and courts defer to such expertise or should they limit bureaucratic discretion in order to keep these unelected officials accountable to elected officials and judges? At what point does bureaucratic discretion become bureaucratic license? Throughout American political development fears about an excessively intrusive and arbitrary bureaucracy have warred with desires to make government efficient and effective. This chapter pays particular attention to the struggles that have taken place to make the bureaucracy democratically accountable while preserving its ability to perform the functions for which it was intended.

## Contemporary Portrait of the Federal Bureaucracy

This section provides a portrait of the current federal bureaucracy. It examines what it does, how it is organized, and what tools are available to the president to coordinate its activities and exercise control (a list of cabinet departments appears in Chapter 8).

Members of the public have direct contact with the federal bureaucracy in many different ways. The national parks they visit are run by the National Park Service. The U.S. Postal Service delivers their mail. The elderly and the disabled receive monthly checks from the Social Security Administration. Taxpayers file their federal income tax returns with the Internal Revenue Service. The person at airport security telling people to take off their shoes and put their laptops in a separate bin works for the federal Transportation Security Agency.

Figure 10.1 shows how many civilian employees the federal government has and what functions they perform. Notice that only two functions – delivering the mail and providing for the national defense – account for almost half of all federal civilian employment.

Three million workers may sound like a big number until one realizes that Wal-Mart, the United State's largest private employer, has more than 2 million. The U.S. population exceeds 300 million. Therefore, there is less than 1 civilian federal employee per 100 persons. The size of the federal government workforce remains relatively small because most federal agencies and departments supervise the work of others. They work indirectly by issuing grants and negotiating contracts with state and local governments, universities, nonprofit social service agencies, and private companies to do a whole host of things that Congress wants done. They write guidelines that grantees, contractors, and state regulatory agencies must follow; they monitors the performance of those non-federal entities to make sure that those guidelines are being followed. The total state-government workforce exceeds the federal workforce by more than 800,000. The local government workforce, which exceeds 10 million, is more than three times the size of the federal workforce. Therefore, the federal civilian bureaucracy is not nearly as big as those of other rich nations, adjusting for population size. But when one includes state and local government workers, many of whom are doing work contracted for by the federal government, the gap between the total government U.S. workforce and that of other rich countries narrows substantially.

As we have seen, even among civilians, defense is the largest component of the federal government workforce. The military component is far larger. The United States has approximately 1.5 million persons in uniform. Only China has a larger military. As we discussed in Chapter 1, the United States is the reigning superpower. That role requires it to devote a great deal of effort to maintaining its power and prestige worldwide. U.S. troops and aircraft are stationed on almost every continent as well as in bases on U.S. soil. The U.S. Navy patrols sea lanes around the globe. To maintain such a huge military effort requires enormous amounts of resources and a complex bureaucracy to manage it. The military has its own bureaucratic structure with the *Joint Chiefs of Staff* at the top. And, as one would expect from a nation born with a fear of standing armies, the military command must answer to civilians. Although military personnel work at the Pentagon, the headquarters of the *Department of Defense (DOD)*, the secretary of defense, the DOD senior management team, and many

| FEDERAL GOVERNMENT CIVILIAN EMPLOYMENT | | | |
| --- | --- | --- | --- |
| BY FUNCTION: March 2010 | | | |
| Payroll in whole dollars. | | | |
| (Detail may not add to total because of rounding) | | | |
| Total | Full-Time | March | |
| Function | Employees | Employees | Payroll |
| TOTAL – ALL FUNCTIONS | 3,007,938 | 2,583,768 | 16,238,227,775 |
| Financial Administration | 128,114 | 123,183 | 804,272,358 |
| Other Government Administration | 25,361 | 24,406 | 165,515,967 |
| Judicial and Legal | 63,159 | 60,317 | 443,812,519 |
| Police | 182,573 | 170,235 | 1,220,406,887 |
| Correction | 37,589 | 37,432 | 216,338,667 |
| Highways | 2,941 | 2,848 | 23,029,679 |
| Air Transportation | 48,525 | 48,178 | 433,888,179 |
| Water Transport & Terminals | 5,010 | 4,727 | 14,450,261 |
| Public Welfare | 8,341 | 8,084 | 70,513,554 |
| Health | 158,439 | 147,165 | 1,134,683,530 |
| Hospitals | 201,323 | 183,665 | 1,307,251,400 |
| Social Insurance Administration | 68,757 | 66,807 | 415,254,206 |
| Parks and Recreation | 27,113 | 24,615 | 141,817,076 |
| Housing and Community Development | 15,397 | 15,153 | 110,218,501 |
| Natural Resources | 187,091 | 177,614 | 1,180,536,412 |
| Nat Defense/International Relations | 773,978 | 747,467 | 3,057,052,574 |
| Postal Service | 658,016 | 538,184 | 3,646,256,435 |
| Space Research & Technology | 18,540 | 18,329 | 173,653,143 |
| Other Education* | 10,218 | 9,745 | 80,308,379 |
| Libraries | 3,871 | 3,710 | 27,602,179 |
| Other and Unallocable | 383,582 | 171,904 | 1,571,365,870 |
| The Department of Homeland Security (DHS) | | | |
| was formed in 2003. Below we provide detail | | | |
| for the largest agencies within the DHS. | | | |

**Figure 10.1.** Federal Government Civilian Employment. Retrieved from http://www2.census.gov/govs/apes/10fedfun.pdf.

| U.S. Coast Guard | 8,138 | 7,998 | 56,177,536 |
|---|---|---|---|
| U.S. Secret Service | 6,849 | 6,714 | 54,304,250 |
| Bureau of Customs and Border Protection | 57,588 | 57,223 | 361,577,357 |
| Federal Emergency Management Agency | 16,257 | 7,477 | 102,081,893 |
| Transportation Security Agency | 59,459 | 48,396 | 266,343,143 |
| All Other | 37,004 | 36,449 | 284,088,429 |
| Total Department of Homeland Security | 185,295 | 164,257 | 1,124,572,607 |
| * Includes Department of Education and the National | | | |
| Science Foundation, plus parts of the Bureau of Indian | | | |
| Affairs | | | |

**Figure 10.1.** (*cont.*)

DOD employees are civilians. The Joint Chiefs of Staff are accountable to the secretary of defense.

The United States maintains embassies and consulates in almost every country. Their employees belong to the Foreign Service, a division of the *State Department*. Those outposts of the United States overseas issue visas to foreigners who want to visit the United States, assists American nationals living or traveling abroad, and facilitates business deals to export to or import from the United States. In addition to performing these services, the embassy houses the ambassador, the official representative of the U.S. government in that particular nation. But the most important function of the State Department is to generate and analyze information. Its Washington headquarters houses bureaus devoted to monitoring and interpreting the political, economic, diplomatic, and military activities of every foreign nation. The reports these bureaus produce are read and distilled by the higher levels of the State Department bureaucracy and serve to inform the critical foreign policy decisions that the president and his chief diplomat, the secretary of state, must make. They are also the basis for the extensive briefings that the State Department provides to members of Congress.

Information that is directly related to American national security and that may well be obtained secretly is called *intelligence*. Each branch of the military also maintains its own intelligence agency, as does the Department of Defense. There is also the *CIA*, which is not part of either state or defense. The NSA, unlike the other intelligence services, does not make use of undercover operatives or informants, but relies on information technology to analyze huge amounts of raw data from foreign nations and break the codes that seek to render much of that data unintelligible to eavesdroppers. In 2004, Congress gave the president the authority to appoint a Director of National Intelligence (DNI) to serve as his principal advisor on intelligence matters and coordinate the activities of all the other intelligence agencies. However, the DNI was not actually given authority to manage any of the existing intelligence agencies, so it is not clear how and to what extent the DNI is actually able to coordinate those activities.

Information is also a critical component of the work of the domestic bureaucracy. The *Census Bureau* counts the number of Americans and provides critical data about where and how they live. The Bureau of Labor Statistics tracks changes in prices and employment. The *EPA* keeps track of changes in air and water pollution levels. The *National Oceanic and Atmospheric Administration (NOAA)* monitors changes in ocean currents and patterns of fish migrations. These mounds of information are vital to scientific research, business decision making, and philanthropic activity as well as to informed public policy formation. Indeed, the federal bureaucracy comprises the single most important source of information about who Americans are, how they live, and how their economy functions.

## The Organization of the Federal Bureaucracy

For the most part, the federal government bureaucracy is organized into departments, each of which is headed by a secretary appointed by the president and confirmed by the Senate. Each department has a specific function – the Labor Department deals with issues relating to workers, the Agriculture Department deals with farming, and so forth. But this is not the entire story; many functions overlap. For example, the EPA has responsibility for managing the nation's wetlands, but so does the Army Corps of Engineers. And some agencies are not in the department whose function they share. For example, the National Forest Service manages public lands, a function that is mostly assigned to the Interior Department. Yet the Forest Service is in the Agriculture Department. NOAA is primarily an environmental agency, and yet it is in the Department of Commerce, not in The EPA. Also, many important agencies, such as EPA, The National Aeronautics and Space Administration, and the Peace Corps, are not housed in departments at all – they report directly to the president.

These exceptions cannot be explained logically. Each one is the result of a specific set of political circumstances. For example, When Nixon had to decide to whom to give the authority to implement the major air and water laws that Congress had passed in the early year of his presidency, the obvious choice was the *Department of the Interior (DOI)*. The DOI already had jurisdiction over most of the environmental issues the government dealt with. But Secretary of the Interior Walter Hickel had become unpopular both within the administration and with a large portion of Congress and the media. Nixon did not want to tarnish his great accomplishment by putting Hickel in charge. Rather, he hoped to gain a great deal of good publicity from signing these powerful laws, so he chose to create a new agency, the EPA, to implement them. To maximize his identification with this popular cause, he had the new agency report directly to him. Likewise, John F. Kennedy sought to maximize his identification with the Peace Corps by establishing it as an independent agency reporting to the president.

When the Forest Service (then known as the Forestry Bureau) was created, it was put in the Department of Agriculture because its original function was to give technical advice to commercial tree farmers. When it acquired its land-management responsibilities, Chief Forester Gifford Pinchot resisted efforts to move to the Department of the Interior, which already housed the Bureau of Land Management and would soon acquire the Parks Service, because he was a foe of the Interior Department Secretary. Because the Forest Service was the only land-management agency in the Agriculture Department, the department hierarchy tended to leave it alone and trust the judgment of the chief forester. Therefore, Pinchot's successors staved off attempts to move it to Interior even though they had no personal animosity toward later secretaries of the interior. As these example indicated the haphazardness of federal bureaucratic organization is a very important clue regarding the nature of bureaucratic politics. Where an agency rests in the organization chart will inevitably give advantages to those political interests whose access to and power over the agency is advantaged by that placement. Conversely, handicaps are created for those whom the placement restricts access to and denies levers of power.

The terms used to designate the different organs of the federal government obey no clear logic. As the examples discussed illustrate, there is no clear difference between an agency, as in the EPA; an administration, as in the Food and Drug Administration; a service, as in the Forest Service; and a bureau, as in the FBI. Therefore, when discussing the functioning of government organizations in general terms, this book uses the generic term "agency."

The agencies we have discussed so far have one very important thing in common: their leaders either report directly to the president, in the case of cabinet secretaries and the heads of agencies such as the EPA and the Peace Corps, or indirectly to the president via a chain of command that leads up to a cabinet secretary. However, as their name implies, the *independent regulatory commissions* are not fully under presidential control. The most important of these are the Federal Communications Commission (FCC), the Federal Trade Commission (FTC), and the SEC. Each has five commissioners who make their decisions by majority vote. The president can appoint no more than three commissioners from the same political party. The FCC and SEC commissioners serve five-year terms. In the case of the FCC this means that a president has to wait until the second year of his first term to replace those appointed by his predecessor. The

SEC commissioners have staggered terms, meaning that only one of them can be replaced per year. The FTC commissioners enjoy seven-year terms, thus a president has to be elected to a second four-year term before he can appoint the commission majority. Perhaps the greatest of all the barriers to presidential control of the independent regulatory commissions is that the Supreme Court has ruled that the president cannot remove a commission member.

These limits on presidential authority have been imposed by Congress because it did not intend these commissions to operate as normal executive agencies. Congress did not want to politicize such sensitive and technically complex issues as awarding of radio and TV broadcasting licenses, scrutinizing corporate financial disclosure reports, and investigating charges of anticompetitive business activities. It wanted the government bodies making such determinations to be governed by experts. Congress did not fully trust the president to place a concern for expertise above political concerns in making such appointments, and even more importantly, in deciding whom to remove. The Congress favored the commission form for the same reason. Any one commissioner might misunderstand the technical merits, or be swayed by partisan bias or personal feelings. Sound technical decisions were more likely to occur if five experts were involved and the decision was made by the majority of them.

As Chapter 4 discussed, the effort to place expertise above politics dates back to the Progressives, who displayed a deep distrust of partisan politics. Progressives believed that many public policy questions had scientifically derivable right answers and that those questions should be settled by experts, whose training would enable them to come up with those right answers. The continuing role of independent commissions in the operations of the federal government, and state governments as well, shows how dependent on Progressivism the path of American government continues to be.

## Presidential Control

The federal bureaucracy is so unwieldy and sprawling that the president has enormous difficulty in controlling it. To assist the president in coordinating the efforts of the disparate agencies and rendering them accountable to the president, the *EOP* was created (see Chapter 8, Figure 8.2).

The two most important arms of the EOP are the *OMB* and *National Security Council (NSC)*. OMB is the biggest component of the executive office of the president. It is the critical tool the president uses to coordinate the disparate parts of the federal bureaucracy. It performs specific functions: budget planning and development; management improvement; regulatory analysis; and legislative clearance. Its single most important function is to assist the president to develop the annual budget he submits to Congress. Because the budget provides specific requests for funds for every federal government activity, it is the concrete embodiment of what the president plans to have the government actually do in the upcoming year. In order to make specific funding recommendations, OMB evaluates agency programs, policies, and procedures and judges amongst competing funding demands within and among agencies in order to establish funding priorities. This budgetary authority also provides it with a powerful tool to influence agency behavior. In the course of its budgetary reviews it makes recommendations to agencies about how they should adjust their policies to bring them closer into line with the president's priorities. Agencies have no legal obligation to bow to OMB pressure. But if they do not, they know that OMB might well retaliate by cutting their future budget requests.

Congress has the final say in determining the federal budget. The CBO does its own analyses of agency performance and spending priorities. But the CBO is no match for the OMB in terms of the comprehensiveness and depth of its investigations. Indeed, the CBO depends to a large extent on the data and analysis the OMB provides. Therefore, even though the budget Congress passes may differ in significant respects from what the president asked for, OMB's fingerprints will be found all over the final budged document. Once Congress passes a budget, OMB is responsible for making sure that federal agency spending conforms to budgetary guidelines.

Historically, the federal government has lagged far behind the corporate world in developing effective management tools. It has been slow to adopt state-of-the-art techniques for analyzing data, buying supplies, improving the skills of its workforce, and communicating with the public. OMB is the leading force within the federal government for modernizing management. It mounts government-wide efforts to encourage agencies to improve their information systems, strategic planning, financial management, procurement procedures, and personnel training. These efforts become ever-more important as the federal bureaucracy continues to grow in size and complexity.

This chapter has already mentioned that much of the work of federal bureaucrats is to put laws passed by Congress into practice by issuing detailed regulations that tell other entities – states, cities, firms, or individuals – what to do to obey the law. OMB reviews drafts of all regulations that agencies as diverse as the EPA, Department of Health and Human Services, and Department of Agriculture propose. It does so to ensure that the regulations are faithful to the statutes they are implementing; that the proposal is superior alternative ways of accomplishing that purpose; and that it does not conflict with other regulations or statutes already on the books.

In order to make sure that the legislative proposals drafted by individual agencies conform to the president's wishes and complement one another, OMB circulates them to other affected agencies and reviews them itself. If it has objections, or objections are voice by other agencies, it oversees a process of interagency consultation to reconcile the divergent points of view. Only when it is satisfied that the key points of controversy have been resolved does it transmit the bill to Congress.

OMB also tries to influence and improve management practices all across the government. Its Office of E-Government and Information Technology is in charge of a government-wide initiative geared to making more and better use of Web-based technologies. Its Office of Federal Procurement Policy devises methods to enable government agencies to lower the cost and improve the quality of the goods and services they buy. The Office of Performance and Personnel Policy devises better methods by which agencies can evaluate their workers and plan for their future staffing needs.

The NSC is chaired by the vice president. Its members include the Secretary of State, Secretary of the Treasury, Secretary of Defense, and Assistant to the President for National Security Affairs. Because the members often supply differing and even contradictory information and advice, the president relies on the Assistant for National Security Affairs to sift through the ideas and information those departments provide to help him understand the nature of the disagreements and assess them. In support of this effort, the NSC has a staff of its own who report to the Assistant to the President for National Security Affairs.

In order to penetrate into the actual workings of the other federal agencies, both the OMB and the NSC have had to create bureaucracies of their own. The staffers of both agencies pride themselves on being as knowledgeable about the policy issues at hand as the bureaucrats they are scrutinizing. They do not limit themselves simply to coordinating and elucidating information from the other departments; they offer information and ideas of their own. Therefore, the NSC and OMB serve both to help presidents control the bureaucracy and as additional bureaucratic competitors for presidential attention and favor.

## Congressional Control of the Bureaucracy

As Chapter 7 pointed out, Congress has enormous power over federal agencies. Its budgetary control is so strong that agency officials try very hard to do what the chairs and senior members of key committees ask of them. Their behavior is subject to strict scrutiny by legislative oversight committees who grill agency officials to ensure that they are obeying what the members understand to be the law, even if their executive superiors are pressing them to interpret the law differently. Congress must agree to any plan put forth by the president to reorganize federal agencies. Later on this chapter will show that Congress has used that power to keep presidents from implementing changes that would increase presidential and decrease congressional control. This wide array of tools available to Congress to intervene in the management of the executive branch is yet another example of the powerful path dependency of constitutionally imposed checks and balances.

## POLITICAL DEVELOPMENT

### Path Dependency: Anti-Bureaucracy

The United States was born hating bureaucrats. In theory, the American Revolution was fought against the British king. But it was the agents of the king, British soldiers and tax collectors, whose offenses drove the colonists to rebel. From the beginning, less effort was expended to create an efficient and forceful government apparatus than to establish strict methods for limiting bureaucratic license. By European standards, the American bureaucracy has always seemed incompetent. But it is also less intrusive and despotic. In bureaucracy, as in so many other aspects of political life, Americans opted for liberty even at the price of effective government (Figure 10.2).

For most of America's history, this liberty was obtained less by wrapping the bureaucracy in red tape than by simply having less of it. Minimizing bureaucracy was part and parcel of the broader commitment to limiting government that the Declaration of Independence and the Constitution proclaim. Because the Constitution limited the powers of government, those tasked with implementing public policies had relatively little to do, at least in peacetime. Their numbers were small. Their tasks were few and simple. As we have seen in previous chapters, the twentieth century witnessed a great expansion in the tasks assumed by government. As those ambitions grew, the size of the government bureaucracy grew with it. But the antipathy to bureaucracy evident at the birth of the Republic did not change. This chapter will chart the course of American bureaucracy concentrating on the tension between the expanding role that bureaucracy has come to play and the strong animus that Americans continue to display toward it.

### Critical Choice: The President's Removal Power

The Constitution provides only a sketchy account of administration. The executive power vested in the president is not defined. The Constitution does not explicitly grant the president control over the heads of executive departments. Rather, it authorizes the president to require their opinion, in writing, on subjects pertaining to their departments. The president is instructed to appoint heads of departments, subject to Senate confirmation, but the power to appoint lesser officials is left unsettled. Congress may choose to let the president make

**Figure 10.2.** "Weeding 'Em Out": An 1893 cartoon by Louis Dalrymple representing Secretary of Agriculture Julius Morton weeding bureaucracy from the national government. Credit: The Granger Collection, NYC – All rights reserved.

such designations, vest them in the courts, or grant them directly to department heads. The first Congress had to sort out the meaning of these ambiguous constitutional provisions.

The first critical choice in the history of American public administration came only three months into the first congressional session. Congress took up the problem of establishing executive departments, beginning with Foreign Affairs (later to become the Department of State). The key question was whether departmental control would be shared with the president. Some members of Congress argued that the constitutional requirement that the Senate approve department heads implied it should also approve a presidential decision to remove them. Depriving the president of the *removal power* would have greatly increased bureaucratic independence. To resist removal, a bureaucrat could cultivate strong ties to Congress. Thus, the bureaucrat could maintain a great deal of personal discretion by skillfully playing the president and Congress against one another.

James Madison supported giving the president exclusive removal power on democratic grounds. Citizens did not vote for department heads, but they did vote for the president. If the president could not fire executive officials, those officials would feel free to ignore the president's instructions. It would be impossible to hold them publicly accountable for their actions. Congress eventually accepted this argument. Although it would later try to challenge the president's administrative preeminence, it never regained this crucial aspect of administrative power that it gave away at the outset. As a result, the heads of executive departments were considered assistants to the president, and a chain of command was established within the executive branch with the president at the top.

## Effectiveness versus Liberty: Citizens versus Soldiers

The earliest point of tension between hatred of government agents and the need for public action occurred with regard to national security. The colonies had been forced to abide garrisons of British troops and suffer their swaggering arrogance. This dreadful experience reinforced the deep antipathy that the colonists already felt toward professional armies. The Bill of Rights forbids the quartering of troops in people's homes during peacetime without their permission and allows it during wartime "only in a lawful manner." However, this antipathy had to be reconciled with the recognition that the new nation faced grave security threats. Despite signing a peace treaty, the British retained strategically located military installations in North America from which they could very plausibly stage a new invasion. The United States had hostile relations with several Indian nations, and many frontier settlers faced great risks from Indian raids.

The first impulse of the new nation was to adopt nongovernmental means, local and state militia, to provide national security. A militia is composed of ordinary citizens prepared to fight in the event of a military emergency. They train and drill on a part-time basis. Unlike soldiers, they are not agents of the government. To the contrary, they stand armed and ready to defend against any threat to their local liberty and security, whether it is posed by marauding Indians, foreign armies, or the national government itself. Support for the militia and hatred of standing armies is at the core of the Bill of Rights. The Second Amendment states that "a well regulated militia being necessary to the security of a free State, citizens must retain the right to bear arms."

Although militias did participate in the American Revolution, the bulk of the fighting was done by the Continental Army. At war's end, public sentiment was strongly behind disbanding the army. However, it soon became clear that as currently organized, the militias were inadequate for responding to the growing threat of attack by hostile Indians. In 1791, a 1,400-person force composed of militia and some hastily recruited volunteers, commanded by General Arthur St. Clair, was annihilated by a smaller army of Miami Indians. In the wake of this catastrophic defeat, Congress endorsed President Washington's request for a 5,000-man army composed of regular soldiers to fight the Indians. That new army, under the brilliant leadership of Anthony Wayne, succeeded where St. Clair's poorly organized and trained army had failed.

Wayne's victories convinced Congress to maintain a permanent professional frontier patrol to ward off Indian attack. But it refused to create a permanent standing army comparable in size to the massive European ones. As this initial effort to keep the nation safe illustrates, America would adopt key trappings of a modern bureaucratic state but only in a reluctant, minimal fashion. The people clung to their constitutional right to bear arms. They sought to keep the independent power of that most powerful of all bureaucracies, a standing army, to a minimum.

## Critical Choice: The Spoils System

In Chapters 4 and 8, we discuss the crucial democratic changes that occurred during the Jacksonian era, including the expansion of voting rights, the development of a political party system, and the withdrawal of government from previous efforts to place control of the economy in the hands of a privileged few. Nowhere was the impact of this democratic transformation felt with greater force than within the government bureaucracy itself. The creation of a mass electorate challenged the principle of the "rule of gentlemen." The greater political influence of ordinary citizens made them less tolerant of rule by people they no longer considered their betters. They demanded to be governed by people more like themselves. And many of them looked forward to improving their lot by going to work for the government.

Washington made his bureaucratic appointments on the basis of character. He recognized that local post and land offices were the only points of federal government contact that most citizens would ever have. Therefore, he took pains to appoint to these offices people of superior moral character who enjoyed the respect and affection of their neighbors. Thus, he could ensure the reliability of the federal service and also enhance the reputation of the federal government as a whole among the citizenry at large.

Despite the lack of an extensive administrative apparatus, the small size of the federal bureaucracy enabled the president to keep track of administrative performance. Traditional social arrangements were still strong. Most communities had an upper class to which the rest of the people paid deference and respect. It was from this stratum of "gentlemen" that Washington recruited his administrators, and he relied on them to serve as effective ambassadors of the federal government to their hometowns. Because he was so confident of their character he did not feel the need to construct regulations and other control mechanisms to limit their discretion.

As the leader of the first real political party (see Chapter 11), Jefferson chose to replace many of Washington and Adams' appointments with Republican loyalists. But he did not deviate from his predecessors' preference for appointing gentlemen. Although Jefferson invented the *spoils system*, it was Jackson who made use of it to transform the character of American public administration by insisting that federal bureaucracy could and should be staffed by ordinary people.

Andrew Jackson's first annual message to Congress in 1833 highlighted the threat to democracy that was posed by allowing public officials to remain too long in office:

Office is considered as a species of property and government, rather as a means of promoting individual interests than as an instrument created solely for the service of the people. Corruption in some and, in others, a perversion of correct feelings and principles, diverts government from its legitimate ends and makes it an engine for the support of the few at the expense of the many.

In other words, if bureaucrats were not closely subject to presidential control they would treat their office as their own property and do as they pleased. In order for them to be true public servants, they should serve at the pleasure of the public, and therefore of the public's tribune, the president. The best way to preserve this spirit of democratic subservience was through rotation in office. A new president should be free to appoint a new team of public officials who reflected the new president's point of view and who would therefore be more responsive to the majority of voters who put that president in office.

This approach was nicknamed the spoils system, but that term is misleading. "Spoils" places the emphasis on the opportunity for enrichment that public office provides. But Jackson's chief concern was party loyalty, not spoils. By appointing only those who shared the outlook of the electoral majority and firing those who did not, he would make the government obey the will of the people. He would appoint only Democrats, recognizing that if he were defeated for reelection, his opponents would, and should, appoint only Whigs.

Jackson did not, and could not wield the spoils system to centralize power in his own hands. As we discuss in Chapter 11, Jackson was beholden to state and local Democratic Party leaders. They dictated who was appointed to federal posts in their own bailiwicks. Thus, rotation became a valuable tool for strengthening bonds between citizens and their government. As the tradition of deference to one's social superiors waned, the government needed new means of solidifying its hold on the loyalties and energies of the citizenry. This problem was greatly aggravated by the rapid westward expansion of the country, which increased the emotional as well as physical distance that separated citizens from the nation's capital. It became even more important to improve the levels of trust and respect for the government that were accorded by the increasingly far-flung citizenry. Ceding control of federal appointments to local Democratic political organizations decreased the psychic distance between Washington and the hinterlands. It gave the national government a friendly, recognizable local face.

Jackson understood that the success of the rotation system required limited government: "The duties of all public officers are, or at least admit of being made, so plain and simple that men of intelligence may readily qualify themselves for their performance." Delivering the mail, collecting tariffs, and selling off public lands were all tasks that ordinary men could perform. Because government did not do many ambitious and complicated things, it did not need a highly skilled and experienced workforce and therefore its employees could be easily and painlessly replaced. In later years, as government expanded and the demands placed on the bureaucracy grew ever-more complex, this basic assumption on which the principle of rotation rested became less and less plausible.

The spoils system ended the era of government by the elite and initiated the full democratization of American public life. Now, in addition to juries and other purely local activities, the bureaucracy itself would become a schoolroom for democracy, educating hundreds of thousands of Americans in the mundane realities of politics. The greatest compliment paid to this system came with the defeat of Jackson's protégé, Martin Van Buren, for reelection as president in 1840. The new Whig president, William Henry Harrison, although opposing most of Jackson's policies, openly endorsed the principle of rotation in office; he removed thousands of Jacksonians and replaced them with Whig loyalists. At this next stage of the development of American public administration, party discipline replaced good character as the solution to the problem of bureaucratic license.

The spoils system flourished throughout most of the rest of the nineteenth century. As the number of federal jobs expanded, dispensing them in return for political support became an ever-more important aspect of party politics. The late nineteenth century was the heyday of congressional dominance of American government (see Chapter 7). Congress, not the president, became the de facto ruler of the public service. Administrative personnel and budget decisions were determined in congressional committee and in coordination with the congressional leadership.

But even as the spoils system was growing in prominence, its democratic luster began to fade. Because Congress was seen less as the voice of public opinion than as the errand boy for powerful business interests, its servant, the bureaucracy, acquired a similarly sinister reputation. Patronage appointees – postal workers, customs collectors, and land agents – were viewed not as public servants but simply as hacks, people who were concerned only with personal gain. The prestige of the federal government faded as it came to be seen as a hotbed of incompetence and favoritism.

Despite its tarnished image, the federal government grew rapidly. Between 1870 and 1880, the number of federal employees doubled from 53,000 to 107,000. By 1890, it grew an additional 50 percent, to 166,000, and by 1901 it reached 256,000, almost a fivefold increase in thirty years. European immigration, the populating of the western territories, economic growth, and technical change all conspired to accelerate demands on the public sector. The federal government did not add many new functions during this period. Rather, this explosion of personnel resulted from expansion in the volume of existing types of federal business and from the growing pressure on the political parties and their representatives in Congress to produce more jobs for partisan loyalists.

The government in Washington was in the happy position of being able to respond to these demands without imposing greater tax burdens. The bulk of federal revenue came from tariffs on imported goods, which grew as the economy grew, providing ample funds to hire more federal workers. Although the post–Civil War Republicans were not big government advocates in the modern sense, they did not adopt Jackson's strict construction of the limits on federal power. As a result, the size of the federal government grew dramatically, and with it grew the opportunities for poorly trained and inexperienced workers to abuse their discretion. The spoils system degenerated because subsequent presidents violated the system's original basis on limited government. Party discipline proved inadequate to the task of checking bureaucratic license, setting the stage for a more rule-oriented form of control and the inevitable red tape that reliance on rules and regulations brings about.

## Critical Choice: Progressive Reform

The beginning of the end of the spoils system came with the passage of the 1883 Civil Service Act (Figure 10.3). The Act extended only to employees of the executive branch in Washington or in major customhouses and post offices around the country. The vast majority – all but 14,000 of 131,000 federal officeholders, including many postal workers – were not covered. Nonetheless, the Act set a critical precedent by expanding the existing but rarely used system of competitive examinations for public posts. It stipulated that appointees would have to be chosen from among those with the highest exam grades. To oversee the examination system and investigate abuses of it, the act created a three-member, bipartisan *Civil Service Commission* consisting of one Democrat, one Republican, and one independent; these members were appointed by the president, subject to Senate confirmation.

The catalyst for dissolving congressional resistance to civil service reform was the 1881 assassination of President James A. Garfield by an unsuccessful office seeker. The direct connection between the patronage system and such a heinous crime, the second presidential assassination in less than twenty years, galvanized public outrage and forced a reluctant Congress to commit itself to civil service reform.

During the next three decades, reform efforts widened beyond the appointments process to encompass the very mission of public service and the role of public administrators in pursuing it. This expansion was an aspect of the rethinking of the relationship between government and society undertaken by Progressivism (see Chapter 4 for a fuller discussion of Progressivism). Woodrow Wilson was the first and only political science professor ever elected president of the United States. He, more than anyone else, framed

**Figure 10.3.** For Their Own Good: An 1895 cartoon depicting President Grover Cleveland reforming the U.S. civil service. Credit: The Granger Collection, NYC – All rights reserved.

the Progressive understanding of public administration. In his classic essay "The Study of Administration," published in 1887, Wilson explained that the role of public administration had to greatly expand in order to respond adequately to the economic transformation that had begun in the aftermath of the Civil War.

As we discussed in Chapter 5, the economy, no longer the domain of small farmers and family businesses, was now dominated by giant monopolies whose new production methods threatened to cause class warfare. According to Wilson, the federal government was the only institution capable of taming these despotic economic powers and diffusing the conflict between management and labor. Because these new responsibilities were so weighty and difficult, Jackson's axiom that administrative tasks could be kept simple enough to be performed by inexperienced amateurs no longer held true. "To straighten the paths of government, to make its business less unbusinesslike, to strengthen and purify its organization and to crown its dutifulness" wrote Wilson, would require a whole new science, the science of administration.

Underlying this new science was the separation of politics and administration. A more active and expert administrative corps would not threaten liberty and democracy because political control would remain the exclusive domain of popularly elected officials. These politicians would set the broad course of public policy and leave it to expert administrators to implement those policies efficiently and effectively.

Wilson likened the distinction between politics and administration to that between the head of a household and the kitchen staff: "Self-government does not consist in having a hand in everything any more than housekeeping consists necessarily in cooking dinner with one's own hands. The cook must be trusted with a large discretion as to the management of the fires and the ovens." The head of household remains in control because he or she is the one who tells the cooks what sort of food the family likes, provides them with a firm budget for food and kitchen maintenance, and fires them if they make lousy meals. Having established broad policy principles and performance guidelines, the head of household stays out of the kitchen, enabling the cooks to make full use of their special talents and expertise to put tasty and nutritious food on the table.

During the Progressive Era, both the study and practice of public administration changed along the lines proposed by Wilson. In 1914, the University of Michigan established the first graduate program in municipal administration. Soon, other state and private universities began to offer degrees in public administration for the purpose of training students for public service careers. The faculties of such programs also did research aimed at establishing a scientific basis for such critical administrative tasks as budgeting, contract compliance, financial auditing, and personnel management. In 1916, the Institute for Government Research, later renamed the Brookings Institution, was created as the first private research institute devoted to the systematic analysis of issues relating to governmental performance and public policy.

Progressive reform of administration was particularly noteworthy in the area of natural resource management. The federal government was the nation's biggest landlord. It owned vast tracts of forest and grazing land, particularly in the West. In 1898, Gifford Pinchot was appointed to head a new Bureau of Forestry in the Department of Agriculture that was dedicated to improving forest conservation. This conservation program would manage the nation's timber and mineral resources to maximize the benefits they would provide over the long-term. Because the United States had no forestry school, Pinchot had gone to Germany for his professional training. He would later found the Yale School of Forestry. In 1905, authority for managing 60 million acres of western federal forests was transferred from the Department of the Interior to the Bureau of Forestry, renamed the Forest Service. In 1911, the Forest Service was granted authority over all federal forests.

Pinchot was determined that the Forest Service break the mold of corruption and ineptitude that had enveloped federal public administration. He sought to establish an organization in which personnel at all levels were committed to its goals and competent, energetic, and skillful enough to attain them. Forest rangers received special training and were encouraged to think of themselves as professionals. They were expected to respond to orders from regional and national service headquarters, not to demands of local citizens or politicians living near the forests they were managing. This quasi-military mode of organization was in stark contrast to the Jacksonian mode in which public servants were expected to identify closely with their local community, have no strong sense of professional identity, and remain loyal to their political party leaders, not their bureaucratic superiors. As their distinctive uniforms proudly proclaimed, the forest rangers were an elite corps. The democratic threat posed by such elites within the public service was presumably outweighed by their expertise and dedication.

Wilson's principle of separating politics and administration required that elected officials provide broad policy direction for the bureaucracy. Congress was simply too large and unwieldy to provide such guidance, and so, increasingly, that responsibility was borne by the president. The Budget Act of 1921 provided the president with a powerful tool for performing that task. It created the *Bureau of the Budget*, which later became the OMB housed in the treasury department. The chief task of this new agency was to prepare a budget for the entire federal government. It would review the requests of all federal programs and agencies, assemble those requests, and then suggest to the president how the requests should be pared down to keep overall federal spending in balance with expected revenues.

This notion of an executive budget has become so deeply embedded in the operations of the federal government that it is hard to believe that no such organizing principle for federal spending existed for the first 130 years of the republic. Spending decisions had been a haphazard affair in which, for the most part, individual federal departments made up their own budget proposals and took them directly to Congress. Creation of a budget bureau enabled the president to establish spending priorities and maintain some degree of financial control over his administrative subordinates.

Congress still preserved its constitutionally mandated power of the purse. It could choose to modify the president's budgetary proposals or even to ignore them altogether. But the sheer existence of an overall budgetary plan gave the president the initiative in policy planning and enabled him to appear fiscally responsible. Congress was put on the defensive. If it chose to deviate from this comprehensive blueprint, it bore the onus of demonstrating that its alternative was not a "budget breaker."

## Critical Choice: Programmatic Rights

President Wilson had only limited opportunity to put his vision of a new science of administration into practice. The Great Depression opened far greater possibilities for Wilson's disciple, FDR. The Depression ushered in the modern era of big government and thus gave FDR a larger canvas on which to impose Progressive notions of administration.

FDR had considerable administrative experience; he had served as Wilson's assistant secretary of the Navy, and he then succeeded one of the greatest of all Progressive executives, Al Smith, as governor of New York. To implement New Deal innovations in banking, labor relations, social insurance, and many other fields, FDR relied heavily on seasoned administrators who had pioneered similar programs in progressive-minded states such as Wisconsin and New York. The depth of the crisis and the verve of FDR's response to it greatly increased the attractiveness of government service to students and graduates of the most prestigious professional and graduate schools. Not since the early days of the republic had the government been so successful in attracting members of the elite to serve the government in peacetime.

Graduates of Yale, Columbia, and Harvard law schools and departments of economics flocked to Washington to work for new agencies such as *SEC, Federal Deposit Insurance Corporation, NLRB*, and the Agricultural Adjustment Agency as well as expanded and reinvigorated organizations such as the Antitrust Division of the Justice Department and the Department of the Interior. Their bosses were often their own former professors. These highly trained professionals were able to apply their knowledge of such arcane subjects as securities and banking law or labor and resource economics to the daunting task of restoring prosperity.

As we discussed in Chapter 8, FDR's effort to reorganize the executive branch failed. However, Congress did significantly expand his ability to manage the increasingly massive and specialized federal bureaucracy. It created the EOP, which provided him with a well-staffed nerve center for obtaining information about the activities of the various executive departments and planning and coordinating them. At the EOP's core was the Bureau of the Budget, which had been transferred to the EOP from the Treasury Department. The purpose of this reorganization was to fulfill the democratic as well as scientific promise of Progressive administration. An expert bureaucracy would be rendered accountable to public opinion by providing the representative of public opinion, the president, with sufficient political and managerial tools to control and direct it. FDR declared, "The day of enlightened administration has come."

But the New Deal was not simply Progressivism writ large. FDR's approach to putting the unemployed back to work had more in common with the older spoils system. Although it might have been more efficient to simply give money to the unemployed to alleviate their misery and encourage consumer spending, FDR rejected this approach. He was as concerned about the self-respect of the unemployed as he was about their economic condition. Therefore, he determined that the bulk of New Deal relief for the poor would come in the form of jobs. He established a series of job-creating relief agencies; the largest and most successful was the Works Progress Administration (WPA), which put millions of people to work in a remarkably short span of time.

Harry Hopkins, head of the WPA, insisted that the WPA create simple jobs that any able-bodied person could do. Skill and expertise were sacrificed to the greater cause of putting Americans back to work. This approach resulted in a lot of wasted effort and misallocation of resources, but it also enabled millions of Americans to hold their heads high. They were not paupers seeking handouts. They were full-fledged Depression fighters, working hard to build a better country. The WPA and its sister agency, the Civilian Conservation Corps (CCC), left a brilliant legacy of accomplishment. Common cultural and recreational opportunities were greatly expanded. Parks were built; hiking trails blazed; murals painted; and concerts performed. By creating simple jobs on a massive scale, the New Deal relief programs were more in keeping with Jackson's view of democratic administration than with Wilson's view of administration as a science.

FDR distinguished between the permanent bureaucracies he was establishing, which would function along Progressive lines, and the emergency relief agencies, which would be terminated when the economic crisis had passed. The massive spoils system instituted by the WPA and CCC did not survive the Depression, but they did leave an indelible mark. Before the New Deal, people did not expect the government to help them if they lost their jobs. The success of the WPA and other relief agencies altered those expectations. Congress acknowledged this new understanding of the responsibility of government when it enacted the Full Employment Act of 1946. This act charges the federal government with the specific responsibility of maintaining prosperity.

As we explained in Chapter 8, FDR (Figure 10.4) insulated his most important New Deal reforms from repeal. Even as he increased presidential power by creating the EOP, he tied the hands of future presidents by transforming his policy goals into a new set of rights. By virtue of being "unalienable," these rights-based programs would be buffered from temporary shifts in public opinion and political power. FDR further constrained his successors by extending civil service protections to his federal appointees. As long as they lived, the committed, youthful New Dealers that he appointed to implement these new programmatic rights would remain in charge of the federal bureaucracy.

FDR's effort to create an administrative state in service to the new programmatic rights was in tension with his desire to strengthen the presidency. This conflict has permeated American government and politics ever since. The democratic principle that policy should bend to the popular will as championed by the president has coexisted uneasily with the liberal principle that rights are immune from change. Thus, FDR's efforts to protect his key accomplishments from being undone by future presidents by establishing them as rights created a new source of conflict between bureaucratic discretion and democratic accountability.

## Post–WWII – A New Critical Path?

The modern federal bureaucracy is vastly bigger and engages in a much wider set of activities than its pre–WWII counterpart. Before the war there were only

**Figure 10.4.** FDR and His Children: 1935 cartoon by Clifford Berryman showing President Franklin Delano Roosevelt encircled by some of the New Deal agencies. Credit: The Granger Collection, NYC – All rights reserved.

eleven cabinet departments; today there are eighteen. The creation of new agencies, commissions, and other forms of federal bureaucratic activity has occurred at a still more rapid clip. And previously existing agencies such as Agriculture and Labor have taken on a whole host of new responsibilities. It may still be true that Americans harbor negative views about bureaucracy, but it is no longer true that those sentiments translate into a successful effort to minimize bureaucratic intrusion.

The most important causes of this expansion have been war, both hot and Cold, and the decline of the *legitimacy barrier* as an obstacle to new statutory initiatives. The legitimacy barrier refers to the constitutional insistence on limited government. In the original understanding of the Constitution, a policy was not legitimate if it did not have a clear basis in the Constitution's enumerated powers. A policy did not just have to serve a legitimate public purpose; it had to be constitutionally legitimate. The success of the Progressive Movement and the New Deal served to greatly diminish the principle of enumerated powers as a barrier to legislation. As we have seen in Chapter 9, a vast number of Progressive, New Deal, and post–New Deal laws were justified under the Commerce Clause. And the Supreme Court did not over turn a single one of those between 1936 and 1995. The older interpretation of the Commerce Clause would not have countenanced such major and expensive programs as health care reform, NCLB, or the Americans with Disabilities Act (ADA).

The ADA requires that all public buildings provide easy access for the disabled. Each of these, and a multitude of other statutory initiatives, require a great deal of implementation Someone has to write the specific guidelines that determine what does and does not constitute a disability, and what does and does not constitute easy access. For example, if a member-owned sports club allows guests to play, must it put in an elevator and a handicapped toilet even if none of the members of the club are disabled? Does its guest make it a public building and therefore subject to the easy-access provision of ADA, or is it a private club and therefore exempt? This and thousands of equally thorny questions like it must be addressed to make the ADA effective and workable. Although the question may ultimately be settled in court, the task of interpreting the law and translating it into specific guidelines to address this sort of question falls first to bureaucrats.

The vast expansion of government activity also changed the environment in which bureaucrats operated. Congress, the courts, and interest groups have all become much more active and influential in bureaucratic affairs. Normally one thinks of politics as creating policies. Interest groups lobby Congress to obtain new forms of aid or otherwise further their objectives. But it is equally true that policies create politics. Once the legitimacy barrier was lowered, Congress frequently created programs even in the absence of strong lobbying from interest groups. It passed strong environmental laws and major new science and educational funding programs before lobbying groups for such programs had become politically powerful. Once those programs were in place, however, the beneficiaries quickly organized themselves to lobby Congress to protect and expand the programs themselves and the agencies that implement them. Superficially, these support efforts may sound like harsh criticism: environmental groups will criticize the EPA for not meeting deadlines or Department of Education for not doing enough to support Special Education. But the purpose of the criticism is actually to assist the agencies; to obtain more personnel for the EPA so that it can act more quickly or to gain more funding for the DOE so it can more amply support Special Ed.

As we saw in the Congress chapter, Congress has sought to compensate for its loss of legislative initiative to the executive by becoming more active in oversight of executive agencies. By threatening to reduce agency appropriations or by exposing agency failures to the glare of publicity, Congress has used its powers to conduct investigations, hold hearings, and appropriate funds to exert substantial influence on the day-to-day conduct of the bureaucracy.

The shift away from centralized leadership control and toward the standing committees and their chairs facilitated these expanded congressional oversight activities. Legislators became careerists, solidifying their hold on their districts by using their committee assignments to oversee executive activities of special concern to their constituents. The Legislative Reorganization Act of 1946 provided members of Congress with expanded staffs to aid their bureaucratic probes. As members' terms of service lengthened their own policy expertise and knowledge of departmental folklore often matched, or even exceeded, that of the administrators they were scrutinizing (see Chapter 7).

The diffusion of authority in Congress that began in the 1970s further diffused political control of the bureaucracy. Bureau chiefs and agency heads found that their budgets, their lifeblood, were controlled as much by congressional committee and subcommittee chairs as by their department heads or OMB. This dual control opened new doors to the interest-group constituencies of federal agencies. If they lacked influence with the president, they could still obtain favored treatment from the bureaucracy by persuading the relevant congressional committee chair to be their champion.

In the 1970s, the federal courts also expanded their influence over the bureaucracy. Previously, the courts had shown great deference toward bureaucratic judgements in recognition of the bureaucrat's claim to expertise and impartiality. But in a series of important cases, courts substituted their own judgement for that of a government agency and ruled that the agency had been insufficiently scrupulous in its implementation of the law. For example, in *Calvert Cliffs Coordinating Committee v. the Atomic Energy Commission* (AEC) a federal appeals court ruled that the AEC had not performed a sufficiently thorough environmental impact analysis of the proposal to build a nuclear power plant at Calvert Cliffs Maryland.

The AEC was the very model of a Progressive regulatory agency. It was established in 1947 to oversee the development of atomic energy for peaceful purposes. In order to give it maximum flexibility to hire the best nuclear scientists and engineers, Congress exempted it from many federal civil service requirements. Among its responsibilities was the licensing of nuclear power plants in order to ensure that they would operate safely.

In 1969, Congress passed the National Environmental Protection Act that required all federal agencies to conduct an *environmental impact statement (EIS)* for each project they were conducting, sponsoring, or licensing. It does not specifically instruct the agencies about what they are supposed to do with the statements once they have been conducted. The AEC did commission an EIS of the Calvert Cliffs project, but it did not make substantial use of it during the license approval process. The federal appeals court ruled that the AEC's perfunctory treatment of the EIS violated the Act's intent and commanded it to reconsider granting the license in the light of a full consideration of the project's environmental impact. In the end the AEC did approve the plant, but the court had made its point. It would feel free to intervene in agency decision making even if the agency involved was composed of physicists, nuclear engineers, and other highly trained experts.

The courts often worked in tandem with constituency groups to press agencies to act more quickly. Public Interest Groups (see Chapter 11) would file suit against a regulatory agency such as the OSHA or EPA claiming that the agency was not living up to its statutory responsibility to issue a particular set of regulations speedily. The courts would then order the agency to move faster, imposing specific guidelines and timetables. Sometimes the agencies themselves actually welcomed these court orders because it enabled them to demand more cooperation from their reluctant political superiors. But just as often the judicial mandates wreaked havoc inside the agency because they forced the agency to reorder its own priorities and reassign funds and personnel away from projects it thought more important to the one the court had ordered it to accomplish at a more rapid clip.

## The Military-Industrial Complex

World War II, the Cold War, and the War on Terror each made major contributions to the expansion of the federal bureaucracy. World War II's daunting logistical challenges led to an intimate partnership between government and the private sector. Confronted with the massive challenge of providing supplies, munitions, and transportation to fight a war on two separate fronts, FDR briefly considered nationalizing the war-related sectors of American industry. But he quickly realized that the government lacked sufficient knowledge and the management skill to run those industries. Instead, he relied primarily on voluntary cooperation from private suppliers. Government restricted its involvement mostly to stimulating such cooperation by paying high prices. Even so, a great deal of direct interaction between government and suppliers was necessary to ensure that the right things were being produced in a timely fashion. To facilitate such coordination, suppliers loaned experienced managers to government for the token price of $1 a year. These "dollar-a-year men" became vital cogs in the war machine, helping to achieve rates of ship, plane, tank, and munitions production that America's enemies had not thought possible.

To hasten production, government contracts were often written on a *cost-plus basis*, which meant that suppliers could recover their full costs plus a specified percentage of profit. Therefore, war industries had no material incentive to keep costs down. Indeed, the greater their costs, the greater the absolute amount of profit they would obtain. Working for the government for $1 a year did not cause managers to forget who really paid their salary. Throughout their government service, they retained a strong loyalty to the companies from which they came and to which they would return.

With the onset of the Cold War, these dollar-a-year men became valued intermediaries between the government and industries whose ability to produce armaments and related supplies and equipment were vital to the United States' ability to compete militarily with the Soviet Union. For the first time in American history, the high levels of war-related industrial production continued during peacetime. As the technology of warfare grew in complexity, government came to depend on science. Grants from the federal government to university physics, chemistry, and engineering departments became a crucial supplement to corporate research and development as a means for stimulating militarily useful scientific discoveries and technological advances.

The executive branch was ill equipped to handle the strategic, scientific, and management complexities created by the Cold War. The Army and Navy each reported to the president via separate cabinet departments. The Army was part of the War Department headed by the Secretary of War, whereas the Navy had its own department headed by the Secretary of the Navy. Nor was there any mechanism for integrating, planning, and forcing deployments involving both the Army and the Navy. Such efforts took place on an ad hoc basis. To give the president a better tool for protecting national security, in 1947 Congress passed legislation merging the Navy and War Department into the Department of Defense (DOD). The Secretary of Defense was given authority over all branches of the military including the newly established U.S. Air Force (previously part of the Army). The Marine Corps remained part of the Navy. The DOD is also in charge of two intelligence agencies, the NSA, created in 1952 and the Defense Intelligence Agency, established in 1961.

The increasingly close relationship between the DOD, corporations, and universities led to the creation of a *revolving door* by which the military and civilian bureaucrats who issued defense contracts and grants would leave to work for the very companies or universities who had won those awards. In his farewell address, President Dwight Eisenhower, the great American hero of World War II and himself an architect of the Cold War, warned of the dangers posed by this new, increasingly unaccountable "military-industrial complex." Eisenhower recognized that government dependence on outside expertise and the increasing interpenetration between government and profit-making corporations was undermining the Wilsonian notion of a scientific administration subservient to executive authority.

The 9/11 attacks on New York and Washington DC destroyed the comforting illusion that war was something that only happened on foreign soil. Before September 11, the nation's antiterrorism effort resembled the early republic's effort to provide military security through militias. Airport security was supervised by state and local governments and performed by the airlines themselves.

Investigation of biological threats was largely in the hands of local public health departments. In the wake of the attack on the World Trade Center and Pentagon and the anthrax attacks that took place in the months that followed, the demand for federal intervention drastically increased. The militia phase was over. The federal government would create a standing force to provide home-land security.

The new *DHS* created in response to September 11, which we discussed briefly in Chapter 1, represented the most ambitious reorganization of the federal government since the creation of the Department of Defense a half-century earlier. As noted in Chapter 8, President Bush had initially resisted forming another government department. After considerable prodding from Congress, however, the Bush administration agreed to support legislation creating a vast new department to cope with the domestic threat of terror. The DHS, established in 2003, is the third-largest cabinet department in the U.S. federal government after the DOD and Department of Veterans Affairs. As of 2010, it had more than 180,000 employees and an additional 200,000 private contractors. Most of those employees are not new; they were transferred to the new department from existing departments including treasury, agriculture, energy, transportation, state, commerce, and health and human services as well as such previously independent agencies as the Federal Emergency Management Agency.

## CONCLUSION

This chapter has chronicled the difficulties of making the bureaucracy effective and respectful of American liberties. It has shown how at different eras in American political development different methods for accomplishing these goals have been relied on, including: choosing people of good character; rotation in office; civil service examinations; professionalism; executive oversight; congressional oversight; and judicial review. It has also emphasized that the expansion of the bureaucracy that has taken place has been accomplished grudgingly. One has only to travel to France or Germany, or even Canada, to realize that not all people are as resentful of bureaucratic intrusion and bureaucratic authority as Americans are.

The American disaste for bureaucracy has not prevented major bureaucratic expansion, one so vast that it may well have pushed the nation off the critical path of bureaucratic minimalism. But the antipathy toward government continues to give the American bureaucracy a distinctive caste. Instead of establishing a federal bureaucracy large enough to implement the myriad responsibilities now assigned to it by Congress, the president, and the courts, many federal agencies function mostly as supervisors, overseeing the work done by state and local officials, non-governmental agencies, and private companies. And there still exists a strong impulse to keep bureaucrats from exercising discretion. Congress, the courts, and the president all strive to exert direct influence on the workings of federal agencies.

As the last section showed, the dual impact of the decline of the legitimacy barrier and the relentless pressure of national security has pushed the United States off the path of limited government and therefore of minimal federal bureaucracy. The larger and more complex the bureaucracy, the more discretion will devolve to nonelected officials and the greater the problem of reconciling ambitious government and democratic accountability will become.

## CHAPTER SUMMARY

☆ Throughout American political development fears about an excessively intrusive and arbitrary bureaucracy have warred with desires to make government efficient and effective.

☆ The civilian component of the federal bureaucracy is surprisingly small. Most of what it does affects the public only indirectly. Much of the actual work the federal government inspires is done by others either in response to grants and contracts issued by the federal bureaucracy or in response to regulatory demands issued by federal agencies.

☆ The Congress exerts very significant controls over the federal bureaucracy, sometimes thwarting the president's effort to coordinate the efforts of various parts of the bureaucracy.

☆ The haphazardness of federal bureaucratic organization is a very important clue regarding the nature of bureaucratic politics. Where an agency rests in the organization chart will inevitably give advantages to those political interests whose access to and power over the agency is advantaged by that placement. Conversely, handicaps are created for those the placement restricts access to and denies levers of power.

☆ Antipathy to the intrusion of British governors and the British army set the United States on a path designed to limit the scope and ambition of the new federal bureaucracy.

☆ The first critical choice in the history of American public administration was Congress's decision to grant the president the power to remove federal officials.

☆ Thomas Jefferson invented the spoils system, but it was Jackson who made use of it to transform the character of American public administration by insisting that federal bureaucracy could and should be staffed by ordinary people rather than "gentlemen."

☆ The combined impact of civil service reform and Progressivism transformed the bureaucracy by replacing political patronage with examinations and introducing a greater emphasis on expertise, professionalism, and impartiality into the staffing and management of the federal bureaucracy.

☆ The creation of the EOP strengthened the president's ability manage the federal bureaucracy.

☆ The programmatic rights created by the New Deal serve to insulate the agencies that implemented them from all forms of political control.

☆ The modern federal bureaucracy is vastly bigger and engages in a much wider set of activities than its pre–WWII counterpart. The most important causes of this expansion have been war, both hot and Cold, and the decline of the "legitimacy barrier" as an obstacle to new statutory initiatives.

## MAJOR TERMS AND CONCEPTS

| | |
|---|---|
| Civil Service Commission | Civilian Intelligence Agency (CIA) |
| Department of Defense (DOD) | Department of Homeland Security (DHS) |
| Environmental Impact Statement (EIS) | Environmental Protection Agency (EPA) |
| Executive Office of the President (EOP) | Federal Deposit Insurance Corporation |
| Food and Drug Administration | Foreign Service |
| Independent Regulatory Commissions | Joint Chiefs of Staff |
| Legitimacy Barrier | Militia |
| National Labor Relations Board (NLRB) | National Security Council (NSC) |
| Office of Management and Budget (OMB) | Removal Power |
| Revolving Door | Securities and Exchange Commission (SEC) |
| Spoils System | State Department |

## SUGGESTED READINGS

Arnold, Peri. *Making the Managerial Presidency: Comprehensive Organization Planning, 1905–1996*, 2nd ed. Lawrence: University Press of Kansas, 1998.

Cook, Brian. *Bureaucracy and Self-Government: Reconsidering the Role of Public Administration in American Politics*. Baltimore, MD: Johns Hopkins University Press, 1996.

Derthick, Martha. *Agency under Stress: The Social Security Administration in American Government*. Washington, DC: Brookings Institution, 1990.

Derthick, Martha. *Policymaking for Social Security*. Washington, DC: Brookings Institution, 1979.

Goldsmith, Stephen, and William Eggars. *Governing by Network: The New Shape of the Public Sector*. Washington DC: Brookings Institution Press, 2004.

Goodsell, Charles. *Mission Mystique: Belief Systems in Public Agencies*. Washington, DC: CQ Press, 2011.

Hoffer, Williamjames Hull. *To Enlarge the Machinery of Government: Congressional Debates and the Growth of the American State, 1858–1891*. Baltimore: Johns Hopkins University Press, 2007.

Kaufman, Herbert. *The Forest Ranger: A Study in Administrative Behavior*. Baltimore, MD: Johns Hopkins University Press, 1960.

Kettl, Don. *The Transformation of Governance: Public Administration for Twenty-First Century America*. Baltimore: Johns Hopkins University Press, 2002.

Landy, Marc K., Marc J. Roberts, and Stephen R. Thomas. *The Environmental Protection Agency: Asking the Wrong Questions from Nixon to Clinton*, 2nd exp. ed. New York: Oxford University Press, 1994.

Moynihan, Daniel P. *Maximum Feasible Misunderstanding: Community Action in the War on Poverty*. New York: Free Press, 1970.

Rosenbloom, David. *Building a Legislative-Centered Public Administration: Congress and the Administrative State, 1946–1999*. Tuscaloosa, AL: University of Alabama Press, 2002.

Selznick, Philip. *TVA and the Grass Roots: A Study in Politics and Organization*. Berkeley: University of California Press, 1984.

Skowronek, Stephen. *Building a New American State: The Expansion of National Administrative Capacities, 1877–1920*. New York: Cambridge University Press, 1982.

White, Leonard. *The Federalists: A Study in Administrative History*. New York: Macmillan, 1948.

White, Leonard. *The Jacksonians: A Study in Administrative History*. New York: Macmillan, 1954.

White, Leonard. *The Jeffersonians: A Study in Administrative History, 1801–1829*. New York: Macmillan, 1951.

White, Leonard. *The Republican Era: A Study in Administrative History, 1869–1901*. New York: Macmillan, 1958.

Wildavsky, Aaron. *The New Politics of the Budget Process*, 2nd ed. New York: Harper-Collins, 1999.

Wilson, James Q. *Bureaucracy: What Government Agencies Do and Why They Do It*. New York: Basic Books, 1989.

# Political Forces

# Parties, Campaigns, and Elections

## CHAPTER OVERVIEW

This chapter focuses on:

☆ A contemporary portrait of parties, campaigns, and elections.
☆ The role parties play in the functioning of the American democratic republic.
☆ The origins of party and the path dependency of the party system.
☆ The impact of Populism and Progressivism on political parties.
☆ The critical choices that transformed the parties during the New Deal.

In 2001, Michael Bloomberg, a lifelong Democrat, deserted his party to accept the Republican nomination for mayor of New York City and was elected. In statewide and national elections, the city votes overwhelmingly for Democrats, but Bloomberg's predecessor, Rudolph Giuliani, was also a Republican. In July of 2002, Bloomberg named a charter revision commission to recommend amendments to the city charter, one of which would be for the purpose of adopting nonpartisan city elections. In a statement accompanying the announcement, Bloomberg explained that *nonpartisan elections* had already been adopted by a number of American cities, including Atlanta, Boston, Chicago, Denver, Detroit, and Los Angeles. Instead of *party primaries*, candidates for all city offices would be chosen in a single primary open to all voters. In both the primary and the general election, candidates' names would appear without party label. Bloomberg claimed that abolishing partisan elections would "prevent the small number of people who vote in party primaries from determining the course of the election.... We should not let party bosses dictate who gets into office." This attack on political parties echoed the decades-old refrain of Progressive reformers that citizens should "vote for the man, or woman, not the party"(Figure 11.1).

Of course, Bloomberg had a practical reason for ending partisan city elections. Because the Republican Party is vastly outnumbered in New York City, his

**Figure 11.1.** Jumping Ship: A 2007 cartoon depicting the mayor of New York City Michael Bloomberg leaving the Democratic Party.

*Source*: Political Cartoons. Com 39217. Retrieved from http://www.politicalcartoons.com/cartoon/c7dfb428-af49-431b-ae48-9cedec333215.html.

reelection chances would improve if he did not have to identify himself with it. His advocacy of nonpartisan elections does not necessarily make him a hypocrite. When the rules of the political game change, someone always benefits and someone always loses. Perhaps, in this case, what would be good for Michael Bloomberg would also be good for New York City.

Is Mayor Bloomberg correct in thinking that New York City would be a freer and a more democratic place if it were governed on a nonpartisan basis? Supporters of political parties would dispute him. They see political parties as an essential means for enabling democracy to operate effectively on a mass scale. They point to the depressing effect that removal of party labels has on voter turnout and the difficulty that voters have in distinguishing between candidates who cannot be identified on the basis of party.

The United States has the oldest continuously operating political *party system* in the world. Every president since 1852 has either been elected to office as a Republican or Democrat. Both houses of Congress have been controlled either by the Republicans or the Democrats since 1849. As of 2012, the president, all the members of the House of Representative, 98 of 100 Senators and 49 of 50 governors were either Republicans or Democrats. And yet when people talk about "party politics," it is usually in a scornful tone. Many voters register as independents. According to a study by the Pew Research Center, as of 2010 approximately 37 percent of American voters described themselves as independent or unaffiliated, whereas 34 percent said they identify themselves as Democrats and 28 percent said they were Republicans.

Although influential political scientists such as V. O. Key, Jr., have stressed the importance of robust political parties for strengthening and maintaining democracy, many voters agreed with Bloomberg that parties are run by "bosses" and that party control of the electoral process stifles the voice of the people. This chapter examines the mystery of political party and its strong but testy relationship with democracy and liberty. A study of the development of political parties helps the reader think about whether a democratic republic as big as the United States can function without them and whether the democratic claims made for them are believable. Because parties are essentially devices for winning elections, they cannot be understood apart from the political campaigns they wage and election outcomes that determine their fate. That is why this chapter is called "Parties, Campaigns, and Elections." It treats all three as interrelated phenomena. First it takes an extensive look at contemporary parties, campaigns, and elections. Then it examines the origins of party; the development and dominance of the party system; the impact of Populism and Progressivism on political party; the transformation of parties during the New Deal; and the complex pattern of decline and resurgence that has characterized the parties since the 1950s. The chapter concludes with a reconsideration of the key democratic and liberal functions that political parties are supposed to perform and some questions about their continued ability to perform them.

## A Contemporary Portrait: Parties, Campaigns, and Elections

The question of who is a Democrat and who is a Republican is difficult to answer. Unlike parties in Western Europe, even those who consider themselves to be very loyal party members, do not officially join a party. They do not carry membership cards, and levels of party loyalty vary. Some who think of themselves as party loyalists may still vote for another party sometimes, or just stay home if they do not like their party's candidate. In the South, many voters almost always votes for a Republican for president, still voting for Democrats for Congress and statewide offices. Does that make them Democrats or Republicans? In the Northeast and Midwest the pattern is somewhat reversed, with voters supporting Democrats for president and Congress but frequently voting for Republicans for governor. In many states voters can vote in whichever party primary they choose. Therefore, primary voting is not a good measure of party strength or loyalty. Because parties are not popular institutions, even those who routinely support one particular party may not claim to identify with that party.

Nonetheless, there are identifiable segments of the population who do continue to support one or the other parties by large margins. Such blocs of voters form the party's *coalition*. One can get a pretty good idea of which kinds of voters identify with one or another of the parties by seeing which ones gave a larger percentage of their vote than the national average to either the incumbent president Barack Obama, a Democrat, or the Republican challenger, Mitt Romney. The total popular vote went to Obama by a margin of 52 percent to 47 percent.

## Party Coalitions

Later in the chapter we shall discuss the formation of the most enduring majority party coalition ever assembled, the New Deal Democrats. Key voting segments who forged that coalition still remain staunchly loyal to the Democrats. In 2012, 93 percent of African Americans voted for President Obama, as did 69 percent of Jews. Labor union members' support has declined in recent decades, but President Obama still received 58 percent of union votes.

The most severe defection from the New Deal Democratic coalition has taken place in the South. Before the 1965 Voting Rights Act, southern whites voted overwhelmingly for the Democrats, whereas almost all southern African Americans were precluded from voting. Since 1965, southern African Americans have adopted the Democratic party loyalty of their northern brethren, whereas southern whites have departed the Democrats. The Republicans now hold almost all the U.S. Senate seats in the southern states and the vast majority of House seats, governorships, and houses of the states legislatures. Romney carried every southern state except Florida and Virginia, the two southern states with the most northern migrants. The South is still "solid," but now it is solidly Republican.

The other large voting bloc comprising the New Deal coalition was the Catholics. They are no longer reliable Democratic supporters. In 2012 Catholics supported Obama by a narrow 50-48 margin. However, this result is largely the result of a 75–21 percent majority for Obama among Hispanic Catholics. White Catholics, who had constituted the vast bulk of the New Deal Democratic Catholic majority, supported Romney 59–40 percent.

The Democrats have compensated for their losses in the South by making very strong gains in other parts of the country. As the map of the electoral college votes cast in the 2012 presidential election shows, the Democrats now dominate the Pacific Coast and the northern and middle segments of the Atlantic Coast. Beyond the solid South, the Republicans also dominate the Great Plains and Rocky Mountain states. Although the Democrats won most of the Midwestern states in 2012, their winning margin in most of them was small. From an electoral standpoint, the Midwest remains by far the most competitive region in the nation. Figure 11.2 provides an electoral map of the 2012 election.

**Figure 11.2.** 2012 Electoral Map. Retrieved from http://www.pbs.org/newshour/vote2012/map/all_results.html.

Like the Democrats, the Republicans also retain critical segments of the electorate whose loyalty it has held for decades. Whereas the Democrats do very well in big cities, Republicans continue to do better in small towns and rural areas. President Obama won 69 percent of the vote in cities with populations over 500, 000. By contrast, Romney won 56 percent of the vote in small towns and 61 percent of the vote in rural areas. The Republicans carried almost all the states in which farming dominates. Owners of small businesses also continue to show loyalty to the Republicans.

In the past, income and education were a reliable indicator of which party a person belonged to. The richer and better educated were Republicans. Income is still a predictor of party affiliation. The poorest Americans, the 17 percent of the population making $30,000 or less, gave President Obama 63 percent of their vote. The richest, the 8 percent making more than $200,000, supported

Republicans by a margin of 64 percent to 34 percent. Fifty-seven percent of voters making between $30,000 and $50,000 also supported Obama. Romney carried the vote of those making $50,000 or more. The relationship between level of education and presidential preference is no longer straightforward. Obama did especially well at the highest and lowest education levels. He won the support of 64 percent of high school dropouts and 55 percent of those who attended graduate school On the other hand, Romney garnered 51 percent of the vote among college graduates.

The coalitions of each party are also composed of those with strong views about matters that have not traditionally divided the parties because they have only become politically relevant in recent decades. Most prominent among these new sources of partisan divide are religiosity, marriage, abortion, sexual preference, and guns.

## Religiosity

As we have seen throughout this book, religion has often been a divisive element in American party politics. But the electorate now divides less over which religion one belongs to than how frequently one attends church, any church. Because most Americans claim to be religious, the Democratic party leadership has sought to erase its image as the secular party. Like previous Democratic candidates Bill Clinton, Al Gore, and John Kerry, Barack Obama publicized his strong religious attachments. Nonetheless, Republicans are much more united in their support of proposals to give federal grants to religious schools and religious social service providers and less reticent in identifying with religious causes. Fifty-nine percent of those who attend religious services weekly voted for Romney in 2012, as did 63 percent of those who attend more than once a week. By contrast, 55 percent of those who attend religious services only a few times a year voted for Obama, as did 62 percent of those who never attend them. Because African Americans and Hispanics attend church in large numbers and vote overwhelmingly for the Democrats, the relationship between church attendance and party affiliation only holds for whites. Sixty-nine percent of white Protestants voted for Romney, as did 59 percent of white Catholics.

## Gender, Marriage, Procreation, and Sexual Preference

For the first fifty years that women had the right to vote, they voted for the two parties in the same proportion as men. But in the last thirty years, women have tended to vote for the Democrats more than men do. In 2012, 55 percent of women voted for Obama, whereas 54 percent of men voted for Romney.

However the gender gap actually reverses itself among whites. Fifty-six percent of white women voted for Romney and only 42 percent for Obama. Marriage also trumps gender when it comes to voting. Fifty-three percent of married women voted for Romney. On the other hand, 56 percent of unmarried men voted for Obama. The relationship between gender and political party only holds for married men, who voted 60 percent for Romney, and unmarried women, who voted for Obama by an even more decisive 67 percent.

Over the past decade, prominent Democratic party leaders and office holders had taken up the cause of gay marriage. During the 2012 presidential campaign, President Obama announced his support for gay marriage. On the other hand, Republican leaders and office holders have been virtually unanimous in their opposition to gay marriage. It is not surprising therefore that 76 percent of those who identified themselves as gay, lesbian, or bisexual voted for Obama. Seventy-four percent of those who opposed gay marriage voted for Romney.

Prior to the Supreme Courts decision in *Roe v. Wade* (see Chapter 9), views about abortion did not divide the parties. But in the wake of that decision, which declared that women had a right to an abortion, most Democratic politicians came out in support of the decision and most Republican politicians opposed it. Therefore, the issue became increasingly linked to party politics. In 2012, 67 percent of those in favor of legalized abortion voted for Obama, whereas 77 percent of those opposed voted for Romney.

Attitudes toward gun control divide sharply along party lines. In 2011 The Pew Research Center asked Americans whether they thought it was more important to protect the right to own guns or control gun ownership. By a 72–22 percent margin, Republicans said protecting gun rights was more important, whereas Democrats placed a higher priority on gun control by a margin of 70 percent to 26 percent. As Nate Silver reported in his polling blog, 538, only about 25 percent of Democrats say they have a gun in their home, whereas almost 60 percent of Republicans say they do. As Silver points out, "Whether someone owns a gun is a more powerful predictor of a person's political party than her gender, whether she identifies as gay or lesbian, whether she is Hispanic or whether she lives in the South."

## *"Swing" Voters*

In order to gain political strength, both parties seek to recruit new blocs of voters. Hispanics are the fastest-growing ethnically identifiable segment of the population. Between 2000 and 2009 the Hispanic population grew from approximately 35 million to approximately 48 million. Therefore, the parties have been particularly active in pursuing them. However, many Hispanics are not citizens, and even those who are register to vote in lesser numbers than other groups do. Hispanic Americans currently constitute only about 10 percent of the electorate. But as their number grows and they assimilate to life in the United States, this percentage is expected to grow substantially. It is already much higher in several of the most populated states, including the three largest – California, New York, and Texas. Republicans believe that the strong religious and family ties and work ethic of Latinos make them very susceptible to Republican appeals. But so far, these Republican hopes have not borne fruit. In 2010, a year in which Republicans scored huge victories in the congressional elections, Hispanics still gave Democratic candidates 60 percent of their vote. In 2012 Hispanics voted even more decisively for the Democrats: 71 percent of Hispanics voted for President Obama.

### Political Party Organization

Political parties are organized at the local, state, and national level. State and local political parties vary enormously in their level of ambition and effectiveness. In some states they may be very active. They may engage in voter registration drives and seek to mobilize volunteers for national as well as local and statewide candidates. They may also try to maintain and instill party loyalty by hosting speeches by public officials of their party and celebrating party holidays – Jefferson-Jackson Day (Democrats) and Lincoln's Birthday (Republicans). In others they may exist in name only.

The national parties exist in two different forms. Each party has a national committee and also a House and Senate campaign committee. The national committees raise funds to spend to help party candidates and support registration drives and other marketing activities aimed at promoting the party's electoral prospects. They also organize and stage their respective presidential nominating conventions.

Even though the conventions no longer have an active role in choosing the presidential nominee, they retain considerable political importance. They are one of only two occasions during the entire presidential campaign season when many millions of people actually pay attention to the race. The other occasion is provided by the presidential debates. In an age of ten-second sound bites and thirty-second ads, the conventions are an opportunity for the public to have a more lengthy and thorough opportunity to hear why each party and its nominee claim that they should be entrusted with the presidency. In 2012 the major television networks accorded the conventions one hour of prime time for four successive nights. The parties carefully orchestrated their choice of speakers and the content of those speeches to highlight the themes they sought to stress to voters. Despite the deep policy differences dividing the presidential candidates, each party sought to use the event to humanize their candidates in the voters' eyes and show them to be devoted to the dominant elements of American political culture – equality of opportunity, the common man and woman, family values, and freedom (see Chapter 2).

The most important convention event is the candidate's acceptance speech. It provides a relatively lengthy occasion for the candidate to define himself to the voters and explain why he is the superior choice. Second in importance are the speeches that nominate the candidate. These speeches expand on the themes that the candidate will later take up in his acceptance speech and also visibly demonstrate that key leaders, representing various elements and factions of the party, are giving him their enthusiastic support. In deference to the growing importance of the Hispanic vote, both parties gave prominent speaking roles at their 2012 conventions to young, attractive Hispanic politicians. The Republicans featured Marco Rubio, U.S. Senator from Florida. The Democrats featured Julian Castro, mayor of San Antonio, Texas.

Off camera, the business of the convention includes determining the party platform and listening to many nonbroadcast speeches. These activities are often of great importance to the delegates and the speakers themselves. They are a vital part of the secondary function of the convention, which is to stir up the enthusiasm and improve the morale of party loyalists whose help is desperately needed by the candidate during the campaign. The platforms are a catalog of the various stances on public policy questions that a majority of the party delegates choose to endorse. Candidates are not necessarily bound to support every plank of the platform. As the two parties have come to be more ideologically distinct from one another and internally cohesive, the platforms have become less politically relevant because the public already has a pretty clear idea regarding what the parties differ about.

The House and Senate campaign committees are organizationally separate from the national committees. Each campaign committee is chaired by a member of their respective branches who is elected by a caucus of all the elected members of their party. In addition to providing funds and logistical support to incumbent party members, the campaign committees aid challengers to incumbents of the other party and those nominated to seek open seats. Also, the committees work actively to recruit candidates particularly in districts where the opposition incumbent appears vulnerable or where an open seat appears winnable.

## Election Campaigns

Individual candidates look to the party apparatus for financial support and other forms of assistance, but they do not rely on it. They set up their own campaign organizations that assume the primary responsibility for raising money, organizing volunteers, scheduling and holding events, advertising, polling, and cultivating the support of outside groups.

Raising funds is the first campaign priority because money is needed to carry out all the other campaign objectives. Staff members organize fund-raising events; scour for possible donors; keep financial records; and solicit by phone and over the Internet. However, the chief fundraiser are inevitably the candidates themselves. Persons considering making substantial donations want to establish a personal relationship with the candidate. In between scheduled events, the candidate is continually meeting with and phoning donor prospects.

The Center for Responsive Politics estimated that the 2012 presidential election campaign cost more than $2.6 billion and that the total of all 2012 campaign spending was $6 billion. Television is the most important device by which candidates reach out to voters. More than $3 billion was spent on television ads. Campaigns hire consultants to write and film the ads. Because television time is so expensive, it needs to be bought strategically. Campaign consultants determine when and where TV ads should air. Thus, in 2012 both the Obama and Romney campaigns saturated the airwaves in the "battle ground," whereas TV viewers in safe states such as Massachusetts (Obama) and Mississippi (Romney) saw very few campaign ads.

Political campaigns have rediscovered the effectiveness of canvassing. *Canvassing* means talking to voters, either by phone or in person, in order to find out for whom they are likely to vote. On the basis of this information, the campaign strives to stay in touch with those who support their candidate. On Election Day it repeatedly calls those supportive voters and may even offer to drive them to the polls. Large numbers of volunteers are needed to knock on doors, make telephone calls, and drive voters to the polls. Facebook, Twitter, and smart phones greatly facilitate the task of enlisting volunteers, using volunteers to recruit other volunteers, and deploying volunteers in an efficient and effective manner.

Campaigns seek fund-raising and canvassing help from outside groups. Democrats are particularly dependent on labor unions to provide contributions and campaign workers. Because the Democrats are more supportive of government spending and allowing public employees to unionize and bargain collectively, public-sector unions are particularly generous in making campaign contributions to them. The Democrats also try to mobilize the support of feminist, environmental, and other organizations that espouse liberal causes. Republicans look to evangelical churches, gun clubs, and business associations and groups that espouse conservative or libertarian causes for such support. The person in charge of cultivating and negotiating with these organizations is usually called the *political director*. This same person also maintains relations between the campaign and various local and state party organizations as well as with the national party leadership and staff.

It is more difficult to make use of outside organizations in primary elections because as loyal party supporters they may feel it necessary to shun intraparty contests. But sometimes these organizations owe sufficient debts of loyalty to incumbents that they will help them defeat a challenger. Or an organization may feel that particular candidates are so closely identified with its cause that it will fight for them against their less enthusiastic rivals.

The campaign does its own polling because it needs types of information that it does not want to make public. In addition to measuring the preferences of voters, campaign polls may test the popularity of specific messages that the campaign is contemplating using in speeches by the candidate and in ads. The campaign pollster may also seek to obtain information about very specific subgroups of the population – for example, Hispanic males and stay-at-home mothers – that the campaign hopes to cultivate.

The candidates spend much of their day addressing crowds. Not only are such occasions important in their own right but they form much of the coverage of the campaign that appears on national and local TV news. They enable the candidate to appear on television for free. It is imperative, therefore, that the events be well staged, and, especially, that they look good for the camera. The task of organizing such events and ensuring that no glitches occur is the job of the *advance person*. This person has to excel at problem solving because glitches do inevitably occur and it is critical that neither the crowd nor the media become aware of them.

Because the functions performed by the campaign are so varied and complex and the staff needed to perform them is so large, the campaign takes on the character of a complex organization that requires leadership and management. The *campaign manager* is the chief executive officer with responsibility for the overall success of the campaign and recruiting and managing the persons in charge of the specific campaign functions. The campaign manager is in constant touch with those who create and disseminate the campaign message, orchestrate events, raise funds, and mobilize volunteers to ensure that these various operations mesh together to most effectively promote victory.

### Elections: A Study in Federalism

The regulations and procedures that govern elections embody the full complexity inherent in Federalism (see Chapter 5). All levels of government are involved in a manner that continually causes them to intersect and intermingle. The U.S. Constitution sets eligibility rules for voting. The Twenty-Sixth Amendment declares all U.S. citizens over the age of eighteen to be eligible to vote. The Fifteenth Amendment prohibits denial of the suffrage on the basis of race, and the Nineteenth Amendment guarantees voting rights to women. But these guarantees are not absolute. Many states bar convicted felons from voting; some states bar felons only while they are in prison, others until they have completed their parole or probation, and still others bar them for their entire lifetime.

State governments regulate the voter registration process as well as party primaries and state elections. They also determine the shape of congressional as well as state legislative districts. States determine how long the polls will remain open, but individual localities provide and manage the locations where people vote and in some states decide what sort of voting process is used. Some localities use paper ballots, whereas others use one or another variety of voting machine. In 2000, Palm Beach County, Florida, became notorious because the design of the ballot it used, the so-called butterfly ballot, so confused elderly voters that many voted for candidates other than the one they intended to vote for. Local elections are even more diverse. Some cities have party primaries, others conduct nonpartisan elections, so there is no primary. Rather, most nonpartisan elections have a preliminary election. If a candidate wins more than 50 percent of the vote that candidate wins. Otherwise, the top two finishers go on to a final election in which the top vote-getter wins.

Citizens are not automatically registered to vote; every state except North Dakota requires them to register. The actual registration process is usually carried out by a county or local election office. Most states insist that one register at least thirty days before an election, but a few allow one to register on Election Day. But registration is no longer entirely a state and local function. The U.S. Justice Department monitors the process to ensure that no racial discrimination occurs. And since 1993 the federal government has also intervened in order make registration easier and encourage more people to do so. Congress passed the National Voter Registration Act of 1993 (the "Motor Voter" law). It requires states to increase the number and variety of voter registration opportunities. Because registration is now available at motor vehicle bureaus, and welfare offices, people do not have to make a separate trip to register. They can do so when they apply for a driver's license or have an interview about their welfare status.

In order to making voting easier and reduce crowding on Election Day, thirty-four states provide for early voting in person. A registered voter may go to specified polling places and cast a ballot in advance of election day. In Texas, for example, early voting starts seventeen days before election days and ends four days before. Absentee voting is permitted in twenty-eight states. In twenty-two of them one needs an excuse to do so. Valid excuses usually involve being out of town on Election Day because one is attending school elsewhere, serving in the military, living abroad, or for some other acceptable reason.

Oregon uses mailed ballots as its primary voting method. In 1998, voters passed a ballot measure directing all elections to be conducted by mail. A pamphlet with information about each measure and candidate in the upcoming election is mailed to every Oregon household three weeks before each statewide election. Ballots are mailed to every registered voter fourteen to eighteen days before the election. Voters fill out the ballot, sign it, and mail it back. Mailed ballots are accepted anytime until 8:00 PM of Election Day.

States make the rule governing how parties choose their candidates. Most states employ primaries. Primaries are preliminary elections in which voters choose among candidates of the same party. In some states only voters who register as party members vote in their party's primary. But other states allow independents to choose which primary to participate in and still others allow any registered voter to participate in whichever party primary she chooses. Some states, Iowa for example, use a caucus system to choose their delegates to the national presidential nominating convention. The entire state of Iowa is divided into 1,784 precincts. In each precinct, each party holds a *caucus*, a meeting that can be attended by any voter living in that precinct who has registered with that party. The precinct caucus elects delegates to the party's ninety-nine county conventions. These county conventions then select delegates to the congressional district conventions. At this point the rules for each party diverge. The Republican county conventions elect delegates to the state party convention, which then chooses the state's delegates to the national convention. The Democrats also elect delegates to the state convention, but most of the delegates to the national convention are actually chosen by the congressional district conventions.

The process governing the choice of presidential candidate begins well before the first convention delegates are chosen. Political scientists James Ceaser and Andrew Busch call it the "invisible campaign" because it takes place away from the public eye. It is the time when would-be candidates try to assess their chances. They talk to potential campaign donors, conduct private polls, and test out campaign messages. They hold private discussions with consultants and seasoned operatives whom they would consider hiring if they do in fact run. The "visible" campaign starts when individuals announce their candidacies and begin to set up their national campaign organizations and field organizations in the individual states.

In 2012, President Obama did not face any challenge for renomination, whereas the battle for the Republican nomination was hard fought. Mitt Romney, the presumed front-runner, was opposed by several rivals, each of whom claimed to be more conservative than he. The conservative cast of the Republican primary voting public was evidenced by the fact that each of Romney's rivals was for some period of time ahead of him in the polls. Each proved to have a fatal flaw as a candidate. Perry proved insufficiently skilled as a debater and insufficiently knowledgeable about national and world affairs. Cain was accused of sexual harassment and adultery. Gingrich's abandonment of his second wife and his controversial connections to various corporations and lobbyists made him less than fully credible as either a fiscal or a moral conservative. Santorum suffered initially because he was the least magnetic of the challengers to Romney. He only rose to the fore after the others faded. By that time, Romney had proven to be a strong campaigner and had broadened and deepened his bases of support sufficiently to stave off Santorum's strong challenge.

Romney was declared victor in the first nominating contest, the Iowa caucuses held on January 3, 2012. A subsequent recount gave the victory to Santorum, but this happened weeks later, too late to prevent Romney from capturing headlines as the winner. Romney then went on to win the January 10 New Hampshire primary. He lost to Newt Gingrich in South Carolina January 21, but defeated Gingrich in Florida ten days later. March 6 was called Super Tuesday because eleven primaries were held in states representing every region of the country. Romney triumphed in seven of the eleven primaries, winning at least one in each region. Most significantly he won the hotly contested Ohio and Virginia primaries. Although Santorum remained in the race for another month, Romney's excellent showing on Super Tuesday, particularly his victory in the hotly contested Ohio primary, assured him of victory.

During the general election campaign the candidates tour the country, spending most of their time in the states with many electoral votes that are being most hotly contested, the so-called battleground states. In 2012 the battleground states were Florida, Virginia, Ohio, Iowa, Wisconsin, New Hampshire, and North Carolina. Obama won all of them except for Florida and North Carolina. Those state received far more frequent visits from Romney and Obama and were barraged with television ads from the two presidential campaigns.

The four 2012 candidate debates – three presidential and one vice presidential – were held over a three-week span in October. Seventy million viewers watched the first debate, the highest rating ever recorded in the entire history of presidential debates stretching back to the 1960 Kennedy-Nixon debate. The debate appeared to alter the course of the campaign. Obama appeared tired and distracted, whereas Romney was energetic and forceful. Most polls indicated a decisive shift in support from Obama to Romney. Throughout the rest of the campaign some of the major polls continued to show Romney ahead but others gave the edge to Obama. Therefore, Obama's decisive victory came as a great surprise to many pollsters and most Republican commentators who had remained confidant of a Romney victory.

### The Birth of Parties

The United States prides itself on being a constitutional republic, and yet its most important political organizations are not even mentioned in the Constitution. All the other key components of the political order – Congress, the executive, the judiciary, and the states – are described in the Constitution, but political parties are not. This omission is no accident. The drafters of the Constitution disagreed about many things, but they all shared Mayor Bloomberg's antipathy to parties. The Framers tried their best to produce a governing blueprint that would make parties unnecessary and difficult to form. Thus, the new republic was set on a nonpartisan path.

The root of the word "party" is "part." The Founders were concerned about the "whole." They saw parties as efforts to form majority *factions* that would substitute partial interests for the common good. The elaborate structure of separation of powers and checks and balances in the Constitution was designed to keep such a majority faction from forming. The very idea of the large republic described in *Federalist Paper* No. 10 was conceived as a defense against party (see Appendix 3). The republic's size would encourage factions to proliferate and thus would keep any single one from growing large and strong enough to dominate. Those in favor of democracy as well as those who were wary of democracy both found reasons to oppose party. The Framers who most feared tyranny of the majority believed that party would enable the untutored masses to deprive others of their liberty. The Framers who feared elitism expected defenders of privilege to cunningly manipulate party to deprive the people of their liberty and democratic powers.

And yet, unwittingly, the founding generation created electoral laws that favored the very thing they so desperately opposed. The Constitution itself does little to specify how national elections are to be conducted. Presidential electors were to be chosen by the states, but state legislatures were free to choose them as they wished as well as determine the "time, place and manner" of holding elections for senators and members of the House. Likewise, they had complete discretion about how to choose their state legislators and governors. They could have adopted a proportional method for choosing state legislative and congressional representatives, but instead, they created legislative and congressional districts in which a single representative was chosen on a plurality basis.

*Proportional representation* encourages the growth of several political parties because it does not require a large fraction of the vote to elect at least one representative to office. *Single member districts* favor two parties because only one candidate can win. Therefore, the "outs" have a strong incentive to band together in support of a single challenger to defeat the incumbent. Awarding victory to the candidate with the most votes, even if the candidate lacks a majority, avoids the need for a runoff election between the two top finishers. Therefore, it deprives smaller parties whose candidates came in third or worse of the political leverage they would have had if one or the other of the top finishers needed their support to gain a majority in the runoff. The decision of almost all states to also award presidential electors on a winner-take-all plurality basis played precisely the same role in discouraging multiple parties that single-member districts and plurality election played in legislative races. These three choices regarding the ground rules for conducting elections are a large part of the reason that, with only a few brief exceptions, the United States has always had a two-party political system.

## Critical Choice: Forming a Party

Despite the Founders' opposition to party, a party formed during the very first years of the Republic. By 1800, Thomas Jefferson, the leader of the first full-fledged party – the Republicans – had been elected president. That party was the direct ancestor of the modern-day Democratic party; today's Republican party has other roots.

James Madison changed his mind about political parties as he watched Secretary of the Treasury Alexander Hamilton – his former partner in the writing of *The Federalist Papers* – strive to amass greater power for the national executive. Madison decided that this centralization of power in the hands of the few was an even greater threat to liberty than a tyranny of the majority. The only way to combat this evil was to organize the many to take power away from Hamilton and his cronies, and so the Republican Party was born.

Because prevailing opinion was so hostile, Madison and Jefferson's party-building efforts were very circumspect. In May of 1791, these two Virginians went on a "botanizing" expedition to the Northeast. Why would Secretary of State Jefferson and Congressman Madison take time out from their important governing responsibilities to look at northern plants unless those flowers and shrubs happened to reside in the backyards of important political personages whose support the two Virginians sought to cultivate? By August of 1791, Jefferson was writing letters to men he had identified as opponents of the Washington administration, urging them to run for Congress. He convinced Madison's friend, Philip Freneau, to start an opposition newspaper in Philadelphia, funded in part through printing contracts awarded by the State Department, of which he was the head. To create a truly national party, these two southerners needed to cement alliances with budding northern political organizations such as the one Aaron Burr was creating in New York. The bond that these men established between New York and Virginia was critical to the infant Republican Party.

At the same time that an opposition was forming among prominent politicians, ordinary citizens were protesting the pro-British tilt of the Washington administration. In more than thirty cities, Democratic-Republican Societies arose to support America's sister republic and Revolutionary War ally, France (see Chapter 12). These societies soon died, but their members gravitated to the Republicans, providing the party with new members and leaders. Schooled in the societies' lively debates and discussions, they transferred this same democratic spirit to their party activities.

These different strands of opposition were woven together into the durable thread of party by a single catalytic event – the Jay Treaty. The treaty was designed to solve outstanding disputes with the British regarding prewar debts, British occupation of forts on the Northwest frontier, and the British Navy's seizing of sailors aboard American ships. But it failed to settle most of these outstanding issues. Madison, Jefferson, and their supporters saw it as a virtual capitulation to the British and a sellout of the French.

In the temporary national capital, Philadelphia, an informal committee formed to coordinate opposition to the treaty. For the first time, a major constitutional debate was organized on a party basis. The Constitution grants the power to ratify a treaty exclusively to the Senate. But the power to provide or withhold the funds necessary for implementing the terms of the treaty rested largely with the House of Representatives. A caucus of all Republican congressmen was convened to oppose the appropriation to implement the treaty. Nonetheless, the appropriation passed and the intent of the Constitution was preserved.

In the election of 1796, a coordinated effort was made to defeat members of Congress who supported the treaty. Of the seven legislators targeted, four were defeated and two reversed their positions. Only one unrepentant incumbent was reelected. This success in punishing disloyalty shows that less than a decade after passage of the Constitution, a political organization had come into being that possessed all the crucial attributes of a political party – a mass membership, an ability to coordinate its activities, and mechanisms for encouraging party discipline.

## A Test of the Electoral College

The Constitution's original method for electing presidents was profoundly and permanently changed during the early 1800s. The Framers had intended the electors to be independent, exercising their own individual judgment about who would make the best president. But in 1800, the Republican leaders in the capital coordinated with party organizations in the various states so that electors were selected as instructed agents of the party, and pledged to vote for Jefferson. In 1800, most electors were selected by the state legislatures, but by 1824 and forever since, ordinary voters had the opportunity in most states to elect a slate of electors who were pledged to one or the other party's candidate.

In the original Constitution, the electors were to vote for two candidates for president. The candidate who received the most electoral support, provided it was a majority, became president, and the second place finisher became vice president. Such a mechanism introduced an element of unreliability into the creation of a party ticket as demonstrated by the 1800 election. The Republicans' choice for president (Jefferson) and vice president (Aaron Burr) received the same number of electoral votes, thus throwing the contest to the House of Representatives. The Federalist-controlled House flirted with selecting Burr rather than Jefferson as president. To ensure against a repetition of such a crisis, the Republicans pressed for enactment of the Twelfth Amendment to the Constitution, ratified in 1804. It required electors to cast separate ballots for president and vice president, enabling the Republicans to create a party ticket.

## Presidential Party Leadership

In the Jay Treaty debate, party mechanisms were used to undermine constitutional intent, but Jefferson's presidential party leadership showed that party could also be used to protect the Constitution. He sought to democratize the government, but not at the expense of the rights he himself had declared inalienable in the Declaration of Independence. To accomplish this tricky task, he needed political support both to push his democratizing initiatives and to keep them from being pushed too far. By imposing party discipline, Jefferson enabled his party allies in Congress to greatly curtail government but to do so without undermining the constitutional checks and balances that protected liberty. Jefferson's Revolution of 1800 abolished all taxes except the tariff, provided for a swift repayment of the national debt, and greatly reduced federal expenditures, but it also left the constitutional governing structure untouched.

Although the term "spoils system" is associated with Andrew Jackson, this method of party discipline was first instituted by Jefferson. During his first two years in office, Jefferson replaced more than half the federal officeholders with Republican appointees. By the end of his second term, only one-third of the holdover federal officials were still there. Jefferson's ruthlessness in hiring and firing on the basis of party loyalty gave his supporters second thoughts about opposing his plans and policies. When the Republican leader of the House of Representatives, John Randolph, opposed him, Jefferson denied favors to Randolph's allies and awarded them to defectors from Randolph. The rebellion was crushed.

Although Madison and Jefferson created a political party, they did not believe in the virtues of party; they viewed their party as the "party to end party." By triumphing over Hamilton and his allies, the Republicans hoped to restore the power of the Constitution to direct-and-control American government. They believed that strict adherence to constitutional principles, especially Federalism and enumerated powers, would sufficiently restrict the role of the national government so that the sort of differences over governmental policies and objectives that give rise to party competition would not arise. Therefore, once proper constitutional government was restored, parties would disappear, including their own. Jefferson said as much in his first inaugural address when he declared, "We are all republicans; we are all federalists."

By the end of Jefferson's two terms, he had converted moderate Federalists into Republicans and destroyed the Hamiltonians. During the administrations of

Madison, Monroe, and John Quincy Adams, the country functioned on a non-partisan basis. In 1820, Monroe was unopposed for reelection. In homage to the lack of partisan rancor, this period of one-party government, which lasted until the election of 1828, was called the Era of Good Feelings.

## The Limits of Nonpartisanship

The Era of Good Feelings was hardly that. It sparked a variety of bad political feelings that are all too likely to arise in the absence of vigorous party life and discipline. In the face of weak central leadership and attachment, sectional differences grew. The West became increasingly disgruntled at the financial dominance of the East and the seeming unconcern of the national government toward the threat posed by the Indians. The South shared the West's resentment of Eastern bankers and was becoming increasingly defensive about mounting northern opposition to slavery. A division of the country into three or four separate nations seemed a real possibility as public interest in and concern for the idea of American nationhood seemed to ebb.

Within the government itself, the principle of separation of powers was in decline as executives and legislators intermingled their functions, rendering neither accountable. Congress increasingly involved itself in the details of administration. Cabinet officials paid less and less attention to presidential dictates and pursued their own departmental agendas through direct contact with congressional committees. Thus, both the authority of the president and of the leadership of Congress were undermined.

This political decline was accelerated by the presidential election of 1824, which cast doubt on the legitimacy of the presidential office itself. No candidate received a majority of the electoral vote. As specified by the Twelfth Amendment to the Constitution, the House of Representatives chose the winner from among the top three finishers – Andrew Jackson, John Adams, and William Crawford. In addition to having the most electoral votes, Jackson was also far ahead in the popular vote. He tallied 153,000 votes, almost 50,000 more than the second-place finisher, Adams. Nonetheless, the House voted to make Adams president. Clay, eliminated as a presidential contender, served as president maker. He used his authority as Speaker of the House to obtain votes for Adams. Adams then named Clay secretary of state. Because this position had been the traditional stepping-stone to the presidency since Madison assumed the office in 1809, Clay was virtually anointed as Adams's successor. No evidence existed that Adams had bribed Clay with the offer of secretary of state. But the result inspired widespread public outrage because, in contrast to all previous presidential elections, the most popular candidate did not win. Jackson accused Clay and Adams of making a "corrupt bargain."

*Critical Choice: Parties Revitalized*

As the "victim" of antidemocratic forces, Jackson, already a military hero, became the foremost spokesman for the rapidly expanding popular discontent. Although many hoped that he would serve as the voice of the people, others feared that he would prove to be a demagogue, exploiting his popularity to assume dictatorial powers. This possibility was greatly enhanced by the expansion of the suffrage that had taken place during the previous few decades. By 1828, virtually all white male citizens in the United States were eligible to vote. Martin Van Buren, a senator from New York and the leader of a powerful New York political faction, sought to take advantage of Jackson's popularity and curb his demagogic tendencies by making him the candidate of a reinvigorated Jeffersonian party.

After meeting with like-minded politicians from Virginia, Van Buren was able to resurrect the powerful New York-Virginia alliance that had proven so valuable in electing Jefferson. It would support Jackson in exchange for his promise to accept party discipline. Jackson agreed. Although he might well have won anyway, the solid support of New York and Virginia, added to his strength in the South and West, ensured his victory. Of course, Jackson could easily have reneged on his bargain with Van Buren after the New Yorker had delivered on his part of the deal. But Jackson was a man of honor. And, he admired the discipline and sense of purpose embodied by the victorious party, renamed the Democratic Party. He authorized the first national, major party convention, held in 1832 for the express purpose of lining up support for Van Buren's nomination as vice president, thus ensuring that Van Buren would be his successor.

Jackson made vigorous use of the Democratic Party to decentralize and democratize political and economic power. He vetoed the Second National Bank of the United States, which ended the cozy relationship between government and the eastern economic establishment that the bank had cemented. He reintroduced, indeed championed, the spoils system, using it to enable ordinary people to serve in government (see Chapter 10). Although his enemies decried his aggressive use of presidential power, that power was employed for the purpose of limiting and reducing governmental intrusion. Therefore, on the whole, the democratizing impact of this reborn political party was compatible with the preservation and even the expansion of liberty.

## Taming Presidential Ambition

Van Buren, unlike Jefferson, did not believe that threats to the Constitution would disappear once his party came to power. The danger of despotism was a perennial one. The Constitution might provide for the indirect election of the president, but the events of 1824 revealed that the people expected to make the real decision. Nothing could prevent would-be demagogues from making direct appeals to the people and exploiting their own popularity for tyrannical ends. Taming presidential ambition would require buttressing the Constitution with the collective restraint and discipline that only party could impose.

Having witnessed the demise of Jefferson's party, Van Buren recognized that one-party rule would eventually turn into no-party rule. The long-term health of a party depended on the existence of a strong and healthy opposition party. Only the continual threat of defeat, and its occasional reality, could keep a party vigorous and cohesive. For a system to endure, it must have rules. Each side must be willing to accept defeat grudgingly, if not gracefully. Neither side must fear that, if they lose, their most cherished values and interests will be destroyed, because under those circumstances neither side will graciously and peacefully accept defeat.

## A Two-Party System

Van Buren as the prophet of the party system triumphed at the expense of Van Buren the politician. Having won the presidency in 1836, Van Buren was defeated by William Henry Harrison in 1840. Harrison ran as a candidate of the Whig party, which, as Van Buren had predicted, grew up in opposition to Jackson and the Democrats. The name "Whig" was chosen to identify this new party with the English party of the same name that had deposed the autocratic English King James the II in the late seventeenth century. Like their namesake, the new Whigs promised to vanquish the heirs of "King Andrew the First" and remove any trace of the monarchism with which he had endowed the presidency.

To defeat Van Buren, the Whigs used the same partisan techniques that had proven so successful for the Democrats. They staged rallies, published party newspapers, and wielded symbols in an effort to excite and mobilize masses of voters. In this election, the modern notion of an election "campaign" was born. "Campaign" was a military term, and its application to elections implied that they would now acquire the hard-fought, tactical, and disciplined character associated with warfare. Parties would provide the troops and the logistical support for these political wars.

## "All Liberals, All Democrats"

Although the Democrats identified more closely with "the common man" and the Whigs had more support among the wealthy, they were not "liberal" and "conservative" parties in the modern sense. They were both liberal in that they both favored free enterprise and protection of private property and adhered to the basic principles of the Constitution and the Declaration of Independence – natural rights and limited government. And they were both democratic. The Whigs had abandoned the Federalists' efforts to promote indirect rule. Indeed, by attacking the "monarchic" presidency of Jackson, they claimed to be more democratic than the Democrats.

The Whigs favored using government to build canals, roads, and other physical improvements that benefited interstate commerce. And they wanted to raise the tariff on imported products to fund those projects and protect domestic manufacturers. They also favored the establishment of a national banking and financial system that would provide greater availability and security of credit and facilitate all manner of commercial transactions. In modern terms, such enthusiasm for activist government would be called "liberal." But the Democrats claimed that these activities were inevitably "illiberal" because they were designed to benefit a select few. Government insiders and their friends would always be better positioned to enjoy the fruits of government-funded projects and obtain governmentally sponsored bank credit. Democrats believed that the ordinary person had a better chance for equal opportunity in a competitive marketplace than in one dominated by government subsidies and favoritism.

Both parties were truly national in scope. Two of the four Whig presidents were southerners: John Tyler and Zachary Taylor. Two of the three Democratic presidents during this same period were from the North. In states such as New York, Illinois, and Pennsylvania, the two parties were intensely competitive, with frequent alternations in power occurring between them.

## A Force for Decentralization

Although created for the purpose of winning presidential elections, the party system that developed in the 1830s actually served to promote political and governmental *decentralization*. Because electoral votes were allocated state by state, the partisan apparatus created to win presidential elections also had to be constructed state by state. In order to maintain the support of the state parties that had brought a president to power, that president had to reward them and be disciplined by them. The spoils system thrived during this period, as state parties demanded what they deemed their fair share of federal jobs.

The dependence of national officeholders on state parties was duplicated by the dependence of state party leaders on local ones. To win statewide elections, party leaders had to rely on local party organizations in cities, towns, and counties to turn out the vote. Therefore, localities held the key to both statewide and national political success and could make powerful demands on higher political authorities. Because the two parties were so evenly matched, they could not afford to ignore even small localities because such seemingly insignificant places might well provide the margin of victory in a close election. This localizing political pressure served as a brake on national political power and a powerful protection of the individuality and diversity of states and localities.

In an era before mass media, local party life was not only a source of spoils but of entertainment, as well. Political parties held picnics, rallies, parades, and other public spectacles. These occasions were intended to be lighthearted, even frivolous, but they also served a crucial democratic function. As Tocqueville had remarked, large republics increased an individual's sense of isolation, weakness, and vulnerability. The instinctive reaction to such threatening feelings was to withdraw from public life into the relatively safe private world of self and family. Local party life was sufficiently unthreatening and pleasurable to encourage tentative steps out of the private and into the public realm. Parties provided a link to the wider world of politics that more impersonal and drab governmental entities could not provide, and parties were therefore a critical stimulus for democratic citizenship.

## The Parties and Slavery

Both parties contained proslavery and antislavery factions. Their desire to survive as national entities, thereby preserving the party system, required them to paper over their internal differences about slavery. This bipartisan effort to suppress the slavery issue was one of the most important factors that delayed the onset of civil war. Ultimately, the pressure to admit new states was so powerful that it overwhelmed the possibility of compromise and made it impossible for either party to reconcile its northern and southern wings. From the mid-1840s onward, regional loyalty came increasingly to outweigh party loyalty. The Democrats became the party of the South, shedding their democratic and egalitarian concerns to focus on protecting slavery. The Whigs could not resolve their differences over slavery and the party died, to be replaced by the antislavery Republicans, who also included antislavery Democrats in their ranks.

Abraham Lincoln, the first Republican president, had been an ardent Whig. He joined the new party only when it became clear to him that the Whigs were not prepared to lead the attack on slavery's expansion. As we discuss in Chapters 5 and 12, during the 1860 presidential election and his presidency, Lincoln gave effective voice to the key Republican principle: incorporation of the ideas of liberty contained in the Declaration of Independence into the principle of Union contained in the Constitution. In town squares and community halls throughout the North, a constitutional debate took place along party lines. The 1860 election pitted Lincoln against the man who defeated him for the Senate – the Democratic candidate, Stephen Douglas. Douglas sought to hold the proslavery and antislavery factions of his party together by advocating the principle of *popular sovereignty*, which allowed each new territory to decide for itself whether to adopt a proslavery or antislavery state constitution. Lincoln committed his party fully to the principle of no territorial expansion for slavery. He made clear that the constitutional justification for such a radical step was the principle of unalienable rights enumerated in the Declaration of Independence. The voter realignment that followed, which granted the Republican party majority status in most parts of the country except the South, was the political outcome of this party-sponsored constitutional reconsideration that gave deeper import to the noble phrase that all men are created equal.

Lincoln did not succeed through rhetoric alone. He relied on his party to mobilize campaign support for him and maintain support for his program in Congress. He adroitly manipulated patronage and cabinet appointments to reinforce party cohesion. Most important, during the critical election of 1860 and after, he depended on Republicans to carry on spirited and probing discussions at the state and local level, pressing their constituents to understand and accept the profound principles on which Lincoln was basing his effort to re-found the Union.

## PATH DEPENDENCY: THE ENDURING TWO-PARTY SYSTEM

After the Civil War, the two-party system that had been created in the Jacksonian era solidified itself. Although both parties have undergone vast transformations since, one or the other of them has won all the presidential elections and controlled the two houses of Congress for the last 150 years. No other nation has demonstrated this degree of political party stability and endurance.

The most severe test of the strength of the post–Civil War party system was the election of 1876, the outcome of which was inconclusive. The Republicans challenged the results in three former Confederate states – Louisiana, Florida, and South Carolina – charging fraud and intimidation of Republican voters, primarily African Americans. The Democrats also challenged the credentials of one elector in Oregon, claiming that as a federal employee he was ineligible. The number of electoral votes under dispute were enough to deprive either candidate of a majority.

Because the issue was the vote count itself, not the lack of a majority of electoral votes, the Twelfth Amendment stipulating that the House of Representatives should choose the president in the face of the lack of an electoral-vote majority was not applicable. Instead, Congress appointed a commission composed of five congressmen from each party, two Supreme Court Justices loyal to each party, and one Independent, Justice David Davis. Because Davis was then elected to the Senate, he withdrew from the commission and was replaced by Joseph Bradley, a Republican but one acceptable to the Democrats. Bradley sided with the Republicans in a series of 8-7 votes that gave Hayes an electoral majority. Democrats threatened to fillibuster, but ultimately the commission report was accepted because of a compromise worked out by the leadership of both parties. In exchange for accepting the commission's findings, the Republicans agreed to accelerate and complete the withdrawal of federal troops from the South, putting an end to Reconstruction. One party gained the presidency and the other gained a critical policy objective. Thus, the party system proved itself sufficiently resilient to deal with such a contentious and potentially destabilizing conflict (Figure 11.3).

## POPULISM, PROGRESSIVISM, AND PARTIES

As of the late nineteenth century, both major parties were, by contemporary standards, conservative. The Democrats remained true to their Jeffersonian roots by advocating limited federal government and opposing efforts to regulate free markets. The Republicans were less committed to states' rights, but they opposed using government to curb corporate power or reduce income disparities. The Republicans had no real support in the South. The Democrats were very weak in most of New England and the Midwest. But elsewhere, vigorous two-party competition existed. Between 1876 and 1896, the Republicans held the upper hand, but not by much. In this period, they won the presidency five times and the Democrats won twice. The Democrats controlled the House of Representatives for most of this period, and the Republicans held the Senate, but by very slim margins.

It took the creation of third party – the People's Party, known as the *Populists* – to disturb the bipartisan conservative consensus and advocate policies that would today be called liberal. The Populists arose in the economically depressed grain-growing areas of the Midwest. They sought federal laws to protect farmers from the monopoly power of railroads and reduce the gap between rich and poor. As the agricultural recession worsened, Populist support grew. By the mid-1880s, the Populists had elected governors, senators, and representatives in several midwestern states and were also gaining strength among southern farmers. The 1892 People's Party platform was a remarkably progressive document. It called for an expanded coinage of silver to inflate the currency, a graduated income tax, a constitutional amendment that mandated civil service reform, and government ownership of railroad, telegraph, and telephone companies. The People's Party ticket garnered more than 1 million popular votes and 22 electoral votes.

In 1896, the Democratic Party was at a crossroads. It was led by President Grover Cleveland, who had been elected in 1884, lost in 1888, and was then reelected in 1892. Cleveland was a devout believer in limited government. When

**Figure 11.3.** "Another Such Victory, and I Am Undone." A cartoon depicting the dilapidated state of the Republican Party after Rutherford B. Hayes lost the popular vote in 1877. He only won the presidential election by twenty hotly contested electoral votes.

*Source*: Senate Art: Cat. no. 38.00115.001. Retrieved from http://www.senate.gov/artandhistory/art/artifact/Ga_Cartoon/Ga_cartoon_38_00115.htm.

farmers in Texas, who had been forced to eat their seed corn because their crops had been destroyed by drought, asked the president to give them some of the surplus seed corn being kept in government granaries, he refused, saying, "It is the job of the people to support the government, not the job of the government to support the people."

But Cleveland's views were challenged by Democrats who wanted to come to the aid of economically distressed farmers in Texas and elsewhere. Cleveland's victories had been something of a fluke, due largely to factional feuding among Republicans. The Democrats were still the out party and therefore more open to new political trends and ideas. Populist ideas were making greater inroads among Democrats than Republicans. Some Democratic politicians, most notably Congressman William Jennings Bryan of Nebraska, were openly courting Populist support.

The 1896 Democratic convention turned into a pitched battle between pro- and anti-Populists. William Jennings Bryan's Cross of Gold speech tipped the balance toward the Populists. In his speech, he depicted the struggle between rich and poor, creditor and debtor in biblical terms, appealing to the strong religious feeling of many delegates (see Chapter 6 for further discussion). His words electrified the crowd, and Bryan himself was chosen as the Democratic Party candidate for president.

Bryan's campaign moved the Democrats in a new direction. Ever since the debate between Jefferson and Hamilton the party that presumed to speak for the people had been the party most resistant to national power, which it associated with privilege, and most committed to the virtues of local self-government. Preempting the Populists, the Democrats now sought to invoke national power for democratic purposes. Major party adoption of third-party policies and programs has recurred several times since 1896. As we point out later in this chapter, when we discuss the 1992 presidential election, the importance of third parties is greater than their lack of success at the ballot box would indicate.

In response to the challenge posed by the fusion of Populists and Democrats, the Republicans rallied behind the theme of stability. Their support of the gold standard was put in the context of a more general defense of the essential soundness of the American economy and way of life it represented. The two pillars of the Republican platform were sound money and protectionism. Defense of the gold standard resonated not only with the wealthy but also with many industrial workers who feared that silver-generated inflation would lessen the value of their wages. High tariffs also appealed to employer and employee alike. Taxing imported manufacturing products was viewed as the best way to defend American workers and manufacturers against the threat of cheap foreign imports produced by oppressed foreign labor. As consumers of foodstuffs, workers opposed farmers' efforts to raise food prices. The Republicans won the 1896 election decisively and remained the dominant party for the next thirty-four years. During that time the Democrats won only two presidential elections – Woodrow Wilson's victories in 1912 and 1916. They won the 1912 election only because former Republican president, Theodore Roosevelt, ran as a third-party candidate, which split the Republicans.

In crucial ways, 1896 was the first modern presidential campaign. Both sides introduced political innovations that are now fundamental features of the electoral contest. Prior to 1896 no party nominee had actually campaigned for office. It was considered to be undignified. Personal participation in the hurly-burly of rallies and parades would make the candidate seem too common and partisan to be worthy of the nation's highest office. But because Bryan was so little known nationally and his views were so unconventional, he determined that he had to take his message directly to the people. For the first time a presidential contender traveled across the country addressing crowds of voters in an effort to personally win them over.

To counter Bryan's aggressive effort, McKinley's campaign manager, Mark Hanna, made an equally significant change in campaign strategy and tactics. Previously, state and local parties had run the presidential campaign within their borders pretty much on their own. Hanna organized and directed a vigorous national effort. The national campaign headquarters produced massive amounts of campaign literature and introduced a key emblem of subsequent campaigns, the campaign button. More importantly, Hanna put pressure on the factory owners and other large employers who benefited from Republican tariff and subsidy policies to contribute generously to this more ambitious campaign effort and pressure their workers to support McKinley. Although McKinley himself remained aloof from the campaign, Hanna's effort to centralize fundraising and publicity and pressure business to more actively support its patron was crucial to McKinley's victory.

The Republican 1896 victory ushered in a period of Republican electoral dominance that lasted until 1932. The only Democrat elected president during this thirty-six-year period, Woodrow Wilson, won only because of the independent candidacy of Theodore Roosevelt that sapped Republican strength. The Democrats did somewhat better in congressional elections. This decline in party competition appears to be the most important cause of the decline in voter turnout rates that one observes post-1896. This decline has been drastic. In 1896 more than 79% of the voting age population voted. Turnout declined in almost every subsequent presidential election reaching a low of 49.2% in 1920.

Even the return of more competitive parties after the New Deal has not managed to restore the pre-1896 turnout rates. It would seem that the nineteenth-century parties were not only more competitive; because they were so decentralized, they were able to exert a stronger hold on the loyalty and energy of voters.

## Progressivism

As we discussed in Chapter 4, Populism was soon followed by another, more broadly based reform movement: Progressivism. Progressivism's impact on party politics was greatly hastened and expanded by the assassination of President McKinley shortly after his reelection in 1900, which propelled Vice President TR to the presidency. TR, former governor of New York, was among the most prominent Progressive politicians. Anti-Progressive New York Republicans helped TR secure the vice presidential nomination to get him out of the state. They expected him to do little harm in that largely ceremonial role. To their considerable chagrin, fate placed TR in the most powerful political post in the land.

Because most members of Congress, both Republicans and Democrats, were not Progressives, TR was not able to implement the full Progressive agenda, but he did greatly increase the visibility and popularity of Progressive ideas. When he retired from office in 1909, he manipulated the nomination of his chosen successor, William Howard Taft. Taft won the general election easily, but TR considered Taft's approach too conservative. In 1912, TR tried and failed to win back from Taft the Republican presidential nomination.

Rather than support the Republican nominee, TR formed a third party, the Progressive Party, and continued his presidential bid under that label. Free from the need to mollify anti-Progressive Republicans, TR and his new party adopted a much more radical reform agenda. TR did not win. But by depriving Taft of the votes of Progressive-minded Republicans, he ensured the victory of the Democrat, Woodrow Wilson, whom he considered to be the more progressive of the major party candidates. Indeed, Wilson borrowed heavily from the Progressive Party platform. For the second time in a generation, a third party had proven to be highly influential in altering the course of American politics. In 1896, the Populists had furthered their cause by joining with the Democrats. In 1912, the Progressives did so by splitting from the Republicans (Figure 11.4). Ironically, Taft was the first sitting president to emulate Bryan and campaign actively on his own behalf, but this did not prevent him from coming in third. Both TR and Wilson also campaigned actively, making 1912 the first campaign in which all candidates, including the winner, did so.

The Progressives sought to destroy the power of party organizations by draining them of their lifeblood, patronage. Progressives provoked the passage of federal civil-service reform laws designed to replace the spoils system with a merit system, a system that awarded government jobs on the basis of examination scores rather than party loyalty. At the municipal level, Progressives sought to eliminate parties altogether, claiming that there was no "Republican" or "Democratic" way to clean streets or remove garbage, there was only the right way. They prodded many cities to elect local officials on a nonpartisan basis, but to Mayor Bloomberg's chagrin, not New York. As the chapter will discuss later on, by the later part of the twentieth century the reforms begun by the Progressives had expanded and proliferated to such an extent as to transform the character of political parties.

**Figure 11.4.** Fear of the Bull: 1912 cartoon depicting the trepidation of the Republican and Democratic Parties at the entrance of Theodore Roosevelt's new Progressive "Bull Moose Party." Credit: The Granger Collection, NYC – All rights reserved.

## THE NEW DEAL PARTY SYSTEM

Woodrow Wilson's presidency, made possible by Republican party schism, did not revive Democratic party fortunes. From 1920 to 1930, Democrats were a minority in both houses of Congress and lost three presidential elections in a row. They receded to their pre-Wilsonian status of being the party of the South, the big cities, and little else. The opportunity to reverse their fortunes was provided by the Great Depression, which began with the collapse of the stock market in 1929 (see Chapter 4). Voters responded to this catastrophe by punishing the party in power, giving the Democrats a majority in the House of Representatives in the 1930 election and electing FDR in 1932.

### The New Deal Party Coalition

FDR exploited his victory in 1932 to create the enduring majority coalition for the Democrats that we discussed in the beginning of this chapter. It provided the political power to fuel the New Deal conservative revolution (see Chapter 4). FDR's 1936 landslide set the Democrats on the road to long-term political dominance. From 1936 to 1964, the Democrats won six of eight presidential elections, and they controlled the House and Senate for thirty-two years of a thirty-six-year span. This winning record is unparalleled in the history of American two-party politics, reflected widespread popular acceptance of and support for the essential features of the New Deal and important changes in constitutional understanding that it represented. As we discuss in several chapters, the New Deal redefined the meaning of rights to include a right to economic security. This newfound acceptance by government of an obligation to provide such security was the glue that held the New Deal coalition together. Like the election in 1860, the 1936 election was one in which a political party, this time the Democrats, provoked a debate about the meaning of the rights enumerated in the Declaration of Independence and recast the meaning of those rights in a manner that strengthened the ties between liberty and democracy.

FDR succeeded by retaining traditional Democratic adherents, especially southern whites, meanwhile adding large numbers of new recruits. His greatest weapon was his willingness to spend federal money to help people in need. Even conservative southerners did not desert him because they were too dependent on the jobs and other benefits that the New Deal provided. FDR, for his part, refrained from the one provocation that would have caused southern representatives to bolt: a direct assault on racial segregation.

FDR was one of very few influential Protestant Democrats to support the presidential candidacy of his predecessor as New York governor, Al Smith, a Catholic. FDR did so in 1924, when Smith failed to receive the nomination, and in 1928, when Smith succeeded. Going out on a limb in 1924 to identify with Catholic political aspirations, coupled with his pro-Catholic reputation as governor of New York (1928–1932), enabled FDR to retain the support of Catholic voters, even after Al Smith angrily broke with FDR in 1934. Jews were similarly drawn into the Democratic orbit. FDR's administration was the first to appoint many Jews to important posts, most prominently Henry Morgenthau as secretary of the treasury.

FDR also won over the support of organized labor. Before 1932, labor unions had mostly remained politically neutral in national elections. In the 1932 election, prominent labor leaders such as John L. Lewis, president of the United Mine Workers of America, endorsed Herbert Hoover. But between 1932 and 1936, the labor movement mushroomed in size. It made inroads in many of America's largest industries, such as steel, mining, and automobile manufacture. Although FDR did not openly support these organizing efforts, he did support section 7a of the NIRA, which unambiguously gave labor unions the right to engage in them. After the NIRA, including section 7a, became law, Lewis and other labor leaders told workers, "FDR wants you to join our union." Although these statements were not literally true, FDR did not repudiate them. As a result, he came to be viewed by labor leaders and members alike as a friend of labor, the first president of the industrial age to enjoy such a status (see Chapter 6). In 1936, the labor movement strongly endorsed FDR and provided him with the largest source of his presidential campaign funds.

In the 1930s, African Americans were a small but strategically important segment of the electorate. Their voting strength was concentrated in the biggest cities in such large and politically competitive states as New York, Pennsylvania, and Illinois. A strong turnout of African Americans in a close presidential election could swing a large number of electoral votes from one party column to the other. African Americans had been among the most loyal supporters of the Republican Party, the party of Lincoln. FDR pursued cautious racial policies. African Americans participated in New Deal jobs and welfare programs, but not on an equal footing with whites. However, for the first time since Reconstruction, African Americans actually received some help from the federal government. They showed their gratitude by reversing their seventy-year partisan tradition and voting overwhelmingly for FDR in 1936.

FDR feared that southern conservatism would undermine the party's new-found strength among labor union members and African Americans. In order to ensure an enduring progressive Democratic majority, FDR knew that he had to abolish the rule that required a successful nominee to garner a two thirds majority of the delegates. The Southern states accounted for less than a majority of the delegates, but they accounted for more than a third. Thus, they could not determine who the candidate would be, but they could prevent any candidate they opposed from being nominated. At the 1936 convention, when his popularity was at its zenith, FDR stacked the Rules Committee with loyal supporters, and it voted to have nominations determined by a simple majority rather than a two-thirds majority. A change in the rules could be passed by majority vote and therefore the Southern delegates could not prevent this change. The end of the two-thirds rule ensured that future Democratic presidential candidates would be in tune with majority-party sentiment and would not have to bend to the wishes of a single bloc of delegates. Although it would be another generation before the Democratic Party would take up the cause of civil rights, the seeds of that undertaking were sown in the fight over the two-thirds rule that destroyed the South's veto power over the choice of the Democratic Party presidential nominee.

Thus, the Democratic Party became the majority party for the first time since the Civil War. It was capable of winning statewide elections in the Northeast, the industrial Midwest, and parts of the Pacific Coast as well as in the "solid" South. The only regions where it did not have a decent chance to win statewide were New England, the nonindustrial Midwest, and the Great Plains.

## A Party to End Parties

FDR did not seek victory for its own sake. Heir to the Progressive legacy, he sought to exploit the Democrats' large congressional majority to erect a strong and resilient national administrative state capable of sustaining the economic security and stability his New Deal programs sought to achieve. This state would provide on a routine and impartial basis what parties had provided on a discretionary basis. Instead of depending on party patronage, people could rely on a social security pension when they got old, unemployment insurance if they were laid off, and welfare payments if they were poor or disabled. FDR recognized that the new administrative state would weaken political parties, including the powerful one he built and led. For all his skill as a party builder, his attitude toward party was strikingly similar to Jefferson's. The New Deal Democratic party would be a party to end party. Once the welfare state he sought to construct was fully in place, FDR believed, parties would become far less important, if not wither away.

## CRITICAL CHOICE: REPUBLICANS EMBRACE THE NEW DEAL

Like Jefferson, FDR was a better politician than he was a prophet. Parties did not wither away. Indeed, the Republicans scored a great political comeback after World War II. As of 1952, the Republicans had not won a presidential election in twenty-four years. They seemed on the verge of suffering the same fate as the Whigs and Federalists. Instead, they demonstrated a resilience even more impressive than that shown by the Democratic party in the wake of the Civil War. Since 1952, Republicans have won eight presidential elections, the Democrats six. The Republicans have never been out of the presidential office for more than eight years. The Democrats were out of office for twelve years, from 1980 until 1992. The Democrats controlled both houses of Congress from 1954 until 1980. Since 1980, Republicans have held the Senate for most of the period between 1980 and the present, and they controlled the House of Representatives from 1994 until 2006 and won it back in 2010.

Like the Democrats in 1828 and Whigs in 1849, the Republicans revived their fortunes by running a military hero, General Dwight David Eisenhower, for president. In WWII, Eisenhower had led the greatest amphibious landing in history, D-Day. He was so popular that a group of prominent Democrats, including FDR's son James, had tried to recruit him in 1948 to replace Truman, whom they, mistakenly, deemed to be unelectable.

Eisenhower won easily in 1952 and again in 1956. He did not oppose, and thereby tacitly accepted, the key programs of the New Deal, most especially Social Security and the legitimacy of labor unions. And he embraced Truman's cautious but firm internationalist foreign policy that was based on the alliance of the Western powers and resistance to Soviet expansionism. As a result, many independent-minded voters were now willing to consider voting Republican because to do so no longer threatened their economic security, protected by the welfare state, and their security against foreign threat, protected by the Atlantic Alliance. The Republican Party suffered its worst post–World War II defeat in 1964 when these moderate "Eisenhower" Republicans deserted the Republican candidate, Senator Barry Goldwater of Arizona, because they viewed him as an opponent of the New Deal and a foreign policy radical. In his campaign, Goldwater frontally attacked the achievements of the New Deal, including social security.

The magnitude of his defeat revealed the extent to which the American public, including many Republicans, had come to embrace the programmatic rights that were the heart of the New Deal program. In 1968 the Republicans regained the presidency with the election of Richard Nixon. Although Nixon was hated by Democrats, he was in all important respects a defender of New Deal policies. Neither he, nor his successor Gerarld Ford, made any effort to repeal or even cut back New Deal programs or the vast administrative state set up to implement them.

## Feuding Democrats

Republican fortunes were also greatly aided by the feuding among Democrats in 1968 over Lyndon Johnson's conduct during the Vietnam War. Not since the annexation of Texas in 1844 had a foreign policy disagreement proven so divisive. For the first time, an incumbent president faced a serious challenge in presidential primaries. Senator Eugene McCarthy(D-Minnesota), ran against Johnson in the New Hampshire primary. Although Johnson narrowly prevailed, the media interpreted McCarthy's impressive showing as a serious setback for Johnson.

In the wake of this "defeat," Johnson withdrew from the race. A three-way contest ensued between Vice President Hubert Humphrey, who defended Johnson's Vietnam policy; Senator McCarthy; and Senator Robert Kennedy (D-New York), who also opposed the war. McCarthy and Kennedy each won several primaries, but as of 1968 most delegates were not chosen by primaries. Humphrey retained the loyalty of the state party leaders who controlled the delegates in the non-primary states. The night he won the California primary, Robert Kennedy was assassinated. Although Humphrey had enough delegates to ensure his nomination, many antiwar Democrats refused to endorse him or did so tepidly. Tensions were heightened by the antiwar riots during the Democratic National Convention in Chicago. The Republican candidate, Richard Nixon, profited from the image of Democratic disarray that emerged from Chicago.

In 1972, the feud among Democrats rekindled. The presidential nomination was won by a passionately antiwar candidate, Senator George McGovern of South Dakota. McGovern had chaired a commission created at the 1968 convention to rewrite the party's nominating rules to make them more democratic. The commission did so by establishing complex formulas for choosing convention delegates to ensure that those delegates reflected the full racial and gender diversity of the party's membership. The rules also contained devices to ensure that state and local leaders could not exert the same level of influence over candidate selection that they had in the past. McGovern's bid for the nomination was greatly assisted by the fact that he and his staff understood the rules and his rivals did not.

Ironically, the rules designed to make the nominating process more democratic and representative resulted in the choice of a candidate who could not obtain the support of key party leaders and coalition members. Organized labor was so offended by McGovern's antiwar stand that the American Federation of Labor, for the first and only time since it was created, refused to endorse the Democratic nominee. Chicago Mayor Richard Daley and many other party leaders extended only pro forma support. McGovern suffered the worst defeat of any modern Democratic presidential candidate. He was the first Democratic presidential candidate since the Civil War not to carry the South. Indeed, he did not win a single southern state. In every presidential election since 1976, Republicans have won the South. In both 2000 and 2004, George W. Bush carried every southern state.

The 1972 election proved to be a historic turning point in the relationship between party and foreign policy. Since FDR, the Democrats had been the more aggressively internationalist of the two parties. Democratic presidents had led the country in the First and Second World Wars, Korea and Vietnam. A favorite Republican slogan was, "They [the Democrats] are the party of war!" Eisenhower and Nixon fought bitter intraparty battles against isolationism. But ever since 1972, it is the Republicans who have been consistently more aggressive in prosecuting the Cold War, the First Gulf War, and the War in Iraq, whereas the Democrats have fought bitter internal battles over freezing nuclear weapons production, the Gulf War, and the Iraq War. A majority of Democratic senators voted against the 1991 resolution endorsing the Gulf War. Although a majority of them supported the 2002 resolution endorsing the invasion of Iraq, the 2004 Democratic presidential candidate, John Kerry, made opposition to the war his major campaign theme. As we discussed early in the chapter, party polarization over foreign policy continues.

*Critical Choice: Republicans Adopt a New Brand of Conservatism*

The Democrats recaptured the presidency in 1976 with the victory of Jimmy Carter, but the victory was short-lived. In 1980 Carter lost to Ronald Reagan, the first elected president to lose reelection since Herbert Hoover in 1932. Reagan's initial victory was mainly due to Carter's unpopularity. But during his first term, he greatly improved Republican fortunes by devising a new, politically popular approach to taxing and spending. Ever since FDR, the Republicans had been divided into two economic policy factions. Moderate Republicans accepted the Keynesian economic doctrines deployed by the Democrats, meaning that they were willing to live with federal budgetary deficits in times of recession as a means of promoting economic expansion. They preferred to criticize individual Democratic spending programs rather than to attack "big government" in general. Conservative Republicans objected to deficit spending. They wanted large cuts in the federal income tax, but demanded equally large cuts in the budget in order to avoid deficit.

Both Republican positions were politically problematic. The moderate approach was virtually indistinguishable from that of the Democrats, whereas the conservative formula required politically popular programs to be cut. Ronald Reagan departed from both strategies. He accepted the use of deficit spending, but only to enable tax cuts. He turned traditional conservatism on its head by first proposing tax cuts and only then asking Congress for the budget cuts to pay for them. Thus, he was able to do the politically popular thing, cut taxes, first. Although some representatives in both parties doubted the prudence of this approach, few were willing to vote against giving money back to the people. Reagan's tax cut plan of 1981 passed Congress overwhelmingly.

Reagan's subsequent proposals to cut programs did not receive the same enthusiastic reception. Although some reductions were passed, spending and revenue remained out of balance. Nonetheless, by putting tax cuts ahead of spending cuts, Reagan had found a successful formula for gaining political popularity while halting the expansion of federal domestic spending. Deficit pressure was insufficient to reduce the budget, but for the next decade it did restrain additional domestic spending.

The Republicans also gained public support by attacking the Democrats for being soft on crime and welfare. Until the 1960s, crime was considered to be a local problem. But President Johnson and many Democratic mayors and governors responded to the mid-1960s urban riots with what voters perceived as appeasement. This perception enabled Republicans to turn the crime issue into a national, partisan one, identifying themselves as the law-and-order party.

Federal welfare payments to families with dependent children had been relatively uncontroversial since their inception during the New Deal. But during the 1960s and 1970s, skyrocketing levels of illegitimate births and crime waves in welfare-dependent neighborhoods made welfare policy notorious. Because these policies were identified with the Democrats, they provided an inviting target for the Republicans. Strong opposition to crime and generous welfare benefits enabled the Republicans to regain the status they had enjoyed in the mid- and late nineteenth century as the party of hard work, piety, and middle-class virtue.

## "New Democrats"

In 1992, as in 1912, the Democrats were able to regain the presidency after a period of Republican dominance because a third candidate siphoned off Republican votes. Like TR, Ross Perot concentrated his attacks on the Republican incumbent. Perot promised to eliminate the deficit Reagan had created and George H. W. Bush had perpetuated. He garnered 19 percent of the vote, the best showing by a third-party candidate since 1912. He took enough votes away from Bush to enable Clinton to win, even though the Democratic share of the vote was scarcely greater than it had been four years earlier.

Like Woodrow Wilson, Clinton took heed of the third candidate's strong showing and shifted his rhetoric and policy proposals accordingly. He pledged to reduce the budget deficit. He refused to support expensive programs despite their strong appeal to key Democratic Party constituents. The crucial exception to this policy – health care reform – was defeated in Congress, followed by the Republican sweep of the 1994 elections (see Chapter 7), giving them control of both House and Senate for the first time since 1954. Then Clinton returned to the centrist themes and policies he touted in his run for the presidency. The combination of spending restraint and a strong economy enabled a steady decline in the deficit. By late in Clinton's second term, there was actually a budgetary surplus.

Clinton declared himself to be a "New Democrat." Like Reagan, he recognized that his party could not thrive without changing its approach. Not only did he strive for a balanced budget, he also aggressively altered his party's posture on welfare and crime. As governor of Arkansas, he rejected clemency appeals from prisoners condemned to die. As president, he sponsored legislation providing federal subsidies to cities and towns to hire additional police. He promised to "end welfare as we know it," and signed the Republican-sponsored welfare reform bill, even though it was much harsher to recipients than his proposal.

Clinton's reversal of Democratic positions on budget balancing, crime, and welfare enabled him to recover from the 1994 congressional election debacle and win reelection in 1996. Deprived of their most popular issues, Republicans made no gains in the 1998 and 2000 elections despite the scandals that plagued Clinton's second term. As of 2000, the partisan balance was the most even in all of American history. The Republicans won the presidential election on the basis of a court contest over Florida's electoral votes but their candidate lost the national popular vote. As we described in Chapter 7, the Senate majority changed on the basis of the switch of a single Republican senator. The Republicans held only a seven-seat margin in the House of Representatives. In 2002, the Republicans gained two additional Senate seats and six more in the House of Representatives. The 2004 election enabled the Republicans to increase their advantage. Bush defeated Kerry by a 51 percent to 48 percent popular vote margin, and Bush won fifteen more electoral votes than he did in 2000. The Republicans also gained four seats in the Senate and four in the House. But as discussed in Chapter 7, the Democrats won back control of both houses of Congress in 2006. Fifty-four percent of all voters nationwide voted for Democratic congressional candidates, whereas only 46 percent voted for Republicans. This represented a larger margin of victory for the Democrats than the Republicans enjoyed in 2004. The Democrats compounded their 2006 victory by winning the 2008 presidential election, but suffered serious reversals in 2010, losing control of the House of Representatives and diminishing their margin of control in the Senate.

## Party Transformation: The Progressive Path

The last several sections of this chapter have been devoted primarily to the patterns of party dominance and competition that have developed since the New Deal. But this same time period also witnessed major transformation in the character and functioning of the party system itself. The United States is still a two-party system, but it now travels a Progressive path as a result of critical choices regarding candidate nomination, campaign finance and organization, and government personnel policy. These choices were made at various times during the twentieth and into the twenty-first centuries, but their inspiration is to be found in the Progressive Movement of the early 1900s.

Over the course of the twentieth century the Progressive-inspired "merit" system based on objective examinations replaced party patronage as the standard method for awarded jobs and promotions. This shift occurred at the state and local as well as the federal level. It greatly diminished the number of jobs that victorious parties could dispense. Patronage powers did not entirely disappear. Local probate judges, for example, retained the discretion to choose which lawyers to assign to lucrative cases. Highway officials kept considerable freedom in choosing companies to perform profitable highway construction jobs. But the decline in the quantity of patronage sapped party leaders of a critical tool for maintaining party discipline and cohesion.

The Progressive Movement had sought to replace state nominating conventions with primary elections. This shift placed the choice of party nominees for statewide offices, and the presidency, in the hands of the voters not the party leaders. Gradually, over the course of the first half of the twentieth century, the number of states adopting the primary system and number of offices chosen by primary election expanded.

Beginning in 1968, as a result of the battle for control of the Democratic Party discussed earlier, the role of primaries expanded dramatically. As of now, in all states, both parties rely on primaries or voter-dominated party caucuses to choose all their candidates for state and federal offices, including the presidency. As the Progressives hoped, the proliferation of party primaries has greatly diminished the power and influence of party leaders. However, because would-be nominees now have to mount campaigns to win party nomination they must publicize reasons why they are superior to their rivals and why their rivals are inferior to them. This necessity encourages intense and bitter nominating contests that create lasting animosities between the rivals and their supporters. It often proves very difficult to mend the feuds provoked and exacerbated by primary battles, further aggravating the difficulties of maintaining party cohesion, discipline, and morale.

The battles against political corruption waged during the Progressive Era had greatly increased public awareness of and disgust with the increasing role of money in political campaigns (see Chapter 12). In the 1970s public concern was greatly heightened by the Watergate scandal (see Chapter 7). In response to public clamor, Congress adopted a series of major campaign finance reforms. The 1974 amendments to the Federal Elections Campaign Act sought to limit the resources and spending opportunities available to personal campaign organizations. They established strict disclosure requirements for campaign donations; set specific limits for those donations; expanded public financing of presidential elections to include primaries and nominating conventions as well as the general election; set limits on campaign expenditures; and established the *Federal Election Commission* to oversee compliance with the law.

Fueled by the voluntary check off on tax forms (now $3), the Presidential Election Campaign Fund matched up to $250 of each contribution made to eligible primary candidates. In return, the candidates had to promise that they would limit spending to a specified amount. Then, in the general election season, the presidential candidates receive a lump sum in return for not accepting any further private donations.

Contribution limits were set differently for individuals and Political Action Committees (PACs), which were entities that corporations, labor unions, and other types of organizations were required to establish in order to legally contribute to campaigns. An individual was allowed to donate $1,000 to a candidate per primary or general election; $20,000 to any other political committee per year; $5,000 to a national party committee per year, but no more than $25,000 in total. A PAC was limited to $5,000 to a candidate per primary or general election; $15,000 to any other political committee per year; and $5,000 to a national party committee. No limit was placed on its total contributions per year.

The 1974 Federal Elections Campaign Act actually served to increase the financial power of parties because the law did not seek to control or limit donations to political parties that were used to support state and local campaign efforts. Such nonfederal funds came to be known as "soft money" to distinguish them from "hard money," regulated donations to individual candidates and parties. Soft money was intended to be used for party-building activities such as get-out-the-vote drives and the distribution of campaign paraphernalia such as bumper stickers and lawn signs.

Both parties raised huge sums of soft money, which – according to advocates of campaign finance reform – were used to evade the spirit, but not the letter, of the law. In the most controversial action, national parties funneled large sums of soft money to state parties for TV and radio advertising praising party candidates and attacking their opponents. These ads were not subject to campaign donation limits as long as they did not specifically ask voters to vote for or against a particular candidate. Interest groups evaded donation limits by doing the same thing. This sort of legal evasion of the intent of a law is called a *loophole*.

Seeking to close the soft money loophole, Congress adopted new regulations that severely weakened parties. The 2002 Bipartisan Campaign Finance Reform Act, commonly known as McCain-Feingold in honor of its senatorial sponsors, banned soft-money contributions to national political parties. All donations to political parties would now be subject to a $25,000 limit per donor. Recognizing that this ban would reduce the money available to carry out campaigns, the act raised the limit on candidate donations from $1,000 to $2,000. It also sought to reduce the electoral importance of corporations, trade associations, public interest groups, and labor unions from financing "electioneering communications" within sixty days of a general election or thirty days of a primary. An *electioneering communication* was defined as an ad that clearly identified a candidate and targeted his or her state or district, whether or not the ad explicitly asked voters to support or oppose the candidate.

Not only did the soft-money ban reduce the financial clout of the parties, it created a new loophole that advantaged organizational rivals to the parties. McCain-Feingold's limit on donations applied only to political parties, not to other political advocacy organizations. Groups such as NARAL Pro-Choice America (formerly the National Abortion and Reproductive Rights Action League) and the National Rifle Association, can spend as much as 50 percent of their resources on election-related activities. A tax-exempt group organized under section 527 of the Internal Revenue Code can spend unlimited amounts for political activities such as voter registration and mobilization efforts and issue advocacy. The only limitation is that this money cannot be spent for the express purpose of telling people to vote for a particular candidate. It can even be used for ads criticizing a candidate as long as the ad does not ask voters to vote for the opponent. In 2010, 527 organizations spent more than $560 million on political campaigns. The three largest contributors to 527s were all unions. The Service Employees International, a public employee union, spent more than $17 million, four times the sum spent by the second-largest contributor, the United Food and Commercial Workers Union. The third-largest contributor was also a union, the Operating Engineers. By contrast, the largest 501c4 contributors were all supporters of the Republicans. The U.S. Chamber of Commerce gave almost $33 million. American Action Network gave more than $20 million, and Crossroads Grassroots Strategies more than $17 million.

As we discussed in Chapter 9, in 2009 the Supreme Court dealt a severe blow to campaign finance regulation. In *Citizens United* it declared the Campaign Finance Act's prohibition against corporations and unions spending their own money on electioneering communication within thirty days of a primary or general election to be unconstitutional. This ruling further diminished the power of parties by lifting a key restriction on the electioneering opportunities of rich and powerful nonparty entities. Thus, the current state of campaign finance regulation reduces party influence without limiting the role that money plays in politics.

The impact of Progressive-inspired reform on political parties was greatly accentuated by the advent of television. The ability to project a televised image of the candidate to millions of people diminished the importance of the traditional methods of political campaigning that had been the province of local parties – door-to-door canvassing, rallies, and get-out-the-vote drives. The direct communication between politicians and the public that mass media enabled meant that party was no longer a mediator between the two. FDR proved a master at using radio to speak intimately to voters; he encouraged them to think of these one-way discussions as fireside chats. Television connected a face to the candidate's voice and increased the feeling of connectedness between candidate and citizen. The televised presidential debates between John F. Kennedy and Richard Nixon in 1960 demonstrated the power of this new medium. Although Nixon was Kennedy's equal as a speaker, voters were struck by the contrast between his grizzled, harsh face and Kennedy's handsome and serene visage. Kennedy was a Democrat, but the capacity to look good on television and speak with warmth and conviction would benefit candidates from both parties, especially the former movie actor Ronald Reagan, the magnetic, empathetic Bill Clinton, and the dignified, regal Barack Obama.

The combined result of these Progressive-inspired choices, combined with the rise of television, was to marginalize political parties from presidential election campaigning and diminish their role in congressional and gubernatorial elections, as well. In order to win primaries, candidates had to form their own personal campaign organizations. If they were victorious, those personal organizations, rather than party organizations, formed the core of their general election campaign effort. After the abolition of soft money, parties were severely restricted in their ability to raise campaign funds. The manner in which television operated to increase the electoral importance of a candidate's image made him ever-more reliant on the expert image makers he or she would hire from the worlds of advertising and marketing rather than party officials who had no such expertise.

## CONCLUSION: POLITICAL PARTIES, DEMOCRACY, AND LIBERTY

Despite the inroads of civil service reform, mass media, and campaign finance limits, the current party system still performs some of the critical political functions that Martin Van Buren expected it to perform when he championed parties in the 1830s. It encourages political accountability, and because there are only two major parties, voters can readily replace the "in" party with a coherent organization of "outs." The two-party system also simplifies and structures voter choice. The typical Republican candidate has very different opinions about a whole host of issues including abortion, guns, taxes, environmental regulation, relations between church and state, and education than does the Democratic counterpart. Therefore, voters can rather easily distinguish between candidates based on their party label.

But parties no longer perform other critical functions that Van Buren claimed for them. He saw party as a device for restraining presidential ambition. But party leaders do not now exert much influence on the actual choice of presidential candidates. Typically, Republican candidates have very different opinions about a whole host of issues including abortion, guns, taxes, environmental regulation, relations between church and state, and education than do their Democratic counterparts. Therefore, after the election, the winner is not much beholden to party chieftains. Indeed, the roles are reversed; it is the president who anoints the national party chair and dominates the life of the national party.

The two parties are no longer primarily state and local organizations who come together in a convention once every four years to choose a president. Now, the national organization of the president's party is mostly just another tool for raising money and promoting the president's agenda and his prestige with the voters. It is not at all clear what role the other party performs, except to raise money for candidates and wait on tenterhooks for the next presidential election.

Van Buren conceived of parties as a means for overcoming sectionalism. Ever since the Virginian Thomas Jefferson chose the New Yorker Aaron Burr as his running mate, parties sought to encourage national ties and feelings. When they failed to do so in the 1850s, there was civil war. As this chapter mentions, each party is becoming more dominant in particular regions, The Republicans in the South and West and the Democrats in the Northeast and along the Pacific Coast. Fewer states remain competitive between them. The national parties are no longer effective agents for encouraging national unity.

In Van Buren's day parties were essentially local in nature. The association of local parties at the state level and the association of state parties at the national level mirrored the Constitution's federal structure, providing a second important bulwark against oppressive central authority. Parties are no longer deeply grounded locally, so they cannot play this important role. Equally troubling, they no longer command the loyalty of a very large fraction of the people, and that fraction is growing. Party once provided a means for people to escape the chains of private self-absorption and reach out into the public realm, but it is less and less able to do so.

Parties arose to redress key threats to democracy and liberty that the Constitution could not cope with by itself. If parties are no longer as effective in restraining presidential ambition, reducing regional differences, and combating privatism some or all of those threats are likely to grow, and alternative means will need to be found for addressing them.

## CHAPTER SUMMARY

☆  The greatest shift in political support for the two parties occurring in recent decades is that of whites in the South from the Democrats to the Republicans.

☆  Three of the most important indications of contemporary party identification are marital status, church attendance, and attitudes toward foreign policy.

☆  Hispanics comprise the largest identifiable group of swing voters.

☆  The regulations and procedures that govern elections embody the full complexity inherent in Federalism. All levels of government are involved in a manner that continually causes them to intersect and intermingle.

☆  Statewide primaries and caucuses have replaced the party nominating conventions as the key venues for choosing presidential candidates.

☆  The early adoption of winner-take-all elections for Congress and presidential electors greatly favored the rise of a two-party system.

☆  Throughout the nineteenth century, American politics was dominated by the two major political parties, and this party system worked to sustain decentralized government.

☆  The slavery issue overwhelmed the parties' capacity to function as national institutions.

☆    The Progressives sought to undermine the strength of political parties by replacing patronage-based hiring with merit-based hiring and encouraging the switch from partisan to nonpartisan elections.

☆    The party coalition assembled by FDR provided the political energy that fueled the New Deal and ushered in the longest period of one-party dominance in American history.

☆    The resurgence of the Republicans began with Eisenhower's election as president in 1952 and culminated in the party's recapture of the House of Representatives in 1994 after a gap of forty years.

☆    Progressive-inspired reforms regarding primary elections, campaign finance, and the replacement of party patronage by the merit system have transformed the nature and character of party politics.

☆    Parties continue to enable political accountability and simplify and structure voter choice. But they no longer work to temper political ambition, sustain decentralized politics and government, promote national unity, or combat selfish individualism.

## MAJOR TERMS AND CONCEPTS

| | |
|---|---|
| Bipartisan Campaign Finance Reform Act of 2002 (McCain-Feingold) | |
| Coalitions | Decentralization |
| Factions | |
| | |
| Federal Election Commission | |
| Loopholes | Nonpartisan Elections |
| Party Caucuses | Party Conventions |
| Party Identification | Party System |
| Party Primaries | Patronage |
| Polarization | Populists |
| Progressives | Proportional Representation |
| Single-Member Districts | Soft Money |
| Suffrage | Swing Voters |
| Voter Turnout | |

## SUGGESTED READINGS

Aldrich, John. *Why Parties?: A Second Look.* Chicago: University of Chicago Press, 2011.

Burnham, Walter Dean. *Critical Elections and the Mainsprings of American Politics.* New York: W. W. Norton, 1971.

Chambers, William Nisbet, and Walter Dean Burnham. *The American Party Systems: Stages of Political Development.* New York: Oxford University Press, 1975.

Cohen, Marty, David Karol, Hans Noel, and John Zaller. *The Party Decides Presidential Nominations Before and After Reform.* Chicago: University of Chicago Press, 2008.

Hershey, Marjorie Random, and Paul Allen Beck. *Party Politics in America,* 10th ed. New York: Longman, 2002.

Key, V. O. *Politics, Parties, and Pressure Groups,* 5th ed. New York: Thomas Y. Crowell, 1964.

Levendusky, Matthew. *The Partisan Sort: How Liberals Became Democrats and Conservatives Became Republicans.* Chicago: University of Chicago Press, 2009.

Reichley, A. James. *The Life of the Parties.* Lanham, MD: Rowman and Littlefield, 2000.

Wattenberg, Martin P. *The Decline of American Political Parties, 1952–1996.* Cambridge, MA: Harvard University Press, 1998.

Suggested Web SitesAmerican National Election Studies: http://www.electionstudies.org/

"Five Thirty Eight: Nate Silver's Political Calculus": http://fivethirtyeight.blogs.nytimes.com/

Politico: http://www.politico.com/

Real Clear Politics: http://www.realclearpolitics.com/

# Participation, Public Opinion, and Media

## CHAPTER OVERVIEW

This chapter focuses on:

☆ Three critical modes of political participation in America: movements, lobbies, and voluntary associations.

☆ Providing a contemporary portrait of each of those three modes of participation.

☆ Describing how political movements trod in the paths of their predecessors.

☆ Exploring the problems that political movements experience because of excessive zealotry.

☆ Exploring the relationship that participation has with political culture, public opinion, and the media.

Business news is normally reported in a calm, noncommittal manner. But in February of 2009, when CNBC Business News editor Rick Santelli commented over the air on the government plan to refinance mortgages, his remarks sounded more like a diatribe than a news report. From the floor of the Chicago Mercantile Exchange, he hotly accused the government of "promoting bad behavior" by "subsidizing losers' mortgages." He urged the president to use the internet to ask ordinary people what they thought of the bailout:

Why don't you put up a website to have people vote on the Internet as a referendum to see if we really want to subsidize the losers' mortgages; or would we like to at least buy cars and buy houses in foreclosure and give them to people that might have a chance to actually prosper down the road, and reward people that could carry the water instead of drink the water This is America! How many of you people want to pay for your neighbor's mortgage that has an extra bathroom and can't pay their bills? Raise their hand.

Harking back to the Sons of Liberty who dumped British Tea in Boston Harbor to protest British-imposed taxes, he proposed that the Mercantile Exchange traders stage a tea party to gather and dump the mortgage-related securities they were trading into the Chicago River. Instead of displaying contempt for this breach of journalistic protocol, many of the traders cheered. Within hours of the broadcast, two Web sites had been created promoting protest activities under the "tea party" banner. The next day, a Facebook page was created to enable tea partiers to communicate with one another and plan rallies and demonstrations not only against the mortgage bailout but against the stimulus plan, health care reform, and a host of other Obama administration "big government" programs. After a video of the occasion was posted on the Drudge Report it became one of the most popular of all the postings on that very popular site that receives approximately 18 million hits daily. That week, protests against the expanding reach of the federal government had broken out all over the country. The Tea Party was dramatically transformed from a semi-serious remark into a political movement involving thousands of people (Figure 12.1).

As the Tea Party movement grew in size and strength, it moved from simply voicing its dissatisfaction with increased government spending and bailouts to trying to change the direction of American politics to shrink the size and scope of government. Its first great political success came in the January special election called in Massachusetts to fill the empty seat caused by the death of Senator Edward Kennedy (see Chapter 11). Self-identified Tea Partiers were very active and vocal in their support of the surprise winner, Republican Scott Brown. But the Tea Party was not content to serve as an instrument of the Republicans. In several states, its members actively supported challengers to Republican incumbents who had supported some of Obama's programs – the stimulus, health care reform, and/or bank bailout. In Utah, it succeeded in defeating longtime incumbent Robert Bennett. In Nevada it succeeded in nominating the most anti-government of the Republican challengers, Sharon Angle, to incumbent Democrat, Senate Majority Leader Harry Reid. In Delaware, likewise, it rallied support for the more radical Republican senatorial aspirant, Christine O'Donnell, who defeated her more moderate opponent.

The results of the Tea Party intervention were mixed. Republicans easily held the Utah seat but both Angle and O'Donnell lost to highly vulnerable Democrats. However, the Tea Party also helped energize the campaigns of scores of Republican House and Senate nominees. Their hard work campaigning door to door and mobilizing their friends, neighbors, and family undoubtedly contributed to the ensuing Republic landslide.

The Tea Party is not an organization. Several different national organizations and Web sites include those two words in their titles, but none can claim to speak for the movement. In reality, Tea Partiers are whoever shows up at meetings of the local and county organizations that have sprung up around the country and have "Tea Party" in their title as well as those who simply show up

THE DESTRUCTION OF TEA IN BOSTON HARBOR.

**Figure 12.1.** Boston Tea Party: A wood engraving of the 1773 destruction of tea in Boston Harbor in symbolic resistance to the Tea Act. Credit: The Granger Collection, NYC – All rights reserved.

at the demonstrations and rallies these groups sponsor or volunteer to campaign for Tea Party–endorsed candidates.

The Tea Party has no leader. Many nationally prominent conservatives, most famously Sarah Palin, praise the Tea Party and speak at its rallies, but they do not speak *for* the Tea Party. The most important leadership is exercised at the local level by ordinary people who rent the meeting halls, manage the Web sites, and organize the phone banks.

## Three Types of Participation

This chapter examines three critical dimensions of *political participation* in America. The Tea Party is an example of one of these three – political participation "out of doors." *Out-of-doors* politics originates and flourishes outside the halls of power. It mobilizes ordinary people to take part in rallies, demonstrations, strikes, and other forms of protest. It is often noisy, chaotic, passionate, and motivated by a sense of injustice and injury. If, like the Tea Party or Occupy Wall Street it gains lots of members and national prominence, it becomes a *movement*. The very word "movement" evokes the surging energy and intense commitment the Tea Party's predecessors – the Temperance, Labor, Civil Rights, and Feminist causes – embodied.

The Tea Party resembles earlier political movements in several critical ways. As we have seen, the Tea Party was born on cable TV and promoted on Drudge. Web sites and Facebook have served as its most important recruiting, fundraising, and organizing devices. As we shall see, the Progressives and The Civil Rights Movement, among others, also successfully exploited new forms of mass communications. As its name proclaims, the Tea Party links itself with America's past. Likewise, earlier movements have identified themselves with core beliefs and precedents that Americans cherish. They all claim to be part of the American tradition of freedom fighting, constitutional fidelity, and moral and religious commitment. The Tea Party has had a strong impact on a political party, the Republicans, but it is not of the Republican Party. When it considers Republicans to be insufficiently aggressive in opposing big government and insufficiently faithful to the Constitution, it actively opposes them. This ambivalent and tense relationship with one or both political parties is also typical of previous protest movements.

Although it is spoken of as a single entity, the Tea Party is, in reality, a decentralized and diverse array of independent local groups. There is no national hierarchy. Instead, whatever sense of solidarity and coherence the Tea Partiers have rests on the basis of a shared commitment to a few fundamental principles, like the abolitionists, temperance societies, and environmentalists that preceded them. Some of its adherents are famous, but they cannot claim to lead the movement. Great movement figures of the past such as William Lloyd Garrison, Ralph Nader, and Martin Luther King, Jr. did in fact lead organizations, but those entities formed only a small fraction o f the movements with which they were involved. Today as in the past, movement leadership is more diffuse and episodic than the fame of its most prominent figures would imply.

This chapter examines these and other characteristics of political movements in order to understand how and why they form and grow; complex ties they form with *public opinion* and the mass media; challenges they face; and how they influence and are influenced by the broader world of politics and government. It describes how political movements learn from their predecessors. For example, it looks at how and why the anti-Viet Nam War Movement borrowed strategies and tactics from the Civil Rights Movement just as the Civil Rights Movement had adopted organizing principles and techniques from the Labor Movement. It applies these same questions and modes of analysis to "politics indoors."

Compared to the out-of-doors drama of protests, rallies, and demonstrations, indoor politics is calm, even dull. The term most often used to describe such activity, *lobbying*, conveys an atmosphere of low-key, casual encounters in the halls outside of legislative chambers, government offices, and hotel rooms. Of course, the large *trade associations*, public interest organizations, and law firms that are the most powerful lobbyists do not confine themselves to such venues and occasions. For the most part, indoor politics plays out in law offices, judge's chambers, and regulatory hearing rooms. Because they want to demonstrate to their targets that the public is on their side, lobbying organizations intentionally blur the distinction between indoor and outdoor politics. They launch extensive media campaigns aimed to influence public opinion. They also stimulate and assist their local affiliates to send delegations to Washington and choke the in boxes of their congressmen with supportive e-mails. Likewise, out-of-doors organizations establish offices in Washington and the state capitals staffed with lobbyists, lawyers, and researchers. They recognize the need to convert the political energies of their members into favorable policy outcomes. And yet these encroachments on one another's turf do not undermine the essential difference between a movement whose strength lies in its ability to excite the passions of large numbers of loyal adherents and a lobby that relies primarily on expertise, discretion, and the quiet exertion of influence.

Despite the dramatic difference between protest movements and lobbying organizations, they both devote themselves to changing governmental policies and practices. Dating from before the American Revolution, America has also been home to a different form of political participation that seeks not to influence government but to substitute for it. Even today many towns rely on voluntary associations to accomplish tasks that would otherwise be performed by the government, or not performed at all. Instead of employing firefighters, many towns depend on ordinary citizens to organize and staff a volunteer fire brigade. Neighborhoods establish citizen crime patrols to provide a level of surveillance that the city police force cannot provide. Local garden clubs prune trees and plant and tend flowers and shrubs in parks and plazas, work that would otherwise be done by municipal public works employees. These activities tap into the wellsprings of individual initiative and optimism so deeply embedded in American political culture. This civic dimension of political participation also forms a critical aspect of American political development, and is a subject of this chapter.

## Public Opinion

This chapter links participation and public opinion because a central purpose of both movement politics and lobbying is to influence public opinion to make their cause more popular and give them more political influence. Even if the public is, on the whole, favorable to their objectives, political movements seek to dramatize their cause in order to transform passive support into active public pressure geared to force political change. From a political standpoint, the strength and energy with which one holds an opinion is more important than what opinion one holds. A person may favor gay marriage, but unless that opinion is translated into some form of political participation – voting for candidates favorable to gay marriage, contributing money to a gay rights organization, encouraging one's friends to do likewise – it is not politically relevant.

In Chapter 2 we examined American political culture, the core beliefs that form the intellectual, moral, and emotional foundation of the American political order. The relationship between public opinion and political culture is similar to that between weather and the climate. Like the weather, opinion varies a great deal. People change their minds. Political culture, like the climate, remains stable for long periods of time; deserts do not suddenly become rain forests. Likewise, the fundamental aspects of American political belief do not reverse themselves. Climate does change, but slowly, often imperceptibly. Nor is political culture immutable. But it is highly resistant to change, and its alterations happen gradually. If a change in public opinion persists over time it indicates that the political weather has shifted sufficiently to constitute climate change.

Just as the climate constrains the weather, so political culture constrains public opinion. It will not snow in Ecuador. Only rarely does public opinion depart from the four key elements of American political culture identified in Chapter 2: optimism; skepticism of government; attachment to individual rights; and religious conviction. Successful political movements borrow heavily from these core beliefs. Movements succeed when they convince the public that they are faithful to those tenets and they lose public support when Americans perceive them to deviate from those cherished principles. As we shall see, political movements have a hard time maintaining broad public support because they are constantly in danger of breaking free of the boundaries set by political culture. The same passionate and excitable qualities that give these movements their energy and vitality also encourage political extremism. As the chapter proceeds we will observe how various movements and their leaders maintain their members' commitment.

## CONTEMPORARY PORTRAIT

### Outdoors

Many of the political movements that had a strong out-of-doors presence in earlier decades have not disappeared, but in recent years they have operated primarily indoors. Those considered to be on the left – environmental, pro-abortion, feminist, gay rights, and civil rights organizations – actively lobby Congress and the executive and bring lawsuits, but they have not been staging large rallies, demonstrations, and protests. Prior to the Tea Party, the major out-of-doors organizations on the right were those rooted in evangelical Christian churches. They, too, have become less demonstrative even as they maintain a strong political presence in Washington and state capitals.

But such changes can prove temporary. In 2011 and 2012 the most passionate and demonstrative out-of-doors protest organizations were more closely identified with the left. Unlike many of their private-sector counterparts, the growth of public employee unions was more the result of legislation than bitter and violent strikes. In 2011 public employees moved outdoors in response to threats to curtail their bargaining powers. In Wisconsin, newly elected Governor Scott Walker proposed legislation to restrict bargaining to wage issues, excluding such vital matters as pensions and healthcare. Walker's proposal would also end the "union shop" agreement that required all state employees to pay dues to the unions elected to represent them. And a new election would be held yearly to allow workers to reconsider whether or not they wanted the union to continue to represent them.

The state's public employees unions mobilized their members to protest Walker's proposals. In February of 2011 union members staged a massive rally at the Wisconsin state capitol. On the first day of the protest so many Madison schoolteachers called in sick, presumably to attend the rally, that the schools had to be closed. Students at the University of Wisconsin, Madison, skipped classes to join the protestors. Demonstrators disrupted the state senate's effort to consider Walker's proposal by blocking the door to the Senate floor. At the end of the day many of the demonstrators refused to leave. During the next few days the daytime protests grew in size, and at night the halls of the capitol became home to a camp meeting of protesters, chanting, dancing, singing, and waving signs far into the night.

The protests took on greater political import when the Senate Democrats, too, stepped out of doors. Wisconsin Senate rules require that at least one member of the minority party be present for a vote on a matter with fiscal implications. To prevent a vote on Walker's proposal, all the Senate Democrats walked out of the Senate chamber and then disappeared. It was soon learned that they had all fled to neighboring Illinois. Two weeks went by. Then the Republican majority revised the legislation, excising those parts of it with fiscal implications, and passed it. Only then did the Senate Democrats return.

The nightly TV news featured scenes of chanting demonstrators and the capitol lobby strewn with backpacks, sleeping bags, and the increasingly disheveled protestors who slept in them. Stations vied with one another to arrange interviews with the missing legislators in undisclosed locations. These highly publicized events sparked rallies and demonstrations throughout the nation aimed both at showing support for the Wisconsin public employees and protesting efforts to cut employee benefits and bargaining powers elsewhere.

In September of 2011, a left-leaning protest movement, Occupy Wall Street, held its first demonstration in Zuccotti Park, in Manhattan's Financial District. The movement quickly spread to more than 100 cities in the United States and sparked similar demonstrations overseas. One of the movement's manifestos declared that it was "fighting back against the corrosive power of major banks and multinational corporations over the democratic process, and the role of Wall Street in creating an economic collapse that has caused the greatest recession in generations." The protestors remained in the park for many weeks – erecting tents and cooking communally. Similar encampments were established in cities across the nation including Oakland, Boston, and Chicago (Figure 12.2).

## Indoors

A good way to appreciate the diversity and abundance of Washington lobbies is to walk the streets of the nation's capital and read the names on brass plaques mounted at the entrances to the office buildings. One gets the impression that no imaginable activity is too obscure or specialized to be denied representation in Washington. In addition to such large, long-established associations as the National Association of Manufacturers, U.S. Chamber of Commerce,

**Figure 12.2.** Monstrous Wealth: A 2009 cartoon responding to the bonuses offered in the wake of the massive federal bailout to those companies deemed "too big to fail."

*Source*: Political Cartoons.com 70219. Retrieved from http://www.politicalcartoons.com/cartoon/1d1d3ea7-2483-488b-9ce8-bd6392c82150.html.

National Rifle Association, and National Education Association, one finds the Canoe Cruisers Association, The National Cannabis Industry Association, the International Society of Crytpozoology, and thousands more.

Plaques also announce the name of firms whose titles do not reveal their purpose. They typically take the form of Smith, Jones, Doe, and Associates. These firms specialize in lobbying, and doing so on behalf of whoever hires them. Major Washington law firms typically include a division similarly devoted to lobbying for clients. The principals of such lobbying firms, as well as leading trade associations, are usually people who have extensive high-level government experience. Many are former congresspersons, cabinet secretaries, and heads of government agencies. Their key subordinates are typically former congressional staffers and executive branch personnel. They bring their extensive knowledge of how the government operates as well as their extensive friendship network of former colleagues, people who are likely to return their calls and who may owe them a favor.

Major profit-making and not-for-profit institutions such as large corporations, hospitals, and universities do not rely solely on their trade associations. They have such a heavy reliance on and complex relationships with government that they have their own lobbying staffs, usually headed by a vice president for public affairs.

State, county, and local governments are major recipients of federal spending. Therefore, these governments are concerned both in the spending levels Congress sets for programs that subsidize them and the formulas that Congress establishes for the distribution of such monies. Formulas are never entirely neutral in their impact. For example, a heavily populated state such as New York will want spending formulas on the basis of population. A lightly populated state such as Wyoming will seek to ensure that a minimum amount of the grant in question be reserved for each state, regardless of size. Because they have so much at stake, state, county, and local governments maintain their own lobbying organizations. Many cities belong to the National League of Cities. Because big cities have concerns that often differ from their smaller counterparts, big city mayors have their own organization, the National Conference of Mayors. The National Governor's Association and the National Council of State Legislatures lobby on behalf of the states collectively. Specific types of state agencies also form national associations. For example, the Association of State and Interstate Water Pollution Control Administrators lobbies the federal government on behalf of the state and interstate agencies that regulate water quality and water pollution.

Regardless of whom they work for, lobbyists perform three related tasks: they inform; influence; and mobilize financial and political support for their legislative and executive branch allies. The quest for information and the contest between conflicting information is at the heart of the legislative process. Facts do not speak for themselves. Lobbying organizations devote considerable time and effort to assembling data and packaging it in a manner that is most supportive of their legislative objectives. This information is vital even to those legislators who are most supportive of those objectives because they need to understand the issue themselves if they are to make a persuasive case on its behalf. It is also vital as a means for shaping the broader public debate on the issue at hand because those legislators not so closely allied with the lobby will resist supporting the objective if they do not believe it is publically defensible.

Information also drives much of executive branch decision making. Regulatory agencies depend on scientific and economic information to provide the basis for their decisions. They do not have the resources to conduct the research and assemble the data they need. Some of it is provided by research agencies within the government, but a great deal is also provided both by the affected firms and often by public interest groups on the right who try to make the case for less costly and intrusive regulation, and the public interest groups on the left who seek more stringent regulation.

## Influence

Lobbyists exert influence in many different ways. Influence may reside in the lobbyists themselves. One of the authors of this book was told an unverifiable story about a Japanese company who badly needed a prompt favorable decision on a trade regulation matter. It had tried to make its case to the regulatory authorities and had been unable to obtain a final decision. Finally, its own lobbyist advised it to ask a former secretary of state to intervene. That person demanded several thousand dollars to make a phone call to the relevant decision maker. The call lasted only a few minutes, but the company obtained the ruling it needed.

Influence also comes through mobilizing an association's membership. Almost every medium-sized town in America has at least one auto dealership in it. If the National Automobile Dealers is seeking to influence a particular congressperson, perhaps the best weapon at its disposal is to urge all the auto dealers and their employees to show up at the congressman's district office when he is there and remind him just how numerous and locally well connected they are.

Because the public, media, and Congress are impressed by the large impassioned shows of support for a cause that political movements mobilize, public relations firms try to help their clients exert political influence by putting together organizations that simulate such movements but whose expenses, and perhaps its participants, are paid by the firm. This phenomenon has been labeled "astro turf" because it offers the appearance but not the reality of the grassroots. Cable companies are known to have organized and sponsored "concerned citizens" movements when states threaten to change the laws granting them local monopolies. Likewise, tobacco and coal companies have funded citizens group that have protested what they consider to be the excessive health and environmental regulations affecting those industries. Public interest groups have also been accused of astro turfing when the "volunteers" they send door to door to with petitions calling for tougher environmental laws are not volunteers at all but are paid for their labors.

In order to maintain good relations with elected officials whom they hope to influence, lobbyists encourage their clients to make campaign contributions. Such contributions enable lobbyists to have ready access to those officials, but they rarely allow the lobbyists to bully them into taking positions with which they are uncomfortable. Threatening to withhold contributions is dangerous because to do so is to lose access to someone whose help will be needed in the future regarding other issues. Also those on the other side of the question will see this threatened withdrawal of support as an opportunity to offer the embattled politician more support, thereby ingratiating themselves with that person.

## Voluntary Associations

In some instances voluntary associations substitute almost entirely for government. Volunteer fire brigades and neighborhood crime watches may receive training and consultations from fire and police departments, but they organize themselves and perform their firefighting and surveillance activities on their own. In Maine, lobstermen substitute for government agents as regulators of the lobster supply.

In order to prevent lobsters from becoming scarce, it is necessary to control the lobster harvest. The trouble is that no individual lobsterman has an incentive to limit his catch if he fears that at least some of the others are failing to do so. Normally, this sort of problem, known as the *tragedy of the commons*, is solved by government – imposed limits on how much each boat can catch and government inspection of the lobster boats to make sure they are not exceeding their quota. But in 1995, lobstermen won the authority, through local councils, to develop local fishing rules. Limits on the number of traps per lobsterman and how often he may check those are ratified by the district council of lobstermen, who must approve them by a two-thirds vote. The lobstermen are more effective enforcers than government agents because they have participated in creating rules that reflect their intimate knowledge of local conditions.

The second category of civic participation involves partnerships between voluntary associations and government, for example, the Central Park Conservancy. New York's Central Park attracts more than 20 million visitors a year. Until 1995, it was maintained by a government agency, the New York City Parks Department. Because of deep dissatisfaction with the appearance of the park and lack of security provided its users, a group of private citizens established the Central Park Conservancy, which then negotiated an agreement with the City of New York to take over the park's management. The Conservancy provides more than 85 percent of Central Park's annual $20 million operating budget and is responsible for all basic care of the park. Approximately three out of every four Central Park employees are funded by the Conservancy. Conservancy staff nurtures the lawns, ponds, lakes, shrubs trees, and flowers; protects wildlife, controls drainage, erosion, and pollution; and maintains the ball fields, bridle paths, and playgrounds. It has renovated many of the park's most important landmarks and built and staffed new visitor's centers.

Charter schools are another example of public-private partnership. Because parents and teachers in many school districts became deeply dissatisfied with the public schools, states have established an alternative. Educators may apply to establish and run their own schools paid for by the taxpayers. Charter schools must meet government-established standards and choose their students randomly among those who apply, but they are not subject to the specific curriculum guidelines or the hiring, firing, and promotion practices of the public schools.

Voluntary associations also work for government as contractors. Government specifies the purposes and terms of the contract and pays the voluntary association to do the work. Many publically funded mental health, nutrition, emergency relief, drug treatment, and family planning programs are actually performed by such prominent private organizations as Catholic Charities, Planned Parenthood and the Red Cross.

## Public Opinion

The two most important sustained shifts in public opinion over the last several decades relate to African Americans and women. As late as 1972, less than half of Americans agreed that "women should have an equal role with men in running business, industry and government." As of 2008, that number had grown to 84 percent. In 1972, 24 percent agreed that "a woman's place is in the home." By 2008, only 6 percent concurred. In the 1940s, most Americans disapproved of interracial marriage and approved of racial segregation of schools. By the 1990s, a majority approved of interracial marriage and only a tiny fraction opposed racially integrated schools. Gender and racial equality have now become part of American political culture.

Identifying oneself with one or the other of the two major political parties has been a staple of American political culture since the 1830s (see Chapters 4 and 11). But the percentage that who consider themselves Republicans and those who view themselves as Democrats varies over time. Because many states do not require voters to state their party affiliation, it is only possible to discover their party identification by asking them. As of September 2012, polls measuring party identification differed substantially. Figure 12.3 describes the changes in party identification between 1939 and 2012 as measured by the Pew Research Center.

Whereas the Pew poll showed a large identification advantage for the Democrats, the Rasmussen poll showed just the opposite. It found that 37.6 percent of respondents called themselves Republicans, whereas only 33.3 percent called themselves Democrats.

The ideological advantage in public opinion is much more decisive and unambiguous than the partisan divide. Forty-six percent of Americans consider themselves to be economic conservatives; only 30 percent are economic moderates, and 20 percent economic liberals. Likewise, 38 percent are social conservatives; 31 percent social moderates; and 28 percent social liberals. As of October 2012,

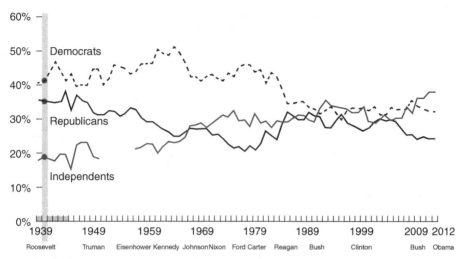

**Figure 12.3.** Trend in Party Identification 1939–2012.

*Source*: Pew Research Center. Retrieved from http://www.people-press.org/2012/06/01/trend-in-party-identification-1939-2012/.

this economic conservative outlook was manifest in the sizeable majority of those who opposed President Obama's expansion of publically funded health care. Most Americans also favored tax cuts and deficit reduction and opposed exempting any working American from paying income tax.

The claim of a majority to being socially conservative is not as strongly supported by public opinion polling regarding specific social issues. A majority of Americans now say that they find lesbian and gay relations morally acceptable. A large majority also approve of abortion, although the larger fraction of those do not favor unrestricted abortion. On the other hand, two-thirds of Americans favor a constitutional amendment permitting prayer in public schools and 73 percent agree with the Supreme Court's decision declaring that the right to bear arms proclaimed in the Second Amendment rendered Washington DC's effort to ban handguns unconstitutional (see Chapter 9). By a two-to-one margin, Americans opposed the decision by the New York City school system to dispense morning-after birth control pills at more than fifty high schools.

The most disturbing trends in American public opinion are those that reveal a loss of faith in their government and those who represent them. Figure 12.4 shows that as recently as 1972 most Americans said that they trusted their government most of the time or just about always.

It is not a coincidence that the largest drop in trust happened between 1972 and 1974. That was the period in which the Watergate scandal erupted (see Chapter 7). As Figure 12.5 shows, 1974 also marked the first time that more

| | '58 | '60 | '62 | '64 | '66 | '68 | '70 | '72 | '74 | '76 | '78 |
|---|---|---|---|---|---|---|---|---|---|---|---|
| None of the Time (vol.): | 0 | ** | ** | 0 | 2 | 0 | 0 | 1 | 1 | 1 | 4 |
| Some of the Time: | 23 | ** | ** | 22 | 28 | 36 | 44 | 44 | 61 | 62 | 64 |
| Most of the Time: | 57 | ** | ** | 62 | 48 | 54 | 47 | 48 | 34 | 30 | 27 |
| Just About Always: | 16 | ** | ** | 14 | 17 | 7 | 6 | 5 | 2 | 3 | 2 |
| Don't Know, Depends: | 4 | ** | ** | 1 | 4 | 2 | 2 | 2 | 2 | 3 | 3 |
| N | 1774 | | | 1445 | 1285 | 1337 | 1497 | 2279 | 2499 | 2859 | 2288 |

**Figure 12.4.** Trust the Federal Government 1958–2008.

*Source:* The American National Election Studies. Retrieved from http://electionstudies.org/ nesguide/toptable/tab5a_1.htm.

| | '52 | '54 | '56 | '58 | '60 | '62 | '64 | '66 | '68 | '70 | '72 | '74 | '76 |
|---|---|---|---|---|---|---|---|---|---|---|---|---|---|
| Agree: | 35 | ** | 26 | ** | 25 | ** | 36 | 34 | 43 | 47 | 49 | 50 | 51 |
| Disagree: | 63 | ** | 71 | ** | 73 | ** | 62 | 57 | 55 | 50 | 49 | 46 | 44 |
| Neither: | - | ** | - | ** | - | ** | - | - | - | - | - | - | - |
| Don't Know, Depends: | 2 | ** | 2 | ** | 2 | ** | 2 | 9 | 2 | 3 | 2 | 4 | 4 |
| N | 1765 | | 1740 | | 1892 | | 1557 | 1289 | 1337 | 1502 | 2689 | 2505 | 2387 |

**Figure 12.5.** Public Officials Don't Care What People Think 1952–2008.

*Source:* The American National Election Studies. Retrieved from http://electionstudies.org/ nesguide/toptable/tab5b_3.htm.

people agreed than disagreed with the statement that "public officials don't care what people think."

The loss of faith that Watergate accelerated has continued to worsen. By 2008, 60 percent of those polled agreed that public officials don't care what people think. Only 23 percent disagreed. By 2008, only 30 percent said they trusted

| '80 | '82 | '84 | '86 | '88 | '90 | '92 | '94 | '96 | '98 | '00 | '02 | '04 | '08 |
|---|---|---|---|---|---|---|---|---|---|---|---|---|---|
| 4 | 3 | 1 | 2 | 2 | 2 | 2 | 3 | 1 | 1 | 1 | 0 | 1 | 2 |
| 69 | 62 | 53 | 57 | 56 | 69 | 68 | 74 | 66 | 58 | 55 | 44 | 52 | 68 |
| 23 | 31 | 40 | 35 | 36 | 25 | 26 | 19 | 30 | 36 | 40 | 51 | 43 | 25 |
| 2 | 2 | 4 | 3 | 4 | 3 | 3 | 2 | 3 | 4 | 4 | 5 | 4 | 5 |
| 2 | 3 | 2 | 2 | 1 | 1 | 1 | 1 | 0 | 1 | 1 | 0 | 0 | 0 |
| 1606 | 1401 | 1921 | 1081 | 1768 | 1963 | 2247 | 1769 | 1496 | 1278 | 1541 | 1312 | 1061 | 1059 |

| '78 | '80 | '82 | '84 | '86 | '88 | '90 | '92 | '94 | '96 | '98 | '00 | '02 | '04 | '08 |
|---|---|---|---|---|---|---|---|---|---|---|---|---|---|---|
| 51 | 52 | 47 | 42 | 52 | 51 | 63 | 52 | 66 | 61 | 62 | 56 | 31 | 50 | 60 |
| 45 | 43 | 50 | 57 | 43 | 37 | 23 | 37 | 22 | 24 | 25 | 33 | 46 | 34 | 23 |
| - | - | - | - | - | 11 | 13 | 10 | 11 | 15 | 13 | 10 | 23 | 15 | 17 |
| 4 | 4 | 4 | 1 | 5 | 0 | 1 | 1 | 0 | 0 | 0 | 1 | 0 | 0 | 0 |
| 2281 | 1397 | 1402 | 2229 | 1082 | 1763 | 1963 | 2247 | 1768 | 1501 | 1278 | 1541 | 1316 | 1061 | 1044 |

government most of the time or just about always, whereas more than two-thirds said they trusted the government only some of the time. If such a radical mistrust in government and its representatives persists, engraining itself in American political culture, it threatens to undermine the public's belief in and commitment to self-government, a belief on which the constitutional order relies.

## POLITICAL DEVELOPMENT

### *Democratic Protest: The Democratic-Republican Societies*

The earliest mass protest movement after the American Revolution erupted during the 1790s. The *Democratic-Republican Societies* considered themselves extra-constitutional agents of the people. As one proponent argued, "the security of the people against any unwarrantable stretch of power" should not be "confined to the check which a constitution affords" nor to the "periodical return of elections; but rests also on the jealous examination of all the proceedings of the administration."

The Democratic-Republican societies saw themselves as the philosophical and political heirs of the Sons of Liberty and Committees of Correspondence that acted as enforcers of republican orthodoxy during the Revolution. Like their predecessors, they, too, held their meetings without asking for government permission and used those occasions to vigorously proclaim their political grievances and demands that government pay more heed to the concerns of ordinary people.

The controversies stirred by the Democratic-Republican societies came to a head with the Whiskey Rebellion in 1794. Secretary of the Treasury Alexander Hamilton's 1791 financial plan included a tax on whiskey. The democratic climate of opinion they fostered emboldened those farmers most aggrieved by the tax to take direct action against it. The rebellion was centered in the four westernmost counties of Pennsylvania, where whiskey was so important to the local economy that it was used, like money, as a medium of exchange. The tax was especially detested because it was levied and enforced by what seemed a distant, indifferent federal government (Figure 12.6).

With support from Democratic-Republican societies in western Pennsylvania, farmers sent petitions to Congress and resisted efforts to collect revenues. A federal marshal and an excise inspector were forced to flee the area, and for two weeks western Pennsylvania was agitated by impassioned meetings, radical oratory, threats to oust all federal authority from Pittsburgh by force, and occasional acts of violence. President George Washington called out the militia of four states and, with Secretary Hamilton and Pennsylvania governor Thomas Mifflin at his side, led an army of 13,000 to confront the rebels. In the face of this massive show of force, the rebellion quickly dissolved.

The Constitution did not discuss whether direct protest in the name of rights against government was legitimate. Washington and the Federalists feared that organizations such as the Democratic-Republican societies were a threat to representative government. Washington denounced them as threats to the well-being of a stable constitutional order. This opposition to the very idea of

**Figure 12.6.** "Tar and Feather": A nineteenth-century engraving depicting the tar and feathering of an excise federal government tax collector during the 1794 Whiskey Rebellion. Credit: The Granger Collection, NYC – All rights reserved.

voluntary political association sparked a heated debate on the nature of democracy and representation. The Democratic Society of Philadelphia, which had condemned the Whiskey Rebellion, now championed vigorous public debate: "If the laws of our Country are the echo of the sentiment of the people is it not of importance that those sentiments should be generally known? How can they be better understood than by a free discussion, publication, and communication of them by means of political societies?"

The Democratic-Republican societies wilted in the face of Washington's denunciation. But many members became prominent Republican leaders and taught the party valuable lessons gleaned from their previous experience. Schooled in the societies' freewheeling activities, they invigorated the party's commitment to popular, mass-based politics.

## Early Voluntary Associations

From the beginning, Americans were actively engaged in governing themselves. In New England, self-government took the form of town meetings in which all town residents were entitled to take part in critical decisions regarding town governance. Throughout the nation it involved widespread active participation in voluntary associations that served as alternatives to formal, representative government. These associations were formed to fight fires, protect public safety, maintain roads and public buildings, sustain the indigent, and provide many other services that in Europe were performed by government officials and paid for by tax revenue.

During his visit to the United States in the 1830s, the Frenchman Alexis de Tocqueville identified the American habit of forming *voluntary associations* as a distinctive and vital ingredient of American democracy: Tocqueville explained how these organizations – rather than threatening the Constitution, as Washington had feared – strengthened political life by correcting for the Constitution's greatest weakness, its insufficient attention to the conditions nurturing an active and competent citizenry:

Americans combine to give fetes, found seminaries, build churches, distribute books, and send missionaries to the antipodes. Hospitals, prisons, and schools take shape in that way. Finally, if they want to proclaim a truth or propagate some feeling by the encouragement of a great example, they form an association. In every case, at the head of a new undertaking, where in France you would find the government or in England some territorial magnate, in the United States you are sure to find an association.

Echoing Anti-Federalist concerns, Tocqueville warned that "if they did not learn to help each other voluntarily," individuals who were obsessed with their privacy and rights would become helpless, expecting government to do everything for them. By participating in voluntary associations, the democratic individual would become part of a vital community that would counter the "danger that he would be shut up in the solitude of his own heart."

## Temperance and Abolition

The Democratic Republican societies of the 1790s represented the beginning of one sort of protest movement that has survived until the present, a movement dedicated to giving the public a wider and louder voice in political decision making. In the 1830s, two other types of movements were born that also remain a part of modern American politics: one involved moral reform and the other civil rights. Both the *temperance* and *abolitionist* movements grew out of a powerful religious movement that swept the country in the 1820s and 1830s. Known as the Second Great Awakening, the movement was characterized by mass meetings, often held out of doors, known as *revivals*. These meetings offered individuals the opportunity to personally accept Jesus Christ as their savior. The theology of the Great Awakening deemphasized the Calvinist notion that God alone determined who would and would not be saved. Instead, each individual was free to choose between sin and salvation. This emphasis on individual responsibility sparked a desire to eradicate evil from the world. In the view of many Americans of that era, two of the worst evils were drunkenness and slavery.

The American Temperance Society, founded in 1826, was devoted to reducing alcohol consumption. Having heard that Americans were dedicated only to their material prosperity, English visitor Edmund Grund was surprised to find that in a single year the New York Temperance Society, devoted to moral uplift, had gained 50,000 members. Its local chapters printed 350,000 circulars and sent them to every family in the state, inviting each to "abstain from the use of ardent spirits, and to unite with a temperance society." They also printed and distributed 100,000 "Constitutions for Family Temperance Societies," which required members to pledge not to use "ardent spirits," keep their friends families and fellow workers from doing so, and place a copy of the constitution in their family Bible.

Although the temperance movement had religious origins and stressed voluntary action, it sought state and national government support. It besieged Congress with petitions asking representatives to promote abstinence. In 1833, Secretary of War Lewis Cass presided over a congressional temperance meeting that adopted a resolution proclaiming Congress's responsibility to aid in protecting public morals. By 1833, the society had 2 million members, out of a national non-slave population of only 13 million. Alcohol consumption had soared after the Revolution and reached a high of four gallons a year per person by 1830, nearly triple present-day levels. By 1845, as the temperance movement gained momentum, consumption dropped to below two gallons a year per person. This success shows how local communities and religion revitalized the American democratic tradition. Although social movements operated outside the formal institutions and practices of the Constitution, they helped galvanize political participation that significantly reduced this space between government representatives and public opinion.

Abolitionism devoted itself to ending slavery and granting civil rights to African Americans. The movement's militancy was exemplified by William Lloyd Garrison. Once a supporter of the American Colonization Society, which favored gradual abolition and returning former slaves to Africa, by the early 1830s his newspaper, *The Liberator*, was advocating immediate, uncompensated emancipation. In what is perhaps the most famous editorial in American history, Garrison told his readers, 60 percent of whom were black, "Urge me not to use moderation in a cause like the present. I am in earnest – I will not equivocate – I will not excuse – I will not retreat a single inch – AND I WILL BE HEARD."

Garrison revolutionized the antislavery movement by linking immediate abolition to African Americans' claim to equal rights. Slavery, he wrote, only violated the "self-evident truth ... that all men are created equal," Calling the

Constitution "a covenant with death and an agreement with hell," he burned a copy of it on July 4. No person or conscience, he argued, should participate in the corrupt political system it formed.

Garrison led the American Anti-Slavery Society, whose determined organizers spread antislavery sentiment in the North and challenged slavery's existence in the South. Before the Civil War, roughly 200,000 people, mostly from New England and the parts of western New York and northern Ohio, settled by New Englanders, belonged to abolitionist societies.

As vital as the American Anti-Slavery Society was in stirring antislavery sentiment, its impact was limited by its fanaticism. Americans were repelled by Garrison's burning of the document so many of them held sacred. And they were frightened by its openness to the use of violence to achieve its ends. Although the Society's Declaration of Sentiments opposed "physical resistance," it also acknowledged that sometimes it was necessary to "wage war against oppressors."

But not all abolitionists rejected conventional politics. Other antislavery militants formed the Liberty Party, which garnered 7,000 votes in the 1840 presidential election. In 1848, many of them supported the Free Soil Party candidate, former president Martin Van Buren, who received more than 300,000 votes, about 10 percent of the total. Abolitionists formed a key part of the new Republican Party that replaced the Whigs as the Democrats' major rival in a realigned two-party system(See Chapter 11) and succeeded in electing its presidential candidate, Abraham Lincoln, in 1860. Thus, the abolitionists helped forge the political transformation that led to the critical choice to emancipate the slaves.

## Parties and Elections

Local temperance and other voluntary associations wrote constitutions and bylaws, elected officers, and formed statewide federations governed by annual conventions of locally elected delegates. These practices became models for political parties, which by the 1830s were governed by local, state, and national conventions that nominated candidates, published platforms, and enacted rules for election campaigns.

Political parties reciprocated, helping sustain the vitality of civic associations by drawing people into political life and cultivating a habit and taste for collective action. The very game of politics, the excitement of competition for votes and the rewards of victory, overcame Americans' natural distaste for working collectively. "A whole crowd of people who might otherwise have lived on their own," Tocqueville noticed, "are taught both to want to combine and how to do so." So, one may think of political parties as "great free schools to which all citizens came to be taught the general theory of association."

Participation in elections became a form of self-expression, an assertion of one's rights, but an individual assertion that took place in concert with other citizens in the collective act of self-government. Voting was not just an opportunity to select public officials. As Philip Nicholas argued on the floor of the Virginia Constitutional Convention of 1829, "It was the right by which man first signifies his will to become a member of Government of the social compact.... Suffrage, is the substratum, the paramount right" on which rested the rights stated in the Declaration of Independence: "the right to life, liberty, and the pursuit of happiness."

By the 1830s, this strong bond between voting and natural rights encompassed virtually every aspect of American life. Club officers, schoolteachers, and team captains were all elected. Democratic principles even penetrated military affairs. Rejecting a standing army as an affront to their egalitarian sensibilities, Americans until the Civil War fought mainly in state militias that selected their own leaders. Foreign visitors, accustomed to the deference accorded to public officials in Europe and Great Britain, were startled by the constraints that elections placed on officeholders. State legislators, and even members of Congress, were expected to return home after every legislative session to talk with constituents about what they had done and what they would do in the future. "Christ how I hate democracy," moaned a weary North Carolina congressman suffering from the ceaseless chase for public approval.

Andrew Jackson was one of the first political leaders to grasp the new politics that celebrated the ordinary citizen; indeed, his presidency signified its ascendance. For the first time, an inauguration was held outdoors, and ordinary citizens gathered in the capitol to celebrate their hero's rise to power. Jackson's opponents claimed that crowds rushed the new president as soon as he took his oath and that Jackson was forced to escape from the back of the Capitol, only to fight past a wall of people to reach the White House. They claimed the executive mansion was swamped by a mob of 20,000 supporters who "spread filth, smashed glassware, vaulted through windows to get at tubs of whiskey on the lawn, and even obliged a makeshift ring of guards to escort the president to safety." In fact, the large crowd that welcomed Jackson to the presidency was mostly well behaved. Jackson himself thought things went quite well that day. The excitement aroused by his election, he sensed, would empower him to use his office aggressively. Democratic elections not only empowered voters, they gave influence to a new breed of politician who appeared to embody the will of the people. As of November 7, 1848, the United States established a standard presidential election day, and nearly 80 percent of all male citizens voted. European nations relied on ancient traditions and folk spirits to unite them;

Americans called on democracy. Walt Whitman, the great poet, declared the rite of selecting presidents "America's choosing day," the Western world's "power-fulest scene and show."

## Media and Public Opinion: The Telegraph

As important as newspapers and pamphlets were as molders of public opinion, they could only travel at the speed of the mails, which in the 1850s and 1860s meant the speed of a horse. Perhaps the single greatest transformation in mass media since the printing press was the invention of the telegraph. Instead of the days or even weeks previously needed for information to travel widely, the telegraph enabled such news to be transmitted instantaneously. As important as the advent of radio, television, and the Internet have proven to be, none of them has achieved as dramatic an increase in the speed of communication as did the telegraph. Although various telegraph schemes had existed since the 1790s, the first real use of the device as a medium of mass communications did not take place until 1844 when the news of the Whig Party's nomination of Henry Clay for president was transmitted over the first long-distance telegraph line, extending from Baltimore to Washington, DC, built the previous year.

The telegraph transformed the Lincoln Douglas debates of 1858 from a series of local occasions into a great national political event. Reporters used short-hand to copy the speeches even as they were being spoken. As soon as each debate was over, they sped to the nearest telegraph office, where telegraphers translated the text into Morse code and transmitted it to newspaper offices nationwide. The next morning, newspaper readers around the country were able to read the debate in its entirety. Although he lost the Senate election to Douglas, the enthusiastic national reception of his speeches made Lincoln a national political celebrity and a plausible candidate for the 1860 Republican presidential nomination. Lincoln was quick to recognize the political potential of the telegraph. It is no accident that his two greatest public utterances – the Gettysburg Address and the Second Inaugural – were remarkably brief. He intentionally made them short so that they could easily be printed and read in the nation's newspapers, which would have quick and ready access to them via the telegraph.

## Populists and Progressives

As we discussed in Chapter 6, the late nineteenth century witnessed the birth of another form of protest movement that continues to thrive in modern America, this one aimed at ending the abuses and curbing the power of "monster" corporations. First the Populists and then the Progressives arose to fight the private economic powers that they believed were oppressing farmers and workers and threatening to undermine individual freedom and democratic accountability.

Because they considered the elected officials of both parties to be servants of the great corporations, Progressives sought to make representative government more democratic. They fought for the Seventeenth Amendment, ratified in 1913, which provided for direct election of senators, and the Nineteenth Amendment, ratified in 1920, which gave women the right to vote. They sought to remove candidate selection from boss control by holding primary elections. The direct primary spread from Wisconsin in 1903 to thirty-nine other states by 1913. By 1920, candidates for virtually every local, state, and federal office (except for the presidency) were nominated directly by the voters. They also championed measures of "pure democracy," such as the initiative, referendum, and recall. The *initiative* enabled citizens to petition to put a specific policy proposal on the ballot. If approved by the voters it would become law even though it was not acted on by the legislature. In a *referendum*, voters are asked to vote on a question proposed to them by the legislature. The *recall* permits citizens to vote on whether to remove an incumbent governor, legislator, or justice from office. All of these measures undermine the power of party organizations and give citizens more direct influence over politics and government in the United States. By 1914, eleven states had enacted some form of initiative and referendum process.

The third-party challenge that TR mounted under the Progressive Party banner emphasized direct popular participation. In addition to the direct primary, initiative, referendum, and recall, the party platform advocated an easier method to amend the Constitution. Sensing that direct democracy was the glue that held Progressives together, TR's defense of it became bolder throughout that critical election year. Toward the end of September, in a speech in Phoenix, Arizona, TR proclaimed that he "would go even further than the Progressive Platform, applying the recall to everybody, including the President."

The Progressives realized that these more democratic procedures would only succeed in keeping the special interests at bay if citizens used them wisely. They did not want merely to empower public opinion but also to educate it. They pressured state governments to make school attendance mandatory. They added a civic dimension to their activities in the form of the social centers movement dedicated to recreating "the neighborly spirit" that Americans knew before they moved to live in large, socially fragmented cities.

This movement started in Rochester, New York, where a former Presbyterian minister, Edward Ward, envisioned public schools as "the instrument of that deepest and most fundamental education upon which the very existence of democracy depends." In Rochester, public schools were used as public baths, libraries, theaters, and forums for debate. In 1912, Ward founded the National

Community Center Association to help proliferate community centers nation-wide. During the 1912 election, both TR and Woodrow Wilson celebrated the use of schoolhouses as neighborhood headquarters for political discussion.

Like abolitionism and temperance, progressivism was strongly influenced by a new religious awakening. The *social gospel movement* that swept through the Protestant churches in the 1890s and early 1900s sought to ally Christianity with the crusade against poverty, corporate abuses, and political corruption. The Progressive Party included many social gospelers in its ranks, lending cre-dence to the claim that the party offered a "fitting medium through which the fervor, the enthusiasm, the devotion of true religion can utter itself in terms of social justice, civic righteousness and unselfish service." TR gave expression to this religious devotion at the Progressive Party convention by characterizing his campaign for "pure democracy" as a "Stand at Armageddon" and a "Battle for the Lord." Observing the reformist speeches punctuated by hymn singing, a reporter marveled that the convention "was more like a religious revival than a political gathering." Progressive morality sometimes degenerated into a narrow and intolerant form of evangelical Protestantism (see Chapter 4). But the social gospel was broad enough to embrace reform-minded Catholics, such as Father J. J. Curran, who championed the cause of downtrodden Pennsylvania coal miners. and Jews, such as Oscar Straus, the Progressive Party candidate for gov-ernor of New York whom reporters spied singing "Onward Christian Soldiers" at the Chicago convention. The most popular Progressive hymn, in fact, was the "Battle Hymn of the Republic," signifying the reformers' civic religion.

Just as secular reformers praised the whole people, social gospelers like-wise proclaimed religious beliefs that downplayed, indeed scorned, particular theological doctrines and denominations. The esteemed social gospeler Walter Rauschenbusch argued, "We have been a wasteful nation. We have wasted our soil, water, our forests, our childhood, our motherhood, but no waste has been so great as our waste of religious enthusiasm by denominational strife. The heed of social service is seen in the fact that as the social spirit rises the sectarian spirit declines." The social gospel thereby invested religious fervor in the Progressive reformers' crusade for a new form of politics that would trans-form America into a national democracy dedicated to social justice and the common good.

Progressivism was greatly aided by changes in the mass media. New, inexpen-sive printing techniques greatly reduced the cost and selling price of magazines, enabling them to greatly expand their circulation. Thanks to the spread of the railroads, they could deliver their issues nationwide in a matter of days. Readers were especially drawn to the exposes that appeared in *Arena*, *McClures*, and others written by a new breed of investigative reporters whom TR nicknamed "muckrakers." Celebrated muckrakers such as Ida Tarbell and Lincoln Steffens cast a critical eye on big business, prostitution, race relations, and even the churches. But their central theme was the corruption of American political life by an unsavory partnership between corporations and politicians. Embracing the Progressive faith in enlightened public opinion, muckrakers appealed to their readers' consciences. As TR's Progressive Party ally Senator Albert Beveridge wrote in 1910, "Party lines all over the country have pretty well disappeared." The cause was clearly "the cheaper magazines, which are circulating among the people and which have become the people's literature."

The Progressive attempt to free voters from partisan, parochial attachments verged over into extremism. Its emphasis on the people as a whole became an excuse for depriving minorities of their rights. Reduced party influence coupled with lower electoral turnout made it easier to whip up public enthusiasm for racist and exclusivist policies that were rationalized on the basis of the distinctive virtues of Anglo-Saxon Christianity. Many states expanded their Jim Crow laws in this era. In 1924, the United States abandoned its tradition of open immigration and shut the door against people seeking to escape poverty and oppression in Europe and Asia.

The prime example of Progressive zealotry was prohibition. Like the temperance movement, this new antialcohol campaign promised a healthier population, fewer abused wives and children, and more responsible working families. But the movement failed to distinguish between these laudable goals and a virulent brand of anti-Catholicism rooted in fundamentalist Protestantism and small-town hostility to the large cities heavily populated by new immigrants. Prohibitionists pointed to the sacramental use of wine by Roman Catholics to prove they were inherently drunkards. Whereas the temperance movement relied principally on voluntary efforts and organizations, Prohibitionism successfully invoked the power of the federal government via the Eighteenth Amendment to the Constitution, which prohibited "the manufacture, sale, or transportation of intoxicating beverages."

In their zeal to reduce corruption and set high standards for political participation, the Progressives imposed strict regulations on voting. The secret ballot, called the *Australian ballot*, swept the country between 1888 and 1896, symbolizing the Progressive ideal of the independent citizen. Similarly, the direct primary, initiative, and referendum encouraged citizens to vote their individual consciences. Appealing to the people as a whole, Progressive reformers disdained partisan entities such as the Democratic and Republican Parties. They also opposed the class-based partisanship – pitting the working class against the propertied class – that developed in Western Europe and Great Britain during the early part of the twentieth century and that submerged "enlightened" voting decisions in favor of group solidarity.

The perverse result of these reforms was to reduce active engagement in the political process. The Progressives' faith in the whole people betrayed them, for it ignored the reality that politics begins with more immediate, particular loyalties. The Progressives' aspiration for a public opinion that transcended family, place, and partisanship was perhaps noble, but it undermined those loyalties and attachments that gave vitality to American democracy. Party organizations had mobilized voters who expressed their partisan and community ties at the polls. Weakening party organization by means of primaries and secret ballots lowered voter turnout. In the presidential election of 1896, 85 percent of eligible citizens outside the South voted. In 1924, the total plunged to 53 percent.

## Participation Moves Indoors

The decline in participation by ordinary citizens increased the power of those well-organized and well-connected groups that had both the skills and resources to operate indoors. Political scientists Richard Harris and Daniel Tichenor have documented the rising influence of lobbying organizations during the Progressive Era. Between 1889 and 1899, 216 groups appeared for the first time ever at a congressional hearing. Nearly three times that many, 622, testified for the first time in the first decade of the twentieth century. During the following eight years, more than 1,000 new groups testified before congressional committees. Nearly every form of lobby increased during the Progressive Era. Growth was especially rapid among trade associations and citizens' groups, reflecting the intensity of the struggles between corporations and insurgents over the shape of the American economy during this period.

## The New Deal: Labor

Just as it transformed the size and scope of American government, the New Deal radically altered and expanded political participation, both indoors and out. Prior to the New Deal, America remained the only rich industrial nation without a strong labor movement. Unionism was mostly confined to the building trades – carpenters, plumbers, brickmasons – and a few other highly skilled but relatively small industries such as cigar making. The one exception was coal mining, much of whose workforce belonged to the United Mine Workers of America.

The 1920s had witnessed a huge boom in manufacturing, resulting in the proliferation of factories across the Northeast and Midwest and a vast expansion of the industrial workforce. But until the New Deal, these millions of factory workers remained unorganized. The condition of these workers deteriorated as a result of the Great Depression beginning in 1929. In response to falling consumer demand, workers were asked to work longer hours for less pay under deteriorating working conditions. The NIRA of 1933 offered half-hearted encouragement to workers' efforts to improve their circumstances. Section 7a of the NIRA proclaimed that "employees shall have the right to organize and bargain collectively through representatives of their own choosing." But these strong sentiments were not accompanied by any mechanism for enabling this to happen.

Nonetheless, the head of the coal miner's union, John L. Lewis, saw 7a as an opportunity to create a new labor movement. He ordered his best organizers to fan out into the auto, steel, aluminum and glass factories and tell workers that "FDR wants you to organize." This was not strictly true, but Lewis gambled that faced with the prospect of hundreds of thousands of workers joining unions in the expectation of support from the president, FDR would be politically compelled to come to their aid. And FDR did. In 1935 Congress passed the National Labor Relations Act, known as the Wagner Act in honor of its chief sponsor, Senator Robert Wagner of New York. The act created a government agency, the NLRB, charged with ensuring fair collective bargaining elections and forcing management to "bargain in good faith" with the unions that won those elections. With government tilting toward their side, Lewis's organizers succeeded beyond their wildest dreams. With their guidance, workers established the United Auto Workers, United Steel Workers, United Rubber Workers, and many other successful labor organizations. Overall union membership jumped from roughly 2 million in 1933 to more than 9 million in 1940.

Although the unions benefited greatly from the labor legislation passed indoors, winning recognition from management and gaining better wages and working conditions resulted from bloody battles waged out of doors. Labor's chief weapon in these battles was the strike. If their demands were not met, workers would withdraw their labor and shut the factory down. Strikes turned violent when strikers tried to physically prevent replacements, whom they called *scabs*, from entering the workplace, and when strikers picketing the factory were attacked by police or gangs hired by management, whom the unionists called *goons*. These labor wars were the most widespread and violent instances of civil unrest since the end of the Civil War.

Because it was so difficult to keep scabs from breaking through union picket lines, the Auto and Rubber Unions borrowed a European technique, the sit-down strike. Instead of declaring a strike and setting up picket lines, workers remained at their work stations at the end of their shift and refused to leave. Management was reluctant to forcibly remove them for fear that valuable machinery would be destroyed in the process (Figure 12.7).

Although its specific objectives were economic – better pay and working conditions – the Labor Movement was imbued with the religious fervor and indignation that comes of being denied one's rights that characterized earlier protest movements. Union rallies embodied the passion and commitment of revival

**Figure 12.7.** "New Technique": A 1937 cartoon by Harry E. Homan depicting the paralyzing effect of the sit down strike on the American automobile industry. Credit: The Granger Collection, NYC – All rights reserved.

meetings. The Labor Movement's unofficial anthem, "Solidarity Forever," was the "Battle Hymn of the Republic" with different words. The coal union song, "Miner's Lifeguard," was taken from the hymn "Life is Like a Mountain Railway." The original refrain:

"Blessed Savior, Thou wilt guide us,
Til we reached that blissful shore;
Where the angels wait to join us in thy praise for evermore

Was changed to:

Union miners stand together,
Heed no operator's tale,
Keep your hand upon the dollar, and your eye upon the scale.

Workers did not simply complain about low wages, they claimed that, like slaves, their civil and human rights were being denied. Asked why they were willing to risk their livelihoods, and even their lives, to fight the boss they often replied, "Because he treats me like a dog." Their nickname for the Wagner Act was Labor's Bill of Rights. This nickname is indicative of the veneration that most American workers paid to American constitutional principles. During the 1930s and 1940s, that veneration was tested as many unions endured vicious internal struggles between the so called business unionists who sought to promote worker interests without challenging classic liberal principles of private property and a market economy and radical unionists who were committed to the class struggle and socialist principles. In almost every case, the business unionists triumphed. As a result, the Labor Movement emerged as a bulwark of support for the American constitutional path of limited government and free enterprise.

By the late 1930s, most major industries had been successfully unionized. For the next several decades, strikes remained numerous. But those strikes rarely took on the violent aspect common in the 1930s. For the most part, workers respected company property and management did not try to break the strike with scabs and goons. Most strikes were settled after a relatively short time. Indoor negotiations replaced violence as the central aspect of union-management relations.

Because labor union leaders were acutely aware of how much their organizations' well-being depended on government policy, the union movement became increasingly active in party politics. As we discussed in Chapter 11, the major national labor organization, now known as the *American Federation of Labor – Congress of Industrial Organizations*, became one of the most powerful and loyal members of the Democratic Party coalition. It established its headquarters in Washington and devoted considerable staff and money to testifying at committee hearings, lobbying individual congresspersons, and other typical indoor Washington political activities.

The greatest Labor Movement successes of the postwar era were won in the state capitals. Union lobbyists convinced many state legislatures to pass laws establishing collective bargaining rights for public employees. As a result, unions were able to enlist state and local government workers as union members and bargain on their behalf. In recent decades the number of manufacturing workers, the original base of union membership, has steadily declined, whereas the state and local government workforce has grown very rapidly. The Labor Movement now has more public- than private-sector members. The nation's three largest labor organizations are all composed of public employees. The biggest, the National Education Association, composed of public school teachers, has more than 2.7 million members. The second, the Service Employees International Union – whose members include hospital workers, mental health care workers, school bus drivers, and custodians – has more than 1.5 million members. The third, The American Federation of State, County and Municipal Employees has almost 1.5 million members.

The New Deal's reach extended to virtually everyone involved in the economy regardless of whether they were farmers, bankers, truckers, manufacturers, miners, or merchants. Therefore, all of these persons and firms came to recognize the need to organize amongst themselves in order to keep abreast of policy developments, fend off adverse government actions, and encourage favorable ones. Notice that the major policy innovations such as the NIRA, Wagner Act, and Securities and Exchange Act preceded the establishment of interested private-sector organizations. Policy created politics as the interested parties formed in response to actions by government.

As the New Deal wore on, these organizations were often able to hire away the very persons who had written the regulations and guidelines the interest groups were now seeking either to sustain or alter. This was the birth of the "revolving door" between the bureaucracy, congressional staffs, and interest groups that has dominated the labor market for lobbyists ever since. This growing interpenetration of government and interest organizations was by no means limited to the business and labor sectors. One of the largest and most influential Washington lobbies, the American Association of Retired Persons, was established to defend the interests of social security recipients. Launched in 1958 with backing from a teachers' retirement group and insurance company, it now has 33 million members, a sufficient base to give it considerable influence over the development of all federal legislation affecting seniors.

## The Civil Rights Movement and the Rights Revolution

The Civil Rights Movement that emerged in the 1950s borrowed key tactics and strategies from the Labor Movement. This was no accident. The coal and auto unions were the large organizations to racially integrate, and many African Americans participated in the epochal labor battles of the 1930s. One of the pioneers of the Civil Rights Movement, A. Phillips Randolph, was the longtime president of the powerful all-black Union of Sleeping Car Porters. Likewise, several important labor leaders, most prominently Walter Reuther, president of the United Auto Workers, were active supporters of the civil rights cause.

The sit-down strike was the model for the approach that civil rights demonstrators took to integrating public facilities. Indeed, the first major outdoor civil rights action, the Montgomery bus boycott, stemmed from Rosa Parks's decision on December 1, 1955, to sit down in the front of a city bus and refuse to move to the back when the bus driver ordered her to do so. Under the leadership of Rev. Martin Luther King, Jr., the black citizens of Montgomery declared that if they could not ride in the front of the bus they would not ride at all. Instead, they pledged to either walk to work or ride in the car-pools that King and his colleagues organized. The boycott lasted more than a year. It received worldwide media attention and did much to arouse national public opinion against Montgomery's racist policy. In November of 1956 the Supreme Court declared Montgomery's city ordinance segregating bus seating to be unconstitutional.

Emulating Rosa Parks, the sit-in was adopted as the tactic for integrating public facilities throughout the South. On February 1, 1960, four students from the Agricultural and Technical College of North Carolina entered the local Woolworths and sat down at the "whites only" lunch counter and ordered cof-fee. When they were asked to leave they refused, and remained in their seats until the store closed. The next day, they were joined by sixteen more students. By the end of the next week, black college students were sitting in at lunch counters in other North Carolina cities – Durham, Raleigh, Winston Salem, and Charlotte. The movement soon spread to Virginia, Kentucky, and Tennessee. On July 25, 1960, Woolworth's desegregated its lunch counters.

Starting in 1961, teams of blacks and whites who called themselves Freedom Riders boarded buses and rode throughout the South, refusing to leave their seats when the blacks among them were ordered to move to the back of the bus. They would also sit down together in segregated bus-terminal lunch counters. The Freedom Riders were often violently removed from their seats and severely beaten by mobs of local citizens and police. Finally, in the fall of 1961, the Interstate Commerce Commission issued regulations requiring the racial deseg-regation of all interstate buses and terminals.

Despite the provocations provided by the mobs that spit and beat them and the mayors, governors, and sheriffs who abetted such behavior, the leaders of the Civil Rights Movement recognized the need to remain within the bounds of civility and constitutionality set by American political culture. Like the Labor Movement, they remained committed to nonviolence and continually reiterated their belief in and support for the American constitutional order and the prin-ciples it was based on. As we discussed in Chapter 2, the idea of an American dream as "yet unfulfilled" was a constant theme of King's speeches and writings. It permeated his most famous oration, the "I Have a Dream" address heard by more than 250,000 people gathered at the Lincoln Memorial during the 1963 March on Washington.

The advent of television greatly increased the movement's ability to influ-ence public opinion. As painful as the beatings and the shocks from the cattle prods were, the spectacle of brave men and women submitting to them and remaining peaceful and dignified was critical in turning public opinion in the movement's favor. Thanks to television, this spectacle was witnessed by tens of millions of viewers nationwide on the nightly network news. Ever since, political movements have orchestrated their out-of-doors activities in order to maximize both the extent and favorability of TV coverage.

It is no coincidence that so many of the great civil rights leaders – Ralph David Abernathy, Fred Shuttlesworth, Joseph Lowery, and Wyatt Walker as well as Martin Luther King, Jr. – were Christian ministers. As we noted in Chapter 11, African Americans as a group are deeply religious. Ever since they were slaves they have looked to Christianity as a source of solace and hope. Churches are among the strongest institutions in African-American communities, particularly in the South. The Montgomery bus boycott and the thousands of sit-ins and rallies it inspired were planned and organized in church basements. In their Sunday sermons, preachers retold the great biblical stories of struggles for freedom, most especially the exodus of the Jews from Egypt, to inspire and embolden the congregants to emulate those efforts.

The leadership that President Lyndon Johnson, a Democrat, provided for the passage of the 1964 Civil Rights Act and 1965 Voting Rights Act cemented the loyalty of the Civil Rights Movement and the African-American voters it mobilized to the Democratic Party. This gain was especially important in the South, where in a matter of only a few years African-American voters went from being disenfranchised to voting in massive numbers. However, the alienation of white southern voters from the Democrats, caused at least in part by the party's aggressive civil rights policies, resulted in a major party realignment in that region in which whites came increasingly to support the Republicans.

The success of the Civil Rights Movement depended on the interplay of the courageous protests and inspiring speeches that took place out of doors with artful indoor lawyering. As we discussed in Chapter 9, *Brown v. Board of Education of Topeka* (1954), which declared school segregation unconstitutional, launched the civil rights struggle that would dominate American politics and government for the next twenty-five years. The Warren court, which rendered this decision, continued the New Deal court's encouragement of citizen groups such as the National Association for the Advancement of Colored People (NAACP), founded in 1909, to turn to the courts to pursue their policy agendas. The NAACP established the Legal Defense and Education Fund in 1939 with a full-time legal staff and eligibility for tax-deductible contributions. NAACP lawsuits against school desegregation finally bore fruit in *Brown*.

Like the Abolitionists, Progressives, and the Labor Movement, the Civil Rights Movement had increasing difficulty remaining unified. As the 1960s wore on many civil rights activists came to question the wisdom of Martin Luther King, Jr.'s adherence to the American creed, a set of principles that they found to be hypocritical in the extreme. They came to believe that freedom for African Americans could best be achieved by separating politically and culturally from the American mainstream and creating their own alternative schools, businesses, and political institutions. They also sought to expel whites from the positions of influence that many had come to occupy in the Civil Rights Movement and they questioned the movement's commitment to nonviolence. They replaced the goal of full integration into American life with the slogan "Black Power." The ensuing split that took place between those who remained committed to peaceful protest and racial integration and those who embraced Black Power sapped the movement's strength. Even as African Americans continued to win crucial legal battles and use their voting power to achieve important public policy victories, the political influence and moral authority of the Civil Rights Movement declined.

## The New Politics

During the 1960s, inspired by the success of the civil rights movement, new protest movements emerged involving college students, war protesters, women, gays, environmentalists, and consumer advocates. Many of the leaders of these various causes had been civil rights activists themselves, and they brought the energy and idealism they derived from their participation in that movement to their new causes. Most importantly, they framed their demands in the language of rights: a right to a decent income; gender equality; healthy environment; and the right of peoples around the world to self-determination.

What the churches had been to the Civil Rights Movement college campuses were to the protest movements of the 1960s. Intellectuals, college professors among them, had been active in all the previous protest movements. One of the greatest abolitionists, Charles Grandison Finney, was a professor and later president of Oberlin College. W. E. B. Dubois, an important progressive and one of the founders of the Civil Rights Movement, was the first African American to earn a PhD at Harvard and spent much of his life as a university professor. But college students had only rarely been active movement members. By contrast, the single most powerful and influential protest movement of the 1960s, the antiwar movement, was born on college campuses and derived much of its support and energy from college students.

In the spring of 1965 the leaders of the antiwar movement decided that the best way to show the size and depth of antiwar feeling was to emulate the epochal march on Washington for civil rights that Martin Luther King, Jr. had addressed in 1963 with their own march on Washington. On college campuses throughout America antiwar activists chartered buses and enlisted fellow students to attend the march, which ultimately attracted between 15,000 and 25,000 thousand participants. Throughout the 1960s and 1970s antiwar marches on Washington filled by college students became a staple of the antiwar movement. To further dramatize their cause, students also engaged in passiveresistance. They occupied university administration buildings on hundreds of college campuses and refused to leave. Videos of war protestors being dragged off by policemen became a regular feature of nightly TV news.

Until the establishment of an all-volunteer army in 1973, male college students were subject to being drafted into the army once they graduated. Much of their motivation for protesting the war came from their strong desire not to serve. However, the antiwar cause was framed in human and civil rights terms, not self-interest. War protestors insisted that the Vietnam War was a civil war and that American support for the South Vietnamese government was depriving South Vietnamese citizens of their right to self-determination. Thus, the protestors claimed the same moral highground, the defense of essential rights, occupied by the Labor and Civil Rights movements before them.

The two other most influential movements that adopted civil rights as their model, the *environmental* and *women's rights* movements, also framed their cause in the language of rights and sought to dramatize their grievances in a media-friendly manner. Environmentalists demanded clear air and water on the grounds that every person had a right to a safe and healthy environment. They fought to protect endangered plant and animal species, claiming that nonhumans, too, enjoyed rights against extinction. Women couched their demands for equal pay and opportunity for hiring and promotion as the fulfillment of the rights crusade begun by the suffragists whose first victory had been obtaining the right to vote. The environmentalists were particularly adept in their use of the media. To protest strip mining for coal they sat down in front of the massive bulldozers that were poised to gouge the mountainsides to remove the trees and soil that covered the coal seams. They produced videos of the wholesale slaughter of baby seals by fur hunters and basement walls turning purple and yellow from the toxic chemicals that oozed into them from abandoned toxic waste dumps.

Unlike the Progressives and the Civil Rights Movement to whom they owed so much, the protest movements of the 1960s did not have deep Christian roots. Many clergy joined them, but their most prominent leaders and most important symbols were either strictly secular or, in the case of environmentalism, rooted in nature worship. It was in this period that religiosity began to acquire partisan meaning. As we discussed in Chapter 11, devout Christians came to see themselves as conservatives. Abortion advocates, feminists, and gays came increasingly to view organized religion as their enemy.

Like their predecessors, these movements were highly successful in shifting public opinion in their favor, forcing government and private industry to improve environmental quality and the status of women. But they, too, were plagued by fanaticism. The public recoiled from anti-logging activists who hid metal spikes in trees in order to destroy logger's chainsaws, animal rights activists who broke into mink farms and released the minks into the wild, and women burning their bras in public.

## The Public Interest Movement

The movements of the 1960s operated primarily out of doors fomenting protests on college campuses: marches on Washington, sit-ins, and demonstrations at city hall. Beginning in the late 1960s, consumer advocate Ralph Nader became the leading innovator of a new form of politics, known as the Public Interest Movement, that shared many of the same objectives of the 1960s movements but relied more heavily on a mix of indoor tactics and muckraking. Nader and his exposé of the automobile industry, *Unsafe at Any Speed: The Designed-in Dangers of the American Automobile*, energized this new reform movement with revelations of corporate malpractice. When Congress responded by creating the National Highway Traffic Safety Administration (NHTSA) in 1970, Nader and other consumer advocates remained vigilant, constantly criticizing the agency for not regulating the auto industry aggressively enough. This political assault continued even after Jimmy Carter was elected president in 1976 and Nader's protégé, Joan Claybrook, was appointed as the head of NHTSA.

The Public Interest Movement resolved its ambivalence about centralized power by gaining influence through the exposure of government's failures, initiating lawsuits on the basis of those exposures, pressing for the appointment of movement loyalists such as Claybrook, and vigorously lobbying Congress and government agencies. As the political scientist Jeffrey Berry has written, "Leaders of the new [public interest groups] wanted to transcend 'movement politics' with organizations that could survive periods of intense emotion." Therefore, despite their antiestablishment rhetoric and profound suspicion of centralized power, public interest activists did not try to get rid of bureaucracy. Instead, they made themselves an integral and permanent part of bureaucratic policy making.

In addition to NHTSA, public interest lobbies fought to establish new agencies such as the EPA and reinvigorate such Progressive Era regulatory bodies as the FTC and the Food and Drug Administration. As Nader urged, regulatory bodies were not to be trusted to act for the public, but were to be directed by administrative procedures to enable public participation "so that agency lethargy or inefficiency could be checked by interested citizen activity." The attempt to marry administration and democracy led to a fundamental redefinition of rights and citizenship. By the late 1970s, statutory mandates and agency regulations provided for higher levels of citizen involvement in agency affairs. For example, Section 101(e) of the Federal Water Pollution Control Act Amendments of 1972 stated that "public participation in the development, revision, and enforcement of any regulation, standard, effluent limitation, plan or program established by the Administrator, or any State under this Act shall be provided for, encouraged, and assisted by the Administrator and the states." Congress also fostered public participation by authorizing direct financial aid to citizen groups who participated in specific regulatory actions of certain agencies, most notably the FTC, EPA, and the Consumer Product Safety Commission. In practice, the citizens best equipped and most interested in availing themselves of these participatory opportunities were the staffs of the public interest groups themselves.

Voter turnout declined dramatically in the second half of the twentieth century. If ordinary citizens find it difficult to muster the interest and time to take part in the relatively simple task of voting, they are most unlikely to participate in the far more complex and lengthy process of bureaucratic rule making. Therefore, the new governmental provisions promoted the participation of these self-proclaimed public interest representatives, not the public at large. For example, public participation funds that supported citizen access at the FTC were concentrated among a relatively few organizations. Consumer activists claimed that genuine grassroots participation in agency rule making was impossible because of the high level of expertise required. Federal subsidy was necessary to enable these activists to represent the public and counter the influence of business and trade groups.

Many public interest advocates were lawyers. Therefore, they naturally turned to the courts as allies in their reform efforts. Courts and citizen activists would appear to be strange bedfellows. As we pointed out in Chapter 9, the Constitution established the judiciary as the guardian of the liberal order, of individual rights against unruly majorities, and gave federal judges life tenure to ensure their independence from public opinion. But the New Deal transformed the meaning of liberalism and the role of the courts. In the 1960s and 1970s, a raft of laws was enacted that couched public policy in terms of entitlements, as statutory rights, thereby inviting the federal judiciary to become a forceful and consistent presence in administrative politics. Lawsuits expanded access to the courts for advocates who claimed to speak for racial minorities, consumers, environmentalists, and the poor. By the 1970s, these *citizen suits* had become a crucial instrument for ensuring democratic control of the bureaucracy and enabling public interest groups to take direct action against lethargic government agencies and unethical corporations.

Joseph Sax, a law professor who educated many public interest lawyers, celebrated citizen suits as "a means of access for ordinary citizens to the process of governmental decision making and a repudiation of our traditional reliance upon professional bureaucrats." Reformers could fight big government and corporations by making innovative legal arguments rather than building political organizations. Of course, ordinary citizens could not do this themselves; they had to rely on public interest advocates to represent them.

The public interest movement gained substantial influence on the policy process, but it did not solidify into an enduring political coalition. Its reliance on lawsuits, media exposure, and single causes was characteristic of what political scientist James Q. Wilson calls "entrepreneurial politics." The movement was dominated by a small number of Washington-based groups. Although it gained numerous supporters through direct-mail solicitations, appeals for donations made little demand on the donors' time, energy, and intellect. As one prominent consumer activist, Michael Pertschuck, put it: "We defended ourselves against charges of elitism with strong evidence that the principles we stood for and the causes we enlisted in enjoyed popular, if sometimes passive support. But if we were 'for the people,' for the most part we were not comfortably 'of the people.'"

## THE NEW RIGHT

Civil rights, environment, and feminism were embraced by the political left and adopted by the Democratic Party. It was not until the late 1970s that movements and lobbies arose on the right to be embraced by the Republicans. The Christian Coalition, National Right to Life Committee, and other organizations copied their opponents' legal, lobbying, and marketing tactics to oppose court and agency decisions that mandated school busing for racial balance, affirmative action to increase the number of minorities and women in higher education and the workplace, and abortion. These conservative organizations resembled their liberal forebears in crucial ways. They, too, spoke the language of rights – the right of a fetus to live; the right of a child to pray; equal opportunity for all, including white males. They, too, found ways to exploit the news media, producing compelling images of human fetuses followed by horrifying footage of those fetuses being removed from the mother and destroyed.

The *Christian right* added a new weapon to the media arsenal of protest movements by producing television series of their own. Several of their most prominent leaders – Reverends Jerry Falwell, Oral Roberts, and Pat Robertson – hosted their own weekly television programs. They combined prayer, hymn singing, and sermons on traditional biblical topics with ringing denunciations of abortion, feminism, and other liberal causes and appeals for funds and volunteers for their efforts to restore religious sanctity and the integrity of the family. Later, conservative spokesmen created vast nationwide audiences for themselves by resuscitating a neglected media vehicle, AM radio. FM had increasingly replaced AM as the preferred medium for music broadcasting. AM stations were becoming increasingly desperate to find programs with popular appeal. At the same time, many conservative citizens were becoming increasingly dissatisfied with what they took to be the liberal bias of the mainstream media – network television news, National Public Radio, and the major newspapers. Conservative talk radio filled the needs both of the stations for programming and conservatives for alternative sources of news and opinion. Rush Limbaugh and Glenn Beck became the most prominent national conservative talk-radio spokesmen, but dozens of others attained great popularity in regional and local media markets. Conservatives also copied the left's indoor approaches. The nonprofit public interest law firms and lobbying organizations they founded proved equally adept at winning seminal Supreme Court cases and convincing Congress and the executive branch to adopt their policy proposals.

## Polling, Public Opinion, and Political Culture

Because a commitment to democracy is such a powerful aspect of American political culture, every political cause wants to claim that the public opinion is on its side. If their view does not prevail they claim that public opinion has been ignored. But how is one to know what the public really thinks? The Progressives supported initiatives and referenda as a means to make public decision making responsive to popular sentiment. Public interest advocates relied on citizen suits and greater public participation in agency rule making to accomplish that same result. But none of those methods are fully satisfactory as gauges of public opinion. Low voter turnout makes initiatives and referenda unreliable as guides to what ordinary people think. The citizens, egged on by the public interest groups themselves, who initiate suits and testify at public hearings may or may not embody majority opinion. Beginning in 1935, George Gallup pioneered the use of *public opinion polls* as a more effective way of measuring public opinion. Gallup saw the poll as a way for ordinary citizens to gain control of their representatives because those representatives could no longer claim to be the best judges of what their constituents thought. His triweekly surveys appeared in newspapers that reached about 8 million readers.

Public opinion surveys are based on the simple statistical truth that a relatively small sample of a population can provide reliable information about the population as a whole. The information is reliable only if the sample is *random*, meaning that it does not differ in any important respect from the population as a whole. In 1936, the Literary Digest poll predicted that the Republican, Alfred Landon, would be elected president. The poll failed to predict FDR's landslide victory in that election because it was based on ballots sent to telephone and automobile owners, who in those days were wealthier than average. The rich were one of the few segments of the population to favor the Republicans in 1936.

Once telephone ownership became widespread, the pollster's reliance on a random sample of names plucked from telephone books become less problematic. However, those who rely strictly on cellphones are not named in telephone books. As the number of such people increases, polls may again suffer from serious sampling error. At present, the most serious problems that pollsters face have to do with obtaining responses, framing questions, and determining which of those people who say they will vote will actually do so. Bombarded with calls from telemarketers, many people refuse to talk to pollsters. Such technical innovations as caller ID enable people to screen calls and refuse to answer those that come from unfamiliar phone numbers. It is unlikely that people who take calls from pollsters are otherwise identical to people who do not. Therefore, the sample of people who respond to the poll may be significantly different from the sample of people originally picked for the poll.

The framing of questions raises two serious difficulties. First, the poll assumes that people actually have an opinion about the matter at hand. No one likes to seem stupid, so people often answer yes or no even when they really do not know or care about the question they are being asked. Second, the way in which a question is phrased can significantly determine the response. A person who is asked "Should the government help poor mothers and children?" is far more likely to answer yes than is a person who is asked "Should the government spend more money on welfare?" This result occurs despite the fact that the program known as welfare mostly goes to help poor mothers and children.

It is much easier to frame poll questions about candidates than about issues because the voter is being asked to make a simple choice between individuals. But a person's opinion of candidates is only meaningful if the person actually votes. Pollsters try to determine how likely it is that a poll respondent will actually vote by asking such questions as "Did you vote in the last election?" and "Do you know where you have to go to vote?" Ordinarily, these questions are successful in enabling pollsters to limit their sample to real voters. But sometimes a campaign proves so exciting that many unlikely voters vote. Or, the race is so dull or dispiriting that even likely voters stay home, or so inspiring that unlikely voters turn out. Under those circumstances, polling, even when conducted close to election day, can prove inaccurate.

During the 1970s, polling became a huge industry. In 1965, the *New York Times* ran fewer than fifty stories reporting poll results. Ten years later, it ran 500, and that number continued to rise in later decades. Such intense exposure to poll results has transformed public opinion surveys from measures of public sentiment to powerful forces shaping it. Here again political culture is crucial. The American belief in democracy exerts strong pressure on individuals to join the majority. When polls show a particular opinion to be popular this result serves to encourage those who are indecisive or only weakly hold the opposite opinion to adopt the majority view point. When polls show a candidate to be ahead, this proof of popularity makes it far easier for the candidate to gain additional supporters and contributors. Thus, polling and public opinion have entered into a dynamic relationship with each one influencing the other.

## CONCLUSION

As this chapter reveals, the three different modes of participation have fared very differently over the course of American political development. Protest movements have changed the least. Although the modern ones have access to modes of communications media beyond the wildest dreams of the earlier ones, their essential character has remained the same. From the Democratic-Republican Societies to the Tea Party and Occupy Wall Street, political movements have all appealed to a mounting sense of resentment and indignation among large sections of the public. They have all spoken the language of rights, not self-interest. They have all sought ways to dramatize their cause. And, they have all had a major impact on one or the other of the major political parties.

Lobbies have changed the most. Although people have always sought to influence Congress and the executive branch, it was not until the twentieth century that large numbers of organizations established permanent offices in Washington staffed by professionals devoted to the exertion of political influence on a continual and persistent basis. The extraordinary profusion of lobbies that has taken place since the New Deal is essentially a by-product of the ever-expanding role of the national government. Once people recognize how dependent they are on the spending and regulatory decisions made by Congress and executive agencies, they are impelled to organize to protect policies that benefit them and defeat those that threaten them with harm.

The most complex case is posed by voluntary associations. They exist in profusion and perform very valuable services, but they are much less likely to substitute for government than they were when the principle of limited government prevailed. In the post–New Deal Era, the presumption has become that if a task is worth doing, government should provide it. Today, voluntary associations are far more likely to be an adjunct than an alternative to government, partnering with it to provide valuable public services or performing specific tasks at the government's behest.

### CHAPTER SUMMARY

☆ Many of the political movements that had a strong out-of-doors presence in earlier decades have not disappeared, but in recent years they have operated primarily indoors.

★ Lobbyists exert influence by dint of: their own personal prestige and prominence; mobilizing an association's membership; and by getting their clients to make campaign contributions. Campaign contributions enable lobbyists to have ready access to the recipients but do not allow the lobbyists to bully them.

★ In some cases voluntary associations substitute for government. In others cases they form partnerships with government. In still other cases they serve as contractors for government.

★ The earliest mass protest movement after the American Revolution erupted during the 1790s in the form of the Democratic-Republican Societies. These out-of-doors organization were considered illegitimate by George Washington and the Federalists.

★ The American political creed's commitment to limited government encouraged the establishment of voluntary associations to perform tasks that in Europe were performed by government.

★ Both the Temperance and Abolitionist movements grew out of the Second Great Awakening.

★ Perhaps the single greatest transformation in mass media since the printing press was the invention of the telegraph, which enabled news to be transmitted nationwide instantaneously. Later movements, too, benefited from media innovation: the Progressives from cheaper printing costs and delivery via railroad; and the Civil Rights Movement and the movements of the 1960s from television. The Christian right rediscovered the value of AM radio.

★ In the late 1800s, first the Populists and then the Progressives rose to fight the private economic powers that they believed were oppressing farmers and workers and threatening to undermine individual freedom and democratic accountability.

★ The Progressives did not want merely to empower public opinion but also to educate it. They added a civic dimension to their activities in the form of the social centers movement dedicated to recreating the neighborly spirit that Americans knew before they moved to live in large, socially fragmented cities.

★ The Labor Movement owed the success it achieved during the 1930s both to the aid it received from the federal government and the strikes, sit-ins, and demonstrations it staged out of doors.

☆   The Civil Rights Movement adopted key strategies from the Labor Movement and bequeathed them to the student, feminist, and environmental movements. All of these movements framed their demands and protests in the language of rights.

☆   The Labor and Civil Rights movements became key supporters of the Democratic Party.

☆   All the major political movements discussed in this chapter were subject to serious internal battles between the faction that sought to work within the existing political order and uphold key constitutional principles and those who favored more radical objectives and tactics.

☆   The public interest movement that emerged in the 1970s shared many of the same objectives as the 1960s movements, but relied more heavily on a mix of indoor tactics and muckraking.

☆   The Christian right became a key supporter of the Republican Party.

☆   Intense and continual public exposure to opinion polls has transformed them from measures of public sentiment to powerful forces shaping it.

## MAJOR TERMS AND CONCEPTS

| | |
|---|---|
| Abolitionists | American Federation of Labor – Congress of Industrial Organizations |
| Civil Rights Movement | Christian Right |
| Democratic-Republican Societies | Environmental Movement |
| Labor Movement | Lobbying |
| Mass Media | Movement |
| Political Left | Political Participation |
| Political Right | Public Interest Movement |
| Public Opinion | Public Opinion Polls |
| Social Gospel Movement | Temperance Movement |
| Trade Associations | Tragedy of the Commons |
| Voluntary Associations | Women's Rights Movement |

## SUGGESTED READINGS

Baumgartner, Berry, Jeffrey M., Marie Hojnacki, David C. Kimball, and Beth L. Leech. *Lobbying and Policy Change: Who Wins, Who Loses, and Why.* Chicago: University of Chicago Press, 2009.

Burns, Nancy, Kay Lehman Schlozman, and Sidney Verba. *The Private Roots of Public Action.* Cambridge, MA: Harvard University Press, 2001.

Ellis, Richard. *Democratic Delusion: The Initiative Process in America.* Lawrence: University Press of Kansas, 2002.

Gerstle, Gary. *American Crucible: Race and Nation in Twentieth-Century America.* Princeton: Princeton University Press, 2002.

Key, V. O. *Public Opinion and American Democracy.* New York: Knopf, 1961.

Keyssar, Alexander. *The Right to Vote.* New York: Basic Books, 2000.

Lippmann, Walter. *Public Opinion.* New York: Harcourt Brace and Company, 1922.

Putnam, Robert. *Bowling Alone: The Collapse and Revival of American Community.* New York: Touchstone Books, 2001.

Schudson, Michael. *The Good Citizen: A History of American Civic Life.* Cambridge, MA: Harvard University Press, 1999.

Shklar, Judith N. *American Citizenship: The Quest for Inclusion.* Cambridge, MA: Harvard University Press, 1991.

Skocpol, Theda, and Fiorina Morris, eds. *Civic Engagement in American Democracy.* Washington, DC: Brookings Institution, 1999.

Verba, Sidney, Kay Schlozman, and Henry Brady. *Voice and Equality: Civic Volunteerism in America.* Cambridge, MA: Harvard University Press, 1996.

Wiebe, Robert. *Self Rule: A Cultural History of American Democracy.* Chicago: University of Chicago Press, 1995.

Zukin, Cliff, Scott Keeter, Molly Andolina, Krista Jenkins, and Michael X. Delli Carpini. *A New Engagement?: Political Participation, Civic Life, and the Changing American Citizen.* New York: Oxford University Press, 2006.

Web SitesGALLUP/Politics: http://www.gallup.com/poll/politics.aspx

Pew Research Center: http://pewresearch.org/

# Concluding Thoughts

This book began with Martin Luther King, Jr.'s dream that one day this nation will rise up and live out the true meaning of its creed. Thus, King acknowledged that Americans do in fact have a creed, a set of cherished principles to which they claim to adhere. And he found that creed to be so excellent that Americans could conquer racism simply by living up to it. He wound his speech around the Declaration of Independence because it is both the simplest and the most profound statement of the creed, "We hold this truth to be self-evident, that all men are created equal and they are endowed by their creator with certain unalienable rights that among these are life, liberty and the pursuit of happiness."

When Lincoln, at Gettysburg, sought to explain to the American people why the Union cause was worth dying for, he gave his own gloss to the Declaration. He proclaimed that the issue at stake was whether a nation "conceived in Liberty, and dedicated to the proposition that all men are created equal" would endure.

Although it may not always be self-evident, the persistence of this creed and its central place in American political culture is the main pillar of American political life. And yet the American creed has been, from the beginning, at odds and in tension with other very powerful contending forces – above all racism, which has also been present in American life from the very beginning. Racial slavery constituted the deepest threat to the predominance of the American creed. After its abolition, the persistence of racial segregation and bigotry mocked the Declaration's fine words.

The American creed has also faced challenge from the centralization and collectivization of economic power that the industrial revolution brought to post–Civil War America. Although this phenomenon is largely responsible for the extraordinary economic growth and prosperity America came to enjoy, it also threatened to undermine the creedal principles of equality, liberty, and the pursuit of happiness.

The political divide between those who stood to benefit from economic collectivization and centralization and those who viewed it as a threat to their liberty existed long before the Civil War. During the 1790s, Jefferson opposed Hamilton's efforts to merge economic and political power. In 1832, Jackson vetoed the Second National Bank of the United States, which he referred to as the Monster. After the Civil War, the growth of the railroads and the rise of massive industrial combinations in such fields as oil, steel, and banking put the economic question center stage. A nation of small farmers, merchants, and mechanics came to be dominated by massive factories, financial giants and interstate railroads owned not by individuals families or partnerships but by corporations with hundreds if not thousands of faceless anonymous stockholders. Powerful social movements arose among those who felt victimized by the economic giants. The Populists fought the railroads. The Progressives sought to bring all forms of corporate power under the discipline of government.

Today, both left and right continue to view economic centralization and collectivization as a threat to the American creed. They differ, however, about which aspects of centralization and collectivization are most threatening. Modern Progressives, like their forebears, focus their attention on private economic power. The Obama administration's efforts to exert greater control over banks and investment houses are grounded in that tradition. Modern-day Progressives champion environmental, occupational safety, and consumer protection regulations as necessary means to protect the public interest from abuses stemming from corporate greed. By contrast, conservatives are more concerned with the power exerted by labor unions, especially public ones, and the ever-increasing economic power of the federal government. They claim that labor unions deprive individuals of the right to bargain on one's own behalf and that public employee unions obtain excessive protections and benefits for their members at taxpayer expense. Their opposition to "Nanny State" is grounded in the belief that an impersonal collective entity, the government, is usurping the privileges and obligations that rightfully belong to individuals and families.

The individualistic premises of the American creed also place it in tension with the communitarian and congregational principles that derive from other cherished sources of American political culture, especially biblical religion. The antimaterialism expressed in the Sermon on the Mount is not easy to reconcile with the competitive practices and self-regarding impulses emblematic of the pursuit of happiness. The Puritans believed that all good Christians were indeed their brothers' keepers and that moral and religious virtue was more fundamental than life and liberty. Those views continue to exert a powerful force on American political culture.

In the nineteenth and twentieth centuries the United States was transformed from an essentially Anglo-Saxon and African-American country to a nation of great ethnic, religious, and racial diversity. Many immigrant groups did not believe that adoption of the American creed required them to abandon their group identity. Their efforts to stick together have often put them at odds with the creed's emphasis on individual freedom. They understood that their ability to cohere required that their children marry within the faith and ethnic group.

The high rates of religious and ethnic intermarriage that emerged during the twentieth century indicated that parents often lost such battles, but not without a fight.

Contemporary political movements also frequently find themselves at odds with individual freedom of choice. Although Christian and Jewish fundamentalists on the one hand, and radical environmentalists on the other hand differ about many things, they would all agree that personal liberty must give ground when in it conflicts with transcendent religious, philosophical, and moral principles. The former would argue that people should not always be free to express their sexual preference or abort fetuses. The latter would insist that individuals are not free to use their property as they choose if by doing so they desecrate nature.

But there is also a supportive side to the relationship between these anti-individualist and communitarian values and the American creed. The very survival of such divergent political, religious, and moral outlooks depends on the civil liberties protections and limits on government the American creed set in place. No other democratic republic is as permissive of group differences as the United States. In France, Muslim girls and women are forbidden to wear headscarves to school. In the United States, they may freely do so. On the basis of the free exercise of religion clause of the First Amendment, U.S. law permits some Indian tribes to smoke marijuana because it is an intrinsic part of their religious practice. Similarly, the Amish are permitted to use child labor under conditions forbidden to other Americans. Because the government provides fewer services than in most other countries, voluntary associations, mutual aid societies, and service organizations flourish in the United States as in no other place.

To understand how these principles, conflicts, and tensions have found their way into contemporary political life, this book has focused on American political development. The key concepts for understanding and appreciating how that development has taken place are path dependency and critical choice. Path dependency provides a means for coming to grips with the remarkable persistence of the American creed itself and the key constitutional political and institutional principles that have formed around it. Critical choice focuses attention on the crucial junctures when paths have been decisively altered; altered but not obliterated. We refer to the most important of these critical choices as conservative revolutions to call attention both to the vital principles and practices they transform as well as those they leave in place. Each conservative revolution was revolutionary in that it brought about a major shift in the understanding of the meaning of democracy and equality and the role of government. It was conservative in its fidelity to fundamental creedal, constitutional norms, and principles.

The first conservative revolution was the American Revolution itself. It was radical not only in declaring itself independent of Britain but in abandoning monarchy in favor of a republic dedicated to securing natural rights. The Sons of Liberty and the local militias that sparked the revolution established a tradition of taking politics out of doors that has been perpetuated by social movements seeking radical political changes. These include: the abolitionists, suffragists, and populists of the nineteenth century; Labor, women's, and civil rights movements of the twentieth century; and the Tea Party and Occupy Wall Street movements of the twenty-first century. The Revolution's conservatism is most evident when it is compared to the later French, Russian, and Chinese revolutions, which crushed the existing social, economic, and religious orders and trampled on human and civil rights.

The adoption of the Constitution was likewise a profound choice based on conservative and revolutionary principles. In the words of *Federalist Paper #*10, it established a "new science of politics" based on the innovative idea that an extensive republic would prove more stable and protective of liberty than a small one. And it built on the thinking of such great classic liberal philosophers as Locke and Montesquieu to create practical governing institutions that would divide power and check one another's tyrannical ambitions. Its conservatism rested in the antidemocratic elements it included in its institutional design – especially the Supreme Court and the Senate – and in the provisions it included protecting property rights. Its central premise – that government should be limited to those powers specifically enumerated – was both conservative and revolutionary. It was radical in that it had never been tried before, but conservative in the limits it placed on government's capacity to interfere with how people led their lives.

Each of the subsequent conservative revolutions profoundly altered American political life without deviating from the essential political principles that the Constitution established. The Jeffersonians promoted democracy by endorsing and nurturing those political institutions and constitutional principles they considered to be most democratic in character: free speech, legislative supremacy, and states' rights. The Jacksonians invented a means for sustaining Jeffersonian principles, the party system. Lincoln and the Republican Party removed the stain of slavery from the American creed. The New Deal expanded the concept of rights to include a right to economic security and established an administrative state of sufficient size and capacity to promote that new programmatic right.

The American political development perspective also enables one to appreciate how crucial the choices not made and the paths not taken have been, ones that would have undermined creedal and constitutional principles. In the *Dred Scott* decision, the Supreme Court, egged on by President James Buchanan, sought to put the Union on the path of permanent acceptance of slavery. That choice was ultimately rejected, albeit at the cost of hundreds of thousands of lives. In a series of decisions made in the late nineteenth and early twentieth centuries, the Supreme Court sought to prevent the national government from regulating the economy. This seemingly critical choice was overturned not on the battlefield but at the ballot box, via the election of Progressive presidents and the judicial selections they made. And yet when FDR sought to solidify his New Deal program by packing the Court, Congress and the public defeated this attempt to undermine the hallowed constitutional doctrines of separation of powers and checks and balances.

As these false moves demonstrate, there is plenty of room in political life for folly, narrow mindedness, and just plain evil. But this book is also full of examples of wise and even noble politics. Good politics relies heavily on leadership and rhetoric. For example, John Marshall used his position as Chief Justice of the Supreme Court to succeed in establishing the Court's right to assert its right to determine the constitutionality of statutes, establishing it as a truly coequal branch of the national government (see Chapter 9). As head of the Forest Service, Gifford Pinchot enabled the agency to break the mold of corruption and ineptitude that had enveloped federal public administration and attain a high level of competence, effectiveness, and expertise (see Chapter 10). John L. Lewis spearheaded the creation of the modern labor movement (see Chapter 12). Elizabeth Cady Stanton's Seneca Falls Declaration of Sentiments was critical to launching the women's movement (see Chapter 2).

As we said at the very beginning of this book, in a free society, most of political life is lived through speech. The various forms of speech that politics employs – argument, explanation, exhortation, and discussion – are what give it its distinctive character. Just as clay is the medium of sculpture, words are the medium of republican and democratic politics. The book began with Martin Luther King, Jr.'s noble words explaining and defending the cause of racial justice. Likewise, the speeches of Webster and Lincoln gave the public the language and concepts they needed to understand and elevate their devotion to the cause of Union. FDR's fireside chats created homely metaphors enabling ordinary people to make sense of the New Deal's programs. By declaring the Soviet Union to be an Evil Empire, Ronald Reagan made clear why the sacrifices and fortitude the Cold War required were worth the trouble.

These fine words and deeds are the work of great political men and women, but leadership is not only exerted by the powerful nor is rhetoric confined to the famous few. The joy and challenge of politics in a free country is that it is open to everyone and it is everyone's obligation. Because the well-being of a democratic republic ultimately rests on the shoulders of its ordinary citizens, they, too, must be leaders and spokespersons. This book has shown that American government rests on strong philosophical and cultural foundations, but also that it is subject to deep stresses and strains. America's ability to sustain its commitment to life, liberty, and the pursuit of happiness depends on the capacity of its people to nurture and develop the political wisdom and skills that successful democratic-republican citizenship demands.

# Index